To Rob,
Happy fiftieth!
— Friederike.

ARKHIVE TWO
THE BOOK OF MASKS

*There is an edition of one hundred
numbered copies of this book
in a special binding
and slipcase*

———

ATLAS ARKHIVE TWO

An Anthology of French Symbolist & Decadent Writing based upon The Book of

MASKS

by REMY DE GOURMONT

With texts selected and translated by
ANDREW MANGRAVITE

And Illustrations by
FELIX VALLOTTON

Additional translations by Iain White, Stanley Chapman, Terry Hale, John Harman & others.

ATLAS PRESS, LONDON, 1994.

DOCUMENTS OF THE AVANT-GARDE

ATLAS ARKHIVE
DOCUMENTS OF THE AVANT-GARDE
NUMBER 2: FRENCH SYMBOLISM

❧

Series editors:
Alastair Brotchie
Malcolm Green
Antony Melville
Terry Hale
Chris Allen

❧

Published by Atlas Press.
BCM Atlas Press, London WC1N 3XX.
© Atlas Press, 1994.
Printed in the UK by The Bath Press.
A CIP record for this book is available from The British Library.
ISBN 0 947757 81 3.

❧

Our thanks to The Arts Council of Great Britain & The French Ministry of Culture for their help with this project.

Arts Council Funded

❧

Copyright acknowledgements are listed in full on page 299 (after the notes). Here we offer our thanks to the publishers concerned: Rougerie, Gallimard and Mercure de France.

THE ATLAS ARCHIVE SERIES ❧ The Arkhive series exists to examine and publish previously unavailable material relating to issues, or neglected groups, within the avant-garde "anti-tradition" of the last 100 years. Where possible they take a documentary format, being either anthologies based on collections assembled by the groups themselves, or co-edited with participants.

Number one, *The Dada Almanac* is still available: this, and forthcoming issues, are described at the back of the present volume.

THIS ISSUE ❧ This Arkhive is loosely based upon the two volumes of Remy de Gourmont's *Le Livre des Masques* which was made up of critical essays on individual writers, accompanied by Félix Vallotton's portraits, published originally in 1896 and 1898. De Gourmont quoted extensively from the authors' texts in his essays, but obviously expected his audience to be familiar with the works from which he was quoting, or if not, they were all easily available. The present book takes a different approach: texts by the authors discussed form the basis of this anthology and de Gourmont's essays are edited so as to preserve their central arguments and observations while omitting references to works which are now very difficult to find, even in French. Furthermore, de Gourmont is frequently more concerned with poetry, while this selection is dominated by prose —luckily one of the Symbolists' favourite means of expression was the prose poem, which submits to translation more readily than their often formally complex verse. A few exceptions have been made, where good contemporary translations could be found, or when it proved difficult to find interesting or representative prose works.

Only the authors discussed by de Gourmont are included in this selection (apart from de Gourmont himself). He made some surprising omissions: Rodenbach, Valéry, Jarry (the latter due to a personal feud*). However, not all the authors covered by de Gourmont are included: it proved impossible to find anything of interest by some writers.

Vallotton's "masks" precede each author's contribution. Behind the mask a later portrait of the author follows, when available, from André Rouveyre's *Visages des Contemporains*, 1913. Rouveyre was a close friend of de Gourmont, who prefaced this book of drawings: his portraits are rather less generous than Vallotton's. Beneath this portrait is a brief biography of the author, beside which will be found the translation from de Gourmont's essay.

The symbols separating authors' texts are those used by the principal Symbolist publishing house, the *Mercure de France*, in place of numbers on non-limited editions of their books. They were usually drawn or selected by the author himself, and were recently collected and published by *Éditions du Fourneau* & the *Cymbalum Pataphysicum* (*Justifications de Tirage du Mercvre*, 1992). A ❧ is employed otherwise.

Uncredited translations are by the editor, Andrew Mangravite; the biographies are by Alastair Brotchie.

A list of anthologies and critical works in English devoted to Symbolism will be found at the back, before the notes which are marked in the text by an *.

CONTENTS

Editor's Preface . . . 7

Remy de Gourmont • Texts from *The Book of Masks, Colours, Proses Moroses* and *Le Latin Mystique* . . . 11

Paul Adam • From *Tea at Miranda's, Second Evening: The Hague, pearl-grey...* and *At The Railway-Station* . . . 23

Jean Moréas • From *Tea at Miranda's, Second Evening: La Faënza* . . . 29

Léon Bloy • *Salamander The Vampire* . . . 37

André Gide • *The Tractate Narcissus, (Theory of the Symbol)* . . . 43

Paul Claudel • Five texts from *The East I Know* . . . 51

Francis Jammes • *Of Things* . . . 57

Laurent Tailhade • *Aristophanesque Poems* . . . 61

Pierre Quillard • *Conversation Concerning the Life and Death of Ravachol* . . . 67

Rachilde • *Frog-Killer* . . . 73

Alfred Vallette • *In Perpetuum* . . . 83

Félix Fénéon • *The Bird-Charmer, and selected 3 Line Novels* . . . 89

Camille Mauclair • *Thus the Blood of the Spirit Cried Out...* . . . 93

Georges Eekhoud • *Chardonnerette* . . . 99

Maurice Maeterlinck • Poems from *Hot-Houses* . . . 107

Tristan Corbière • *Paris by Night, and Paris by Day* . . . 113

Jules Laforgue • *The Aquarium* . . . 117

Arthur Rimbaud • *Vowels, and Farewell* . . . 121

Adolphe Retté • From *Thule of the Mists: Nightfumes* . . . 125

Robert de Montesquiou • Poems from *Blue Hydrangeas, and Goldsmith & Glass-maker* . . . 133

Ephraïm Mikhaël • *Miracles, and Armentaria* . . . 139

Stuart Merrill • *Miracles: Ecstasy, Apocalypse* . . . 145

Joris-Karl Huysmans • *Saint Lydwine of Schiedam*, and *Chlorotic Ballad* . . . 149

Pierre Louÿs • *A New Sensation* and extracts from *The Young Girl's Handbook of Good Manners* . . . 157

Albert Samain • From *Hyalis the Blue-Eyed Faun* . . . 167

Jehan Rictus • From *Fil-de-Fer* . . . 173

Hugues Rebell • *Dizzy Spells: Surprises, Night* . . . 177

Jean Lorrain • *The Gloved Hand* . . . 183

The Comte de Lautréamont • From *Les Chants de Maldoror* . . . 189

Édouard Dujardin • *The Iron Maiden* . . . 195

Gustave Kahn • Prose Interludes from *Nomadic Palaces* . . . 199

Paul Verlaine • *The Signpost* . . . 205

G-Albert Aurier • *Nocturne* . . . 214

Stéphane Mallarmé • *With Upraised Nails...* and *The Supposed Old Woman* . . . 215

Henri de Régnier • *The Story of Hermagoras* . . . 223

Jules Renard • From *Natural Histories* . . . 229

Maurice Barrès • *Hate Conquers All* . . . 233

Saint-Pol-Roux • Prose poems from *Pauses in the Procession* . . . 239

Francis Poictevin • *Jacques: Dreams, Reveries* and *Parisian Sketches* . . . 249

Paul Fort • *The Queen of Queens & her Lover the Great Blue Lake* . . . 257

Ernest Hello • *The Night-time Washerwoman* . . . 261

Émile Verhaeren • *The Horse-Fair at Opdorp*, and *Rain* . . . 269

Villiers de L'Isle-Adam • *Swan-Killer* . . . 277

Marcel Schwob • Four stories from *The Book of Monelle*, and one from *The King in The Golden Mask* . . . 279

Omitted authors . . . 293
Notes . . . 295
Bibliography . . . 299
Future issues of *The Arkhive* & other Atlas publications . . . 301

PREFACE

Andrew Mangravite

Symbolism and Naturalism were the first movements in that great wave of artistic experimentation which is now known as Modernism. Naturalism, represented by the likes of Zola, has always been very well known and translated, its apparently straightforward descriptive narratives pose no great problems of comprehension, and Impressionism, which is almost Naturalism-on-canvas, has always been among the most beloved schools of modern art. Symbolism, whose "essential character consists in never going straight to the conception of the idea itself"[1] by contrast has been relatively neglected, perhaps because it often opposed the entire rationalist basis of Naturalism, or because it was too closely identified with the scandalous young men of "The Yellow Nineties" who actively, though briefly, championed its goals on English shores. The Symbolists actively feuded with the Naturalists and were often too easily dismissed as "fantasists," while the Naturalists nowadays are seen as being healthy and "sane": as early as 1875, Zola himself, writing in the *Messenger of Europe*, had dismissed Symbolism as "a retrograde movement."

Symbolism was a romantic and visionary movement drawing freely from several varieties of idealist philosophy and was itself interested in fixing the finer shades of things unseen. The Symbolists had certain points in common with the Surrealists. (Though the Surrealists' Freudian and Marxist interpretations necessarily caused them to assign different values to otherwise similar experiences.) Symbolism was the larger movement in terms of membership—and this, as it turns out, was as much a curse as a blessing. The Symbolists never had a common programme to which every Symbolist subscribed. Rather, their ranks included anarchists and monarchists, Catholics and Satanists, believers in extreme experimentation and "Romanesque" neo-classicists. All these differences of opinion lessened the movement's total impact, and made it all the easier to ignore its very real achievements—which a fresh and unprejudiced look can reveal.

Far from being "evanescent as the dew," Symbolism was a fairly long-lived movement, the years 1885 to 1905 being its heyday, though, of course, the first generation of proto Symbolists—Baudelaire, Rimbaud, Verlaine—were active much earlier. One can date Symbolism as a movement, rather than as the ideas of these few individuals, from the publication of Verlaine's *Les Poètes maudites.* The publisher Vanier commissioned the articles on Corbière, Rimbaud, Mallarmé, Villiers de l'Isle-Adam, the Romantic actress/poet Marceline Desbordes-Valmore, and the self-portrait "*pauvre Lelian*" that went to form this collection from Verlaine in 1883, and this book in turn defined for the younger generation the poet's place in society. After the turn of the century, Symbolism had become the accepted literary norm and the more spirited of the younger poets found themselves in reaction against it, but the actual crisis-point for the movement came much earlier, in the early to mid-1890s. In 1892 the revolutionaries of the Anarchist Movement turned from agitation to bomb-throwing, the Symbolists' support for this campaign, though hardly unanimous, transformed them in the public's eye from harmlessly naïve young men to fellow-travellers in a dangerous criminal enterprise. Félix Fénéon, friend of Seurat, peerless art critic and contributor to the leading Symbolist journals, was actually brought to trial in connection with a series of anarchist outrages, while Laurent Tailhade, "the terrible

Tailhade," had marked himself as a heartless malcontent when he used the occasion of an anarchist attack upon the Chamber of Deputies to coin a *bon-mot*[2]. Ravachol, one of anarchism's great martyrs, and a man who had boasted that he had killed as many bourgeois as he had fingers on his hand, was an assassin and a complete madman to the public at large, which could only look askance at such Symbolist productions as Pierre Quillard's prose eclogue concerning him.

The Symbolists, as a group, did not all rally to Ravachol's defence however. Too many of them were themselves comfortably middle-class to find much solace in such anarchist war-chants as "It will come, it will come,/Every bourgeois will have his bomb."[3] The Ravachol Affair, however, was nothing compared to the Dreyfus Affair (1894-1899) which split the movement as deeply as it split France. Quillard, Fénéon and Tailhade were Drefusards while Barrès and Adam sided with those who rallied to the army as symbol of the Republic. Even though the most famous of the Dreyfusards was no Symbolist at all, but rather the arch-Naturalist, Emile Zola, the feeling remained that these Symbolists were not for the right things—the Army, the Church and France. What was needed was less seeking after obscure truths and more of the guide-book exoticism and well-behaved meters of the Parnassians (the verbal adjunct to the grandiose and middlebrow art of the Salon)—or better still, more from good, grey (and mostly dead) Romantics, all of whom had become accepted and acceptable literary lions. These were hardly propitious times to flaunt one's difference. Every new school of artists and writers finds itself tried in the kangaroo court of public opinion, and the Symbolists did not escape it. Their sincerity was challenged in such satires as *Les Déliquescences d'Adoré Floupette*[4], their love of country was challenged, and, of course, so were their sexual proclivities—though there were no outright purges like the one to which Oscar Wilde and Aubrey Beardsley fell victim.

Where public opinion failed to scatter the members of the movement, their own egos and private inclinations succeeded. Jean Moréas, who had been a leading theorist and practitioner of Symbolism, turned against his colleagues an in 1891 had established the "Ecole romane" in opposition to them.[5] The resultant vision of Greco-Roman classicism proved especially attractive to those disaffected pro-nationalist and pro-monarchist members of the school, still smarting from the collapse of General Boulanger's attempted coup d'état in 1889. By 1899, one of Moréas' co founders, the young poet Charles Maurras was helping to found the *Action Française* group, which nowadays would be described as neo-fascist.

Some members simply "grew out" of their earlier convictions—Adolphe Retté, for instance, began as a fervent anarchist, became converted to Socialism, and died in the arms of the Church, a writer of religious tracts. Rachilde, th most successful of the Symbolist romancers was, by the beginning of World War I, an extreme nationalist and very much the opposite of her Symbolist-era self.

Another split within the movement, and one that was even more inevitable than the first, revolved around the style and manner of the writing. We have already seen that Moréas broke ranks to follow a simpler, cleaner lyrical line. In a way he was simply following the advice of Paul Verlaine, the movement's first "Prince of Poets," who had, in his famous verse manifesto *Art poétique*, counselled his readers to "Take Eloquence and wring his neck!"[6] But Verlaine could be quoted as righteously by the more experimental-minded, in the role of a poet who had spent his entire career seeking out fine shades of meaning, composing the most exquisite and subtle verbal music.

The movement had progressed far beyond its spiritual father, Charles Baudelaire, whose theory of "correspondences" had come to seem absolutely primitive beside the esoteric theories of such experimenters as Gustave Kahn and René Ghil.

Another split within the movement concerned the concept of Decadence. Mainstream Symbolism, with which the

THE BOOK OF MASKS 8

century ended, was rather like the Romanticism with which it began in that it had a "black" component to it. It is almost as though an overweening preoccupation with matters spiritual and idealistic must give rise to a "mirror-image" which mocks all ideals and twists the spiritual into its most perverse form. In any event, both the Symbolists and their dark twins the Decadents regarded themselves as being adrift in the world, and constantly in search of the true way.

The Symbolists put their faith in their philosophies and even in religion itself. The mystic order of the Rose + Cross was pleased to state that, "there is no other Reality but God. There is no other Truth but God. There is no other Beauty but God."[7] The reverse of that point of view would be held by those Decadents who, out of boredom or a sincere search for a power that could move them, attended the Black Mass or undertook experiments in "magic." Some of this ceremonial magic was harmless enough, but in other cases was driven by desperate human needs. As I said earlier, the Surrealists, in some ways the successors to the Symbolists in the great quest for an art that could transform life, had the benefit of more rigorous political and psychological theories which lent more disciplined procedures to their researches. For the Decadents, there was only the empty allure of a magic that promised mighty powers but delivered only disappointment, and a confused anarchist philosophy which failed to deliver concrete results.

There were other Decadents, of course, who put their faith in neither Satan nor magic. Their methodology of escape was an old, old one—one that Baudelaire knew well. These were the seekers of "artificial paradises," conjured out of wine, hashish or opium.

If all of this sounds a little bit desperate in a theatrical sort of way, we must remember that the end of any century tends to be seen as "a time of crisis" by those who are living through it. How much more must this be true when the century's end also heralds the approaching end of a millennium? The rational mechanism that had been so carefully built up by the philosophers from the time of the ancients to the Enlightenment, seemed to have ruptured its mainspring, faith in "progress" began to falter. There was an anxiety in the air that went deeper than the nagging fear that Nietzsche's assertion that God is dead, and Proudhon's challenge that property is theft, might conceivably be true. The anarchists waited for the universal rising up of the oppressed. Science seemed to have reached an end-point, mechanistic explanations of the universe held the promise (pre-Einstein!) of describing everything, all that was required being rather tedious application. Yet other scientists were convinced that entropy meant the world had grown old and the sun must be dying out! Under such circumstances, it should hardly surprise us that the Symbolist quest led down some strange paths.

NOTES.
1. Jean Moréas, *Manifeste de Jean Moréas*, Figaro, September 18, 1886.
2. "What matter the victims if it's a fine gesture?"
3. Quoted in *The Proud Tower* by Barbara Tuchman, Macmillan, NY, 1965, p. 80.
4. A collection of Symbolist and Decadent satires by Gabriel Vicaire and Henri Beauclair, "*Floupette*" which appeared in 1885 was rather like Owen Seaman's home-grown anti-Decadents satire *The Battle of the Bays* in its original intent, except that the French collection actually made readers curious enough to seek out and read the "originals."
5. The American poet and man-of-letters Vance Thompson, who seems to have known most of the Symbolist poets personally, offered this purportedly verbatim account of what Jean Moréas planned to replace the "abolished" Symbolism with: "I have found another name for my school, and now my poetry is the *poésie Romane*. That name expresses my intention. It covers the art of the Midi of Europe—that art which has reached its highest development in French literature. Today my culture has attained such a height that I can comprehend this development from beginning to end; there is no line marking off the Middle Ages from the Renaissance; there is no hiatus between the folk-lore of the land of *Romanie*, and my poetry, which is the perfection of art; they are of the same race and family; thus it is that I bring back the *poésie Romane*..." From *French Portraits* by Vance Thompson, Badger, Boston, 1900, p. 95.
6. Paul Verlaine, *L'Art poétique*, trans. C.F. MacIntyre.
7. Joseph Sâr Péladan, quoted in *Symbolists and Symbolism* by Robert L. Delevoy, Skira/Rizzoli, NY, 1978, pps. 89, 90.

"Literature of the Decadence!" —Empty words that we often hear dropping, with all the resonance of a flatulent yawn, from the lips of those sphinxes-without-a-riddle who stand guard before the holy portals of Classical Aesthetics. Each time that dogmatic oracle echoes forth, you can be certain that you are in the presence of something more entertaining than the Iliad.

—Charles Baudelaire

11 Remy de Gourmont

Remy de Gourmont (1858-1915). The most obvious omission from the original *Book of Masks* is, of course, de Gourmont himself. A scholar and critic of unusual intelligence, de Gourmont became the "arbiter of elegance" of the Symbolist school after its first champion, Moréas, abandoned it. He worked in virtually every genre of Symbolism: poetry, drama, novels, short stories, essays, philosophy, even book-design and typography and was highly regarded in the English-speaking world, particularly the USA, where many translations of his books appeared, including Richard Aldington's 700 page selected works.

He began his professional life as a librarian at the Bibliothèque Nationale, but was dismissed in 1891 for writing an anti-patriotic article in the *Mercure*. At around the same time he suffered a skin illness that left his face permanently disfigured, he became something of a literary hermit henceforth, rarely leaving his book-lined apartments, which became the destination of a literary pilgrimage by his most illustrious contemporaries

The selections here show the theorist turned practitioner, after the two introductions to the original *Book of Masks*, the first two stories are from *Couleurs* (1908) and the rest are from *Proses Moroses* (1894, *Prose for a Poet* is dedicated to Saint-Pol-Roux). The unusual final text is not by de Gourmont at all, but by the eleventh century monk Godeschalk; it is taken from de Gourmont's *Le Latin mystique* (1892), a highly influential work of scholarship in which de Gourmont explored the strange and fetid productions of the early Latin Christian poets.

THE BOOK OF MASKS 12

REMY DE GOURMONT

Introduction to the first Book of Masks

It is a difficult thing to characterise a literary evolution at a moment when its fruits are still uncertain, when the blossom has yet to spread throughout the orchard. Precocious trees, late-blooming trees, questionable trees and those that we even now hesitate to call sterile: the orchard is very diverse, very rich—too rich; the close-packed leaves engender shadows and shadows discolour the flowers and make the fruits seem pale.

We shall go walking through this opulent and shadowy orchard, pausing now and then to sit at the foot of the strongest, most beautiful or most agreeable of the trees.

When they merit it owing to their importance, their necessity, their suitability, these literary evolutions receive a name; this name very often has no precise significance, but it is useful: it serves as a rallying point to those who receive it, and a target for those who bestow it; thus battles rage over a purely verbal banner. What does *Romanticism* mean? It is easier to feel this than to explain it. What does *Symbolism* mean? If we take it in a narrow and etymological sense, hardly anything; if we go beyond that, it can mean individualism in art, the abandonment of handed-down formulas, tendencies toward that which is new, strange and even bizarre; it can also mean idealism, disdain for social anecdotes, anti-naturalism, a tendency to snatch from life only its most characteristic details, to pay attention only to the acts by which a man distinguishes himself from other men, to wish to realize only results, only the essential; in short, symbolism, for poets, seems bound up with free, that is to say unswaddled, verse, whose youthful limbs can caper comfortably, freed from the impediments of swaddling clothes and bonds. All of which has only a casual bearing upon the syllables of the word—for it ought not to be insinuated that this symbolism is nothing more than a transformation of the old allegorism or the art of merely personifying an idea in a human being, a landscape or a story. Such an art is total art, primordial and eternal art, and a literature released from this concern would be unspeakable; it would be null and void, its aesthetic significance suited to the clucking of guinea hens and the braying of a wild ass.

Literature in fact is nothing less than the artistic development of an idea, the symbolising of the idea by means of the imaginary hero. These heroes, or these men (for every man is a hero in his own sphere) are only sketched out by life; it is art which completes them by giving them, in exchange for their poor sick souls, the treasure of an immortal idea, and the most humble of men can be called to this participation, if he is chosen by a great poet.

Humble men like Aeneas, burdened by Virgil with all the weight of serving as the idea of Roman might, and Don Quixote, on whom Cervantes imposed the frightful load of being at once the mad Roland, the four sons of Aymon, Amadis, Palmerin, Tristan and all of the knights of the Round Table! A history of symbolism would be a history of man himself, since man is unable to assimilate ideas, except in a symbolised form. This point must be insisted upon or we might otherwise think the young devotees of symbolism are unaware of the *Vita Nuova* and the character of Beatrice, whose frail and pure shoulders nevertheless remain unbowed beneath the complex load of symbols with which the poet overwhelms her. Where, then, has this illusion come from, that the symbolising of an idea is a novelty? Here is the answer.

We have been gifted, in recent years, with a very solemn literary tome, a study based upon contempt for the idea and scorn for the symbol. We know about the theory, which seems culinary: take one slice of life, etc. Monsieur Zola, having invented the recipe, neglected to avail himself of it. His "slices of life" are awkward poems with a muddy and tumultuous lyricism, popular romanticism, democratic symbolism, but always filled with an idea, always heavy with allegorical significance, *Germinal**: the Mine, the Mob, the Strike. Still the idealist revolt was mounted not against the works (unless against the nightsoil-works aspect*) of naturalism, but against its theory or rather against its pretensions; returning to the prior necessities, the eternals, of art, those in revolt believed they were affirming new, and even surprising, truths, in professing the wish to reintegrate ideas into literature; they not only rekindled the torch, but, all about them, lit up a great many ancillary smaller candles besides.

A new truth, and such a one has recently come into our literature and art, is entirely metaphysical and *a priori* (in appearance), it is quite young since it has come about in this century, and truly new, since it has not yet served in any aesthetic order. This truth, evangelical and marvellous, liberating and renovating, is the principle of the ideality of the world. In relation to man, the thinking subject, the world, everything that is exterior to the ego, exists only according to the idea that it has become. We know only the phenomena, we reason only about appearances; all truth in itself escapes us; the essence is unassailable. This is what Schopenhauer has popularised in that formula, so simple and so clear: The world is my representation. I do not see what is; what is, is what I see. So many thinking men, so many diverse and perhaps different worlds. This doctrine, which Kant left unfinished to rush to the rescue of a shipwrecked ethics, is so beautiful and so supple that we can transpose it, without offence, from the liberal logic of theory to the most exacting practice, a universal principle of emancipation for all men capable of understanding it. It has revolutionised not only aesthetics; but we are speaking only of aesthetics.

They still offer a definition of the beautiful in handbooks; they go farther still: they present formulas by which the artist can arrive at an expression of the beautiful. There are institutions in which these principles are taught, principles which are only the average and the resumé of ideas of previous appreciations. Aesthetic theories being generally obscure, examples are added to them, the ideal type, the model to follow. In these institutions (and the civilised world itself is but a vast Institution) all novelties are held to be blasphemous, and every personal affirmation becomes an act of dementia. Monsieur Nordau*, who, with a strange patience, has read all of contemporary literature, propagated this villainously destructive idea that all intellectual individualism is "non-conformist" and a capital crime in a writer. We differ violently in this regard. Conformism, imitativeness, submission to rules and to teachings is the writer's capital crime. The work of a writer must be not only the reflection, but the larger reflection of his personality. The only excuse that a man has for writing is to write about himself, to reveal to others the sort of world that is mirrored in his own glass; his only excuse is to be original; he must speak of things not yet spoken of in a form not yet formulated. He must create his own aesthetics—and we must admit as many aesthetics as there are original spirits and judge them for what they are, not for what they aren't.

Let us admit that symbolism is indeed excessive, indeed unseasonable, indeed pretentious, the expression of individualism in art.

This definition, unduly simple, but clear, will suffice us provisionally. In the course of the following portraits, or perhaps later, we will doubtless have occasion to complete it; still its principle will serve to guide us, and by spurring us to seek out not what ought to have been wrought, according to terrible rules, according to tyrannical traditions, by these new writers, but what they have wished to create. Aesthetics too has become a personal talent; no one has the right to impose them ready-made upon others. We can only compare an artist to himself, but there is a profit and a justice in taking notice of the dissimilarities: we shall endeavour to indicate, not how these "newcomers" resemble each other, but how they differ, which is to say, how they live and breathe, for to exist is to differ.

This is not being written in order to claim that there are not, inevitably, obvious similarities of thought and technique between them, but such inevitabilities as these are without interest. Nor must it be insinuated any longer that this flowering is spontaneous; before the flower, there is the seed, itself fallen from a flower; these young people have their fathers and their masters: Baudelaire, Villiers de l'Isle-Adam, Verlaine, Mallarmé and others. Living or dead, they love them, they read them, they listen to them. What foolishness to think that we despise them now! Who has a heart more admiring and affectionate than Stéphane Mallarmé? And has Villiers been forgotten? Or Verlaine forsaken? Now, something ought to be said about the order in which these portraits are presented, neither completely arbitrary nor according to any classifications or prize-lists. There are even some notable absentees from the gallery who shall be brought back on some other occasion; there are empty frames and empty places as well; as for the portraits themselves, if anyone judges them to be too sketchy and incomplete, we shall respond that we wanted them that way; laying claim only to offer directions, merely to indicate the way with a wave of our arm.

Finally, in order to reunite yesterday with today, well-known faces have been interpolated amongst the new figures: and, in such cases, rather than re-tracing the lines of a physiognomy familiar to many, we have sought to throw light upon some more obscure point in preference to the whole.

Introduction to the second Book of Masks Should the reader feel the need to understand the general method which has guided the author of this second series of "Masks," he should consult the pages placed at the head of the first volume.

Goethe reflected:

"When one fails to speak of things with a partiality that is filled with love, the words spoken aren't worth repeating." Perhaps that goes too far. Negative criticism is necessary; there aren't enough pedestals within the human memory to accommodate all the idols: perhaps it is still necessary to smash and hurl a few unjustified and overly insolent bronzes into the melting pot. But that's a dreary chore; one need not casually invite the crowd to the execution. When we shall call out to them, it will be for them to participate in a feast of glory.

Certain critics always have the demeanour of judges who, having handed down their sentences, hasten to attend the execution.

"Hop-la! The headsman! We've made a cheery fire, let's dance around the ashes of our loves!"

There's no further need of butchers for all the worthless books; the flames in fireplaces are good enough.

The following pages are not criticism but psychological and literary analysis. We no longer have principles and there are no more models; a writer creates his own aesthetic and his own works: we are reduced to appealing to sensation rather than judgement.

In literature, as in all else, the reign of abstract words must cease. A work of art exists only for the emotion it gives us; it will suffice to determine and characterise the nature of this emotion; that will suit anything from the metaphysics of sensuality to the pure idea of physical pleasure.

There are enough chords in the human lyre! It's already a chore to count all of them.

Mauve Pauline was passing a very agreeable half hour at confessional. As the heavy fruits of sin were dropped one by one the lightened tree straightened its bowed branches and resumed its springtime symmetry.

"It is also," she was thinking to herself, "like having Amelie wash my hair. The more the cool stream pours over my head the lighter it feels, as though it had washed away a heavy veil—the crepe of care."

And then she felt ashamed for having allowed her thoughts to wander, when they should have been devoted to contrition and the impulse of repentance urged by the indulgent questioning of the priest.

"But it is lovely, really," she mused, "and this feeling of well-being proves that the sacrament has acted upon the sinner."

She then related, without exultation, but also without reticence, everything that had happened to her during two years.

"I have sinned against chastity."

"Was it by yourself?"

"No."

"With your husband?"

"Oh, no!"

"Well, go on."

"I have sinned in my thoughts, in my speech, and in my deeds."

"Was he a steady lover? Was there only one, or several?"

"Only one."

"Did you have a passionate desire to see your accomplice, did you long to embrace him and to yield yourself to him?"

"Yes."

"Often?"

"All the time."

"And when you were together, did you indulge in unseemly speech with him?"

"Oh, no!"

"Unseemly sentiments,—that is to say endearing words?"

"Yes."

"Very well, and now as to caresses: were they natural?"

"..."

"Did he caress you over your entire body?"

"Yes."

"For long?"

"Yes."

"And what did you do?"

"I did the same with him."

"And it was then that you experienced the extreme voluptuous sensation?"

"Sometimes."

"Well, this is a serious matter. Was it with your full consent, or against your will?"

"Oh!"

"You permitted it, then?"

"Yes."

"This is terrible. You merit the fires of hell."

"But, Father, I have repented. I have repented greatly."

"Go on. Was any effort usually made to avoid procreation?"

"..."

"You satisfied your passion without thought of anything else, as the beasts do—to quote the words of St. Paul the Apostle?"

"..."

"You mingled your flesh thoughtlessly, without any other reason than bestial pleasure?"

"Oh!"

"Without considering your conduct, without one regret, without one thought of the precepts of the Holy Church?"

"Alas!"

"Without shame?"

"I am ashamed now."

"Then continue. Both of you were naked, entirely naked?"

"Yes."

"Unblushingly?"

"Alas!"

"You are no better than a demon."

"Oh!"

"Only demons refuse to blush for their nakedness."

"I am blushing now."

"Did you yield to the force of a very amorous temperament?"

"..."

"And always with passion?"

"Yes, I loved it."

"And you neglected to resort to the sacraments, to pious exercises?"

"I am doing so now."

"How did he entice you?"

"I cannot tell exactly. By his glances, his smiles, his words..."

"Did you struggle against your desires?"

"I loved him."

"Is it over now?"

"Yes."

"You will not see him again?"

"Never."

"Very well, go on."

And they proceeded to review the other sins: gluttony, idleness, lying, and Pauline recalled the delicacies eaten after their furious feasts of love, the falling asleep in the arms of her lover, the complicated stories they invented to fool her husband. It was a dream! It was nothing but a dream! She began to cry.

"Since your repentance is sincere, I will give you absolution, though it might be advisable to postpone it; however, tears wipe out many things. Ask God to forgive you from the depths of your heart, for you have grievously offended Him."

Her emotion was redoubled while the Latin words fell one after another upon her blonde head, through a jaunty mauve hat that matched her dress, which was of the same colour though of a lighter shade.

When the ceremony was ended, she bowed without the slightest embarrassment to the priest, whom she recognised. They chatted for a moment about the latest charity affair and its marvellous success, and the poor man was powerless to abstain from considering—without desire, of course, but with a certain complaisance that was surprising—this charming young woman, refined and pretty, who no doubt knew more about the inmost secrets of voluptuousness than the most cunning casuist.

"Oh, Woman! Woman! Here she is with two little children as pretty as the angels, whom she takes to mass and whose catechism she conducts herself. Her husband preached a holy war, and her lover has abandoned her for Madame de Ruel, who tells everybody: 'I am madly in love with God!' Oh, Woman! Woman!"

Pauline, returning to her carriage, thought of the wonderful orchids which a hand she knew well had brought her that very morning.

"I am all pure, without a stain—what a comfort! This orchid, with its little rosy tail like a corkscrew, is like love! It is he, assuredly, it is he. Six o'clock already! Oh, I hope he is not there ahead of me! Goodness! Isn't religion a lovely thing! I am so happy!"

—*Translated by F. R. Ashfield.*

R G.

Green After having remained silent for eight days, after having disdainfully resisted all the tortures of solitary confinement and all the strategies and endless questionings of the third degree, Catherine, who was accused of having poisoned Madame W, her mistress, suddenly gave way and said:

"Oh, well, I might as well admit that I did it, but I am not to blame. I lived alone with her and she was of such an unbearable disposition that no one could remain with her for more than a couple of hours, and then only in the morning. There is no one else to accuse except myself; I have thought it over and realise that. Until now, I had thought to save myself by keeping silent, by appearing mute and unmoved before you and all other judges; but I realise now that my silence has condemned me. It only became clear to me when I woke up this morning; until then I seemed to be living in an impenetrable night, and I dreamed that if I remained hidden there I would be forgotten. When you ordered me brought before you, I heard your words without understanding a single one, but I smiled I think, because your voice was pleasing. And so, last night, I thought it all out, and have decided to tell you just how it happened and why I am not to blame."

Catherine seemed out of place; there was nothing of the coarseness usually to be looked for in one in her equivocal situation. Her position had been something between a lady companion and a servant. She had formerly been a governess and came from a poor but respectable family. She was tall, and her face was pale under her dark-brown hair, which had a tawny tinge, while her eyes were green. When she raised her head defiantly, the judge regarded her green eyes somewhat fearfully.

"She has green eyes," he said to himself, "the eyes of a cat, of a monster!"

She lowered her eyes and awaited a response; and then raised them questioningly.

"They are green, but what a beautiful green—so soft and profound," thought the judge, "the eyes of a passionate woman. It is evident that there is a man in the case. She is trying to shield her lover. Her eyes proclaim that she is in love and her beauty vouches that she must be loved. What misery justice causes; and what difference does it make to the world if an old woman has been done away with, if it has brought happiness to those eyes? How beautifully they must glow when they grow mad with passion! . ." he mused. "But I, myself, seem to be going mad . . ."

He frowned and merely said:
"I am listening."

But Catherine, knowing well what was going on in his mind, and conscious of her effect as a woman, made herself even more feminine.

"Two years ago I entered the service of Madame W in the capacity of a companion, but I soon perceived that I would be compelled to devote the greater part of my time to humbler duties. Maids seldom stayed more than a week; the bickerings, the suspicious and constant bad humour of their mistress, discouraged them. And having had my fill of the same sort of treatment, I had often thought of leaving, but when I noticed that she was a little afraid of me and that with a little skill I would be able to manage her, I determined to stay. Toward the end, I used to call in a poor neighbour to do the heavy work, and in this way I kept the whole house without the help of any servants. Thus I obtained some peace and quiet and was able to smile despite the surly way in which she spoke to me. She never addressed me in anything but an arrogant and insolent manner, but I disregarded it and let things pass. I was able to endure this life so long, because I used to go out frequently . . ."

"Did you go to your lover?"

"Yes, sir. I went to my lover every day, and I will go again to him every day, if you will let me . . ."

Her green eyes became so tender and at the same time so ardent that the judge could not endure their brilliance. He lowered his head and said:

"Go on, please."

He was toying with a pencil, scribbling at random upon a large sheet of paper.

"I will speak," went on Catherine, tranquilly, "about her suspicions. The meals were brought in to us, and it was natural for me to serve them; they passed through my hands and I was responsible for them. As we did not have the same tastes, she let me cook separate dishes for myself. This was the cause of my trouble, and also hers," added Catherine viciously.

"In what way?"

"Eh! Because she began to be afraid—afraid . . ."

"She feared something that was going to happen?"

"Yes, sir, she began to fear that which was fated to happen, that which she had brought on herself—not with her hands, perhaps, but with her words at least. She would suddenly push her plate away, and cry: 'Catherine, are you trying to poison me?' And I would reply calmly: 'Why, Madame, the idea has never entered my mind, as you well know.' She would keep it up and say: 'Then taste this.' And I had to resign myself to take a morsel from the rejected plate. Then she would be satisfied and go on with her repast, murmuring to herself: 'Well, it will not happen today, at any rate.' These words, so often repeated, acted upon me like a command. I would hear them at night in my dreams, and sometimes even when I was awake. I should have gone away, but, alas, I stayed on. And then, about the same time I suffered a grievous disappointment. My lover fell ill and was compelled to leave Paris. I went out of my mind—if an obsession be insanity—and one morning I found myself repeating, like a litany: 'It is going to happen today! It is going to happen today!'"

The judge looked at his watch and got up hastily.

"We will take this up later. Calm yourself. Do not say another word."

Two hours later, the judge was alone with Catherine in her cell, and was saying to her:

"My child, there are no other proofs against you except the admissions you might possibly have made. Therefore I shall not question you further. Some other time, you can tell me the rest."

"Some other time?" exclaimed Catherine. "Do you think that we will ever meet again?"

"I would like to see you. Haven't I been kind to you? My child, I have no right to say it, but I will not only save you from death, but probably from prison and certainly from disgrace. Do I not deserve your friendship?"

"My life," said Catherine, "is worth so little! And now? The prison frightened me—but now I am afraid of freedom."

She covered her face with her hands and burst into tears.

"Your lover waits for you," said the judge, his voice trembling slightly.

"Would I be crying," said Catherine, "if a lover were waiting for me?"

"Then I am free to love you! Would you like me to love you?"

"Can I prevent it?"

"Thank you; but could you love me?"

"I? . . . I? . . . Perhaps I might love you, if you were to sentence me from jealousy, so that I might be parted from a lover."

"But I already know that you no longer have a lover. Judges have knowledge of many things."

"He is dead, and his death proved that he was false to me ... Leave me, please leave me to myself..."

"I will see you another time, and then you can tell me the rest of the story. But here," he continued in a whisper, "not another word. You will be given the address of a house where you will be expected tomorrow."

The judge became the possessor of the smile of those eyes which had enchanted him, and the white, slim body of Catherine, with its rosy flowers and russet shadows. She was an agreeable mistress, but so melancholy that at times she seemed like a statue in a dream. Then suddenly awakening, she would catch hold of the hand that lay upon her shoulder and kiss it.

The matter of her story's ending never came up between them. The judge knew it; he knew that the poison had been poured out, that the crime was the consequence of a word like a command which must not be mentioned.

One day he asked for a drink.

"Never," said Catherine, "shall you eat or drink here. Never."

"Don't you love me?" asked the judge.

"Perhaps I do not love you enough to believe in your love."

"What would you have me do then, my child?"

"Forget... Do you wish to drink now."
He did not answer.
"You see?" said Catherine.

—*Translated by F.R. Ashfield.*

R G.

Hell In his humble cell, traversed by strange glimmers which came neither from the nascent dawn nor the moribund lamp, the illustrious Heretic wrote.

At the head of his fleet Monitory, he had set down this undeniable aphorism, basis for all truly serious morals:

HELL EXISTS.

Now, in the red-glowing retorts, he distilled foul sulphurs, stirred up in devils' pots, soups of pitch, sauces cooked from bitumens, measured out rations of boiling oils, drenched in resin, for the birthday illuminations, the blonde hair of the Well-Beloveds and the beards of Lovers; he poured out vast pools of alcohol where, like lemon slices in a punch, demoniacs floated, surmounted by green flames; he basted skulls rebellious to the eternal Word with molten lead, and the devoured flesh regenerated magically to sizzle beneath the immortal rain of fire yet again; here, a terrible chopper chopped at the hands of liars; there, a scraper with a superhuman mechanism scraped the sterile flesh of the foolish virgins from their groaning bones—and their hearts fell beneath an infernal millstone pressing them even as grains of wheat.

The illustrious Heretic, not forgetting the souls, had burnished, with utmost care, the pitchforks of fear, the arrows of remorse, the collars of anxiety, the hammers of terror, the chains of shame, the pincers of desolation.

Next, he brought forth proofs.

He evoked the sinister damned, the lamentable cadavers appearing suddenly and speaking with eyes filled with an infinite terror: "*I am in Hell!*" Ratbod, king of the Frisians, emerged from the bottom of the abyss, tried to shake off his handcuffs of red-hot iron right in front of the surprised officers. Likewise, Count Orloff, released for an instant from his gehenna, thanks to his strange presence in slippers and dressing gown, demonstrated the truth of an inferno denied by general incredulousness. And the others, how many others, momentarily rejected by the abyss, marked upon the living, upon their furnishings, upon their tapestries, the carbonised tracings of their fiery fingers, or else, with a joviality truly demonic, amused themselves—like that famous damned one of whom Pierre the Venerable, Abbot of Cluny, spoke—by returning to sprinkle upon innocent creatures a liquid more corrosive than piss, crying out in voices not devoid of a certain irony: *Behold the cold water that refreshes us in Hell.*

....

Clouds covered the heavens; the humble cell was traversed by glimmers which came from neither the veiled sun nor the dead lamp.

The illustrious Heretic had leaned his meditating head upon the table; now suddenly he roused himself and seized with dolorous cackles, he uttered a few syllables:

I, TOO, SHALL BE IN HELL.

...And hearts fell beneath the infernal millstone, pressed even as grains of wheat.

R G.

Prescience She opened her window:

It was a springtime landscape, young, not yet exhausted, a landscape of lingering dawn and expectant glimmerings—of skies palely blossomed, the reverse of a brocaded silk, an embroidery of young leafs upon mauve tulle...

There was a pause, before the certain exaltation of expected glimmerings. Some clarifying thing was about to surge into an impending benediction. The mystic Star gave birth to the Sun of Love...

She closed her window, saying:

"And I await The One who will never arrive."

R G.

Earliest Joys

What do you want with me, shadow of my early Joys, and why do you return to obsess me after so many years at this very hour, at the final hour?

...Perfumes of lindens and scattered mignonettes, the spell of columbines in their mourning colours, fringes of ferns! Coolness of the clear brook beneath the jealous alder trees, of mint where the angelic frog with its gentle eyes lies hidden!...

"All that," the Shade said, "is to remind you of the odour of the hemlock also, and the supreme hemlock cut off in its morning verdure; to remind you of the hemlock and its scent... exceptional... criminal..."

R G.

Prose for a Poet

"Think," said the Poet, "think of the pale abandon..."

You should know that she wasn't young and hardly pretty—amid the artificial blonde glazing of the fine hairs, white streaks were set as in a sky inflamed with the precursors of twilight, primroses dying amid incandescent cares.

You should know all that the Poet knew: only this, that a sad fancy was leaving that no longer young and hardly pretty woman abandoned: "He no longer loved her!" Ah! even with a great calmness of tone and with It-can't-be-helped-what-d'you-expect gestures, there were sobs enough there, though not quite moving enough to rise to the occasion of assaulting his paltry heart...

You should also know that she said, after a silence: "Now I'm all alone. It remains to pull oneself together, to arrange one's life," and that, so saying, she contorted her arms into unwonted poses—oh! still beautiful and even relatively haughty, relatively so as regards inconstant youth—her arms widowed of the so dearly loved neck she would have had so much joy in strangling so that it might never again submit to the embrace of arms other—oh, yes! it might be said—than her own!

You should also know that there was a real, deep sorrow in her pantomime of obligatory pretences—because, alone or not alone, isn't that the same thing, eh?—and that, had she been alone, she would have wallowed on the carpet, would have got drunk on bitter tears, and with "Oh God!" every other second, and "What's going to become of me?" in the intervals, and then, because she's got religion, with "Blessed Virgin Mary, bring him back to me!"

There remains nothing else to know, save this, that the Poet had plenty of talent, and that he made verses, verses, "Ah! My sweet! Such verses! Oh! What grace! What charm! In short, admit it, they're good. Caresses, yes really, inexpressible, caresses, such caresses..."

"Think," said the Poet, "think of the pale abandon..." And the not-so-young and scarcely pretty woman became quite graciously pale at last—like a sky glowing with the precursors of twilight which fade away towards the pale tints of the day's dying—perfectly, perfectly white...

Ah! beware of consoling poets; beware of the Word, of the magic of realisations; beware of Words that rise up and live, of improvised evocations, of creative incantations; beware the logic of Eloquence; not all syllables are ineffectual.

The Poet said:

"Think of the pale abandon of old and solitary lilies."

From Godeschalk's *In Communi Virginum*

They offer the Lord the holocaust of their bodily wholeness, those chaste and elegantly adorned virgins who have chosen Christ for their immortal spouse. —O marriage of felicity unspotted, without the grave pains of childbirth, without any go-between, any tiresome wet-nurse. —When Christ leaves their beds, angels, guardian angels, enclose them, for fear that incest introduce its pollution, and armed with naked swords, ward off the impure. —For it is in these beds, it is with the Virgins that Christ comes to sleep, happy sleep that refreshes the faithful Virgin clasped in the arms of the divine Spouse... —Clothed in white linen, clothed in Purple, in their left hand lilies, in their right hand roses... —Flowers in which the Lamb delights, flowers His only food... —The Lamb plays and runs, and he leaps in their midst, —and with them he rests in the midday's fervent heat. —He lies down, at midday, on these Virgin's bosoms, —He makes his nest between the Virgin's breasts, —for, a virgin, born of a virgin, —he loves and seeks above all virginal laps, —and it is sweet to him to rest his head on breasts—so pure that nothing blemishes or stains His fleece. —This is the canticle dedicated to the distinguished college of devout Virgins; —may our devotion make of it a further ornament for the temple of the Lord.

Paul Adam

Paul Adam (1862-1920). Adam's first, naturalist, novel *Chair Molle* (*Soft Flesh*) was prosecuted for immorality and earned him a heavy fine and a suspended prison sentence. Soon after he changed his allegiance to Symbolism and wrote two books in collaboration with Moréas, the selection here being from the first *Le Thé chez Miranda* (*Tea at Miranda's*) published in 1886. As one of the first books of the new movement it was critically dismissed as the work of madmen (a verdict with which de Gourmont agreed), but proved influential nevertheless. Two years later Adam pseudonymously compiled a dictionary of Decadent and Symbolist terminology which derived much amusement from the arcane and obscure vocabulary that he and Moréas had done so much to promote. His move from rather socialist beginnings towards the political right occurred during the next decade and culminated in a spasm of patriotism during World War I. His literary output increased during this period, but his later works are of little interest.

Tea at Miranda's is divided up into "evenings": each begins with a prose poem rather like an overture, printed in italics (here, *The Hague...* by Adam) which is followed by a story from each author, here Adam's *At the Railway Station* and Moréas' *La Faënza* (*La Faënza* being the first of these two stories in the novel). These three texts constitute the novel's second evening.

Monsieur Paul Adam is doubtless a precocious talent, but there are limits to precocity, above all in an author destined to tell of life as he sees it and as he feels it. It is necessary that the education of the senses should have the time to perfect itself and experience have fortified the spirit in the art of comparisons and choices, the association and dissociation of ideas. A novelist still has need of a large erudition and of ideas of every sort, which are acquired in a reliable form only slowly, by chance, by the goodwill of circumstances and the kindness of events.

...Ill-informed literati have long thought that Adam's novels were like everyone else's. They are quite different. Different in style: Paul Adam uses a vigorous language, compact, filled with images, its novelty even extends to its establishing new syntactical forms. In observation: his keen eye penetrates things and souls like the sting of a wasp; it reads through flesh and caskets like those new photographs.* His imagination allows him to evoke and bring to life the most diverse, characteristic and personalised individuals; like Balzac, he has a genius for giving these beings not just a life but also a personality, to make them real individuals, endowed with a particular soul all their own... Different, lastly, in their inventiveness, an inventiveness not merely linear and neatly laid out as furrows, but an inventiveness which makes even the least of his works significant.

THE BOOK OF MASKS 24

PAUL ADAM

The Hague, pearl-grey...

The Hague, pearl-grey, where closed-up facades merge. At the zenith, the white incandescence of a pierrot sun has a dusty look. Beside the mirror-moiré of the lake, heart of the city, the houses, lined up perpendicularly, taper towards the watery depths.

Helmeted with leather, his round face swarthy and close shaven, except for the unique goatee like a paintbrush, a fisherman offers live seals to the corpulent tradeswomen. And there, in the hampers, are the oblong beasts with their oily sheen; he points out their mouse-coloured coats and their soft little frightened eyes, and feline moustaches.

In the depths of the greenish-blue landau, dreamy Miranda, outstretched, reclines: slender, sexless forms. She allows one of her hands in long chamois gloves to hang outside; the other unravels the last lock of her blonde plait, blonde as newly-threshed hemp. And the plait curves toward her neck, close to her little bloodless ear, where nary a jewel darts its gleams. But two sapphires fasten the stiff collar of her plush, iron-coloured dress. And, in the folds of the pleats, the material gives off glimmers of clear steely light which encase her like an armour as far as her enigmatic eburnean countenance. Her feet are not visible beneath the brown-bear skin that covers her from the knees down.

Outside the town. The youthful birches stand up white upon the red carpet of the lawns. A foliage powderises coquettishly on high, and seems to see, and quivers. A sort of boudoir with multiple white columns, with red velvet-pile carpets. Without birds. Silently.

Inside. The Vyverberg. Its massive trees, which the leafy branches unite. There, the sun is sifted, drops down, blots the ground with violet spots, with a purple so little violet it is almost mauve. And the reddish houses peer through the frames of their blank windows as if through two quadrangular eyes, eyes of a statue, without pupils.

Beneath a glass-case, the Limoges enamels and their electric wanness, and their stormy skies with the tones of ruined ink; further off, some historical gentleman's cane with a Dresden-china handle.

Rembrandt: a yellowish-brown ray that glistens in a fantastically brown temple, a yellowish-brown ray in which the hand of the high priest emerges from a dalmatic of orphrey, where the Virgin appears in azure habit, and Saint Joseph, bearer of doves.

The dunes. Hilly, undulating yellownesses; crouching and round like the croups of fat cattle; and squeezed together like a great herd; innumerable.

The sea. Naked immensity; and it slobbers. Emerald mottling sprawls across its silver skin, like meadows; or sometimes surges from soapy crests that go and overflow.

And the firmament curves in above, forever there, a white page always uncommenced.

Miranda alights. She leans upon the arms of her initiated dear ones, and her rosy lips delight in the rustling freshness of the air; and her bushy eyebrows, pale, frown at the briny slap in the face of the spray. She speaks. Her Elsewhere voice, very low, dominates the roaring sea.

"...It pleases me that this suits us and that our eyes indulge themselves to contemplate this mad boiling that wishes always to issue from itself, strives and cannot be... human! Meanwhile you read me the tales in the white Euchology. See how I have invited you to the symphony of the northern whitenesses."

And this is the white transfiguration of things. An illuminant rises from the farthest reach of the waves; and spreads. It blends into and appears through every colour. Even the pearl-grey mists, towards the city, it watercolours with lactescent whitenesses. The foam of the waves seems like splashes of chalk, and the white glimmers play over the cambered sides of the tarred ships, the roundnesses of the yards and the masts. They hang heavily upon the sailors' starched pennants; they dull the silver that shines far away, laid out on the tablecloth of the sunlit sea.

Among the wooden weekend cottages, set in the dunes, whose scanty little gardens are wasting away behind the straw matting that protects them from the sands, there stands a small dwelling with a peristyle.

Miranda pushes the wrought-bronze gate open, and bestows a pitying glance on the withering blooms in the minuscule flowerbed.

The interior of the one large room, all in varnished deal that gleams like lacquer. Frozen dark mirror, with twilight perspectives in which individuals' profiles shrink.

Some white furs, white and grey of polar monsters, conceal the floor. Footsteps sink into them. A door-curtain of white velvet spangled with silver falls in pleats filled with shadows that shade into blue.

On the side looking out onto the sea, there is only a plate-glass window, framed in snow-white silk. And on some trestles of varnished deal, furs again, beds of fur for resting on.

Miranda removes her gloves, which fall like slaughtered birds; and lie there.

At the Railway Station

Still four minutes.

The sergeant slipped his watch away under his jacket; the other gendarme got up, swinging to and fro with the motion of the train, forced to steady himself against the cushions of the compartment. To the accused, Professor Lucien Tordel, that announcement of the approaching station was a relief. Douai, the court of assizes; that would mean the end of his detention under remand, and of his anxieties. Inwardly he goes over his speech for the defence, repeating to himself the key sentences that will be his benchmarks. Fully-rounded periods in the manner of Bossuet, they will resonate with power beneath the sonorous ceiling of the courtroom. They will tell, to begin with, of a mad passion for Alice, the wealthy student, the bold hopes of the poor private tutor, his deferential timidity. Then the thrust of the narrative will soften with plenty of tenderness in the substantives, and emotion in the epithets after the manner of Zola in his *The Sin of Father Mouret* phase. Lucien Tordel imagines himself already declaiming them: pale, righteous in his severe frock-coat grown grey with wear and tear. And, for the benefit of the ladies, he will let this slow gesture stray towards the audience.

As for the jurors, upstairs, self-made men, they too will sympathise with the miserable pedagogue's obligatory humility at that point; a dollop of gall, two or three mordant assertions in the style of Vallès. —And not too much about the abduction. In a few very simple, concise words he will acknowledge his guilt: he will ironically stress the technical charge of "seduction of a minor," like a man who considers human justice a stupidity, inevitable as sudden showers or... the nonsensical falling of a tile upon a new hat. —For the rest, the conclusion of his speech, some Proudhon, from any of his works. This passage will begin with a masterly rough sketch of contemporary society: "a mouldiness." He will brand the hypocritical reprobation of free loves; and then he will bring up the grandiose personification of Prostitution and Adultery. And the whole thing will conclude with a dilemma, a triumphal dilemma posed with hoarseness in his throat, while bringing the handkerchief to his lips with an automatic, all but somnambulistic gesture.

Most certainly, Tordel will not allow old Peyrebrune to take charge of his defence. That talentless, pettifogging advocate would stammer out a mass of obscure quibbles. Besides, a condemnation would be profitable: the affair would be noised abroad, the press would reprint his defence; he would enter into journalism through the front door. Superb prospects. And he would finish *Les Veules**, his poems. This book will admit him, will make him richer. Alice will share the glory with him, the easy life, she who has sacrificed everything, family, reputation, for his love. Perhaps it will be a painful bondage: to trail that woman about everywhere with oneself? —But no; she has proven herself intelligent and devoted. —How long before the delights of their first reunions and the infinite quiverings of their naked flesh?...

After a succession of muffled shuddering shocks, the train comes to a halt. The sergeant leans out over the door; then he warns Tordel:

"Monsieur Peyrebrune is over there."

Peyrebrune, the great Peyrebrune, the man with the blond side-whiskers rushes forward, grips his friend's hand, crying out:

"Excellent news, dear fellow, charges dismissed."

"Eh?"

"Ah, yes. Little Alice had been sleeping with Bergelette, and Bovardy too, you know, the cavalry lieutenant, the dandy of dandies. In the search certain torrid letters came to light, really hot stuff! You've no idea..."

And he related all of the steps he had taken to obtain that search. He went on and on, proud of his success.

Lucien Tordel smiled to put a good face on it.

At the first words that were destroying the order of his life, his unique passion, he felt himself outside of things, far removed from everything. Abandoned. The advocate's verbose tittle-tattle concerning his mistress' escapades stupefied him, killed the future for him. From time to time he protested: "Surely not!" at the more improbable debauches. And soon he was no longer listening, the words of his friend seemed to be addressed to someone else. Meanwhile in his breast, through all his members a nervous tension was rapidly becoming aggravated. Close to rage, he spat out:

"Bloody whore!"

And a spasm shook him from his feet to his jaws, lodging itself there, in the teeth that he kept clenched. Tordel was broken-hearted at these words and at the wasted effort; and then: despair. After such a scandal, he would no longer be able to give lessons. It was poverty, then; or else, after the dismal voyage across the dreary oceans, teaching classes of piccaninnies, between four white walls, far from art and fame, once and for all.

But these images very rapidly vanished. He was no longer thinking about her, with her languid hair, with her childish pout. Others now possessed that beloved flesh. He saw her, the officers' quarters, crushing her mouth against pointed moustaches, and he suffered at each position she was obliged to assume, each limb she bared, shameless... glutted, according to the allegations... She stood there before him, mocking, on the lustreless connecting-rod of the locomotive, among the water that was pissing briskly from the boiler, and she burst out laughing amid the crackling of a lump of coal that fell and flickered out.

A rage overcame Tordel. It impelled him to thoughts of murder. And always the unremitting image of Alice allowing her skirts to be turned up.

Peyrebrune was prattling along. An account, now of the inn, in which she was caught out.

Lucien is thinking: she took off her corset, unfastening the busk from the bottom up; the crumpled chemise became visible on her belly, with her breasts peeping out above it. A clean smell, one of elegance, fills the air and, in that room which he visualises as being completely impregnated by her, he himself is not there. An animal in heat, she surrenders herself to the embraces of a man both embarrassed and self-satisfied.

The lover's breast swells and subsides with a painful precipitancy. Evil sweats, flowing from the nape of his neck, along his back, bathe him. His joints contract into a bunch, a nervous seizure, a tension of passion, as if for some enormous effort.

"Bloody whorrre !"

He finds relief in those rrs that whistle between his clenched teeth. To some extent it is the draining away of that useless contraction that grips him, tormenting him.

Within him a drama is playing itself out so intensely that the external world seems factitious to him, artificial, contrived: the greenery, dull; the trees, blue as in old landscapes; the sky, a false, chimerical light; the clinker between the lines, a black daub; the rails, like dashes of a quill; the tunnels, a pasteboard masonry, a toy.

And he forces himself to lead his thoughts elsewhere, to escape from the frightful phantasm of his mistress lying in a swoon on a filthy divan next to a gleeful rake.

"Bloody whore!"

Then he lingers over discovering faults in her, finding her ugly in order to build up for himself reasons for indifference. She had freckles on her face and throat; her brow was wrinkled; but her eyes, but her hips, but her lips mingling with the moustache of an old soldier!

Peyrebrune is still going on. In the empty immensity of the engine-shed the combative sparrows were fluttering, cheeping. A clatter of spanners resounds, the rumble of a baggage cart and, always, uninterruptedly, the irritating activity of the electric bell.

—*Translated by Andrew Mangravite & Iain White.*

29 Jean Moréas

Jean Moréas (1856-1910). Moréas, a French-speaking Greek, wrote the first manifesto of Symbolism in 1886 for the literary supplement to *Le Figaro*; it gave the slowly forming movement a name as well as an attitude. Moréas' poems were more decadent in feeling, he was often parodied for his use of outlandish neologisms, and the manifesto was in part an attempt to substitute the word Symbolism for Decadence, an epithet he disliked.

After the two novels he co-authored with Adam (from one of which this story is taken: see previous biography of Adam) he sought a return to the simplicity of classicism by founding his *École romane* (whose penchant for the past is so deftly skewered by de Gourmont in his remarks here). The portrait by Rouveyre was drawn a few days before his death.

...arrived in Paris like any other Wallachian or Levantine student, and already full of love for the French language, Monsieur Moréas betook himself to the school of the Old French poets, and especially kept company with Jacot de Forest and Benoît de Sainte-Maure*. He wished to take the road to which every ambitious young man who wants to be a good harper ought to vow himself; he swore to accomplish the entire pilgrimage: to date having started out with the Chanson de Saint-Léger,* he has, it is said, arrived at the XVIIth Century, and all that in just ten years: this is not as discouraging as might be believed. And, now that the texts are more familiar, the road shortens itself: henceforth fewer halts, Moréas will pitch camp beneath Hugo's old oak tree and, if he perseveres, we shall see him attain the goal of his journey, which is, without doubt, to catch up with himself. Then, casting aside the staff, often exchanged and cut from diverse copses, he will rest upon his own genius and we shall be able to judge him, if that is our pleasure, with a certain confidence.

All that we can say today, is that Mr. Moréas passionately loves the language and the poetry of France and that the two sisters with haughty hearts have more than once smiled upon him, content to see at their feet a pilgrim so patient and so chivalrous and armed with such good-will...

JEAN MORÉAS

La Faënza   In the world of the high-life she called herself by the Italianised name of La Faënza, because of her complexion which seemed burnished by the sun of Naples and her big black eyes that would lay you low like blunderbusses from the thickets at some godforsaken crossroad of the Abruzzi. She was born, for all that, in the province of Indre-et-Loire, where she was married at scarcely sixteen years to a certain Verdal, a respectable attorney and a man of fifty, who, after fourteen months of married life, left her a widow with a little boy on her hands and in a thoroughly problematical financial situation. Some time later, wearied by that sad and monotonous life in the provinces, haunted by dreams of luxury and easy pleasures, she allowed herself to be taken away to Paris by a sacked sub-prefect, who soon deserted her to marry the daughter of a rich merchant of the rue du Sentier.

As her twentieth year dawned, her big lively eyes carried hearts away, her hair, without actually touching her heels, descended well-nigh past her hips which were round and dancing, she had ample occasion to throw off all restraint in fashionable cabarets. Her stock was soon priced pretty high on the stock exchange of gallantry, and the respectable barons, who so profitably pursue the white slave trade under the noses and beards of the police, were offering golden bargains to her.

Before long every pasha fleeing hanging, every boyar in the mood to eat up his estate, every flash adventurer and billiard-hall philosopher having any pretensions to the respect of his fellows, was manoeuvring for the honour of depositing handfuls of golden *louis* on the rose marble of the mantelpiece in her bedroom. She had her town house, just like an actress with *eleven hundred* francs worth of income, valets in knee-breeches and coachmen of an unlikely obesity.

Then a time of splendour commenced for the beautiful La Faënza, that lasted for more than ten years. It was the old, old story of all those pretty girls landed up on the streets of Paris with breasts too large for their slight scruples. In her salon she wore ruinous outfits, extravagant hats, fabrics from the Orient fit to make a shah squint, and in her boudoir, she had Venetian mirrors bordered by gems in which to admire the sweeping curve from the majestic small of her back to her buttocks. She possessed the very essence of that self-styled Parisian spirit one encounters while sucking crayfish in the stale atmosphere of the private rooms of expensive restaurants. The young reprobates, anxious to earn their spurs, and the old rakes, jealous of their hard-won fame, contended for the glory of paying off her dressmakers' bills, her villas at Nice and her cottages in Normandy. In short, in the midst of all those intoxications of her victory, without realising it, she was overtaking the sad epoch of obstinate wrinkles, loose teeth, and the hair that disappears as sadly as the autumn leaves. To tell the truth, she really had no reason to realise it, for, despite her thirty-four years, her skin was perfectly smooth and marmoreal, her teeth were of a whiteness that was insolent, and cascades of hair intractable to the most murderous combs fell from a head as charming as that of a virgin by Giorgione.

At this point we recall that La Faënza had had a son from her marriage. This child was brought up by an aged aunt. His mother saw him only once, when he was eight; after that her only concern was to send him some money in letters filled with that type of false sentimentality common among whores. The aged aunt, wishing to conceal the mother's conduct from her son, arranged for him to enlist in a regiment stationed in Africa, where, at nineteen, he was a non-commissioned officer. Having distinguished himself during the latest uprising there, he was awarded the Military medal, but unhappily his wounds obliged him to leave the army. At the news, La Faënza felt herself moved by a subtle and immeasurable maternal affection, and she resolved to renounce the pleasures of paid love in order to consecrate the remainder of her existence to the happiness of that abandoned child. Having sold her town house, her jewels and her carriages, she withdrew to Touraine, to a property offered to her years before by a rightist deputy. And so La Bella Faënza became once more Madame Verdal, the widow of an honest attorney, the mother of an exemplary family, a pious and charitable lady.

II.

Philippe was a handsome young man of nineteen or twenty, with a fine moustache, a young girl's waistline and the eyes of a dove. Without the least suspicion of the past life of his mother, who invented a thousand ingenious lies to explain to him their unduly long separation, he began adoring her with all the ardour of a heart closed until then to familiar development. La Faënza, for her part, was literally mad about her son, her beautiful Philippe.

The property where the former courtesan determined to expiate her little failings was a charming villa with green shutters about which convolvulus and nasturtiums with bleeding calyxes coiled like serpents. A small wood, growing wild, enveloped it with an air of exquisite mystery in its fleeting shadows. In its darkest corner, beneath the parasol of a big polonia, the twittering of the green woodpeckers mingled with the tinkling of the water a nymph's urn poured out into the little marble basin gnawed at by moss and yellow lichens.

For many months the mother and son led a sweet and peaceful life there. They did all the little nice things for each other, beside excessive endearments interspersed with make-believe sulking, perhaps to a ridiculous degree. La Faënza had completely forgotten about her former existence: the grandstands at the races and the pit-tier boxes at the little theatres, the climbing trips in the Pyrenees and the yachting parties at Trouville, the lavish dinners in her splendid town house in the Parc Monceau, and the little suppers in small, fashionable restaurants, where the carafes of champagne and chartreuse of all colours made her incredible tight-fitting costumes seem even more nonsensical than was natural.

Nevertheless, in spite of all their mutual affection, the intimacy, that intimacy free and full of abandon, between the mother who has spanked her child and the child that has grown up around his mother's skirts, did not come about. And that was natural. As we know, since her flight with the sub-prefect, La Faënza had seen her son only once while he was still a brat. All at once she met him again as a tall young man with a fearful moustache and a martial scar across his temple. For her son, the mother was a stranger; it was almost as if he was seeing her for the first time. That being so, one can easily understand why they were rather hesitant for a while to speak to each other in familiar terms and retained in their relations with each other an inscrutable reserve and an unnecessary politeness.

Madame Verdal had cast off La Faënza, the hetæra in her was definitely dead. Her attire was severe: black silk dresses with jet trimmings. A few rings and earrings of a ravishing modesty. She adopted centrally parted plaits as her hairstyle and used a modicum of rice powder as her make-up. One supposes that the neighbours in the countryside had not been able to refuse her their esteem, so alike were they in modes of conduct and yearly income. Among the ex-courtesan's good connections, the Mouflet family—comprising the father Evariste Mouflet, a venerable notary and an insipid provincial touched by a mania for subterfuge, the mother, Olympe, a decent and respected woman, who had taken as lovers no more than three or four of her husband's clerks, and their three daughters, not bad looking, to tell the truth, for the daughters of a notary—were certainly the foremost.

The Mouflets' eldest daughter, Mademoiselle Clémentine, would have been extremely pretty without those odious dresses of gosling-shit-green vicuna from the shop of some subprefectural Worth. Two great big startled eyes beneath a helmet of hair of a becoming chestnut colour; and, with that, a seventeen-year-old's bosom that had the air of intending to keep promises.

The ex-courtesan and the notary's family often visited one another to take cups of tea, to play innocent games and twist a few opera-arias out of shape on more-or-less out-of-tune pianos. Philippe, who had not learned to be particular about matters of dress in his hunting-grounds at Koumir, found Mademoiselle Clémentine's gosling-shit-green dress strong for his taste, everything in him preferring to it the treasures that it concealed. Mademoiselle Clémentine, for her part, did not feel an insurmountable aversion to his brown moustaches. Needless to say the Mouflets daily discovered new qualities in the only son of a mother enjoying an income of five thousand *livres*. Thus they chastely courted, under the eyes of La Faënza, who suspected nothing. One evening in July, the entire Mouflet clan found itself assembled in the ex-courtesan's dining-room. After some polkas tapped out by the youngsters, and some trifling exchanges of conversation, the scrivener proposed, in view of the insupportable heat of the atmosphere, a stroll beneath the cooling foliage of the garden. Everyone accepted with alacrity.

The evening was superb. The full moon was shining like a fantastic *louis d'or* in the cloudless sky. They scattered through the paths where, now and then, some glow-worms perhaps sparkled.

La Faënza had been searching several minutes for her son, when she thought she made out two shadows intertwined upon a stone bench in the darkest corner of her garden. She paused, watchful. It was really as if the sound of kisses were mingling with the plashings of the water falling into the marble basins. Holding her breath, she advanced almost to the bench itself, behind a hedge of red rose-bushes. Her son Philippe was engaged in murmuring the sweetest things in Mademoiselle Clémentine's ear.

A strange sentiment then invaded the ex-courtesan's heart; she experienced a moment of vertigo; then the pupils of her eyes dilated and, choking with rage, starting up to her full height in front of the poor, totally bewildered lovers, she addressed Mademoiselle Mouflet in virulent terms:

—She certainly was stupid not to have noticed long ago that they'd been coming here to steal her son. And on top of that she'd been forking out her money to feed a corrupt notary and his street-walker daughters. And as for Ma Mouflet, why, she was only a good-for-nothing who bedded with her domestics! Everybody in the countryside knew about it. They'd better not, all those stoney-brokes, ever set foot in her house again; she'd chase them from her doorstep with a broom....

Completely forgetting herself in her rage, Madame Verdal again became what she formerly had been and crushed the Mouflet family, drawn to the scene by the noisy dispute, with the filthiest possible invectives.

Mouflet led his wife and his frightened-to-death daughters away, after having responded with an indignant tirade.

Philippe remained standing there, wild-eyed, uncomprehending.

La Faënza went back into the house in a state of indescribable exasperation. She wept, sobbed, rolled about in the carpet, foaming at the mouth. Then, suddenly, rising, she began kissing her son full on the lips, all the while laughing like a madwoman.

IV.*

After a few days of sulkiness, the mother and son were reconciled, with a renewal of tenderness. And every day there were long walks through the fields, from which they returned like last night's lovers, their hands full of bunches of broom. In the morning they would go off for hours at a time, on horseback, in the woods, and in the evenings they would go sculling with a canoe on the calm waters of a nearby pond in the romantic moonlight. And here's something odd! Since the incident in the garden, a noticeable change had taken place in La Faënza's habits. Breaking with the severe attitude she had adopted since her conversion, she cast aside the honest woman's inelegant frock to dress again in ruinously expensive fabrics in startling colours, ostrich-plume hats, and very long doeskin gloves. The gems she hadn't wished to part with were taken out once more from their garnet-red velour caskets to adorn her fine long hands and her regal neck. Rice powder no longer sufficed her as an embellishment and she recalled the subtle tints and the precious aromatics that confer youth. She took particular care regarding the choice of her undergarments, in the deceitful promises of which she was an expert: antique lace on silk chemises, pale rose pink stockings with bows or with diamonds darting fire from their facets. The modest furniture of her boudoir and bed-chamber was completely changed. Calling to mind again the exciting pomp of her courtesan's alcove, she surrounded herself with low-built and softly velvety furnishings that entwined one like voluptuous arms, with Syrian fabrics, with Karamanian carpets, and with striped tiger skins on which naked feet frisked, offered for vibrant kisses. Perfumes smouldered continuously in the richly carved incense-burners and armfuls of white roses mingled their last exhalations with the indifference of the tree trunks in the lofty fire-place.

Outfitting her son also occupied her enormously. She would say: "This isn't chic," or, "That looks good on you;" "This frock-coat wrinkles down the back," or, "That jacket has a nicely snug fit." She would part his hair and pomade his moustache, just as she had done with her lovers in the days when she was kept by obese bankers.

Sometimes at evening, in the late hours, she would summon him to her bed chamber, and there, in the dying light of the pink wax candles, her sculptural fingers scarcely shielded by the cambric chemise with its impudent scooped neckline, planting herself bolt upright before the tall mirror of her dresser made from West Indian hardwood and jutting out her dazzling breasts and the insolent curve of her statuesque haunches, she would speak to her son, with insinuating glances:

"Don't you think that I'm still beautiful? Don't you think that you'd be mad about me if I weren't your mother?"

Then she would laugh, peals of laughter that made the burnished splendour of her teeth shine like those of a wild beast. Casually, entwining, sinuous and feminine, she would seat herself on Philippe's knees, while he, flustered and with unconscious lasciviousness filling his eyes, barely dared to look at her. After having spent some minutes twirling her son's moustaches, kissing his lips and his carefully waved hair, she would wallow on the tiger-skin rug that pointed the way to her bed, crunch a few biscuits. swallow a glass of port at a gulp; then, with the leap of a gazelle, she would bound between the sheets, bordered in *broderie anglaise*, she would deliciously close her glossy eyelids, with long and shivering eyelashes, saying with a faint movement of her lips:

"Off you go to bed, Monsieur, it's late and I'm sleepy!"

When Philippe's nerves and his poor little heart finally revolted, their tranquillity was definitively ruptured. He frequently left the house before dawn, on a restive horse, over the meadows, without knowing quite where his reckless ride might take him, or he would go shooting wild duck for days on end in the typhoid-infested marshes. Nervous, temperamental and irritable, for some time he had tried to find ridiculous reasons for an argument with his mother, saying that this life of idleness had finally begun to get on his nerves, that it was shameful for a young man of his age, that he would certainly return to his regiment! Then there would be touching scenes, tears, pardons begged for, protestations of filial love, followed by long caresses and swooning kisses on the mouth.

V.

That day they had dined—it was a whim of La Faënza's—in the little boudoir, hung with mauve satin. A sad twilight palely filtered through the panes of the narrow window. La Faënza had said: "Don't let's light the candles, this half-light is very pleasant." She fell silent, with a vague frown. Scents of magnolia hung in the heavy air. She lit a Dubèque cigarette, he his simple soldier's pipe. Nearly ten minutes passed in an embarrassed silence.

La Faënza spoke without turning her head:
"Are you worried?"
"No."

A few more minutes of silence. Suddenly, tensing her limbs in a supreme effort, La Faënza fell at her son's knees and, embracing him frantically, she said to him, almost upon his lips:

"Philippe, you don't love me!"

He kissed her on the head without responding. Then, with an abrupt jerky movement, she rose, paced the room feverishly; then, stopping short, she said in a hollow voice:

"Oh! my God, how awful this is! I must finish it. Listen to me, Philippe; you see it, you sense it, I love you; and it isn't a mother's love that I have for you, but that of a woman in love, of a mistress, do you understand? Oh yes—I want you and you will be mine!"

She giggled like a madwoman, then began anew:

"I'm your mother—and what of it? A fine affair! Is it that I know you? I've only seen you once when you were seven; you are a stranger to me, a nice boy, and you've turned my head... As if you don't desire me too! Take a good look at me, I'm as beautiful as I was at twenty. But then there's morality! Ah, morality! I laugh at it myself! And besides, you don't know; your aunt kept everything from you... I have been... kept; I've been what's called a tart! All of my income, and yours, comes from that... So you really might not have the right to be so scrupulous. We are both in the mire, Philippe, let's stay there..."

He stared at her stupefied. She went on, more and more possessed:

"You've seen me in my chemise, you know that I have superb breasts that princes have paid their weight in gold for... We'll be happy, my Philippe, don't you want that? Oh! I'll love you, and we'll die together... of love..."

She threw herself upon her son with the frenzy of a Maenad, and, carrying him with her in her vigorous arms, she tumbled with him onto the chaise longue, panting the intoxication of her breath into his face. He felt himself lost in voluptuous annihilation. Then, suddenly, disengaging himself from that embrace with a desperate spasm of his will, standing erect and stiffening his hams, he looked about him wild-eyed.

La Faënza completely beside herself, threw herself once more at her son. Then, his features contracted, his lips frightfully clenched, Philippe seized a Japanese dagger whose slender blade glittered upon a round pedestal table with bizarre inlays, and struck her a violent blow in the throat.

She fell upon the carpet, without a cry, gushing torrents of blood.

37 Léon Bloy

Léon Bloy (1846-1917). Characterised by Philippe Jullian as "the Catholic polemicist who shuddered with horror while reading Lautréamont" and yet created tales that are "a literary counterpart to Antoine Wiertz's pictures."*

Léon Bloy was one of those writers who vividly embodied the paradoxical nature of "Decadence." He remained a devout, rather stiff-necked, Roman Catholic even when the content of his stories verged on the Luciferian: an illustration of Mario Praz's contention that "Sadism and Catholicism, in French Decadent literature, became the two poles between which the souls of neurotic and sensual writers oscillate."*

Bloy's two great collections of stories are *Histoires désobligeantes* (1894) and *Sueur du Sang* (1892), from which the present tale is taken.

Monsieur Bloy is a prophet. He took care, in his writings, to certify himself as such for us: "I am a prophet." He was able to add: and a pamphleteer as well... The prophet makes hearts bleed; the pamphleteer flays skins; Bloy is a flayer of skins.

Not an elegant torturer who, Roman or Chinese, decorticates a breast, a cheek, removes half a scalp, in accordance with the science of animal pain; but a butcher who, after a circular slash, tears away the entire hide, like a tight dress. Many of his victims, still alive, still cry out as loudly as at the moment when the tender robe of flesh was ripped from them; the man is perfectly naked and, through the transparency of his second skin we see the double cloaca of a putrefied heart. Deprived of their hypocrisy, men peeled in this way truly appear as over-ripe fruits. The vintage-time has gone by; all they are good for now is the dung-hill....

The pamphleteer has need of a style. Bloy has a style. He has gleaned the choicest seeds from the garden of Barbey d'Aurevilly and from Huysmans' little plot, but the spruce has grown—sown in that earth of metaphors—into a mighty forest that scales the summits, and the pungent pink, into a field glittering with magnificent poppies. Bloy is one of the greatest creators of images that the earth has born; that anchors his work, as a rock anchors the shifting soil; that puts his thoughts in relief like a chain of mountains. He lacks for nothing to be a very great writer except for two ideas, because he only has one: the theological idea.

Monsieur Bloy's genius is neither religious, nor philosophical, nor humane, nor mystic: Monsieur Bloy's genius is theological and Rabelaisian. His books are as if written by Saint Thomas Aquinas in collaboration with Gargantua. They are scholastic and gigantic, eucharistic and scatological, idyllic and blasphemous. No Christian can accept them, but no atheist can rejoice in this. When he insults a saint, it is for his mildness, or for the innocence of his charity, or the poverty of his literature... But it befits a prophet to grant himself immunities: he allows himself to blaspheme, but only out of an excess of charity.
Monsieur Bloy's blasphemies are, in any case, of a perfectly Baudelairean beauty, and he himself says: "Who knows, after all, if the most active form of adoration is not blasphemy out of love, which might be the prayer of the abandoned?"

...It is unfortunate that Bloy's theological notions are not discussed anymore; they are curious because of their vain tendency toward the absolute. Vain, because the absolute is the profound peace in the depths of the silent immensities, it is thought contemplative of itself, it is unity.

LÉON BLOY

Salamander The Vampire

It is said that after the death of Alaric, the Goths mourned him as a hero of their nation and that in accordance with the custom of the Northern Barbarians, who lavish great attention upon the tombs of their outstanding men, they diverted the course of a little river near Cosenza as part of his funeral rites. Having excavated in its bed a grave resembling a well-shaft, they laid there the corpse of their king, together with a quantity of treasure, filled in the hole and then allowed the waters to resume their natural course. To assure the secrecy of the tomb, they cut the throats of the prisoners who had been employed in this task.

The instinct of that race has so little changed such that, fifteen centuries later, we have seen similar scenes repeated among us, stripped of all grandeur, to be sure, but strangely demonstrative of a certain leaden childishness of that Germanic people which all the cudgels of all its masters and the prattling of all its pedants could never make more manageable.

Prussia's slaves, mechanically disciplined, have imported into France, in the baggage trains of their bum-bailiff infantry, the most age-old mustiness of their origins.

How many times have we asked ourselves in vain how it could be that *uhlans*, evidently slain or at least very badly wounded by our marksmen, whose paths were plainly marked in drops of blood, should remain in their saddles and vanish?

Some have claimed that they were tied there, others that their comrades carried them away. This much is certain, that these savages had the inexplicable power to conceal their dead and their wounded from us. If straps were fitted to their saddles, we would expect that these served to secure the rider in such a way that, even if his mount fell, the man would be instantly freed. I recall that this deceptive and complicated business of stirrup leathers was called, at the time, *the Prussian question.*

It has been asserted that they burned their dead. I have never seen this, and I doubt that at any time during the war, these odious brutes who so efficiently burned our wounded and our old people would have had the leisure or the means to extend such Teutonic practices to themselves.

But frequently, when they were unable to carry off their dear departed, they certainly did inter them in the manner of Alaric, with every imaginable reverence and all the sense of mystery that can inform such brains; burying them, for instance, between two apple-trees in which they would make an incision, in the hope of being able, a little later on, to recover their precious carrion.

Many a stray dog knew the miracle of tracking down and devouring them, scratching at the earth of those shallow graves.

There was, among us, a man we had adorned with the ironic nickname of *the Salamander*, because he was half-burned.

I do not suppose I shall ever see a more apalling face. Before encountering him, I had not been aware that the physiognomy of a living being could express so much hatred, so much hopelessness, and could so well duplicate the faces of those who had fallen into "the fire that dieth not."

They told the story, in almost hushed tones, of this unfortunate who had been listed as missing from the first corps of volunteer riflemen, of how he never forgot having seen his wife and daughter raped and murdered by a gang of fifty German louts quartered in his farmhouse in Morsbronn, the same evening as the grievous battle of Froeschwiller.

Through a thoroughly Prussian refinement that Bismarck himself had applauded, he was bound *to the foot of the bed.* A punishment for the enormous crime of having failed to speak respectfully to one of these bandits. He had to go on living with that in his heart!..

Twelve days later, at Saint-Privat, he fought many hours like a man gone berserk, and was the cause of that great cry of sorrow which arose from the midst of the Germans, when they saw the interminable rush of blood ebbing from their dead.

Struck by a ball a few moments before the close of that terrible day, and cast at random into the church where our wounded were piled high, it was his destiny to be one of the miraculous survivors of the nameless catastrophe that the military historians have feared to recount, and for which a whole people will one day have to answer, when sacred Justice makes an appearance.

Maréchal's hasty retreat not having permitted the evacuation of this temporary field-hospital, the three or four hundred poor devils abandoned to the mercy of the conquerors were condemned to be burned alive by that horrible cretinoid bastard Steinmetz, who wished thus to revenge himself upon them, in advance, for the splendid drubbing he received that infallibly forced upon him a foolish waste of his own troops.

I do not know whether it is easier to picture it to oneself or to describe such a horror. Our Salamander, who had been its witness and its victim, having only with great difficulty escaped the supreme penalty, would at times interrupt his grim monastic silence to speak from the depths in which he cloistered his soul.

Then he spoke a few very brief words that made one's hair stand on end, but the stigmata which his body displayed were even more eloquent than his silences.

He had been able to save his eyes, now lacking eyelids and resembling two spikes of dark metal thrust into two bloody swellings; but his nose, his lips and ears: all were gone, and three quarters of the face was blackened, carbonized, as if a paintbrush of burning lava had passed over him.

It had been necessary to amputate three fingers of his left hand, and his chronic limp, complicated by bizarre tics, led one to suppose that the rest of his body had also sustained the cruelest familiarities of the firebrand.

He used to say, "I was browned in the grease of those poor buggers."

For the fire had ended by setting light to that mass of human corpses upon whom the burning timberwork fell...

And were those terrifying flames touched off by jets of petrol, as at Bazeilles? God alone knows. Nevertheless, the Germans were old hands at this, and it is an unspeakable blot upon their armies, a shame not seen since the days of the Byzantine Empire, that regiments of Baden or Bavaria, armed with cans and paint brushes soaked in petrol, were assigned the task of burning down buildings or enclosures...

A profitable lesson which was not lost upon the joyous Communards of 1871.

At all events, the unfortunate village of Saint-Privat could easily be pillaged, all night long, in the white clarity of that terrifying lamp of sorrow.

The Salamander, so called because he had been able to escape an agony whose horror flouts the imagination, had managed to shelter himself in a sort of sepulchral vault where the inferno pursued him in the atrocious form of fiery liquids—mineral oil or human axle-grease, he was unable to say—and in the darkness of that place, The Pit, it calcified for him his phantasmagoric face.

So hardy a cripple was he, that four months had barely gone by when this man, whom death evidently had not wanted at any sort of a price, found himself among us in the capacity of a volunteer. He was really very good! As good as any of us, especially during the night attacks, when the sudden looming up of his demonic face often caused a panic.

His sole intact hand was, I believe, as good as ten and it seemed to multiply itself. Unsuited to the various ways of handling a rifle, it was none the less, the best in the world for knifings or bludgeonings.

At those times his macabre mouth would open in a sort of laugh that did not spread to the rest of us, I assure you, and he would cry out hysterically and voluptuously, like a lover.

When his pleasure was exhausted and it was time for us to withdraw from combat, nothing, but nothing, could convey an idea of the sadness of the unfortunate who would be heard weeping softly for the rest of the night. It issued from him like a black flower, a gloomy tuberose of melancholy that suffocated us...

Very mild, in other respects, as soon as he no longer saw Prussians, a good-natured spectre and an excellent soldier who never grumbled; we accepted the moral and physical oppression of his redoubtable presence out of pity as much as out of fear. The fact is, he was not a nuisance and passed the hours, immobile, seated on the ground, his chest pressed into his drawn together knees and his face lost in the hollow of his two arms.

One of his compatriots explained that he had been a worthy man, a respectable husbandman, loving his wife and his daughter as a fanatical bonze loves his idols; and, having been himself transformed into a phantom, he now chattered familiarly with their phantoms.

I have often asked myself what could life, country, even God have meant to one as profoundly wretched as he...

We only found out when it was too late—and everything was over—how complete a spectre he was, when we discovered that our Salamander was a passionate despoiler of graves.

Having lived for several months with only his hatred of the Germans to sustain him, nothing was able to assuage this unique passion, not even their deaths, on which he lavished care, and which he knew how to prolong under certain circumstances. Even these deaths barely satisfied him.

He wished that he might have the power to lay hands on that which does not die, that which some call their immortal soul—if, that is, it were possible that such brutes might possess one.

Unable to evoke the fluid spirits of the dead before

his executioner's heart by supernatural means, he turned his attention to their corpses, horribly persuaded that the *Requiescant in pace* is not an idle formula, and that he could, in some way, torment the dead by defiling their tombs.

In any case, this way he had the possibility of inflaming the grief of those who had survived them, and wept for them.

Among the evidence gathered after the extermination of the vampire are details that are such as to defy understanding.

They found bundles of papers on him, plundered from the corpses, and letters in his own hand that might well have been posted from hell. These letters, composed in the mournful style of funeral announcements and almost too disgusting to touch, informed the mothers, the widows, the children, the friends or the fiancées, living in Germany, of certain sacrilegious acts inflicted in the darkness upon the wretched disinterred bodies of their dearest ones, according to the satanic discernment of this ghoul...

Naturally, he knew of the Gothic custom of secret inhumations of which I have spoken, and he had a jackal's flair for rooting out such buried treasures.

He died in his sin, at the commencement of the armistice, his existence no longer having any object.

"What's the good of hanging on now?" he said to himself.

This is how we have, by means of induction or deduction, pieced together the facts concerning his fate:

During the especially fierce combat waged in the environs of the unfortunate little town of Belleme, in the *département* of the Orne, the Prussians, having seen one of their youngest and best-loved officers die, had contrived to bury him clandestinely, according to their custom, in a wooden trough, found in a peasant's pigsty.

They laid him in this bizarre coffin, his sword at his side, and beside him, on the bare earth, as if to guard his body for eternity, a simple soldier killed the same day. The soil of the double tomb was carefully tamped down, and the emplacement marked with the greatest precision.

Two months after the signing of the armistice, three Germans came before dawn to visit the funereal spot and discovered, by the side of the open grave—which was emitting an unbearable odour—the Salamander crouching over the two corpses, which he had mutilated, sneering at their putrefaction.

Teterrima facies daemonum!... The apparition of this frightful face, in such circumstances, in such an hour and in such a place, must have been terrible for these barbarians, since the physician declared that one of the Germans had died on the spot from a ruptured aneurism.

As for the other two, they bravely gave of everything they had of the blood in their veins—and their bodies, pierced repeatedly, were only with the greatest difficulty separated from the spasm-wracked corpse of Salamander the Vampire.

43 ANDRÉ GIDE

André Gide (1869-1951). This early text by Gide (1892), previously untranslated, is simultaneously an exegesis and demonstration of Symbolist theories of literature. Though a little flawed by youthful enthusiasm, it is a courageous attempt to explain the more hermetic concepts that underline Symbolist ideas: Platonist influences being particularly evident. Although *Narcissus* is dedicated to Paul Valéry it is more influenced by Mallarméan concepts, in particular his "Garden of Ideas." Pierre Louÿs introduced Gide to Mallarmé in 1891 and he became an enthusiastic disciple, attending his famous weekly *soirées* in which Symbolist doctrine was elaborated. This text, and the one following it, by Claudel (and perhaps even the final piece by Saint-Pol-Roux), attempt an evocation, rather than a definition, of the essence of Symbolist thought.

Gide's abandonment of Symbolism dates from his trip to Tunisia in 1895, although its influence pervades many of his works, in particular *Paludes* and *Le Voyage d'Urien*. Gide's subsequent literary career hardly needs recapitulation here.

A writer's talent is often only the terrible ability to retell the eternal clamourings of a mediocre humanity in phrases that seem beautiful and eternal; even geniuses and men of gigantic talent, like Victor Hugo or Adam de Saint-Victor were destined to offer us an admirable music whose grandeur conceals immense deserts of vacuity; their souls are like the unformed, docile soul of the sands or of a crowd; they love, they dream, they crave loves, dreams, the desires of every man and beast; poets, they cry out magnificently that which is not worth the effort of being thought of.

The human species, without doubt, in its entire aspect of a hive or colony, is only pre-eminent over the bison species or that of the kingfisher, because we are a part of it; here and there man is a sad automaton; but the superiority of man lies in the fact that he is able to arrive at consciousness: a small number attain it. To acquire full consciousness of self, is to know oneself so much different from the others that one is no longer conscious of men except through purely animal contacts: and yet among souls of this degree there is an ideal fraternity based upon differences—while the social fraternity is based upon resemblances.

This complete consciousness of oneself can be called the originality of the soul—and all of this is only to point out that group of rare beings to which André Gide belongs...

ANDRÉ GIDE

The Tractate Narcissus (Theory of the Symbol)

Perhaps books are not all that necessary; originally a few myths sufficed; a religion contained them all complete. The people, amazed at the appearance of these fables, and uncomprehending, worshipped them; the attentive priests pondered the depths of these images, and slowly fathomed the inner meaning of the hieroglyph. Then the need to explain them was felt; books have enlarged upon the myths—but a few myths sufficed.

Thus the myth of Narcissus: *Narcissus was perfectly beautiful, and that is why he was chaste; he scorned the Nymphs, because he was smitten with himself. No breath troubled the spring, where, peacefully reclining, all day long he contemplated his image...* You know the story. But we tell it still. Everything has already been said; but since nobody listens, it must always be repeated.

Now there is neither bank nor spring; neither mirrored flower nor metamorphosis; there is nothing then, but Narcissus alone, dreaming and holding himself aloof in the greyness. He is uneasy in the useless monotony of the moment, and his restless heart questions itself. He wants at last to know the exact form his soul possesses; he senses that she must be excessively adorable, he judges this to be so because of her protracted trembling; but her face! her appearance! Ah! not to know whether one loves oneself!... not to know her beauty! I merge into this landscape without paths, that does not contrast its planes. Ah! Curse this inability to see oneself! A mirror! a mirror! a mirror! a mirror!

And Narcissus, who does not doubt that his form may be somewhere, rises and goes in search of the wished-for contours wherewith to envelop his great soul.

Narcissus has halted at the edge of the river of time. Fatal, illusory river in which the years pass by and flow away. Simple banks, like a rough frame in which the water is set, like a sheet of plate glass; where nothing could see behind itself; where, behind, empty ennui might spread itself. A dreary, lethargic canal, an almost horizontal mirror; and nothing to distinguish this dull water from the colourless ambience, if one did not sense its flow.

From a distance, Narcissus has taken the river to be a roadway, and as he is bored, all alone in all this greyness, he draws near in order to watch things pass by. Now, his hands upon the frame, he leans over, in his traditional pose. And, as he watches, a slender appearance suddenly dapples itself upon the water. Flowers on the banks, trunks of trees, reflected fragments of blue sky, a flight of rapid images that only awaited him in order to be, and that take on colour beneath his gaze. Then hills open up and forests space themselves out across the slopes of the valleys: visions that undulate in accord with the water's flow, that the waves diversify. Filled with wonder, Narcissus watches; but hardly comprehends because, whether his soul guides the stream or the stream itself is the guide, they balance each other out.

Where Narcissus watches: it is the present. From the more distant future, things, still potential, hurry toward being; Narcissus sees them, then they pass; they flow into the past. Narcissus soon discovers that it is always thus. He questions; then ponders. The same forms always pass by; only the surge of the wave differs. Why several? or indeed, why the same? It is because they are imperfect that they always begin anew... and, he thinks to himself, all strive for and seek an original, now-lost form, crystalline and paradisiac.

Narcissus dreams of paradise.

I.

Paradise was not vast; each form, perfect, blossomed there only once; and all were contained in a garden. If it was, if it was not, to us what matter? But it was as it was, if it was. Everything there crystallised into a necessary blossoming, and everything wasn perfectly as it ought to be. Everything remained motionless, because nothing wished to be better. Calm gravitation alone carried out the revolution of the whole.

And, since no momentum ceases, in the Past or in the Future, Paradise was not becoming: it simply and forever was.

Chaste Eden! Garden of Ideas! where forms, rhythmic and certain, revealed their number effortlessly; where everything was as it appeared; where to prove was pointless.

Eden! where melodious breezes undulated in anticipated curves; where the sky stretched out blue above symmetrical lawns; where birds were the colour of time and butterflies on flowers created providential harmonies; where the rose was pink because the rose-chafer, who happened to land on it, was green. Everything was as perfect as a number and scannedlike a poem; an accord emanated from the rapport of its lines; a constant symphony hung over the garden.

At the centre of Eden, Yggdrasil, the logarithmic tree, plunged its roots of life into the soil, and spread across the lawn the thick shadow of its foliage where only Night lay extended. In the darkness the book of Mystery, in which the truth that must be known may be read, lay propped against its trunk. And the wind, breathing all day long into the leaves of the tree, spelled out the necessary hieroglyphics.

Religious, Adam listened. Still unsexed, unique, he lived seated in the shadow of the great tree. Man! Hypostasis of Elohim, instrument of Divinity! for him, through him, forms appeared. Motionless and central amid all this enchantment, he watches that which unfolds.

But he, ever an obliged spectator at a spectacle where he has no role other than to watch, grows weary. He knows that everything is for him—but himself... he never sees himself. But what, then, does all the rest matter to him? Ah! To see himself! Certainly he is powerful, since he creates and the entire world hangs on his glance—but what does he know of his power, in so far as remains unaffirmed? By dint of contemplating them, he no longer distinguishes himself from these things: not to know where one stops—not even knowing where one goes! Because finally it is slavery, if one dares not risk a movement without disturbing the whole harmony. Too bad, then! this harmony and this always-perfect accord irritate me. Movement! a little movement, just to know—a discord, devil take it!—Right then! something unexpected.

Ah! grab it! to grab a branch of Yggdrasil between his infatuated fingers, and let him break it...

It's done.

...An imperceptible fissure, at first, a cry, but it sprouts, spreads, becomes exasperated, whistles shrilly and soon groans like a tempest. The tree Yggdrasil, withered, totters and snaps; its leaves, where the breezes played, shivering and curled up, contort in the squall that rises up and carries them far away—toward the unknown of a nocturnal sky and toward the hazardous regions, where the scattering of pages torn from the great sacred book, also stripped of its leaves, fly away.

Into the sky a vapour rises: tears, clouds that drop down again in tears and which rise again in storm-clouds: time is born.

And terrified Man, androgyne split in two, trembled in anguish and horror, feeling, with a new sex, a restless desire welling up within him for that nearly identical half of himself, that female suddenly present there, whom he embraces and of whom he wishes to regain possession —that woman who, in the blind effort to recreate through herself the perfect being and there to limit that breed, will cause the unknown-one of a new race to stir in her womb, and soon a new being will emerge in time, still incomplete, and which will not suffice unto itself.

Sad race, who will disperse yourselves over this land of twilight and prayers! the memory of Paradise lost will come to desolate your ecstasies, the Paradise you will search for everywhere—which prophets will come again to tell you of—and poets, here, will piously gather up the leaves torn from the immemorial Book in which one may read the truth that must be known.

II.

If Narcissus turned over, he might, I think, see some green bank, perhaps the sky, the Tree, the Flower—something stable at last, and enduring, but whose reflection falling upon the water breaks up and is dispersed by the fleetness of the stream.

When will this water cease its flight? and finally resigned, stagnant mirror, show me, with the same purity of image, the lineaments of these fatal forms—so confusingly alike—or even become them, at last.

When will time, ceasing its flight, allow this flux to rest? Forms, divine and perennial forms! which only await repose in order to reappear, oh! when, in what night, in what silence, will you re-crystallise?

Paradise has always to be restored; it is not in some far-off Thule. It remains beneath appearances.

Everything is in potential possession of the intimate harmony of its being, as each salt, in itself, possesses the archetype of its crystal—and a time of tacit night comes when the densest waters descend: in the imperturbed gulfs secret crystal-clusters will flower...

Everything strives towards its lost form; it is apparent, but soiled, warped, and dissatisfied with itself, because it always commences anew; hurriedly, embarrassed by neighbouring forms which also strive, every one of them, to appear—because, to be is no longer enough: one must prove it to oneself—and pride infatuates them all. The passing hour overwhelms them.

Since time flies only through the flight of things, each thing clings fast and tenses itself in order to slow this course a little and so be able the better to appear. It is during these periods then, when things are moving more slowly, that time rests—one imagines—and as noise ceases, with movement—everything is quiet. One waits; one comprehends that it is a tragic moment and that one must not stir.

"There was silence in heaven;" prelude to apocalypses. Yes tragic, tragic moments, in which new eras commence, in which the heavens and the earth meditate, in which the book sealed with seven seals begins to open, in which everything begins to be set in an eternal position... but suddenly an obtrusive clamour arises; upon the blessed plateaux where it is said that time goes to end itself, a few ever-avid soldiers share the vestments between themselves and cast lots for the tunic—as ecstasy immobilises the holy women, and as the rent veil will betray the secrets of the temple; when all of creation finally contemplates the Christ who congeals upon the supreme cross, speaking the last words:

"It is ended..."

No! for all things are to be made anew, eternally made anew—because one of those casting lots has not checked his vain gesture, because a soldier wished to win a tunic, because someone did not watch.

Because the fault that again loses Paradise is always the same: the individual dreams to himself while the Passion ordains itself, and he, proud supernumerary, fails to subordinate himself.*

Inexhaustible masses, every day, in order to put Christ back into agony, and the public in the mood to pray... a public!—when it would be necessary to prostrate the whole of humanity: then *one* mass would suffice.

If we knew how to watch and wait...

III.

The Poet is he who watches. And what does he see? — Paradise.

Because Paradise is everywhere; let us not believe in appearances. Appearances are imperfect: they stammer the truths that they contain; the Poet must take the hint—then reiterate these truths. Isn't this what the Scientist does? He also seeks out the archetypes of things and the laws governing their succession; in the end he recombines an entire world, ideally simple, in which everything arranges itself naturally.

But the Scientist searches out these primary forms by means of a slow and timorous induction, through numerous examples; for he halts before appearances and, desirous of certitude, he refrains from intuition.

The Poet, himself knowing that he creates, guesses through each thing—and one thing is enough, being a symbol, to reveal its archetype; he knows that appearances are only a pretext, a concealing vestment to defeat profane eyes, but which shows us that It is there.*

The pious Poet contemplates; he leans over symbols, and delves deeply, silently, into the heart of things—and when, visionary, he has perceived the Idea, the intimate harmonious Number of its Being, which supports the imperfect form, he seizes it, and then, heedless of the transitory form which it dons in time, he knows how to restore an eternal form to it, *its* true Form at last—crystalline and paradisiac.

Because the work of art is a crystal—partial paradise in which the Idea flourishes anew in its superior purity; in which, as in vanished Eden, the natural and necessary order has arranged all forms within a reciprocal and symmetrical dependence, in which the pride of the word does not supplant the thought—in which the sure and rhythmic phrases, still symbols, but pure symbols, in which words make themselves transparent and revealing.

Such works do not crystallise themselves except in silence; but sometimes there are silences in the midst of crowds, in which the artist takes refuge like Moses upon Sinai, isolating himself, escaping things, time shrouding him in an atmosphere of light above the busy multitude. The Idea slowly settles on him, then, lucid, blossoms outside of time. And as it is not within time, time will be able to do nothing to it. To go on: one asks oneself if Paradise, itself outside of time, was perhaps never more than this—that is to say, only ideally...

Meanwhile Narcissus contemplates from the bank this vision of an amorous desire transfigured; he dreams. Childish and alone, Narcissus falls in love with the fragile image; he leans over, with a need to caress, in order to quench in the river his thirst for love. He leans over and now, suddenly, this phantasmagoria disappears; now in the river he sees only two lips in front of his own, offering themselves, and two eyes, his own returning his stare. He understands that it is he—he alone—and that he is in love with his own face. All around, an azure emptiness, which his pale arms, sinking into an unknown element, split asunder, straining with desire towards the shattered appearance. He raises himself slightly; the face disperses. The surface of the water, as before, is dappled and the vision has returned. But Narcissus tells himself that to kiss it is impossible, he does not need to desire an image; a gesture to possess it, will tear it. He is alone. What to do? Contemplate.

Religious and grave, he recovers his calm serenity: he remains—a symbol that grows—and, brooding over the semblance of the World, vaguely feels the transient generations of humanity re-absorbed into him.

Perhaps this treatise is not all that necessary. At first, a few myths sufficed. Then came the desire to explain; priestly pride that seeks to reveal mysteries in order to be adored—or else a lively sympathy, and that apostolic love which brings it about that one discloses, and in displaying them profanes the temple's most secret treasures, for worshipping alone is painful and so one wishes for fellow worshippers.

Certainly it will be neither the irksome laws of men, nor fears, nor modesty, nor remorse, nor respect for me or for my dreams, nor you, sad death, nor terrors from beyond the grave, that prevent me from joining that which I desire; nothing—but pride, knowing something so strong, yet feeling myself stronger still and able to defeat it. But the joy of one such haughty victory is still not as sweet, not as good, as to yield to you, desires, and to be vanquished without a fight.

When springtime came this year, I was tormented by her grace; and as desires made my solitude painful, I came out in the morning into the fields. All day the sun shone forth upon the plain; I walked dreaming of happiness. Certainly, I thought, it is from other lands than these disenchanted regions that I led my soul to graze. When shall I be able, far from my morose thoughts, to stroll in the sunlight filled with joy, and, in forgetting yesterday and so many useless religions, embrace the happiness which will come, vigorously, without scruples or fears? And I dared not return that evening, apt to imagine too many new anxieties; I walked towards the woods where, already, in times past and often, my sorrow had vanished. Night came, and moonlight. The woods became tranquil and filled with marvellous shadows; the wind shivered; the nocturnal birds awakened. I started down a deep path where the sand glowed beneath my feet, and this haunted whiteness guided me. Between the more widely spaced branches, when the wind stirred the trees, one could see the elusive shapes of mists floating over the path; and, as if in the middle of the night, the dew dripped from the leaves, and the scents of the forest became amorous. There were tremblings amid the grasses, each form searching, finding, becoming harmonious; the flowers swayed, and the pollen floated, lighter than the mist, like powder. A secret and swooning joy felt itself murmur beneath the branches. I waited. The night birds lamented. Then everything fell silent; it was the meditation before the dawn; joy became serenity and my solitude boundless, there in the colourless, counselling night.

Paul Claudel (1868-1955). Claudel worked for many years in the French diplomatic service in China and the Far East. In 1886 he simultaneously converted to Catholicism and discovered the works of Rimbaud, which had a seminal influence upon him. He was principally known as a poet and a dramatist (and it is in this latter role that de Gourmont wrote about him in *The Book of Masks*).

The present texts come from his collection *Connaissance de l'Est* (which can be unsatisfactorily translated as *The East I Know*, 1900) which he referred to as *"a book of exercises"* written as an application of Mallarmé's rule: *"Learn to see."*

We have always seen superior men, once they have no taste for running civilisation, live outside of it. This one, whose name is practically unknown, has never rubbed shoulders with his brethren; at the first opportunity he left us, dedicated, fierce, for a distant consulate; for his retreat, he has an abandoned pagoda and, certain that they do not see into his soul, he allows his eyes to wander amid the yellow ants....

But it will be fifty years before even these details interest anybody; the author of Tête d'or *is here or there, as he has chosen to be. For ships it matters whether the wind blows this way or that; for books not at all: they set out from all sides at once, they arrive everywhere, waifs that shipwrecks wrap in eternal swaddling-clothes.* Tête d'or *was launched one day by a man who wrote in French, and with genius, seven or eight years ago, and who has since been silent.*

THE BOOK OF MASKS 52

PAUL CLAUDEL

The Religion of Letters

Let others discover in the range of Chinese characters either the head of a sheep, the arms and legs of a man, or the sun setting behind a tree. For my part I seek a more difficult clue.

All writing commences with a symbol or line which, considered as a whole, is a pure characterisation of the individual. Either the line is horizontal, like all things which, in simply conforming to the laws of their being, find sufficient reason for existence; or it is vertical, like the tree and the man, indicating acts and laying down affirmations; or, if oblique, it marks movement and the senses.

The Roman letter has had the vertical line for its principle; the Chinese character seems to have the horizontal as its essential trait. The letter with an imperious down-stroke affirms that a thing is so; the character is the very thing that it signifies.

One symbol or another is equally a sign. Let us take figures for example. They are all equally abstract images, but the letter is essentially analytic. Each word is an enunciation of successive affirmations that the eye and the voice spell out. Unit is added to unit on the same line, and the Protean syllable changes and is modified in a continual variation. But the Chinese sign develops the figure, and, applying it to a series of beings, it differentiates their characters indefinitely. A word exists by a succession of letters, a character by the relation of its strokes. May we not imagine that in these the horizontal line indicates, for example, the species; the vertical, the individual; the oblique, diverse of movement, that group of traits and energies which gives meaning to the whole; the period, distinct on the white page, signifying something that can only be implied? One can therefore see in the Chinese character a completely developed being, a written person, having, like a person who lives, his nature and his moods, his own acts and his inner individuality, his structure and physiognomy.

This explains the piety with which the Chinese regard writing. They burn with respect the humblest paper marked with a vestige of this mystery. The sign is a being; and, from the fact that it is common to all, it becomes sacred. With them the representation of ideas is almost an idol. Such is the foundation of that scriptural religion which is peculiar to China. Yesterday I visited a Confucian temple.

It was in a solitary quarter where everything spoke of desertion and decay. In the silence and burning heat of the sun at three o'clock, we followed the sinuous street. Our entrance is not to be by the great door where the proud rot in their enclosure, where that high column marked with an official inscription in two languages guards the worn sill. A woman, short and round-backed as a pig, opens a side passage for us; and, with echoing footfalls, we penetrate into the deserted court.

By the proportions of the court and of the peristyles which frame it; by the spacious intercolumniations and the horizontal lines of the façade; by the repetition of the two enormous roofs, which lift their massive black curves with a single sweep; by the symmetrical disposition of the two little pavilions which are before it and which lighten the severity of the whole with the agreeable grotesques of their octagonal roofs; the building (to apply the essential laws of architecture) is given a learned aspect, a classic beauty in short, due to an exquisite observation of rule.

The temple is composed of two parts. I suppose that the passages with their rows of tablets on the walls, each one preceded by a long, narrow altar of stone, offer to a hasty worship the primary series of precepts. Lifting our feet to avoid the sill which it is forbidden to tread upon, we penetrate into the shade of the sanctuary.

The vast high hall has the air of holding an occult presence. It is utterly empty. Here silence sits veiled in obscurity. Here are no ornaments, no statues. On each side of the hall we distinguish, between their curtains, great inscriptions; and, before them, altars; but in the middle of the temple, behind five monumental pieces of stone, three vases and two candlesticks; under an edifice of gold, a baldachin or a tabernacle which frames it on all sides; four characters are inscribed upon a vertical column.

Here writing possesses this mystery: it speaks. No moment marks its duration, no position. It is the commencement of an ageless sign. No mouth offers it. It exists; and the worshipper, face to face with it, ponders the written name. Solemnly enunciated in the gloom of the shadowy gold of the baldachin, the sign, between the two columns which are covered with the mystic windings of the dragon, symbolises its own silence. The immense red hall seems to be the very colour of obscurity, the pillars are hidden under a scarlet lacquer. Alone in the middle of the temple, before the sacred word, two columns of white granite seem its witness; the very soul, religious and abstract, of the place.

P. C.

The Melancholy Water

There is an intelligence in joy, I admit it. There is a vision in laughter. But that you may comprehend, my friend, this medley of blessedness and bitterness which the act of creation includes, now that the melancholy season begins I shall explain to you the sadness of water.

The same tear falls from the sky that overflows from the eyelid. Do not think to accuse the cloud of your melancholy, nor this veil of vague showers. Shut your eyes; listen! The rain falls.

Nor does the monotony of this constant sound suffice to explain it.

It is a weary mourning whose cause is within itself. It is the self-absorption of love; it is the effort in labour. The heavens weep over the fruitful earth. Not only autumn, and the future fall of fruit whose seed she nourishes, draws these tears frown the wintry cloud. Sorrow is in the summer; in the flower of life is the blossoming of death.

At the moment when the hour before noon is ended, as I descend into the valley filled with the murmur of various fountains, I pause enchanted by the gloom. How abundant are these waters! And if tears, like blood, have their perpetual source in us, how refreshing it is, listening to this liquid choir of voices, deep or shrill, to harmonise from them all the shades of grief! There is no passion but could borrow of your tears, O fountain! And since the brightness of this single drop, falling from on high into the basin upon the image of the moon, satisfies my particular desire, not in vain shall I have learned to love your sanctuary through many dreamy afternoons, O sorrowful valley!

I return to the plain. On the doorsill of his hut—where, in the inner darkness, gleams a candle lit for some rustic fête—a man sits, holding in his hand a dusty cymbal. It rains heavily. In the midst of this damp solitude, I hear only the cry of a goose.

P. C.

The Temple of Consciousness

I have devoted more than one day simply to the discovery of it, ensconced upon its steep cliff of black rock, and it is not till late afternoon that I know myself to be upon the right path. From the giddy height where I climb, the wide rice-fields seem designed like a chart. The brink along which I move is so narrow that whenever I lift my right foot it is

THE BOOK OF MASKS 54

poised over the yellow expanse of the sown village fields spread out like a carpet below.

Silence. By an ancient staircase covered with a hoary lichen I descend in the pungent shade of the bay trees, and, as the footpath at this turning is suddenly barred by a wall, I arrive at a closed door. I listen. No word, no voice, no drum! In vain I shake the wooden handle of the door, and beat upon it rudely with both hands.

Not even a bird cries as I scale the wall.

This place is inhabited after all; and while, sitting upon the balustrade where domestic linen is drying, I sink my teeth and fingers into the thick rind of a haddock stolen from the offerings, the old monk inside prepares me a cup of tea. Neither the inscription above the door nor the dilapidated idols who are honoured with a thin spire of incense in the depths of this humble cave seem to me to constitute the religion of the place, any more than the acid fruit that I munch; but here—on this low platform, which encloses a piece of muslin—this circular straw mat where the *bhiku* will come soon to squat for meditation or sleep —is everything.

Let me compare this vast countryside, which opens out before me as far as the double wall of mountains and clouds, to a flower of which this seat is the mystic heart. Is it not the geometric centre where the scene, united into an harmonious whole, virtually takes on existence and a consciousness of itself; and where, to the studious contemplation of the occupant, all lines converge?

The sun sets. I clamber up the steps of velvet whiteness where open pine-cones are strewn like roses.

P. C.

The Tomb

On the pediment of the funereal portal I read an order to alight. On my right are some broken statues in the reeds, and an inscription on a formidable pillar of black granite gives with wearisome detail the laws relating to sepulchres; half obliterated by moss a threat forbids the breaking of vases, loud cries, or the spoiling of ceremonial basins.

It is certainly later than two o'clock, because I see that the dim, round sun is already a third of the way down a dull and lurid sky. I can only mount straight onward, to survey the arrangement of the cemetery; and, preparing my heart, I start out on the road the funerals follow across this home of the dead, in itself lifeless. First come, one after another, two square mountains of brick. Their hollow centres open by four arches on the four points of the compass. The first of these halls is empty. In the second a giant tortoise of marble, so high that I can scarcely reach his moustached head with my hand, supports a panegyric column. "This is the porch and apprenticeship of the earth," I thought. "Here Death halted between the double thresholds, and here the master of the world received supreme homage between the four horizons and the sky."

But scarcely have I gone out by the Northern door (it is not vainly that I leap this rivulet!) than I see open out before me the country of the shades.

Forming an avenue of alternate couples, monstrous animals appear before me, facing each other, successively repeated kneeling and standing in pairs; rams, horses, unicorns, camels, elephants; until, at the turning where the last of the procession disappears, these enormous and ugly shapes loom out against the straggling grass. Further off are ranged civil and military mandarins. These stones are sent to ceremonial funerals in the place of animals and men; and, as the dead have crossed the threshold of life, it would not be suitable to give closer likenesses to such replicas.

Here, where this large cairn—hiding, they say, the treasures and bones of a very ancient dynasty—ceases to bar the passage, the way turns toward the East. I am walking now among soldiers and ministers. Some are intact and standing, others lie on their faces. One warrior without a head still clasps the hilt of a sword in his fist. By a triple-arched bridge the path crosses the second canal.

Now, by a series of stairs where the central hand-rail still shows the imperial dragon, I cross the ravaged site of terraces and courts. These are the walks of Memory, the fugitive traces of lives which, leaving the earth, serve only to enrich it by decay; the steps of sacrifices, the awful garden where what is destroyed attests its whilom existence in the presence of what still remains. In the centre a throne supports, a baldachin still shelters, the inscription of a dynasty. All about, temples and guest-houses have become a confused rubbish among the briars.

And the tomb is before me.

"Between massive projections of the square bastions which flank it, behind the deep-cut channel of the third stream, is a wall which assures us that the end of our journey must be here. A wall and nothing but a wall, a hundred feet high and two hundred feet wide. Eroded by the use of centuries, the inexorable barrier presents a blind face of masonry. A single round hole shows in the centre of the base, the mouth of an oven or the oubliette of a dungeon. This wall forms the front of a sort of trapezoid formation, detached from the mountain which overhangs it. A low moulding, ending beneath an overhanging cornice, stands out from the wall like a console. No corpse is so suspect as to require such a mass being placed upon him. This is the throne of Death itself, the regal exaltation of sepulture.

A straight alley, remounting the sloping plain, crosses a level plateau. At the end there is only the same mountain whose steep slope conceals in its depths the ancient Ming.

And I understand that this is the sepulchre of the Atheist. Time has scattered the vain temples and laid the idols in the dust, and only the arrangement of the place remains, with the idea it expressed. The pompous catafalques on the threshold have not been able to retain the dead. The cortège of his vanished glory cannot retard him. He crosses the three rivers, he traverses the manifold courts filled with incense; nor is the monument that has been prepared for him sufficient to hold him. He cleaves his way further, and enters into the very body and bones of primitive earth. It is merely an animal interment, the mixing of crude flesh with inert and compact clay. The king and peasant are forever consolidated into this death without a dream or an awakening.

But the shadow of evening spreads over this cruel place. O ruins, the tomb has survived you! And the brutal stolidity of this bulk is a perfect symbol of death itself.

As I return among the colossal statues of stone, I see in the dried grass the decaying corpse of a horse, which a dog is tearing. The beast looks at me as he licks the blood which trickles down his chops; then, applying his paws again to the red carcass, he tears off a long strip of flesh. The mangled remains are spread about.

P. C.

Dissolution Again I am carried back over the indifferent liquid sea. When I am dead, nothing can hurt me. When I shall be interred between my father and mother, nothing will make me suffer more. They cannot jeer any longer at this too ardent heart. The sacrament of my body will dissolve in the interior of the earth; but, like a most piercing cry, my soul will repose in the bosom of Abraham. Now everything is dissolved, and with a dull and heavy eye I search about me in vain for the familiar land and the firm road under my feet—and for that unkind face! The sky is nothing but fog, and Space is nothing but water! You see it! Everything is blurred; and all about me I must search in vain for line or form. For a horizon there is nothing but the cessation of colour in darkness. All matter is resolved into water alone, like the tears I feel coursing down my cheeks. All sound is like the murmur of sleep when it breathes to us all that is most crushing to our hopes. I shall have searched in vain, I shall find nothing more beyond me—neither that country which might have been my home, nor that well-loved face!

—*Translated by Teresa Frances & William Benét.*

Francis Jammes (1868-1936). Jammes lived his whole life in a small town at the base of the Pyrennees, far from Parisian literary coteries, who only discovered his verse by accident. There is little else to say of a biographical nature.

The work here dates from 1920 and has an interesting similarity to the later writings of Ponge.

Jammes became a Catholic, but avoided the Nationalism that accompanied the conversion of so many of his contemporaries.

A bucolic poet!... No variety of poet is rarer: he needs to live apart in the honest homes of yore, at the edge of a wood guarded by thorns alone, among black elms, wrinkled oaks and beech-trees with skin as smooth as that of a dearly-loved mistress...

Without a doubt there is no other poet in France today capable of evoking a tableau so serene and so true with words so simple, with phrases that seem like those of an idly wandering conversation and still, as if by chance, form charming, pure and definitive verses...

It is high time, for our good name, to give this poet fame and, for our pleasure, often to breathe in his poetry, which he himself has called a poetry of white roses.

FRANCES JAMMES

Of Things (extract) The belief that things are endowed with life exists among children, animals, and simple people.

I have seen children attribute the characteristics of a living being to a piece of rough wood or to a stone. They brought it handfuls of grass, and were absolutely sure that the wood or stone had eaten it when, as a matter of fact, I had carried it off without their noticing it.

Animals do not differentiate the quality of an action. I have seen cats scratch at something too hot for them for a long time. In this act on the part of the animal there is an idea of fighting something which can yield or perhaps die.

I think it is only an education, born of false vanity, that has robbed man of such beliefs. I myself see no essential difference between the thought of a child who gives food to a piece of wood and the meaning of some of the libations in primitive religions. Do we not attribute to trees an attachment to us stronger than life itself when we believe that one planted on the birthday of a child that sickens and dies will wither and dry up at the same time?

I have known things in pain. I have known some which are dead. The sad clothes of our departed wear out quickly. They are often impregnated with the same disease as those who wore them. They are one with them.

I have often considered objects which were wasting away. Their disintegration is identical with our own. They have their decay, their ruptures, their tumours, their madnesses. A piece of furniture gnawed by worms, a gun with a broken trigger, a warped drawer, or the soul of a violin suddenly out of tune, such are the ills which move me.

When we become attached to things why do we believe that love is in us alone, and afterwards regard it as something external to us? Who can prove that things are incapable of affection, or who can demonstrate their unconsciousness? Was not that sculptor right who was buried holding in his hand a lump of the same clay that had obeyed his dream? Did it not have the devotion of a faithful servant; did it not have a quality which we should admire all the more, because it had the virtue of devoting itself in silence, without selfish interest, and with the passiveness of faith?

Is there not something sublime and radiant in the thing that acts toward man, even as man acts toward God? Does the poet know any more what impulse he obeys, than does the clay? From the moment when they have both proved their inspiration, I believe equally in their consciousness, and I love both with the same love.

The sadness which disengages from things that have fallen into disuse is infinite. In the attic of this house whose inhabitants I did not know, a little girl's dress and her doll lie desolate. And here is an iron-pointed staff which once bit into the earth of the green hills, and a sun bonnet now barely visible in the dim light from the garret window. They have been abandoned since many years, and I am wholly certain that they would be happy again to enjoy, the one the freshness of the moss, and the other the summer sky.

Things tenderly cared for show their gratitude to us, and are ever ready to offer us their soul when once we have refreshed it. They are like those roses of the desert which expand infinitely when a little water brings back to their memory the azure of lost wells.

In my modest drawing-room there is a child's chair. My father played with it during his passage from Guadeloupe to France when he was seven years old. He remembered distinctly that he sat on it in the ship's saloon, and looked at pictures which the captain lent him. The island wood of which it was made must have been stout for it withstood the games of a little boy. The piece of furniture had drifted into my home, and slept there almost forgotten. Its soul too had been asleep for many long years, because the child who had cherished it was no more, and no other children had come to perch upon it like birds.

But recently the house was made merry by my little niece who was just seven. On my work table she had found an old book with plates of flowers. When I entered the room I found her sitting on the little chair in the lamplight, looking at the charming pictures, just as once a long time ago her grandfather had done. And I was deeply touched. And I said to myself that this little girl alone had been able to make the soul of the chair live again, and that the gentle soul of the chair had bewitched the candour of the child. There was between her and this object a mysterious affinity. The one could not help but go to the other, and it could be awakened by her alone.

Things are gentle. They never do harm voluntarily. They are the sisters of the spirits. They protect us, and we let our thoughts rest upon them. Our thoughts need them for resting-places as perfumes need the flowers.

The prisoner, whom no human soul can any longer console, must feel tenderly toward his pallet and his earthen jug. When everything has been refused him by his fellows his obscure bed gives him sleep and his jug quenches his thirst. And even if it separates him from all the world without, the very barrenness of his walls stands between him and his executioners. The child who has been punished loves the pillow on which he cries; for when every one of an evening has hurt and scolded him, he finds consolation in the soul of the silent down. It is like a friend who remains silent in order to calm a friend.

But it is not only out of the silence of things that is born their sympathy for us. They have secret harmonies. Sometimes they weep in the forest which René fills with his tempestuous soul; and sometimes they sing on the lake where another poet dreams.

There are hours and seasons when certain of these accords are most to the fore, when one hears best the thousand voices of things. Two or three times in my life I have been present at the awakening of this mysterious world. At the end of August toward midnight, when the day has been hot, an indistinct murmur rises about the kneeling villages. It is neither the sound of rivers, nor of springs, nor of the wind, nor of animals cropping the grass, nor of cattle rubbing their chains against the cribs, nor of uneasy watchdogs, nor of birds, nor of the falling of the looms of the weavers. The chords are as sweet to the ear, as the glow of dawn is sweet to the eye. There is stirring a boundless and peaceful world in which the blades of grass lean toward one another till morning, and the dew rustles imperceptibly, and the seeds at each moment's beat raise the whole surface of the plain. It is the soul alone which can apprehend these ochre souls, this flower-dust joy of the corollas, these calls, and these silences that create the divine Unknown. It is as if one were suddenly transported to a strange country where one is enchanted by languorous words, even though one does not understand very clearly their meaning.

Nevertheless I penetrate more deeply into the meaning whispered by these things than into that hidden in an idiom with which I am unfamiliar. I feel that I understand and that it would not require a very great effort to translate the thought of these obscure souls, and to note in a concrete fashion some of their manifestations. Perhaps poetry sometimes actually does this. It has happened that mentally I have answered this indistinct murmur, just as I have succeeded by my silence in answering distinctly a sweetheart's questions.

But this language of things is not wholly auditory. It is made up of other symbols also, which are faintly traced on our souls. The impression is still too faint, but, perhaps, it will be stronger when we are better prepared to receive God.

—*Translated by Gladys Edgerton.*

61 Laurent Tailhade

Laurent Tailhade (1854-1925). Destined for the priesthood by his family, Tailhade became one of its chief scourges. Among the most active of the anarchists of his time, Tailhade produced mountains of sarcastic attacks on the church, state, army, fellow writers, politicians, journalists. Fortunately he was as skilled with sword as with the pen which he frequently proved in the numerous duels provoked by his invective. The establishment was delighted when he became the victim of an anarchist bomb at the Foyot restaurant in 1894 so soon after his witticisms at the expense of the Chamber of Deputies bombing. Tailhade eventually lost an eye but this misfortune did not dim his enthusiasm for the cause. (It has been alleged that Fénéon planted the Foyot bomb, whose only casualty was his friend, although more recent research makes this seem unlikely*.)

Tailhade's anarchist prose is too full of contemporary references to translate easily; his poems are somewhat less vitriolic, those following are from his *Poèmes aristophanesques* (1904), a collection of his poetry of the previous ten years.

Individualism which, in literature, gives us such agreeable panniers of novel flowers, frequently enough proves itself sterilised by the growth of the weeds of pride. One sees young men, wholly swelled by a monstrous infatuation, avow their desire to create not only their own work, but at the same time The Work, to produce the unique flower after which the exhausted intellect will have to rest itself to become fertile and collect its thoughts in the slow and obscure work of the restoration of its vital juices. Even in Paris there are two or three "Glory Boys" who have arrogated to themselves the right to pronounce with their mouths alone this word which they have exiled from the dictionary. But that is of little importance, for the spirit blows where it will, and, when it blows into the skins of frogs and causes them to puff up, this is merely entertainment, because the world is sad.

Laurent Tailhade has none of the grotesque blemishes of pride: no one more naturally practices a more natural profession, that of a man-of-letters. The Romans called such men rhetoricians and that meant those who speak, those who master words, those who subject them to the yoke of thought and who know how to wield them, animate them, spur them on to the point of imposing upon them, at the moment of their choice, the rudest uses, the most dangerous and the most novel. Latin by both race and taste, Tailhade has the right to this beautiful title of rhetorician, one who is shocked at the incompetence of the vulgar pedants; he is a rhetorician in the style of Petronius, a master of prose and of verse alike...

The century's ignominy exasperates this Latin in love with the sun and perfumes, beautiful phrases and fine gestures, for whom money is a pleasure that one tosses like flower-petals beneath the feet of lovely women, and not the productive seed that one buries in order that it might germinate. He proves himself to be the proud executioner of hypocrisies and avarices, false glories and all-too-true turpitudes, of money and success, of the parvenus of the Bourse as well as of Fleet Street. Harsh, and even unjust, he whips his own hatreds; for him, as for all satirists, the private enemy becomes the public enemy, but what beautiful language traditional and new at the same time, and what insolence:

The things I write are not for those dull bastards!

LAURENT TAILHADE

Good Friday

A luxury—for pious flocks who've sinned
With parsley sauce to smother their boiled cod—
Is when indulgent charitable God
Blows constipation off with holy wind.

In buses undefiled by blasphemy
Nuns scramble, tangled wimples all askance;
In bible-shops, smug priests hum mournful chants,
Benign through grinning physiognomy.

Lace-surpliced boys—tossed off by doubtful sires—
Trot off to mass behind round-bellied friars
And thrill each cottage with forthcoming trade.

A sandwich-man—whose news blots out the light—
States solemnest cantatas will be played
In sports-grounds, bars and music-halls tonight.

A Ballad on Facing the Prospect of an Imminent Dose of Syphilis

> And you, young man, do not despair, for, whatever you may think to the contrary, in the Vampire you have a friend. And if we include the acarina sarcoptes which produces the itch, why then you have two everlasting comrades.
> —LAUTRÉAMONT, *Les Chants de Maldoror*, I.

When white-sprayed lilac scents the April night
Love's randy rake is never out of work;
His fancy flies fly open at the sight
Of damsels undistressed: tumescent Turk,
Like maypoled Spring his fount of youth will perk
Its head up for the shepherdess who'll faint
In sweet recumbence, pretty as fresh paint,
Till harvest's festival makes antic hay.
Then spotted spoilsports youth's delights must taint—
Love dies a lad; the pox lasts till you're grey.

Sensation-hunters, desperate in tight-
Chained bondage seek relief where vice-dens lurk,
And Venus shields her troth from Cupid's plight
While hellhounds, slashing leashes with bare dirk
Release Pandora's box of poisoned murk.
So listen as your maiden aunts acquaint
You with the wisdom of their chaste constraint:
From domes of Xanadu to Mandalay
Take note of quacks' advice—it's not so quaint:
Love's fancy-free; the pox insists you pay.

You scratch your limbs where tenfold itches bite;
Sin punctures them with a deflating jerk.
Lothario, you fought a lusty fight—
May mercury in magnums, phallic firk-
Ins brimming iodines not deign to shirk
Their duty in restoring health and maint-
Ain innocence licentiousness made feint.
Priapic gods protect you—if they may—
From fairy queens whose bottoms lack restraint.
Love smiles but once: the pox is never gay.

Great Prince of Love, pay heed to this complaint,
Abstain for once, if you can't be a saint.
Read this device whose timely warnings say
Through Valentine's proud sprinkler's peeling paint;
Love comes, and goes; the pox is here to stay.

LAURENT TAILHADE

Barcarole

Running noses still half-wiped,
Half-washed faces still half-washed,
River boats are guttersniped,
Sunday's decks all over-squashed.

They inhale salubrious
Perfumes of suburban dreams
Floating up from dubious
Swollen dogs on stagnant streams.

And their lady wives all swear
Summer heat's too fierce to bear
As, with hides of elephants,

Massive heaving haunches squeeze
Past unsmiling Japanese
Slim in silken elegance.

—*Translated by Stanley Chapman.*

67 Pierre Guillard

Pierre Quillard (1864-1912) A poet and playwright much engaged in the great social issues of his day. He was a tireless defender of Dreyfus, and travelled farther afield than most of his contemporaries in the movement, teaching in Constantinople and covering the war between Turkey and Greece. A fervent supporter of the anarchist cause, he favoured "propaganda by literature" rather than by "deed."

This work, a sort of prose eclogue (published in the *Mercure de France*, September 1892), concerns the anarchist Ravachol, just recently executed after being found guilty of a series of bombings aimed rather inaccurately at members of the judiciary. Ravachol's two trials were major events, his insolent self-possession impressed even those who had most to fear from his beliefs. Sentenced to the guillotine he strolled to the scaffold singing "in a raucous voice":

Pour être heureux, nom de Dieu,
Faut pendres les propriétaires!
Pour être heureaux, nom de Dieu,
Faut couper les curés en deux!...

His cry of *Vive la Révolution* was cut short by the blade of the guillotine. Ravachol's impenitent eloquence at his trials and nonchalance at his execution ensured his snactification as *the martyr of anarchism*, as exemplified by pictures in the anarchist press like the one reproduced on page 72. Subscribers to a fund for the children of one of his accomplices included Régnier, Saint-Pol-Roux, Rictus and Verhaeren from the present volume; Paul Adam wrote an essay comparing him to Christ.

His is a pagan soul, or a would-be pagan soul, for if his eyes avidly seek out perceptible beauty, his dream lingers, wishing to force the gate within which the beauty enclosed within things obscurely sleeps. He is truly more troubled than he vouchsafes to say, and the captives' glances trouble him with more than a mere shudder. He knows all theogonies and literatures,

I have known all the gods of heaven and earth,

since he has drunk at every spring, he knows more than one way to get intoxicated: dilettante of a superior type, when he has chosen his dwelling (no doubt near some old sacred fountain), having gathered enough, having sown enough noble seeds, he will find himself the master of a royal garden and an odorous multitude of flowers,

Eternal flowers, flowers equal to the gods!

PIERRE QUILLARD

> *As I see it, Mathilde thought, only being condemned to death sets a man apart from his fellows; it's the one thing that is not for sale.*
>
> STENDHAL, *The Red and the Black*.

Conversation Concerning the Life and Death of Ravachol

These voices were heard by the sea, on a calm summer night: the men were stretched out, half-naked, on the golden sands, nonchalantly, close by the pretty young women, and, though they were "of today," the dying glimmers of the sun, the soft caresses of the waves, the harmoniousness of the twilight, lent to their words and gestures that charm which it pleases us to attribute, fancifully perhaps, to the sages and courtesans of antiquity, gathered beneath marble porticoes where the noble shade of the oleanders floated in the virile scent of the spindrift. As they did not know that their conversation could be overheard, they no doubt did not feel any pressure to lie, but each seemed instead to speak with the complete sincerity befitting one who agrees to consider a thing without self-deception; and when I recollect this unforgettable conversation to myself now, I ask myself if, in fact, it was not the very charm of those syllables that bestowed on the surroundings the splendour of those vanished times.

THE POET. Thus it is we shall not die without having known, except through our legends and epics, the man superior to the very idea we create of gods, the hero: he who—lacking the omnipotence that we all too willingly grant to supernatural phantoms, remaining a man like us, capable of failure and, yes, of being vanquished too—has sanctified actions vulgar and detestable in appearance, and will deserve that poets in future ages shall praise him in the same way as in former days they did slayers of monsters and prophetic lovers of justice.

THE PHILOSOPHER. Ravachol was certainly a hero. When one day he felt the injustice of suffering from causes that were not of his own making and which the rest of the herd foolishly respected, he accepted a struggle with the Triumphant Beast*, and each time it became necessary, he—at the risk of his life, unhesitatingly dedicated to the inevitable penalty—accomplished the necessary murder.

A YOUNG WOMAN. The necessary murder, you say. Who has revealed to you that this man was not a bloody and rapacious brute, a commonplace assassin, who understood nothing of the grandeur of revolt and killed solely in order to steal?

THE PHILOSOPHER. I don't think so: he understood that he had to kill and had to steal, and thatt it would be despicable and demeaning to beg. The traditional resignation had been preached to him: he had audaciously refused to resign himself and gave an example of liberating anger. Two portraits of him show well enough how a doubt similar to yours first imposed itself on a few reasonable individuals: the one was taken immediately after his arrest, and the other when his normal physiognomy had been restored. The first image is that of a felled beast: the expression upon his face bruised by blows is terrible; the second is of an infinite gentleness, the eyes caressing and magnificent with tenderness and love. No words better capture this peculiar beauty than this phrase from the police psychologist that was reported to me: "His smile is softer than any woman's." That one is the true Ravachol. Imagine that he has set aside his haughty serenity for an instant and wept at seeing the children that he played with in the past coming before the bar; recall with what magnanimous commiseration he welcomed the wretch who had betrayed him, and above all the impassioned farewell addressed to him in the judges' faces by the woman whom he loved, herself a prisoner also, and certain nevertheless that the words would cost her further rigours. His attitude during the double trial had been admirable for its simplicity and nobility, and those who condemned him were obliged despite themselves to recognise in him a generous spirit.

A JURIST. That may be; and nevertheless they had to condemn him because he had broken the law.

A POET. Law... the very word makes me shudder with horror and disgust. That a man assumes the right to judge another already seems to me to be one of the most repugnant follies ever to haunt an obtuse and bestial brain. But that somebody might have determined beforehand that this one or that one will be, by virtue of some imbecilic formula, held to be criminal or lawful, that, for its ferocity and absurdity surpasses all imaginings. There can be no common standard, because two identical acts have never been committed under the sun, and nobody could possibly predict the innumerable multiplicity of characters and circumstances.

A POSITIVIST. I might willingly agree that the notion of good or evil is conventional. But it doesn't seem to me that this convention is arbitrary: it expresses necessary relationships and transposes into human language social fatalities that science has confirmed with total certitude.

THE PHILOSOPHER. There's a very adventurous word. Mathematical theorems alone embody certitude, because they derive from the spirit which is unable to contradict itself. Once the notion of number is accepted, it's a mistake to say that 2 plus 2 doesn't add up to 4. But we can only gratuitously call science a system of nature: your science is a momentary conception of life, a sort of mnemotechnique that is pretty near rational sometimes, but at others more ridiculous, after new discoveries, than the most puerile of errors. As for the so-called social sciences, they are even more vain than the physical and natural sciences, perpetually changing and outmoded, and without which meanwhile, by your own admission, it wouldn't manage to exist: these phenomena are too complex for observation, and at each moment individual whims will run counter to experience and disprove these chimerical laws.

A POSITIVIST. But it's still necessary that these whims manifest themselves with clarity. I have read Ravachol's last statements, and I can scarcely comprehend what dream he had formed for a new world.

THE PHILOSOPHER. In order to know very exactly what one wants, one need only wish for mediocre things and look upon the world as a banal catalogue for a fancy-goods company's warehouse. For that very reason a precise desire is a limited one, while a somewhat confused conception allows for the miraculous roses of the unconscious to bloom in their savage and fierce liberty.

THE MAN OF INSTINCT. I am amazed to hear you speaking so calmly about what others disapprove of, you whose own life is a perpetual negation of violence. Here you are, philosophers, poets, by the shining sea; the mouths of young women do not refuse your lips; you have never known hunger, never felt your teeth chattering on the roads in the winter; you have never killed, you have never stolen, and you go through the world proclaiming the gospel of revolt and destruction. But your hands are too shaky, I fear, to ignite bombs of dynamite or firmly to grasp the haft of a dagger. Others become intoxicated by the hatred you pour forth, and it is they who, in prisons, in penal servitude and on the gallows, suffer lamentably for having listened to you. What have you yourselves done?

THE POET. What! We act according to our nature: without intending to, you have just vindicated us. Yes, men may perhaps eternally allow themselves to go beneath the yoke; they may barely notice that they suffer and that monstrous tyrannies oppress them. We come to rouse them from their sleep and from their cowardice; with our aid they are able to throw down age-old idols, 'til nothing will remain except what they have not thrown joyfully into the abyss. We haven't starved, and we haven't shivered on the wintry highways, but when we kiss the mouths of young women, anguish over this universal sorrow poisons our pleasure, and we suffer because all those we know have been crucified around us. From now on we shall be silent no longer and our outcry will rise, ever more loudly from the earth all the way to the stars: then when the time comes, we shall die, with joyous hearts, struck down perhaps by our brothers who we will have set free.

THE PHILOSOPHER. We shall be struck down by our brothers and we shall die, our hearts joyous, if our deaths, as wise as we are, are as glorious as that of this sublime illiterate, and if we can sing during the final moments of the collapse of all hierarchies and authority.

A YOUNG WOMAN. I think that at least you might compose poems less cynical and with a more pleasing harmony.

THE PHILOSOPHER. What does it matter, provided that we say well what we wish to say. He walked proudly to the guillotine, and the coarser his words, the more they were vomited from the sewers, the more able they are to reach the stupid old man with the white beard, the boss of eternity's chain-gang, the odious "rewarder-avenger" who has weighed upon men through the centuries and filled Moses, Monsieur de Voltaire and the moralist Jules Simon with wonder at his complacent ignominy.

Thus, upon the golden shore, voices alternated, acrid and insidious by turns, and in the dusk the red flower of the sun shed its petals onto the night and the sea.

Ravachol, martyr of the guillotine

73 Rachilde

Rachilde (1860-1953). Marguerite Eymery began using the pseudonym "Rachilde" when she was still a teenager. By 1878, she was living in Paris and, in 1889, she married Alfred Vallette, with whom she co-founded the *Mercure de France*, the Symbolist's most important journal (de Gourmont was among its editors). Their salon quickly became the essential entry-point into literary circles.

Rachilde wrote prolifically: novels, novellas, short stories and plays, though her novels are only now beginning to be translated into English. In her day she was considered decadent, perverse and strange, but by the time of the First World War, she had aged into a doughty patriot and defender of the status quo. The Dadaists mocked her, and she regarded them as Bolshevik/Boche swine. Nevertheless, the present story (first published in the *Mercure de France*, 1900) is one of the most powerful pieces in this book.

Sincerity, what an excessive demand when a woman is concerned. Those most vaunted for their candour were still players, even that lachrymose Marceline*, an actress after all, who wept through her life as through her roles, with the conscientiousness that the public's applause inspires. As long as women have written, not a one has had the good faith to call herself one and to acknowledge herself one in all imperious humility, and the only rudiments that literature possesses of feminine psychology, it must seek out in books written by men...

Whether they try out their charms in perversity or in candour, women succeed better in living than in dissimulation; they are made for life, for the flesh, for materiality—and they realise their romantic dreams with delight if they do not find themselves restrained by the indifference of the male whose more sensitive nerves are damaged by vibrating in the void....

(Some of her pages) demonstrate that a woman can experience phases of virility, write, at such moments, without concerning herself with the obligatory coquettishness or customary attitudes, produce art with no more than an idea and words: create.

RACHILDE

Frog-Killer Tiny, frail, poised over his pale sheet like a water-bug upon the film of a pool, the boy listens in the night. A finger has awakened him, it seems to him it was a moist finger, lightly touching his brow.

It's not that of God, because God is too old now to trouble with children. Silence now supersedes him. God is an invalid no longer able to gallop upon the wind, and he has sent the wind off to the stables where it sometimes snorts from behind the gate.

The vast silence, with its cold index finger, has awakened the boy who listens, startled, discovering how black is this thing that he doesn't hear.

Poised on all fours, his lean little limbs rigid like sheaves of wheat, long thighs, strong hocks, delicate feet, with all the bearing of one about to make a leap, growing smaller his eyes take in everything, his head cunningly lowered, his hair streaming as though he were in a heavy downpour, barring to him the temples of figures more sombre than the night, and beneath his hair his fixed pupils shine, like two luminous veils of crêpe, because this little one, even undressed, still has about him an air of mourning.

He lives in an animal state, going, coming, sleeping, eating, with nothing to say. He possesses a corner of the room, a filthy corner, by the side of the fire-place. It's home to him just as though he were a cricket. In the winter it's heated by the ashes. In summer he gets air from a hole in the roof. His bed is a wattle of willows solidly tied to the ancient canes of chairs. Someone has thrown down a mat of heather and a sheet on top... the same one for the entire year.

Very sensibly, the little one shakes out his sheet each morning while mother boils their soup, because he noticed that fleas don't seem to like fire, and all the vermin either burn up or drown inside the pot.

But on this June night, it's not the fleas that have awakened him. He has sensed someone walking close by him, all but noiselessly. Perhaps the wind has escaped from God's stable? Or perhaps it is a marten? Or perhaps a rat, one of those big field rats, brown and furry, with a smooth snake-like tail? No; it *is* a person...

And the boy creeps forward a bit on his hands and knees, lowers his head again, raises his rump. If he can, with a single leap he'll be standing in the middle of the room with the sole relaxation, in reserve, of his two folded hams. He knows that one doesn't walk about at night as in the daylight. In daylight the beasts are what they wish, but at night they are what they are able to be, and when the birds have closed their eyes, they fold in their wings and, like an unknown species, run with extraordinary leaps, grazing the sun. He knows this and other things as well, this little one, just six years old, who, being left on his own avoids the house, going there only to sleep, and eating anywhere with a savagery that leaves his lips bloody.

He hears nothing; all alone, over by a fence of brooms guarding the garden—cabbages, turnips and some nice onions—*the earth has cried out*. The earth has a truly *terrible* way of crying out. It is almost silent, emitted through grinding teeth. If someone, man or beast, does a forbidden thing, she tries to give warning, and more faithful than a good dog, she doesn't spoil matters with useless noise; a pebble rolling, a grain of sand crushed, the imperceptible sound of a snail's shell weighing it down suffices.

And always and at all times, a cracking of death's three little bones, for the earth is replenished by them. How those little bones of death do protest!

Someone certainly came from the direction of the beans. A robber? After the onions, no doubt. Nude from head to toe, sex and ears pricking up, Little Toniot rose for his habitual leap like a hopping insect or a toad. He had the idea of waking his father, Big Toniot, who sleeps in the other room, who sleeps beneath a hunting rifle hung upon the wall—Big Toniot, so fatigued from his last stalk.

Wouldn't it be a terrible thing to shake a man who was so weary, who had only just gone to sleep without a word?

Little Toniot didn't think of his mother because to him, a man of six, women don't count. He scorned them. His mother would beat him, and he would cry, silently, behind her back; because women open their hands to strike, they only swat a lot of air at you, it doesn't hurt, whereas men slap with a closed hand. Big Toniot slapped that way, and the boy was filled with respect for his father—possessor, moreover, of a real hunting rifle.

Decidedly, it was a robber who had come, seeking onions. Little Toniot could no longer deceive himself on that score. Those bonelets of the dead were starting to protest. Sticky all over as with sweat from bad dreams, the slight body of the boy huddled by the worm-eaten chest where they stored the bread and the lard, those two treasures of the house. Despite his looking like a little wet cat lying in wait for a big rat, he was paralysed with fear; but his carnivorous instinct gave him the keen desire to sniff out prey. If it should prove much larger than he, it would be well to call for Big Toniot directly... as the earth cries out when too heavily trodden upon.

From his corner, Little Toniot saw little more. The room had only the one outside door and the roof-hole. By day, the sunlight entered through the doorway. On certain evenings, the moon reserved the roof-hole for herself, passing her hands through the soot, caressing the suspended kettle and making it shine like silver. This moon always awakened Little Toniot who heard it shine. Ah! why didn't she enter now while his teeth chattered, scared in this corner by the chest? Light is so good! And there—she miraculously opened the door, the door shut with an inside latch. Yes, the moon was good, just like a real person, a beautiful woman, very pale because of the blackness of the night, a completely naked woman, a little fat, the hips rounded and full as befits a star, her breasts high and hard, her entire face veiled in red hair.

Toniot had never feared beasts nor females, but he was terrified by the moon disguised as a woman. Mechanically, he made the gesture of pushing his black hair back from his face like a stubborn child, and he saw, with an inexpressible terror, this gesture repeated across the face of the moon, as though he had seen his own reflection in a mirror.

And it wasn't the moon, this big white reflection of himself: it was his mother. Little Toniot no longer dared stir.

"So! What are you doing here, seed of a toad? Why aren't you asleep at this hour?"

The woman, face to face with the little one, rumbled dully.

"I'm not doing anything," he answered, protecting his cheek with raised elbow.

"Why aren't you asleep, vermin? Why are you nosing around here? And your father—where's he at? Have you caused him to wake up, wretch?"

"No, I haven't bothered him, only I'm awake because I heard crackling in the garden."

"Is this the first time you've heard crackling in the

garden, little pig? At night, everything crackles! Must you catch each passing noise by the tail, snoop?"

"I thought it was after the onions! It sounded like a man's footsteps!"

"Footsteps? Son-of-a-dog!"

And before Little Toniot could think to raise his elbow, the angry female seized him by the shoulder, pushed him toward his bed of heather in the corner of the hovel, from which the cursed little swine wasn't to stir before the proper time. There, dumbly, blindly, balling her fists, she beat the boy, wholly mastered by a frenzy of anger, though he hadn't done anything wrong.

Completely naked, the child received blows to the tenderest places without crying, in keeping with his scornful habit, and, that very night, it came to him that he might perhaps be spared if he complained less to the world.

His mother had a drunken air.

"I'll tie you up, vermin," she repeated in a low voice, clenching her teeth, and even more her fists. "I'll tie you by the legs like they do with chickens for market!"

Then he responded in an equally low voice, guessing that he would have to resign himself to the blows, submitting to an order laid down by the most high.

"What? You still angry? Why aren't you wearing a chemise tonight? Finish this or go to sleep."

The female suddenly stopped, and tossed back her hair.

And Little Toniot imitated her.

They faced each other from the depths of the shadows where the mother's panting sides shone dully. And each was shamed by their paltry nudity.

Cowering on his sheets rubbing his little smarting limbs which would be blue by morning, the boy studied the female with a look of suffering curiosity, protecting his little sex with his left hand, because he greatly suspected that if she struck at him again, it would be the end of the *little toad*, which would emit a squawk and be dead.

Strange; why had she suddenly begun to hit like a man? Was it because naked women have this right? Had such mysteries entered the room along with the brightness of skin? And he shivered with fright.

"Ah, I'm as worn out as if I had just produced you, son-of-an-owl!" the mother murmured, turning her back to him in order to put on her chemise.

It was as if the moon had finally left the room.

Everything grew dark and Toniot began to breathe again.

Big Toniot was dirty and lean. He had the sad mien of one who throws himself into the lion's mouth and frets for want of something better. His trousers of a greyish-brown cloth turning green from lengthy rubbings upon the forest mosses and grasses of the embankments, glided woefully upon his hips like vine-poles, allowing a pretty thong of fawn leather, which had the same skin as its owner, to peek from between his belt and a short patched jacket. (Little Toniot, to imitate his father, designed a similar thong by means of a ligature and he gripped the string 'til he was on the point of bleeding in order to clarify the demarcations.) This man said nothing. He killed beasts, *mole-catcher* by profession. He tended the traps set for foxes, martens, rats, fish, chiefly for game, and as he had no game licence, he took some precautions, such as the moles hung from the back of his jackets and frequently left to rot for weeks, displayed as self-evident insignia.

He owned his hereditary house, stranded in this forest clearing like a shipwreck on a desert isle; he lived there simply, catching everything he was able to devour: the female and the little one unable to demand more of him, since the police would not mix in his affairs. From time to time, he went into a distant neighbouring town to sell some rush baskets. By five, he always brought one back neatly full of horse manure, a trifle to urge the garden vegetables along. He also brought bread and lard which he set down in the middle of the dung, the whole of it covered by an old newspaper, to keep away the flies. He walked about barefoot in winter and in summer, his soles having acquired the hardness of iron. No one knew whether he loved his woman. His woman hated his guts. First, because he never spoke and the woman had a superstitious horror of silence; then, they had a boy and she would have preferred a girl, an ally and an accomplice, a creature more supple, capable of appreciating all the vain phrases which escape from exasperated mothers on rainy days. Moreover, Big Toniot's woman grumbled about him with all the abundance of a foaming torrent to any rare passer-by whom Providence deigned to send her way. When the gatherers of dead wood, the shepherds, the lily-pickers or the dry-goods pedlars accidentally strayed to her door, there was a flux of discourse and lamentation which rambled along, arms waving, from one end of the house, instantaneously vacated by her two men, to the other. Fortunately, Big and Little Toniot were able to escape her, the woods were vast: and, during those times, the red-haired woman, so tired of a life of sloth spent with her two bad boys ("If bad, Madame, then they shall have nothing to eat, just as they have nothing to say!"), recounted her woes in terms that cannot be written down for home consumption, as for example: *He stinks of moles.*

Then, loving to spend money foolishly, she would purchase a faggot, or mushrooms gathered at night, a bunch of lilacs or a penny's worth of thread.

Big Toniot never reproached her for this, but Little Toniot shook his head, scornfully. Is that the sort of thing one buys deep in the woods, mushrooms or lilacs? As for the thread, Little Toniot knew how to mend things with sprigs, having many a time tested their relative strengths on the bird-traps.

One Sunday, it was a pedlar instead of the dry-goods man who came with thread for Big Toniot's woman. This day the conversation in the empty house was less loud. The pedlar spread out his goods. It was very interesting. You could purchase a bee made from honey, and Big Toniot, the following week, noticed that someone had stolen his onions.

"Is it possible," cried the woman, all of her coarse hairs bristling, "is it possible that you are accusing a brave pedlar whose papers are in order? He even showed me his licence! He don't need your onions, dirty owl! He's a very proper man; he wears out his shoe leather every day and, on Sundays, he drinks wine."

What she didn't say was that she had offered him the onions in exchange for some dubious compliments.

Big Toniot lowered his head, sniffed in the direction of the door. In effect, because wine blossomed inside of him, and nothing was added to it, every word cost him cerebral effort. For the rest, when he watched for a beast marauding behind a hedge, he was not so childish as to waste time talking. Not he!

But Little Toniot naïvely promised to himself that he'd keep an eye on the onion s.

That's why, having heard a *crackling* not far off in the garden, he had got up in the night, while the father slept beneath his hanging rifle, his father, the stinking mole shut away by a female grown extremely delicate since she had longed for a night-gown and no longer tolerated the irritating touch of a rough night-shirt against her burning skin...

Poor Little Toniot! Feverish, he's unable to sleep. His turn has come to chase the great beast. He sniffs. He listens in the dark. He turns this way and that on the dry heather, slowly, fearful of making noise. All through the night he listens for something. Something or someone. He's not really certain. The forefinger of silence probes deep in his head. He has calculated that it's a week since he heard the earth cry out. Heavy groans from a breast upon which someone has pressed their knee, deep shudder of revolt going forth in a discreet signal, like the cough of a very old wise person; and the heart of the earth beats in the breast of the little savage on watch, who rises at last, looks straight in front of him, his nostrils sucking in the scent.

With the supple movement of a grass-snake, Little Toniot arrives at the door without checking his mother's bed. He knows full well that Madame la Lune has emerged. What remains there, is her linen chemise swooned upon the brown coverlet, the shroud of one who is dead to him, put from the world a second time beneath the blows of her powerful fists.

So, she's out there with a man on this wicked night, and he has guessed enough to perceive in him an everlasting foe.

To the hunt then!

And he crept out of doors into a mild blue light that bathed him, caressed him, a baptism of courage. The moon has hidden in that part of the swamp where the frogs sing. Yes, the moon's just there beyond the foremost of the tree branches. She is a jolly white form, round all over, who rolls in the nap of the grass; she is veiled by a thick cloud that runs around her waist, seeming to him to eat up her head. And she rolls, and she glistens, all of the light escapes from her in reflections of red hair, of milky throat. Little Toniot crouched low and bent back the grasses with great caution. He has gone beyond the garden, he's almost to the ditch just before the wood where there's a sort of alcove, an ample bed of foliage. He watches, he watches and silently he laughs, in spite of which his heart grows tighter from fright. What he sees there, he will never forget, because it's so funny! He sees a great white frog, yes, it's just like that, this marvellous flexibility of thighs and open arms, this elastic and precise stretching of members so pale that they seemed to be of silver! Now he understood why she'd called him seed of a *toad*, for he really was the son of a frog. He watched, he watched, his eyes ached so much that they burned! He'll look at that thing all his life, inside him, in the dead centre of his heart, he'll be mirrored there like a poisoned wellspring whose reflections are sometimes cruel, sometimes sweet.

He had truly seen enough! He retraced his steps, the little savage, he drew back, re-entered his lair. He ought to have gone back to sleep like an obedient and compliant child, head turned toward the wall, but stronger than himself, the spirit of the earth, that primordial pact drawn up between men for protection against the Enemy, drove him instead to his father's bedside.

Big Toniot, awakened in turn, sniffed at the wind:

"What, boy, what is it? You sick?"

"Nah, pa. Ma's hurt. Fell down. Better help her get up right away, pa."

He said pa as he'd done when he was an infant, and scarcely capable of a wicked thought.

But the father got up, snorting, muttering:

"Oh yes—what's she been up to? The bitch!"

"Stealin' onions, I think." Little Toniot added that part in a low tone, his face filled with loathing in the presence of the inexpressible crime he's explained as best he could.

"Blast it!"

And the father had taken down the rifle.

"It's that pedlar, eh?"

"I dunno! It was a man..."

"Yeah? Well I know! You stay here."

The little one stays put. It's no longer his affair. The father knows his business.

And back to sleep goes Little Toniot, stopping up his ears. He hears it all the same: two shots, reverberating through him endlessly, in the depths of his being where it is always filled with the vision of the great white frog, of Mother Moon wallowing on the earth beneath an unknown cloud. He perceives a cry, two cries...and he stops up his ears. His teeth chatter. My God, what's happening? Will she return, angry enough to kill him with her fists?

She comes back alright, trailing Big Toniot who pulls her along by the hair.

"Here," the father says in a hysterical voice in which all the suffering earth seemed to groan, "meat on the table!"

The big white frog is now striped along the thighs by streaks of blood which spurt from her mouth as well. The motions of the arms and legs, through nervous energy, imitate those of a few minutes past, so that the pangs of her death-throes resemble the writhings of her pleasure.

Then her jaws snap shut.

The great white frog will sing no more.

He has remained all alone completely satisfied with himself. His days go by lying in wait for animals. The police, taking his father from him, had left him the rifle. His mother was buried far away. The good women who had rushed forward like big buzzing flies to offer him eggs, milk, consolation, and had taken pity upon his condition of orphanhood, were infuriated because he had made his horror of talkative people a little too brutally evident. He does his little bit of housekeeping, shakes his sheets, steeps his soup. The place is his, he had almost lost it all through the workings of justice, and when the curate showed up, with his benign air, Toniot fled up the chimney after having bolted the door. But he is now the master of the house, and no longer a child learning his catechism!

Having the fortune no longer to owe anything to anyone on earth, it seems crazy to him to tolerate menaces from the sky. (Besides, as soon as it rained, he went to bed; this always saved him a meal at least!)

Meanwhile, the seasons change. It became necessary for him to look for the old clothes belonging to his father, now in prison, because his child's trousers were unable to grow along with him. And first he weaves two reed baskets, remembering the gear that people display when they go to town... and he hides two rabbits there. The rabbits and the baskets, the one inside of the other would probably bring in fifty pence. A fortune. Lard for six months.

Then he sets out, threading the heaps of the footpaths, proceeding by chance. He'll arrive anyway, and there's plenty of time. Finally, the actual day for the walk to town arrives. He speaks of Big Toniot, the one who had murdered his woman... Now the whole world knows why he's come back. That surprises him. He owes as much to Big Toniot who killed his wife, doesn't he? He learns that it's very rare in town for people to think this. Well! obviously there's more to men than there is to... *frogs*, and he'd need too much lead to plumb them.

He finds his way to the prison and there he obtains his patrimony: the famous trousers of grey-brown cloth, more green than ever, decorated now with reddish stars, and the old short jacket, patched everywhere. Someone explains things to him: his father, all in all, was perhaps not so culpable; he had acted almost within his rights, and surely no one would have condemned him to hard labour for life if he had been a gentleman of the town, rather than a primitive forester and a poacher to boot. So then—to kill a woman and to maim a pedlar—not as grave as hunting without a licence! This last echo of civilised existence filled him with a new stupor. It all becomes a muddle in the poor head of this simple boy. He tosses his rabbits into the manure, no longer daring to sell them. This gives him vertigo. He imagines to himself that he's tossed his father and mother away. He gives his baskets away and runs from the town with his bundles as though he'd killed all the policemen there, not even breathing 'til he reaches the middle of the woods. How will he live without a hunting licence? What now? How often could he furnish explanations for his personal rifle shots? He discovered a grave inequity. Whether he killed rabbits or people, he sinned; that's all. But more important is to live in freedom. And while dreaming of how he will sin, he laughs silently...

...Because they always sang, the bitches! At nightfall he hears them chatter and croak from the depths of every swamp in the forest, the swamps surrounding the house, in the beautiful swamps, cups of glaucous crystal overflowing with moss, full of a mysterious liquor where, in equal doses is mixed the poison of the rotten autumn leaves and the purer honey of the springtime flowers, irises, nympheas, arrowheads and periwinkles, of gloomy periwinkles which weave themselves in plaits for entangling the legs of hunters.

Yes, yes, they murmur, the bitches, implore, cry out in never-ending sadness their search for a king, and forming their foul rings, shining with pleasure at being so stupid, they importune him with sinister vociferations. From every corner of the woods, summer evenings, a concert of maledictions raises itself up and falls in a downpour of long sobs upon the orphan's face.

Yes, he knew quite well what he would fish for! Since he must kill to live, and he wanted to live, he wanted to kill without a sound and to kill those whose deaths would best serve to suffocate noise. So he tried to gather up joyfully those living flowers of the turbid swamps, hatched from the mouths of fools... which he closed one by one.

Returning from town, Little Toniot thought of himself as Big Toniot henceforth, a bit wilder than the other, having inherited a desolate house and the trousers of an assassin. And he stood erect, taken with respect for himself, like a man who has found his way. The rush baskets fetch little, the mushrooms don't last, and the birds are singularly cautious. A field rat furnishes a sorry roast, releasing a fetid odour of musk during cooking... but frog... is like chicken! A true feast for the amateur! He saw, in a blissful dream, the little white thighs lined up on a hazelwood spit, browning in the fire and turning with the docility of little puppets, vaguely ghostlike. He'd eat his fill and sell the rest. Eventually, he would depopulate the countryside of the enervating little animals whose songs, half oaths, litanies of hysterics, haunted his memory fearsomely.

Each day, Toniot leaves his house which the winter wind has ravaged, carrying off the door and splitting the roof. This is no longer his hereditary home, it's his ruin. He goes inside like a night bird swallowed up after a tempest in the hole of an old wall or a crag. He has lost the taste for daylight and for bread. He's unable to shake off his somnolence until the first callings of the frogs. Then he stretches out on all fours, a savage on the scent of war, sniffing at the wind. He crawls; he snuffles; he sucks in the smells of the forest which the tenderness of the morning moistens with its tears. If it's autumn, there's the smell of rosemary, juniper trees, and the acorns of the oak which dry out, exhaling little jets of gold; if it's spring, sage, elder and eglantine, all in full bloom.

Either the beasts begin to flee, or else they intermingle madly.

The only change evident in the man is a bit more sadness, a bit more languor.

But Toniot no longer thinks. He is far from the town, from his parents, from himself. The pernicious ponds, mirrors which have reflected every mystery, attract him, fascinate him, bewitch him. He is the prince of the frogs who call to him with a frenetic passion... without ever getting a better glimpse of their time to die.

And he will go towards them, pole on his shoulder from which a thread hangs (perhaps bought from the pedlar by his mother!) and a little scrap of red cloth as long as a woman's tongue. He goes beneath the boughs, with a methodical step, eyes fixed and dull, his black hair barring his face with heavy lines. He looks like a very old man with the piercing eyes of a young animal. Before the pond he salutes them with his silent laugh. He makes no conversation with them, nor does he offer any gift of joyous accession. They all, in a grand deployment of their mesmeric forces, begin to undulate in broad bands, and pleat the water like soft silk.

Around them, the trees contemplate the drama with bent heads. Their weeping hair spreads out, and the moon that one notices early on in a clear sky is outlined by a crown of amber gradually deepening to the colour of blood. Still later, it will be like the point of an arrow whetting itself upon the agony of the day.

The clamour of the frogs grows frightfully, their yellow eyes, drops of weeping gold, shine like stars. In the midst of this Sabbat they emit human words, shrill interjections in the manner of infants amusing themselves with excess, or make themselves hoarse with puerile anger. These are the little abortions born of unavowable loves, little foetuses immersed in the universe's carboy, who try to break through its transparency with their desperate little hands.

And they crowd one upon the other, poor little monsters, in order to gaze upon the red tongue which draws to them the man at the end of his damnation's thread. It is the fiery tongue of the chimera! They are fascinated, little siren enchantresses, and, in turn, he is fascinated also. The pole drops, the thread lashes empty air, and the atrocious cry of a live plucked bird is heard. The frog, full of curiosity, is seized by the double hook which, from afar, resembles a saving anchor. She shakes her little legs behind her like the thighs of a girl being violated..

The frog hunter gathers them up one by one, tranquilly. He seems to mow them down with the top of his pole. He would take them all if it were possible to take all the frogs in a pond, where each glob of mire receives a charge at birth and every drop of clear water caresses an adult. But night comes.

The moon looks down, a queen who jibes most evilly at those who call themselves her subjects. Whether the frogs sing or die doesn't prevent her from being the only frog's eye that has seen everything from the beginning of the world.

Toniot fills his sack. A long linen sack that he has cut from his mother's lost chemise. His nails are red with blood. The sin at an end, he returns home, pole upon his shoulders and from it hangs the sack whose guts are swollen with little guts who gasp and then die. At home, it's supper time and he handles the fireplace passably well. The wind paws, suffocating the flames. The earth moans, scolding gently. No, people are no longer able to prevent him from eating in his hunger, to live. He is free.

On his knees before the heap of tiny cadavers, he despoils them, removes from them the double loop of their two golden eyes, removes their jolly robes of green satin, their cute panties of white velvet. All these jumbled things glisten like the underwear of dolls, and he leaves the room for as long as those naked thighs, so pale, are shaken by nervous tremors.

...And the fixed pupils of the man have a strange flame in them, shining with covetousness or with hatred, and far, far away dogs are howling at the moon, and dreaming of biting Death in the arse.

83   ALFRED VALLETTE

Alfred Vallette (1858-1935). Married to Rachilde. he was the dominant spirit behind the *Mercure de France*, both the magazine and the publishing house. He devoted his life to this enterprise, supported many writers during hard times (Alfred Jarry being a notable example), and wrote a great deal of critical material for the review. He hardly wrote fiction, the present tale being a rare exception (from the sixth issue of the *Mercure*, 1890).

The merits of the founders of religious orders have been much celebrated... Of these orders, some have been extinguished, having given the world what light they had; others have prolonged down the centuries the lingering death that quietly stifles institutions in disaccord with the tastes of humanity; others, finally, have survived only by modifying, and again modifying, their statutes to meet the transformations, so rapid and disconcerting, of the eternal ideal.

...In like manner one might write curious chapters on the founders of literary reviews, and one might find, no doubt with astonishment, that Saint Philippe Neri and some of our contemporaries have characteristics in common—for example a taste for the unknown and that disinterest which sacrifices present satisfactions for the success of an idea.

...It comes about, in the social sphere, that an association founded by a Breton servant-girl cares for more poor people than the Assistance Publique; and it comes about that, in the sphere of literature, a review founded with a capital of fifteen Louis has more influence on the progress of ideas, and consequently on the progress of the world (and perhaps on the rotation of the planets) than the proud compilations of leading academics and commercial dissertations.

...Identified from the birth of the Mercure de France *with the review to whose inception he had plainly contributed, Monsieur Alfred Vallette subsequently became its real founder, since all the stones set above the first have been touched by his hands alone, and since alone he represents in it, from the laying of the foundation-stone, the principle of continuity which is the principle of life itself. From that time on, then, when he assumed this burden, his literature has been all in deeds; he has exercised only a practical imagination, a criticism with immediate and certain consequences.*

Irony or poetry; everything outside of that is insipidity and platitude. Perhaps we will never know if Monsieur Vallette would have made splendid use of his literary gift, but we know he possesses it. In writing literature it is to be regretted that Life may have intervened and, with a somewhat satanic gesture, upset the inkwell over the newly begun page.

ALFRED VALLETTE

In Perpetuum (A novel)

Preface

Why did the Will one day create the Frog of the game of *Tonneau**?

I.

A little metal poured into a clay mould in which the predetermined shape was hollowed out, and already the embryo, liquid semblance of a being still participating of nothingness, gaped.

II.

But the beastie was born into the light. Someone released her from the silt embossing her limbs, scraped her, trimmed her; and, during these solicitudes for her infancy, unaware of herself and of the world, she gaped.

III.

Time passed, of which she had no notion; after which, one fine morning, gathered together with many of her peers, she found herself gaping—like all the rest. She did not see in this anything more than that it was the mark of her race. But, neither rejoicing in the revelation nor chagrined by it, wholly indifferent, she gaped.

IV.

Meanwhile, by dint of day-dreaming of it sometimes, and as if her understanding were by degrees expanding, she inferred that—this mark clearly not corresponding to anything—the future held things in store... And her imagination aroused, by the rose of the spirit, impatient for tomorrow, she gaped.

V.

What things?... Certainly none of the minor incidents of her present life, little miseries and little joys of no importance... But someone clothed her in a lovely painted robe of green with bronze reflections, and such was her happiness that she thought her destiny fulfilled. Yet she quickly realised that it was not; and more than ever avid of something new, each thought questioning the future, she gaped.

VI.

A great event occurred; someone set her upon a pretty table of green wood pierced by holes and painted ochre, a royal residence she had often coveted when one of her sisters was so adopted, and yet again she imagined herself as destined for her full share of worldly delights. But she accustomed herself to luxury, and, materially satisfied with her condition, she experienced anew the effects of the emptiness in her soul, and she gaped.

VII.

However it led to nothing, and she was gliding through days of monotony with an opaque ennui, when a cart carried her off toward an unknown destination. She felt an intense emotion, which during the trip grew into a perfect fever of anxiety: there could be no doubt, the hour was approaching for something... And she gaped.

VIII.

Someone set her down just two steps from a bowling alley, not far from a swing, beneath an arbour attached to a house whose sign depicted a thin pole planted in a river in which a perch was swimming, a rebus underlined by the following: *The Two Perches**—*Fish-stew and fried fish from the Seine...* But her excitement subsided, because nothing of the things to come was immediately apparent. —Ah! if only she were able to hasten destiny along!... And she gaped.

IX.

All in all, she was not unhappy there, were it not for that irrepressible need for adventures, and the weeks flowed by gently and calmly, free from any notable events: dull. Meanwhile the breezes grew warmer, the sun brightened up the horizons, the greenery of the arbour became spangled with multi-coloured bell-flowers; then, one Sunday, the clouds rained down upon *The Two Perches*. Then she understood that time was passing, and, restless to the point of anxiety, she gaped.

X.

Indeed, something out of the ordinary was underway in the arbour and, all at once, a disc flew by, passing over her head. This was the *fiat lux*: these were the things!... And, while the iron discs whistled around her, sometimes struck against her so as to do her harm, showered down upon the pretty table of green wood and rushed into the holes, her explicit longing became impatient, grew keener. Suddenly, a dazzlement, a swoon of ecstasy, oh! so brief! And, as soon as communicated, the disc was swallowed up... where? Was it no more than that?... And she gaped.

XI.

The chance event often recurred, invariably followed by a melancholy of disillusionment. But soon enough the secret craving rose in her again, and when it was too long in coming, there was a sensation of abandonment within her at first benign, then insupportable, which was succeeded by a black sorrow: the most exquisite emotion, after all, that she had yet experienced. —And she gaped.

XII.

But month followed upon month without anything new happening. Now was this *all* of the things promised to her by the future, and the entire unique reason for her having been brought into the world? That was not all there was to life: it was a reason, no doubt, but not a reason for life... And she gaped.

XIII.

Winter came, and solitude, and boredom, dissipated a little by that first sunlight. Then she recalled the joys of the other summer, along with its melancholies, exactly the same, and also the same regrets. And after a winter and a summer alike, there were another similar winter and summer, to which absolutely identical years were added. —And she gaped.

XIV.

Only she grew old, and the bad weather damaged her home, along with her lovely green robe with reflections of bronze, which had moreover been rent by so many fruitless discs—just as it happens that futile desires wound more deeply than dreams, even when too fulfilled. So her spirit returned more frequently to the past; in life as she had lived it, experience made it plain that the future no longer held anything. —And still she gaped.

XV.

More and more her abode fell into decay, and finally she no longer dared to look at herself, so immense was the sorrow of seeing, through the innumerable holes of her torn robe, the incurable leprosy of the rust with which her body was tarnished, poor body that the discs—now quite rare—had bruised and even crippled, for she lacked a foot. Her day-dreaming took greater delight in her past, whose vision nowadays conjured itself up so pleasantly. —And still she gaped.

XVI.

At last her house, for a long time a hovel polluted by nauseous stenches, collapsed from age. Someone separated her from it, and, after diverse peregrinations of which she was scarcely conscious, she again found herself in a dark place, in the middle of a heap of old scrap iron as rusted as she was. —Ah! her regal home, her beautiful green robe with bronze reflections, her former good health and the communions under the arbour pricked with bell-flowers! They were good times, then, the good old days!... Now, everything was said. —And still she gaped.

XVII.

How many weeks, or months, or years did she lie there, her spirit in her memories, her soul drowned in melancholy, and in spite of all, gaping?... Now, in the presence of the melting-pot in which her dissolved being was about to return to unformed matter, she gaped—someone grabbed her in order to hurl her in: alas! alas! it was the end of all ends, ineluctable! And she gaped—slowly she was pushed into the molten metal, which already halfway encompassed her: she gaped—slowly it reached to the corners of her mouth: she gaped—and slowly, slowly the two extreme points of her spread-apart jaws disappeared, gaping all the while...

Postface

One day the Will created the *Tonneau* Frog *in order to amuse itself.*

André Rouveyre, *the artist, Vallette & de Gourmont at the Mercure.*

Félix Fénéon (1861-1944). A quite remarkable figure, Fénéon was a vital intellectual influence within the artistic, literary and political circles of his time. As art critic he was the most influential advocate of a whole series of avant-garde painters. He more or less invented Post-Impressionism, supported the Impressionists, Fauves, Nabis, Futurists, and was a close friend of most of the important artists of many decades. As chief editor of the most luxurious literary review of the time, *La Revue Blanche*, he introduced and supported a wide variety of writers. But Fénéon's great passion was for anarchist politics, within which he was active for most of his life, writing thousands of articles under dozens of pseudonyms and actively supporting the "propagandists by deed" (bomb-throwers).

Fénéon's anarchism frequently got him in trouble with the state and he was one of the defendants in the most famous anarchist trial of the day: The Trial of Thirty, which resulted from the dynamite campaign of Émile Henry. Despite detonators being found in Fénéon's house he was acquitted, primarily due to his acerbic witticisms which reduced the trial to farce. At one point the judge excused himself after opening a parcel received through the post which contained human excrement; Fénéon remarked: "Not since Pontius Pilate has a magistrate washed his hands with such ostentation."

His several hundred *3 Line Novels* were written as space-fillers for a daily newspaper in 1906, and are true stories. They soon achieved cult status and have been often reprinted.

The veritable theoretician of Naturalism, it is by means of his conversation, through gently sarcastic little remarks that he taught his friends the art of rejoicing in turpitude, baseness and evil. His resignation to life's difficulties was discreetly hilarious: with what fine prudent and contented air have I seen him smoking a foul cigar!...

Never to write, to disdain that; but to have written, to have proven an evident talent in the exposition of new ideas, and abruptly to have fallen silent? I believe there are spirits who are satisfied once they know their worth; a single attempt sets their mind at rest. In this way cool-headed men, having tested their virility, abandon an amusement which, to them, was no more than the quest of a proof. Monsieur Fénéon is cool-headed.

Cool, not luke-warm, because the disdain for writing has not brought about in him a disdain for action: the cold-hearted are the most active and their patience of will is limitless. Thus, having social (or anti-social) ideas, Fénéon decided to obey them even beyond the point of prudence. This man, who assumed the air of an American Mephistopheles, had the courage to jeopardise his life for the achievement of plans that he perhaps judged to be foolish, but also noble and just: such a page in the life of a writer casts its light further and higher than red-glowing writings. One need not render oneself a slave to ideas, to the point of enslaving oneself by living in the vanity of perpetual sacrifice, like a Blanqui*, but it is good to have had the occasion to show some contempt for laws, for society, for the citizen-herd; if, from a vain struggle, one comes away with a wound, the scar is beautiful.

FÉLIX FÉNÉON

The Bird-charmer Five fingers spread wide. The crumbs scatter, high in the sunlight, form into flakes, and are on the point of falling when they vanish, snapped up. The rustle of wings is gone. There the sparrows are, on the lawn, footless, and their grey takes on a purplish tinge against the newly-sprung grass whose viridity the banks of geraniums glorify. Incited by the old man's success, some little girls try to win the confidence of the small creatures, in pretty gestures from which fodder issues. Uselessly. The birds were coming right up at his first advance. Now they take flight again, fearful or disdainful. Only the odd clubfooted pigeon decides to peck about on the path and consents to coo a little. The little girls are amazed: the gentleman has magical powers. They don't know that it is not bread he is distributing to the fastidious beaks—but succulent *brioche*, and that's the whole of his secret. Once again they are in a circle about him, watching the birds come and go according to his movements, eddying about his hat; and suddenly they are filled with wonder: on his sinister nose, a linnet, momentarily perched, is flapping its wings.

Meanwhile, on the pedestals, Spartacus swears, Atalanta decamps, Hercules volunteers, Pomona enbosomifies; we see sailors of the siege, a druidess, a Neapolitan fisherman and, over there, a tiger being devoured by an alligator. (The old gentleman with military moustaches will be back, at nightfall, to sit in the same park, where all the frolics will still not have ceased.)

On the *quais* it is particularly to the cab-drivers that it falls to fatten the birds. Collignon is kneeling on the driver's box; the flat roof is covered in oats and the pecking beaks resound on it like hail. In this way the cab-driver indulges the sentimentality of the guardian of the law who watches over the rank: this worthy driver will not be hauled up for any contravention of regulations. Moreover, moved by the spectacle, a family has swept into the cab and the horse is hobbling off towards the zoo.

A square. About a hideous old biddy, jerky in her movements, and on whom the birds affectionately void their droppings, some ladies have halted. She tells them about the birds' habits, and about how much she loves them: last winter, such a hard one, lots of little sparrows died; she was their Providence; more than once she went hungry on their behalf. And a tear tergiversates, then runs down the facial ravines; the ladies get maudlin, look for their purses.

The foster-mother never goes back home without a few francs that will serve to radically alcoholise her dinner. Next morning, very early, she will be in the garden whose denizens she praises so well. She will stuff two or three pigeons into her shopping basket and they, in their turn, will nourish her. She's the animal-lover.

—*Translated by Iain White*.

3 Line Novels

Monsieur Frachet of Lyon, bitten by a pug-dog and believed cured (Institut Pasteur), attempted to bite his wife and died of rabies.

A dishwasher of Nancy, Vital Frelotte, back from Lourdes, forever cured of his tuberculosis, died on Sunday, by mistake.

Well, well! Neither the *duc*, nor any person representing him at the obsequies of Riehl, crushed at Nancy by the duc de Montpensier's car.

At Clichy an elegant young man threw himself under the wheels of a rubber-tyred fiacre; then, unhurt, under a lorry, which crushed him.

The customs-officer, widower Ackermann of Fort-Philippe (Nord), who was to have been married today, has hanged himself at the tomb of his wife.

Considering his daughter (aged 19) insufficiently puritanical, the Saint-Etienne clockmaker Jallat killed her. It's true he still has eleven other children.

Nothing but silver-plate! The finger of Saint Louis, though, that at least must be genuine: so the burglars of the church at Poissy made off with it.

Too much laudanum only gave the architect Godefoin, gripes in the stomach. Fair enough—he'd drown himself. But they fished him out.

In a dramshop in Versailles the ecclesiastic Rousleot encountered, with his eleventh absinthe, the attack of delirium tremens that carried him off.

Love. At Mirecourt, Colas, a weaver, planted a bullet in the head of Mademoiselle Fleckenger and treated himself with similar severity.

Returning home, the ploughman Vaulthier, of Chapelle-au-Bois (Vosges), found his wife there, drunk, and virtuously strangled her.

The tender feelings of Delalande for his servant-girl were such that he killed his wife with a pitchfork. At the assizes of Rennes: death.

—Translated by Iain White.

93 CAMILLE MAUCLAIR

Camille Mauclair (1872-1945). Mauclair began his literary career as a poet and was co-founder with Lugné-Poe of the *Théâtre de l'Oeuvre* which premièred the plays of Maeterlinck and Ibsen (and Jarry's *Ubu Roi*). He turned to journalism and then became a prolific art critic, a champion of Rodin and the Impressionists. He aged ungracefully: unlike Fénéon, whose influence he deplored, his tastes did not evolve and he later became an implacable enemy of "modern art." His notorious *La Crise de l'art moderne* (1944) allied this enmity to extreme anti-Semitism: Mauclair, a collaborator, celebrated the "disappearance" of the Jewish picture dealers and critics responsible, so he thought, for the perversions of modernism. He contrived to die before the Liberation.

Ainsi Cria le sang de l'esprit appeared in *La Revue Blanche* in February 1894 (dedicated to Rachilde). Although it rather typifies the more melodramatic writing produced by some of the minor figures in the movement in their moments of indiscretion, its very lack of restraint foreshadows some of the modernist writers Mauclair was later to despise so much.

Of an intellectual precocity comparable, as regards the date, to that of Maurice Barrès, man of slow approaches, or Charles Morice, man of meanders and of labyrinths, Camille Mauclair is the man of deductions and of inferences and protractions....

He has been represented merely as a disciple of Monsieur Barrès; as he also was of Monsieur Mallarmé, of Monsieur Maeterlinck, of many styles of art and schools of philosophy, of all new methods of thinking and living. No one has more passionately than he sought the flower that is not to be plucked, that which one gazes upon, whose scent one bears away forever in one's eyes. Whether he sings of the dream or counsels energy, it is because, in the course of his restless excursions, he has encountered the blue irises of the green pond, or two oxen with their horns intertwined. All of a piece, to his latest acquaintance, it is to her that he transfers all his former loves, at the risk of perplexing those who, without having forgotten the day before, listen to the confidences of the present moment.

Mauclair is of superior intelligence. There are no ideas that he is unable to comprehend and assimilate immediately; he clothes them again immediately with a supreme elegance; they seem completely tailored to his cut: there is a singular sorcery here; it is as if, like Cinderella's godmother, he possessed the gift of transforming things into immediately usable objects. He has tried everything and turned everything to account...

If, as the theme of a discourse, he takes this dictum of André Gide: "I call everything that appears, a symbol," we are surprised, but not disconcerted. For we know that from this obscure formula Mauclair is going to deduce a suite of formulae whose elegance will inevitably clarify, to a blazing whiteness, the ambiguous thought which he has chosen for his experiments. He must have it become luminous; he must have it so dazzling that we close our eyes...

Now, and here's where eloquence triumphs magnificently, Mauclair gets hold of this dry and harsh formula, envelops it in the sumptuous folds of his opulent style; he drapes, he adjusts, he regulates, he arranges; the diffuse materials become tunics, robes and mantles; the mannequin comes alive; in truth it smiles and one believes that it breathes; the creature is complete: one sees, admires, and loves it...

Camille Mauclair makes the sense of that old metaphor, "the magic of style," completely understandable. His style is magic, not for the gaudiness of its colours, or for the magnificence of its sonorities, but for the beauty of its unique colour and the purity of its tone. He would seem to be like those rivers which flow, with a rich fluidity, over a bed of golden sand mixed with pebbles whose resistance is resolved into a slow, profound and continuous music. If this is not of its nature totally incomprehensible, I should say that I perceive in that sound metaphysical harmonies and, on the surface, the perpetual gleam of the ideas the river carries along.

CAMILLE MAUCLAIR

Thus The Blood of The Spirit Cried Out...

(If these pages arouse surprise, they present not so much meaning as life itself, a passionate cry, or a force of nature. Thus it is that the spirit of their author strives now rather towards a violent sensibility than towards reason: and that sensibility does not always seem lucid, because it submits itself to the sense of things, which is distinct from the order that our judgement imposes upon them, and effortlessly frees itself therefrom. One never comprehends anything, one cannot guess at the thoughts of others, but one sometimes finds distant sonorities of one's own awareness in the sound of present words: and the author's hope here is but to awaken one of those underlying sonorities in the instinctive responses of the reader—if he can.) C.M.

Men! If I set myself up in your midst, it is not in the manner of a chatterer, setting the spirits, naïve fledglings, squawking among the trellises of his phrases! But I shall stand up like a rock upon your sand, I shall wag my head like a sun, I shall tear my thoughts out from my innermost depths like quarters of meat, and I shall cry out to you: Take, and eat!

For I am not a man of taste, polishing his phrases as he does his nails, nor a man concerned with making himself clear, nor any other of your derisory puppets. I live by my instinct; I have come, enamoured of the enigma of existence, to press my mouth to the old wound of Life; now I must crush my crimson lips against your consciences, as if against strawberries!

Men, I discovered that I was a vast garden. The drops of my blood are the seeds of pomegranates from a miraculous orchard, my heart is an immortal fruit! I wish that my soul should at last appear as it was when I concealed it from strangers: a clearing burnt by a terrible sun, where jets of the living water of sensibility and of happiness spurt out.

I wish to spit out my words, red signs of my cries, as I spat out the beautiful red blood from my breast. I shall mark your faces with this blood! You will walk the streets with these words thickened with blood stuck to your eyeballs! They will congeal on your eyelashes, they will colour your wan tears, they will honour the shameless rouge on your cheeks, they will hang from your lying lips! And you will be so dismayed that your flesh will crack, just to drink in this divine liquor, and you will mingle it with the nauseating body-fluids of your cowardice!

The blood of my spirit flourishes like the seeds of a rowan tree... It is as flavoursome as the peppers of the tropics in which the hidden ardour of the sun boils! I shall not fail to cry out to you the truth of life and its ardour: what does it matter if my head sways like a world halfway extinguished? I rise up like one fated, with the face of Saturn, with the muscles of Atlas, with all the desolate shapes of ancient chaos!

I laugh at your regularities, I create myself according to my pleasure in your midst! I have not come among you to be sculpted like a stone, frozen like sorbet in a mould, handled like a tool, agreed over like a party wall; I do not accept the laying of laws on the curves of my brain like your crossroads-slabs! I no longer wish to confine my enthusiasm in an item of clothing, nor to rhyme my genius to the noise of my heels upon a boulevard, watched over by the yellow rancour of street-lamps! I no longer wish as a man of letters, to suck on the sugar-stick of morals as you do, nor to chomp on a sceptical cigar between the gaps of a smile of blue-tinted teeth!

O reasonable men, I will no longer put up with all this greyness! I am exasperated at passing for a critic, I do not thrive like a vibrio in the blood-corpuscles of others, I come, improbably, to pour my own into your abject probability, I have unloaded an enormous cargo of despair onto your quays! I rise up like a shark from the muddy depths of the ages, I rise with the candour of coral from deep in my fishing-grounds of simplicity!

I pass through your assembly clothed in wonder-inspiring red, guardian of the incomparable red blood, I advance! I am the man who bleeds among those whose veins are filled with dirty water! In your thirsty lands, in the motley hideousness of your cafés, I build an immoderate, incredible aqueduct for blood!

Rush with the others, join the palms of your hands, open your jaws decayed by acidic irony, clamber up my legs like crabs! I pour out on you the red and frothy fountain of War! I have devoured every twilight to tint my elixir, and that which I cause to flow over your tongues bleeds with all the murders of all the suns!

I have faded the dawns for you, I have lain in wait at six in the morning to assassinate the sun, I have run across the sky like a madman, I have hunted down the clouds like cattle! I cut their throats at evening, I wiped my luminous knife on the pastures of the somnolent hills!

Why should I not be thrown headlong amid the dancing stars, as though in the midst of golden bees? I cry out red, I breathe red, I laugh at being incomprehensible, honest or probable! You do not know Life; it is neither a theorem, nor an account-book, nor a heart fluttering like a fan! Life is red, and lords itself over greyness, and shines over all! I am the man who gives his blood, come running with urns! I bestow my immortal consumption upon you to dye tragically the pale bandages of your dying moments!

O women! You whose sensibility flowers above the reason of men as frail birds soar above the worms, I shall contrive to shimmer before you like a jewel. I shall wind about your feet like a bracelet of gems! I shall congeal my horrible blood in necklaces, I shall harden its drops in the interior fire of this old planet to braid them on threads of gold! I shall make myself supple as satin, I shall make myself as diaphanous as tulle, I shall clothe my soul with velour, the better to drape the scarlet of my spirit upon your finery!

For the truth that I bring you will know how to be as beautiful as it is frightening, its rapier will flower like a lily, it will lean toward kisses as the sun inclines toward the occidental groves! It will not limit itself to a single passion, it will not be contained in a lone winepress, but it will burst out like a universal vintage through all humanity's sieves!

Be silent, all of you, so as to consider sensing in silence. Be skilful moulders, occupied with affixing an exact death-mask on the face of the Invisible! And you will stride through life like real men. You will feel you are going out at dawn, skin pink from morning ablutions, and comparing your rejuvenated faces with the pallid features of people coming home from a ball!

You will look at them, those pitiful creatures, with their greenish complexion and their hollow eyes exhibiting in their pupils a shred of tarnished clarity, which the silky lustre of their coats laughs to scorn. And you will be unharmed by the make-up that pleases itself to dirty the faces of men, the first light, dwarf god, infamous dresser of lust: because your strengthened souls can no longer be crushed.

Hop no longer upon the crutches of your logic like chattering insects, but rise up, pure as reeds, towards the ineffaceable sky! That your heart might be a monument, that each of you might be a bronze tablet to which the long horde of secrets comes to surrender! Because you are masters of knowledge, and the stars are the reflections of your spirits!

No longer will there be two troops of truths trudging over the mountain and across the plain. But the firmament's flowers will descend upon their shoulders like wings, and all the birds of life will fly up in a single v-formation to go and fall into the ideal brazier of Orient!

Men! life has champed on its bit, the broken reins have taken fright and gone off to box the ears of the stars! My mysterious word stands like Hyperion in his great chariot! Do not winnow my parables with the fan of your little truth, but abandon reasoning and balance, trample the astrolabe or the compass underfoot: there is no longer time to measure out barley in the sticky shops of existence, there is no longer time to roam about with candles searching for one's shadow! Deliver yourself from the abominable parody of clownish creatures, and behold a virginal sky gushing forth!

Project yourself like a stone from an opened palm, hang the garlands of your efforts from the pillars of Paradise! I come here to vomit out to you the blood that gives strength, and, like an old river-god, I stream in your bodies which are my lands! Let the blood spread through the hidden compost of your muscles, let it swell the trees of your lungs, let it penetrate into your smallest veins, let it come like a warm spring to lurk beneath your skin, so that, by it, you may regenerate your enervated sensibility!

And then uttering a solitary cry, drunk with the honey of nature, raise yourselves up above the world in the breeze, like the oak trees, and enjoy it! Do not despise the little shiver of the highest leaf in the evening, do not scorn the little creature's caress on your pistils, do not forget the sweetness of the water's smile, do not neglect to float upon the frail, hesitantly falling, feather of the swan, any more than you refuse to howl with ecstasy like a crater finally awakened!

Feel, men, take hold of Nature's millions of hands! Go up after her, stand up on her forehead, seize her! For it need no longer be a grey existence, reason burrowing like a mole, and this is no longer the time to revere the straw eminence, to glorify the shrew-mouse! Hah! Haven't you sniffed enough at the repugnant balm of disgust, the clinging oil of ennui, and the shameless sweat of wrinkled monotony? Stand up! Reason is to be drunk with love, down to the dazzling hour of death!

You will either perish like cockroaches, or you will be as resplendent as rubies! That is why I have come to show this strange face to you today, because an unfathomable apocalypse is shaking the frail decor of my naked flesh! Here is the blood; it is time to drink it! I am gaping like a red Fountain of Youth! Rush up like camel-drivers to the curb of the well, lean over, jostle each other, madmen! And when your thirst has been assuaged, and strength has returned to you, when you move apart, the crimson spring will become as calm as a mirror once more, a translucent jewel!

There you will contemplate, instead of the moulded clay of your features, your true and future face, for I am the one through whom you will know your destinies.

André Rouveyre, *Remy de Gourmont.*

99 GEORGES EEKHOUD

Georges Eekhoud (1854-1927). Born in Belgium, he spent his adolescence in Switzerland before bowing to family pressure and entering the army. A small inheritance allowed him to escape military service and begin his writing career. He was associated with the most important Belgian literary review *La Jeune Belgique* between 1881 and 1893, a collaboration he ended when the editors issued a manifesto opposing *vers libre*, he was then the co-founder of a rival magazine, *Le Coq rouge*.

An Epicurean socialist he attempted to rally literary support for Oscar Wilde during his trial and later dedicated a book to him with these words: "To Oscar Wilde, Poet and Pagan Martyr, tortured in the name of Justice and Protestant Virtue." The sympathetic treatment of homosexuality in his novel *Escal-Vigor* (1899) was a continuation of this campaign and resulted in Eekhoud being unsuccessfully prosecuted for "writing an immoral book."

In *Terroir Incarné* (1925) he describes an aspect of his aesthetic: "I aim to concentrate, to symbolise, a whole landscape in one unique but essential individual." A function performed by the heroine of *Chardonnerette* (from *Mes Communions*, 1895) in the story here.

There are a few dramatists among the newcomers, by which I mean fervent observers of the human drama, gifted with that overwhelming sympathy that allows a writer to fraternise with everyone in the world and with all forms of life...

Georges Eekhoud is a dramatist, impassioned, a drinker-in of life and of blood.

His sympathies are many-sided and quite diverse; he loves everything. "Every living thing that liveth shall be meat for you." Obedient to the Biblical injunction, he fortifies himself with every feast the world offers. He assimilates the tender or the harsh savagery of peasants or sailors with as much certitude as the most attenuated and hypocritical psychology of creatures intoxicated with civilisation, the disquieting infamy of eccentric loves and the nobility of devoted passions, the brutal animation of gross popular customs and the delicate perversion of certain adolescent souls. He does not select, but he loves all, because he understands all.

Taking something of a liberty with the word, I have, in defiance of etymology and usage, called him a "dramatist," albeit that he has never written for the theatre... His Cycle patibulaire, *which, reprinted, has again come before the public, and* Mes Communions, *published last year, seem to be the two books by Eekhoud in which that passion most clearly and loudly cries out the charities, the hatreds, the pities, the contempts and the loves of this man who is the third tome of the marvellous trilogy whose first two have as their titles* Maeterlinck *and* Verhaeren...

If sincerity is a merit, it is doubtless not an absolute literary merit; art accommodates itself quite well with falsehood and no one is bound to confess either his "communions," or his repulsions; but I mean here by sincerity that sort of artistic disinterestedness which makes the writer, fearing neither to terrify the average brain nor to grieve either friends or masters, unveil his thoughts with all the calm shamelessness of extreme innocence or perfect vice—or of his passion. The "communions" of Georges Eekhoud are impassioned; he eagerly seats himself and, having been nourished upon charity, hatred, pity, contempt, having tasted the elixirs of love piously concocted through his hatred, he rises, drunk, but not sated, on future joys.

THE BOOK OF MASKS   100

GEORGES EEKHOUD

Char-donnerette
☙

Certain stretches of a city's outskirts can be compared to orphaned lands fallen under the sway of a harsh step-mother. They rejoice in their sense of well-being and rustic quietude even as monopolist industry comes to seize them by the collar in order to blight and exploit them. The vestiges they manage to retain of better times accentuate their sorry state, for if ruined monuments exude a restrained and romantic melancholy, there is nothing more sinister than a landscape gone to seed.

Such is the case with a small valley situated to the west of the city. The little swarded hills of bygone days have been transformed into slopes and embankments where slag heaps and piles of broken bottles take the place of cows sprawled in the high grasses. The bareness of the telegraph poles parodies the elegant *sveltesse* of the white birches and poplars. A streamlet startled by the nearness of a brick-making plant and one of those frightful blocks of workers' flats—proclaiming the abyss between philanthropy and the Gospel—strives to frolic and even to smile at the approach of the sordid tributaries that lie in wait for it yonder, where it will be diverted behind the railway aqueduct the better to be crammed between kilometres of man-made walls. How sad is the final cantina of limpid springs and upstream mills that the condemned rivulet sings to itself!

But it is in springtime that the spoliated area impresses you beyond all telling. My memory never succeeds in detaching itself from an April journey to these crucial provinces. The smile of renewal shone falsely upon them. A radiant and sprightly child, the sun excited the saddened countryside and communicated who knows what forced and artful grace to it.

A morbid spiritual state had dragged my feet to this so sadly transitory region that morning. I no longer felt my aloneness there, even more isolated than elsewhere. Forever deprived of hopes, I was plunged into the emptiness of my former nostalgia; I assimilated myself into this disintegrating region, doubly afflicted, struggling in turn with convulsions of anguish and normal growing pains—just like this land where the brutal union of city and countryside resembled the corrosive and deadly kiss of a rape. It kept me from emigrating, from loosing my way, from dissevering myself once and for all from everything good. Not one normal affinity held me together any longer, not one lawful consolation could come my way and, pending the imminent metamorphosis, I was savouring the complaisance of this final springtime in the sickly and carious industrial suburbs. I was breathing in the fumes of this world in order to arrive at new shores. But which ones? And by what means? My presentiments of an indispensable avatar by no means implied the end of my life upon this earth. Reason told me that, without my leaving this planet, it had the means to create a new world and a new humanity, with other morals and other gods, outside of every tradition.

At this moment in my speculations, descending an embankment, on the point of embarking upon the most intractable defile in this tollgate region, I crossed paths with a young girl, a sort of beggar, a true native of this soil. At once childish and aged, this being assumed a superhuman importance in my eyes. She was caught between twilight and dawn, promise and decline, suggesting at the time both the night to come and a day waiting to be born. She lent charm to and reinforced the impression produced by so local an environment, and I did not doubt that she had issued spontaneously from the accidental meeting of the redeeming sun with the damned suburbs.

Her sexless appearance complicated any determination of her age. Her face could as easily be that of a little boy as of a little girl, her body was as suited to an ephebe as to a female adolescent.

Scrawny, nervous, wan, dressed in tatters sewed together with straw substituted for thread or fastened with thorns in place of pins, she thrust herself upon your attention with one of those faces that have a complex and impassioned expression, a physiognomy at once affectionate and spiteful, ingenious and precocious, sensitive and rebellious, shaped like an elongated oval of livid complexion, rosy in places, with an aquiline and animated nose, an obstinate chin, a smooth brow, almost too genial for a woman, contrasting with the sarcastic pucker of her fleshy lips, alluring although rather faded. This face changed in its expression from a depraved urchin's carefree and ambiguous smile to the ecstatic and languorous melancholy of an angel by some Gothic master.

And in this local physiognomy nothing was as intense and troubling as the eyes of an indescribable blue, by turn beady and sparkling with mirth or clouding over, becoming as velvet in their desolation; eyes a bit bloodshot, all at once bantering and beseeching, deep-set beneath the arch of the eyebrows, shadowed by long pale lashes, circled with violet as though from contusions. Oh that look, that began like the prayer of a child martyr and ended with a prostitute's leer! The better to define the emanation, the aura this dubious creature gave off, I would say that she might well have led the legions of urban and rural *sans-culottes*[*], and that in times of panic and bourgeois reprisals, decent citizens might have stood her against a wall, so much did she exude subversion, anomaly, the spirit of the outsider.

She took up her stand in front of me, barring my passage, stretched out her chapped and callused hand and demanded alms of me in a vulgar voice, chant-like with inflections shaped into fairground rhapsodies, poignant as the roll-calls on a ship in quarantine.

Seeing me moved to the point of searching through my pockets for money, she interrupted her complaint and, taking me by the hand in a very familiar way: "Come on!" she said. "Where?" I stammered. "I'm starving!" she confided to me laughing sorrowfully, while she enveloped me with a carnivorous and coaxing stare. If I had to portray Hunger, I would copy that look of hers!

We took ourselves off, myself completely at her mercy, the liege-man of this social outcast, to a dilapidated little tavern, where once, at the dominical vespers, couples from the city, escaping from cashier's-desks and ell-measures, abandoned themselves and whirled round and round in periodic harmony with the fiddles. I was delighted by her imperious assurance and allowed myself to be guided as if that had been where we were bound for and this stopover in a hovel a thing arranged between us, as if she had been waiting for me this morning, out in the lane on the city's borders.

Chardonnerette—the tavern-keeper had addressed her by this suggestive, almost coarse, name, a name truly fitting for this plant of the wasteland*—devoured the frugal dishfuls that I had served up for her. Occasionally she paused in her eating to turn the unctuous and almost too grateful caresses of her pupils upon me, so grateful were those pupils of hers that they seemed ironic to me and inspired me to remorse for my paltry benevolence: then, immediately after, this velvety and lubricated gaze became hard, withdrawn, almost vindictive. When she had finished her meal, she came to me, as I was settling up, took hold of my hand and, with the resignation of a cornered vagabond who goes off with the peelers: "Go on, give yourself a treat! Then, we're quits!"

With her breasts already bared, she had signalled to the landlady who made to show us the way to a loft. Chardonnerette, her foot set upon the first tread of the staircase, turned round to me. Ah! always that physiognomy with its contradictory expression! If the enigmatic child was beginning to stir up my sensorial being, she was also encroaching upon me, saturating me even to the smallest crannies of my soul. And so it came about that the protector's pity turned bit by bit, to respect, and even veneration. Yet, as my sympathy became love, it was she who began to humiliate me, it was I who became pitiable.

"No, you owe me nothing!" I cried. "That would be frightful!" And all but sobbing: "How you must despise me if you believe me capable of exploiting your hunger!" She shrugged her shoulders: "Go on, don't talk foolish! You'll have a first taste, that's all! Unless you're disgusted!..." "Chardonnerette, I beg of you!"

"Oh yes, and what then? Make up your mind! Come on upstairs and get it over with! Or else make way and give up your place to the next in line..." I seized her arm, hard enough to break it: "You have lovers!" This jealous outburst escaped me like blood spurting from a punctured artery. She laughed a false, hoarse laugh: "Lovers! Now he calls them lovers! All those who come up to me on the highway! Anyone who's walking by!" And, edgily, she made the motions of counting them out on her fingers, which she then flicked as if to shake off an invisible dust whose every grain represented one of her innumerable gallants.

At that moment I simultaneously wanted to cover her with kisses and beat her unmercifully. I understood those desperate ones who, on the point of commission, or even having committed the worst of outrages, massacre the object of their monstrous desire and believe themselves to be less damnable assassins than divine lights; I compared myself to them to the point that, ears roaring, eyes red and filled with tears, with a great effort I reached the door to flee from the temptation of imitating them all the way.

Chardonnerette had thrown herself in front of me and, once more, that long ambiguous stare of caress and menace, prayer and exasperation, drilled into my heart and troubled me to the core of my being. Beneath the force of that stare my fury subsided into a delicious stupor. I swooned away at the pressure of a hand become tutelary, at the heat of a fraternal hip grazing mine and, in her eyes freed of prejudices and lies, I drank in forgetfulness of all things, save for her presence.

Was this the awaited angel, the annunciator of the new world? Marching without speaking, two sleepwalkers, we found ourselves, almost without knowing it, in the open countryside, far from the suburb.

"Let's go back," she murmured to me with a voice hollow and envious. "It's too happy, too healthy here. This whole countryside stinks of butter and fat cabbages. The limp and swollen flesh smells of tallow…"

This rural nature, serene, blissful and salubrious, resigned to the point of servility, accorded poorly with the subversive colour of our thoughts. Recognising my companion's inward feelings of disgust and acidic affinities, I went still further, saying: "Yes, let's return to where people suffer, where people always seem in revolt beneath the constant menace of the pillory or jail, where every licence glorifies us; let's go where love blasphemes, where kisses bleed, where possessions are agonies, where people love in order to kill each other!" At these words the eyes of the pale child appeared more fiery to me, more like Greek fire than ever before.

In place of the rustic steeples dressed in gold, we saw the manufacturers' smokestacks appear once more, unrolling funereal crêpes. The angeluses of peaceful villages were smothered by the factory bells chiming a short-lived deliverance to their gallery-slaves.

Walking at an accelerated pace, in swarms, flasks at their hip, pipes in mouth, ungainly, dusty, they looked my companion over quite shamelessly, as if everyone had rights over her. My wounds were rubbed raw by those contemptuous winks of their eyes. Why hadn't I, so irritable, so inclined to bridle at the least offence, challenged these proles instead of merely looking to get away from them? More eloquent than symbols, true incarnations of easy-going strength or latent revolts, with stout limbs and perfect figures reminiscent of Roman medals, patinated with smoke, their gaudy apparel stuck tight to their sides from the exertions and sweat of labouring—we had miraculously avoided them.

All flesh and muscular curves they, all pupils and physiognomy she, Chardonnerette greeted them by their names, or by a smutty nickname. For this one she had a tender tear, for that, a smile; at one of them she made a lascivious pout, another she gratified with her preferred gesture, she parodied the tic, the vulgar roll of the hips of a fourth and greeted the most surly, frequently the ragged, of her bedfellows who wished her in their own image, brutal and pugnacious with the most trenchant, bitter and callous imprecations of combustive smuttiness. Inexplicable phenomenon! The more storm-battered and miserable they seemed to be, the more she demonstrated her irritating and indelible solidarity with them as she passed. An even more incredible phenomenon: far from being jealous of them I wished to reconcile myself with these pariahs, to affiliate myself to this immense tribe of slaves and rogues; partisan of a sort of polyandry, I would have been content to share Chardonnerette's favours with the very lowest members of the beggars' brotherhood, with the rabble of cant-speaking thieves and tinkers. As if she had read my thoughts, she cried out enthusiastically: "Oh yes!… They're proud rascals, richer in spunk and in blood than cash! They give me a good going-over too; I've had caresses from them that would flatten you completely and leave you splayed like a cabbie's mare!" With a volubility, with a ferocious fever that made her hoarse and breathless, she evoked for me in short, panting phrases, the practices and demands of those men; she depicted siestas in brickyards hotter than sulphur-springs, nocturnal copulations in the hollow of a millstone, and debaucheries in warehouses, and the audacity, the sexual fury of those beggars, unbridled even behind the law courts, not two steps from the constables, while some snuffling and sententious magistrate laid charges against one or another robber of virginities* who had let too much blood from his patients. But still I brought her back to the facts of her personal experience.

She told me of her communions with the underdogs, the pangs of hunger that she had glutted, the thirsts she had quenched. This sublime hussy never set the price of her favours higher than a quid of tobacco, the other consolation of the starveling. How recidivists and incurables, sordid but with aching hearts, had sought a promise of redemption, alms of felicity in Chardonnerette's embrace. To the strikers on perpetual strike, rebounding from the police-court to the county jail, and from the doss-house with its phalansteries* of vagabonds to the wounded of our social gehenna, she represented the moment of balsamic truce, the sweet ointment, the field-hospital always open to them. But sometimes she operated like cauteries and fiery needles. In the imagination of her debtors she stirred up dreams of expiatory cataclysms. She had inoculated herself with the virus of reprisal in order to pass it on through the cupping-glasses of her kisses to too-submissive and too-patient helots. She stirred the good-looking boys of the rabble to the most courageous crimes. And on her breast, heaving with ferocious charity, the most radiant adolescents, still so naïve and so tender that they smiled in their misery and at the inequity of their position, awoke one morning as out-and-out anarchists. In return she impregnated herself with their virile and courageous essence, she modelled herself upon her lovers. The race of the heroic, louse-ridden poor had shaped her feminine charms to suit their benumbed hands, their gross, convulsive mouths of Tantaluses thirsting for goodness and justice.

Her disgrace seems like a black purgatorial splendour to her.

The more she enumerated her ignominies to me, the more I loved her, this total loss, this Madeleine of the loutish idlers. Yes, I loved her. And with an absolute and pantheistic love! In the person of this prostitute I adored all of the people, all their suffering, the infinity of human sorrow, and I wanted to incarnate in this martyr and saint the tragic and rebellious common humanity in order to possess them, to beatify them forever.

My affective aberration reached the stage of displacing into her my nostalgia for a better world. Her nomadic and innumerable loves exalted her in my eyes. Infinitely redeeming and expiatory, she had wiped away more tears than the little virgins at the cross-roads. Like insistent and volcanic ejaculatory prayers, like the prayers of the shipwrecked that turn into curses of despair, the furious declarations of her faithful followers had scourged her. Many a one, drunk, impassioned to the point of epilepsy, in those stages of lovemaking in which, among those of a primordial temperament, the outpourings of tenderness commingled with transports of hatred, had beaten, bitten, bruised her, trodden her underfoot, tattooed her like a jail house wall.

Our Lady of the Chattering Teeth and the Rags, it was with sores and wounds that her truculent pilgrims covered her body during their amorous novenas, by way of votive offerings!

When we entered the tavern I fell upon my knees.

"I adore you," I cried out to her, wetting her chapped and dusty feet with all the tears accumulated within my breast since destiny had first confronted me with this beggar-woman. "Yes! I bear for you an aberrant love... a monstrous love, so my bygone loves, abjured for you, will tell me!... But forgive me my feebleness and my novitiate. It is for you to initiate me into the redoubtable mysteries... See, I humble myself, tremble again at your feet. At this moment you might dispense succour too terrible for my trivial distress, you must be loved to the uttermost degree... The happy cowards still have too great a hold over me. Before entering into the heady dens of revolt, I must shake off in the open air the stale stench of the kennel! Be patient a while until I am reconciled to the fact that for a part of your being I have denied my race, my origins, my family and my marriage, until I have known hunger, proscription, prison chaplains, round-ups, defilements, the outrages of every sort that the wicked rich man lavished upon Lazarus, the shadow of and the foil to his damning prosperity... In order to gain access to the anarchist communion, I hope first for the baptism of the interdict. It is from your union with some ruffian or another, it is from your adolescent bosom, more ruinous than that of the octogenarian in the prophecy that, without a doubt, will emerge the Antichrist, the Incendiary, the Purifier!"

Her rags fell to the earth as a sign of her acquiescence to my forebodings. In her dying consumptive's nakedness, with her poor emaciated arms, her frail and ligneous legs, with her mouth and her womb the oscellated butt of scars, the whole of that exhausted and starving body which would have fitted three times in a child's coffin, she stood there more heart-rending than a strike-day, more consuming than petrol and firedamp, more damnable than a warming-room in a convict prison, and at the same time purer and more lustral than a baptismal font. Her shoulders were so puny that they seemed to bend beneath the burden of her long hair, crowning with a smoky halo of sorrow her seraphic and exhausted face. Her blue eyes, dilated to the extreme, bluer than the sky on the first day of the world, searching as consciences, opened for me onto vertiginous visions of shame and salvation, iniquity and redemption.

Then, torn between horror and fanaticism, wilder than a stealer of holy relics, with all the forces, all the aspirations, all the emotional overabundance of the riffraff and the beggars who had paid tribute to her fermenting in my being, I embraced her, I pressed her to me.

As her lips met mine, a delicious cold, the sapid coolness of a paradisal fruit, spread through the very sources of my life and I felt myself welling up, then drying out eternally in the prayer of universal suffering granted me...

—*Translated by Andrew Mangravite & Iain White.*

107 Maeterlinck

Maurice Maeterlinck (1862-1949). Maeterlinck won the Nobel Prize for literature in 1911 and must be the most translated author in this collection, yet it is doubtful that his voluminous spiritual ruminations are much read nowadays.

Maeterlinck trained as a lawyer, even practising as a barrister for a while, before turning his back on the world of facts for one of nuance and mysticism (he translated Novalis, Emerson, Ruysbroeck...). His first book, published in 1889 by the original Symbolist publisher Vanier was *Serres Chaudes* (*Hot-Houses*), —to modern taste he never surpassed these poems of pure claustrophobic Symbolism, two of which follow. Apart from his essays and meditations Maeterlinck made important contributions to Symbolist drama with plays now rarely performed (*The Blue Bird, Pelléas & Mélisande*) except on the operatic stage.

There is an island somewhere in the mists, and on this island there is a castle, and in the castle there is a great hall lit by a little lamp, and in the hall there are people waiting. What are they waiting for? They do not know. They are waiting for a knock on the door, they are waiting for the lamp to go out, they are waiting for Fear, they are waiting for Death. They speak; yes, they utter words that momentarily trouble the silence, then they listen again, leaving their sentences incomplete and their gestures unfinished. They listen, they wait. Perhaps he won't be coming? Oh! He always comes. He'll be coming. It's late. Perhaps he won't come until tomorrow. And the people assembled in the great hall, under the little lamp, begin to smile, and they are on the point of hoping. There is a knock on the door. And that is all: there is a whole life there, all of life.

In this sense Monsieur Maeterlinck's little dramas, so deliciously unreal, are profoundly living and true; his characters, who have the air of being phantoms, are filled with life, like those globes which appear inert and which, charged with electricity, will flash on contact with a point; they are not abstractions but syntheses; they are states of mind or, still more, states of humanity, moments, minutes that will be eternal: in short, they are real, by dint of their unreality...

Poetry or philosophy, Maurice Maeterlinck's literature comes at a time when we are most in need of being raised up and fortified, at a time when it is not immaterial for someone to tell us that the highest goal of life is "to keep open the highways that lead us from what can be seen to that which we cannot see." Maeterlinck has not only kept open those highways trodden and cleared by so many well-intentioned souls, where the great-minded here and there stretch out their arms like oases, he also seems to have extended into the infinite the profundity of these highways: he has said "such specious words in low tones" that the thorns have made way on their own, the trees have spontaneously pruned themselves and a step beyond is possible, so that today's gaze travels farther than it did yesterday.

Others without doubt have or have had richer language, a more fecund imagination, a gift for clearer observation, more whimsy, faculties more apt for sounding the clarion of the music of words, so be it, but with halting and meagre language, childish dramatic combinations, a technique almost enervated by repetition of phrases, with these clumsinesses, with all of these faults, Maurice Maeterlinck works at books and pamphlets of definite originality, and a newness so truly new that they will for quite some time disconcert the lamentable troop of misoneists, the tribe who pardon audacity, if there is a precedent—almost from a sense of protocol—but who regard genius, which is perpetual audacity, with mistrust.

MAURICE MAETERLINCK

Hospital

Hospital! Hospital by the canal!
Hospital in July!
They're lighting a fire in the ward!
As the ocean liners whistle on the canal!

(Oh! Do not approach the windows!)
Emigrants passing through a palace!
There's a yacht in the tempest!
And flocks of sheep on all the ships!
(Better that we keep the windows closed,
We're almost safe from outside.)
It's like a hot-house in the snow,
Or a woman's churching on a day of thunder,
Plants appear scattered on a woollen blanket
A conflagration of a sunlit day,
And I'm walking through a forest full of wounded.

Ah! the moonlight here at last!

A fountain in the middle of the ward!
A group of young girls open the door!
I glimpse lambs on an island of meadow!
Beautiful plants on a glacier!
And lilies in a marble hall!
A festival occurs in the virgin forest!
And tropical verdure in a grotto of ice!
Listen! the locks on the canal are opening!
And the ocean liners churn its waters!

But look, the sister stirs up the fire!

Along the banks the beautiful green rushes aflame!
A boat filled with wounded pitches in the moonlight!
All the king's daughters are aboard a barque in this storm!
Princesses will die in a field of hemlock!

Careful! Don't open the windows!
Listen: the liner's horns on the horizon!

Someone is being poisoned in the garden!
A great feast celebrated by the enemy!
Stags in a besieged city!
And a menagerie amidst the lilies!
Tropical forests in the depths of a coal-mine!
A flock of sheep crosses an iron bridge!
And the meadow lambs mournfully enter the ward!

Now the sister lights the lamps,
She brings meals to the patients,
She has closed the windows overlooking the canal,
And the doors to the moonlight.

Hot-house

O hot-house in the forest's heart!
Your doors forever sealed!
And everything beneath your dome!
And in my soul in your affinities!

Thoughts of a princess sick with hunger,
A sailor, listless in the desert,
Brazen music at the windows of the dying.

Seek out the coolest corners!
Like a woman fainting during harvest,
There are coaches in the hospice' court;
And far off, an elk-hunter passes by, become a sick-nurse.

Look about you in the moonlight!
(Nothing's in its proper place!)
Like a madwoman dragged before judges,
A warship in full sail on a canal,
Night-birds amidst lilies,
Bells tolling at noon,
(Beneath these panes of glass!)
The sick halted in a prairie,
The smell of ether on a sunny day.

God, O God, when will there be rain,
When snow or wind in this hot-house!

MAURICE MAETERLINCK

Corbière, *Self-portrait*, 1873.

113 TRISTAN

Tristan Corbière (1845-1875). A Breton, Corbière spent most of his short adult life in the resort of Roscoff, where he lived for the sake of his poor health. Consequently he hardly moved in literary circles, paying only short visits to Paris. His most important work *Les Amours jaunes* appeared in 1873 at his father's expense. Verlaine's discovery of these poems, and his subsequent inclusion in *Les Poètes maudits* established Corbière's posthumous fame.

The two poems here were quoted in their entirety in De Gourmont's essay.

Laforgue, in the course of reading, pencilled these notes about Corbière which, though unedited, are all the same definitive; among them:

Bohemian of the ocean—picaresque and droll—abrupt, concise, lashing the line of verse with a riding-crop—strident as the sea-gull's cry and like them never weary—without aestheticism—nothing of poetry and nothing of verse, scarcely literature—sensual, he never displays flesh—Byronic and a loafer—always the frank word—there isn't another artist in verse more distanced from poetic language than he—he has a trade without plastic interest—the interest, the effect, is in the whip-cut, the dry-point effect, the pun, the briskness, the staccato romanticism—he wants to be undefinable, not to be loved, not to be hated; laconic, rejected in every latitude, by every custom, on this side and the other of the Pyrenees.

That is the truth without doubt: Corbière was dominated and guided by the demon of contradiction. He supposed that he had to distinguish himself from men through thoughts and actions exactly contrary to the thoughts and acts of the run of men; there is much of the wilful in his originality; he toiled over it, as women toil over their complexion, during the long afternoons between earth and sky, and when he disembarked, it was to fire broadsides of stupefaction: dandyism à la Baudelaire.

But one can only work at a nature successfully in the sense of ones instincts and penchants; Corbière had to be inherently a bit of what he became, the Don Juan of singularity; there is only one woman whom he loves; he mocks the other with the smart phrase, "the eternal madame."

Corbière has a lot of wit, wit at the same time of the Montmartre wine-shops and the forecastle; his talent is composed of this boastful wit, waggish and baroque, with an impudent bad taste, and with flashes of genius; he has a drunken demeanour, but he is only laboriously awkward; he carves, to make of them absurd chaplets, from miraculous rolled pebbles works of a century-long patience, but in his dizaines, he leaves the little stone from the sea all rough and raw, because he loves the sea, at bottom, with a vast naïveté and because his paradoxical folly yields him, time after time, an intoxication of poetry and beauty.

Amid the never ordinary verses of Amours jaunes, there is much that is very unpleasant and much that is admirable, but admirable with an air so equivocal, so specious, that one does not always appreciate it on a first encounter; then one assumes that Tristan Corbière is, like Laforgue, who is a little his disciple, one of those unclassifiable and undeniable talents who dot the history of literature, strange and precious exceptions -- singular even in a gallery of singularities.

Here are two short poems by Tristan Corbière, forgotten even by the latest publisher of his Amours jaunes:

TRISTAN CORBIÈRE

Paris by Night

The sea it is. Dead flat. The swelling tide—
A gurgling bath-plug—rumbles to subside—
Then hears its wave roll back. The roar withdraws.
Hark! Can you hear the night-crabs' scrabbling claws?

The Styx runs dry. With lantern old Diog-
Enes comes scavenging. A fishing lodge
Finds poets, all perverse as pachyderms,
Recycling their cracked skulls as cans of worms.

A field it is. Fierce harpies, screeching, scoop
For rancid scraps. Their spirals loop the loop.
The mangy midnight rabbit's guttered den
Helps give the slip to springe-heeled garbage-men.

And death it is. Laws snore. Upstairs love sleeps
Siesta-sound. Love's succulent beef keeps
The rich red seal that switched-off kisses make.
Time's all alone. See! Not one dream's awake.

All life is there. Lend ears to living springs
That shampoo Neptune's locks. The triton sings
While struggling through the spinach-slimy tide
From naked morgues, his gouged eyes open wide.

Paris by Day

A copper disk spins shining in the sky—
God's cook-house! In this pan he likes to fry
His manna in his manner up above—
His menu drenched in sweat and drenched in love.

With outstretched palms, gape-mouthed, the famished wait—
And parched throats rattle; clang their empty can.
They queue up for their turn, man after man,
And, listless, listen for the sizzling bait.

Do you imagine that the frizzled sun
Supplies such sustenance for everyone?
Bah! On our heads just black dog stew will fall!

They're on a sunbeam; *we*'re deep in the pit,
Our jug's congealed, half-cracked, our lamp unlit.
Our wits survive on wormwood—and on gall.

—*Translated by Stanley Chapman.*

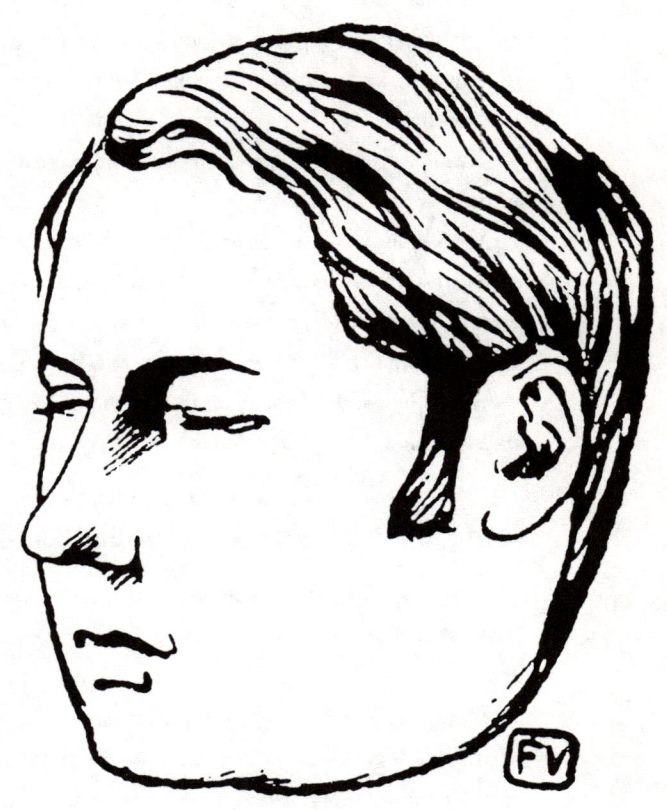

117 Jules Laforgue

He was a supremely gifted spirit, and rich in considerable learning. He had wished to nourish his natural genius made of sensibility, irony, imagination and clairvoyance, on positive knowledge, on all philosophies, all literatures, all images from nature and from art; and even the latest insights of science seemed to have been familiar to him. His was an ornate and flamboyant genius, ready to construct infinitely diverse and beautiful structures, to raise up new ogives and undreamed-of domes; but he had forgotten his winter muff, and he died of cold one snowy day.

That is why his work, already magnificent, is but a prelude to an oratorio ending in silence.

Many of his verses are coloured with an icy affectation of ingenuousness, the language of a child that is unduly loved, a little girl unduly indulged—but an indication, too, of a genuine need for affection and a pure sweetness of nature—an adolescent of genius who would have liked still to rest on his mother's knees his "equatorial brow, store-room of anomalies," but many have the beauty of smoky topazes, the melancholy of opals, the coolness of moonstones, and some pages, like that, for example, which begins thus:

> Black north wind, yelping rain-shower
> And black river, and houses of ill-fame...

have the grace, sorrowful yet still consoling, of eternal confessions; the thing, eternally the same, which Laforgue repeats in such a way that it seems dreamed and confessed for the first time....

There was no present for Laforgue except among a group of friends; he died just as his **Moralités légendaires** was coming out, though still offered to a restricted few, and it was only just granted to him to hear, from a few mouths, that those pages irrevocably destined him to live, to the life of glory, among those the gods create in their own image, themselves gods, and creators.

This is a literature entirely renewed and unexpected, one that disconcerts one and gives the curious (and rare) sensation of our never having read anything like it; the bunch of grapes with all its velvet softness in the early morning light, but with singular reflections and an air as if the grape-seeds had been frozen within by a breath of ironic wind, come from farther away than the pole...

Jules Laforgue (1860-1887). A short, rather tragic life and a little posthumous fame was Jules Laforgue's fate. Born in Uruguay, he was sent to school in France and suffered from chronic loneliness which remained unabated on his eventual arrival in Paris. He travelled to Germany as a tutor and died there of consumption shortly after marrying an English girl. His poems were collected together and published after his death by Fénéon and have been widely translated into English, largely because of the esteem in which he was held by such poets as Pound and Eliot. He also published a volume of short stories (*Moralités légendaires*, 1885, also available in English) and various marginalia of which the present text is one. It originally appeared in *La Vogue* in May 1886.

JULES LAFORGUE

The Aquarium

Do you know the land where silence blooms? Admission costs one franc—less expensive, but less sought-after than the Opera, and two sous for the cloakroom, because it's raining outside and here it is properly, cosily warm.

A maze styled like a grotto, with gallows-like gas-jets in the vault, corridors winding right and left of the luminous glass world of the undersea chambers—this is the Aquarium—twisting and turning day in day out in its cellar to the intermittent rhythm of the pistons that drive the hydraulics—it is the Aquarium where one witnesses the most virginal intimacies—the most far gone scenes from behind the doors of the worlds in question—silent, like the distinguished company in a sick-room; this is the Aquarium that we shall one day see recognised as an institution for public benefit.

Dolmen-studded heaths encrusted with viscous jewels, circles of tiered basalt where (in private, I assure you) crabs with an obtuse and tentative after-dinner goodwill grapple in couples with their deadpan eyes. Oh! that lofty plateau, whence, stuck like a sucker, an octopus, fat hairless minotaur, surveys the whole surrounding world. Then plains of fine sand, so fine that it is lifted by the flapping of a flatfish's tail as it arrives from afar with a fluttering of banderoles, watched as it passes by great eyes at the surface of the sand here and there for whom this is the sum total of the daily news...

Spanned by natural bridges, there are cracks where the slate-roofed carapaces of rat-tailed king-crabs sprawl and masticate, some capsized and struggling, maybe even with themselves? One never knows. (Would I be so out of place on my back among these crabs?)

And fields of sponges, sponges like jettisoned lungs, or beds of orange velvet truffles, a whole graveyard of pearly molluscs, and those precious plantations of asparagus swollen and preserved in the formaldehyde of Silence...

And the desolation of steppes empty but for one tree, blasted and ossified, a cast-off phalanstery where hundreds of sea-horses unpretentiously cluster.

And beneath chaotic, deserted triumphal arches, eels slip away like carefree ribbons...

And all these undersea territories I shall have you observe.

The eggs I know not whose, hang—till when?—like bean-pods tied with corkscrew strings...

Hairy cells migrating to nowhere in particular, a crest of lashes round a frame, which they fan through the boredom of interminable journeys...

And these secluded wells, most secret harems, laboratories for more mysterious experiences, where bubbles float upwards, oh! they're going to burst!... bubbles maybe pregnant, bubbles of bluish jelly tensed by one single perpetual diaphanous spasm.

And plenty more, and better ones.

At last, as far as the eye can see, the prairies; prairies enamelled with white sea-anemones, juicy fat onions, bulbs with violet membranes, by bits of guts scattered about, and, I swear, rebuilding their existence, by stumps whose antennae wink at the coral next to them, a thousand apparently pointless warts: a whole foetal, cloistered flora, fluttering, waving, the eternal digestive dream of succeeding in whispering one day mutual congratulations as to this state of affairs.

Oh! I know what you will say, my friends, as you flatten your sensuous noses against the glass. Yes, put yourself in their place. No day, no night, no winter, no spring, no summer, no autumn or other weathercocks: dreams among the smelly messes of the cradle, sex without moving an inch, at the price of blind imperturbability, in the coolness!

Closing time, and up we go, back out into the muddy, shivery, hackneyed, knock-kneed, runny-nosed, poxy and bellicose daylight of 1886. Oh! before they close, you are down in the under-sea, while we, we are dry with superterrestrial cravings: that is the difference I wanted to make clear. Why aren't the antennae of our senses, too, limited by Silence, Opacity, and Blindness? and why do they suspect possibilities beyond what is allowed for us? and soak as if thirsty forever? and why do we also know how to curl up in our little corner to coddle the dead drunkard that is our little self?

This is what I wanted to say as I leave this *world of smugness*.

Now, O under-sea vacationers, I will make no bones about admitting that among our super-terrestrial cravings we have two fruits that can perhaps match yours: the head of our lady-love, a worn-out flower, closed and asleep among the pallid pillows, her curls limp and sticky with the final sweat, her bruised mouth showing her pale teeth in an aquarial moonbeam (do not pick it, no!)—and the moon itself, a sunflower flattened and desiccated by agnosticism...

But the too-much loved lady is so near and the moon so far, at least at certain times of the night. Well, what is it about certain times of the night? rather than always, always on time?—Dialogue:—Passer-by, pray what time is it?—It's Time, this is the Time (and that may mean at the same time, oh you need not hurry.)

Why just having to bed these things that a conscientious, enlightened alderman should be taking care of...

—*Translated by Anthony Melville.*

Arthur Rimbaud (1854-1891). The facts of Rimbaud's life have the status of legend, but not for de Gourmont, and it is startling to read his thorough reprimand of the poet—on the other hand he was closer to Rimbaud than his subsequent hagiographers and knew many who had had first-hand dealings with him.

After a riotous, and often deliberately squalid life in Paris, and then abroad, with Verlaine in his adolescent years, Rimbaud abandoned poetry around the age of twenty, after the publication of *Une Saison en Enfer* (1873) to indifferent response. A long period of vagabondage followed, in Europe, the middle and far East, until he eventually applied himself to becoming rich through trading in the Horn of Africa. He struggled hard against enormous difficulties but eventually illness, exacerbated by the climate, defeated him. He was shipped back to France in agony to die; the precise cause of his ailment is unknown, but it may have been tertiary syphilis.

Meanwhile, his fame (a matter of total indifference to him it appears) had commenced with the publication of *Les Poètes maudits* in 1884, followed by whatever manuscripts had not been lost in *La Vogue* in 1886, while the next year saw the publication of *Les Illuminations* by "the late" Arthur Rimbaud. His friends knew nothing of his return and final months in France, nursed by his sister, until several months after his death.

His theory of the poet made "Seer" by means of a systematic derangement of the senses proved influential for many decades. All his works are translated into English.

We offer here a new translation of his most famous Symbolist poem (which led a good many of his less able disciples up increasingly arcane blind alleys*), and the final section of *A Season in Hell*, generally seen as the rejection of his past beliefs.

Jean-Nicolas-Arthur Rimbaud was born in Charleville on the 20th of October, 1854, and, from the most tender age, he made his presence felt as a most insufferable street-tough. His brief sojourn in Paris was in 1870-71. He followed Verlaine to England, then to Belgium. After the little misunderstanding that separated them, Rimbaud roved the world, followed the most diverse occupations: soldier in the Dutch army, manager, in Stockholm, of the Cirque Loisset, contractor in Cyprus, trader in Harar, then in the Cape of Guardafui in Africa, where a friend of Monsieur Vittorio Pica would appear to have encountered him involved in the slave trade. More likely than not, despising everything but brutal enjoyment, savage adventure and violent life, this poet, alone among us all, voluntarily renounced poetry... after the age of seventeen Rimbaud had conquered originality, and his work will last, at the very least as a phenomenon. It is often obscure, bizarre and absurd. Quite without sincerity, with the character of a woman, of a girl, innately ill-natured and even ferocious, Rimbaud had that sort of talent that interests us without pleasing us. In his work there are many pages that give us to some degree an impression of beauty such as one might experience before a suitably pustulous toad, a beautiful case of syphilis or the Château Rouge* at eleven o'clock at night....

It is unfortunate that his life, so imperfectly understood, could not be a true vita abscondita*; *what there is of it that can be understood, disgusts us. Rimbaud was like one of those women who fail to surprise us by announcing in a brothel that they will embrace religion; but what is still more revolting to us, he seems to have been a jealous and a passionate mistress: here the aberration becomes debauched, because sentimental...*

But intelligence, conscious or unconscious, even if it lacks all rights, has the right to all absolutions.

> *Who knows if genius*
> *Is not one of your virtues,*
>
> *monsters, be you called Rimbaud—or Verlaine?*

ARTHUR RIMBAUD

Vowels

A black; E white; I red; U green; O blue:
Some day I'll excavate our vowels' birth.
A, sables corsetting the blazing girth
Of flies that storm a stench-charged foul bayou,

Overcast coves; E, mist-clouds, tents' bleached hue,
Ice assegais, white knights, seeds' umbelled berth;
I, purpled spittle, full round lips in mirth-
Ful spite, drunk orgies penance learns to rue;

U, endless rippling viridescent green
Seas, peaceful herd-spread pastures, calm serene
Deep furrowed brows thought's alchemies incise;

O, great last trump's proud clarion's strident shrill,
Worlds' tumbling silences where angels spill—
Omega's ultra-radiant violet Eyes!

—*Translated by Stanley Chapman.*

Farewell Autumn already!—But why regret an eternal sun, if we are to undertake the discovery of a divine light, far from all those who die with the seasons.

Autumn. Our ship rises up out of the unmoving mists and turns toward the harbour of misery, the immense city, its sky stained with fire and mud. Ah! putrid rags, rain-soaked bread, drunkenness, the thousand loves that crucified me! So, she will never be done, that ghoul queen of millions of souls and corpses, *and which will be judged!* Once again I see myself, skin corroded by mud and plague, hair and armpits infested with worms, still bigger worms in my heart, lying among strangers without age, or feeling... I might have died there... Unbearable memory! Poverty disgusts me.

And I dread winter, that season of comfort!

Sometimes I see in the sky endless beaches covered with white nations filled with joy. Above me a great golden vessel, its multi-coloured pennants flutter in the morning breezes. I created all festivals, all triumphs, all dramas. I tried to invent new flowers, new stars, new flesh, new ways to speak. I thought I had acquired supernatural powers. And so! I must bury my imagination and my memories! An artist's and story-teller's fame precluded!

I! Who called myself magus or angel, exempt from all morality, I am flung back to earth with a duty to find, and rough reality to embrace! Peasant!

Was I wrong! Could charity be death's sister for me?

At last I shall ask forgiveness for having fed on lies. Let's get going.

But no friendly hand! and where find help?

Yes, the new hour is at least hard.

For I can say that victory is mine: the grinding of teeth, hissings of fire and pestilential sighs are dying away. All the filthy memories are fading. The last remaining regrets de-camp: my envy of beggars, thieves, death's companions, all those backward creatures. —The damned, and what if I avenged myself!

It is necessary to be completely modern.

No hymns: at least hold onto ground gained. Arduous night! The dried blood smokes on my face, and there's nothing behind me but that horrible bush!... Spiritual battle is as ferocious as the battle of men; but only God enjoys the vision of justice.

Meanwhile this is the nightwatch. Let us welcome all influx of vigour and genuine tenderness. And, at dawn, armed with an ardent patience, we shall enter magnificent cities.

Did I mention a friendly hand! My one great advantage is—I can laugh at old lying loves and put those dishonest couples to shame—I saw the hell of women back there—and I shall be free *to possess truth in one body and one soul.*

—*Translated by John Harman.*

125 Adolphe Retté

Adolphe Retté (1862-1930). After a difficult childhood, and voluntary military service in the cavalry, Retté turned to literature, made the acquaintance of Gustave Kahn and assumed co-editorship of *La Vogue*.

His early writing is marked by an intense rejection of reality, none more so than *Thulé des Brumes* (1892) of which *Nightfumes* is a condensation of the first section. It was not very well received; Maurras wrote that it "marked the extreme limits of inhabitable literature." Another critic, Harold Swan, described Retté's early works: "He has a taste for mystery, a penchant for too-preciously crafted and mystificatory phrasing, a mania for over-elaboration, as for his poetry, I find its sprinklings of affectation and word-play extremely disagreeable." Swan was in fact Retté's own pseudonym! His criticisms of his fellow authors and, especially, a long campaign against Mallarmé, written under his own name, alienated most of his contemporaries.

Thulé des Brumes was written during Retté's anarchist period, when he was also indulging in drugs (probably morphine) and a surfeit of alcohol. His increasingly militant anarchist beliefs gradually eroded his conception of a literature separate from the world, while paradoxically supporting a position of complete liberty for the writer. He was arrested for agitation several times and his political writings (*Réflexions sur l'Anarchie*, 1894) were virulently anti-militarist and anti-Catholic. Ten years later he found himself at an impasse, his writing had failed to acquire a reputation, his politics had moved to Socialism and then apathy, his much abused friends had washed their hands of him. His conversion, described in *Du Diable à Dieu* (1907), dates from this time. A burnt-out case, he ended his days writing devotional guides, making religious pilgrimages and lecturing against the evils of Anarchism and Socialism.

For its richness in poets, the present day—which has already lasted ten years—is barely comparable to any in the past, even the richest in sunshine and flowers. There were quiet early-morning strolls in the dew in the footsteps of Ronsard; there was a fine afternoon when Théophile de Viau's weary viol sighed, heard among the hautboys and the trumpets; there was the romantic day, stormy, sombre and royal, troubled toward evening by the cry of a woman Baudelaire strangled; there was the Parnassian moonlight, and the Verlainian sun rose; and here we are, if you like, at bright noontide, in the midst of a broad countryside rich in everything needful to make verses: grasses, flowers, rivers, streams, woods, caverns, and women, young, and so fresh one would imagine them thoughts newly sprung from an artless mind.

This broad countryside is filled with poets who go their way, no longer in troops, as in Ronsard's time, but alone, and with a somewhat unsociable air; they greet each other from a distance with brief gestures. Not all have a name, and many never will: how shall we call them? Let us leave them to their play, while this one here will welcome us and tell us something of his dream.

He is Adolphe Retté.

...As a poet, Adolphe Retté has nothing other than a sense of rhythm and a love of words; he is fond of ideas, and he loves them new and even excessive; he wishes to free himself from all the old prejudices and he likewise would like to free his brothers from social bondage...

ADOLPHE RETTÉ

Nightfumes

Darkness most merciful, Charity with innocent eyes whose golden lashes filter pale and distant tears, Night ripples waves of pacifying silence upon the city's agitated slumber. Frenzied fingers of subtle spirits stir strings floating from delicate harps on high: gliding over unheard-of epithalamiums for the marriage of a soul to Mystery.

Fountain of all graces, amid lilies of reconciliation; peaceful water, coveted fluid gems wherein the barbarisms of everyday existence are drowned; clear waves, sobbing, cut by luminous gondolas; the mourning murmuring of memorial viols soothes the ennui of a deformed prince who hides himself; mirror of melancholy and oblivion offering nival moirés and blues of solitary moons—after so many burning stations—to the fatigue of a pilgrimage to the basilica of Nut; forests of Gulistan; cool shadows enshroud you, sick soul corroded by too many yesterdays of salt from the Desolate Sea; the good motherly Night caresses the frail childhood of Dream; oh, but she'll never survive the furtive glimmer of a dawn which perhaps reveals the abortion—the blessed starry Night lit with candles for the mass of the Ideal—oh that the brutal fanfares of the sun might never gush forth from the quotidian horizon! For I am embarked upon this Night, may the velvet charm of this mystical Night descend upon me—and you will possess me no more, monotonous Life, hungry nightmare whose maw awaits.

The barking of the pack rolls through the forest. From glades sifted for new gold by a martial sun, to copses where ponds half open mossy eyes, the child hunter's horn has grown hoarse.

Just so, the afternoon, an ephebe on horseback; the shadows elongated, the cries of crows accompany him and the hamadryad (she is the arch centenarian of the centuries) sings to him: "You will not run it down..." His horse gallops.

The forest bleeds twilight; the weary horse has slowed to a walk; the horn has split and the divine rider's halo hangs, rent, in a tangle of low branches.

See—Night ascends, the dogs fall silent and crouch on the ground. Can this beast possibly be caught? Even the horse lies dead.

Joyful at last—after so many years of the chase!—an old horseman stumbles forward, gaping. There is nothing there; nothing but moonlight, solitary, spreading shrouds upon ground.

There was a journey; it happened long ago.

Open, precarious prettiness of fans; slowly, the better to pleasure bleary-eyed Insomnia; very quickly, to agitate in brief rainbows the vapours of your garish aromatics—O city of artifices!

Fans, in the darkness, are bouquets of pale fire, the snow of lunar cascades upon a thicket of asphodels, of noble garlands of the Panathenæa.

A mocking procession hurls itself pell-mell toward the confused course of the clouds and tosses the milky pearls to Her from on high. She doesn't gather them; she knows that in reality they are beads of coloured glass. On certain evenings I do gather them myself, but sooner or later I reject them to grovel at her feet, near the hearth, powdered over with cold ashes.

There—the wind is singing through the chimneys—once again I have a lengthy, luminous dream of galleons rocking upon the blue calm of her eyes and her half-open windows, as the caress goes forth from the cool fans that discreetly lure Insomnia.

Flowering lime-trees scent this night.

In ecstasy beneath the tree of life, I impregnate myself with the floral torments aroused by the breezes of a terrestrial Paradise, and I hear the golden chain that shackles Salammbô's childish ankles.

The branches of the tree swing to and fro; their clatter a maddening zither at a barbarian festival. There are fruits among these branches, beautiful vermilion fruits, but I shall not gather them. My old cousin, the Serpent, hidden in the leaves, has warned me not to.

One… just one… is lying in the grass, ripe, the wind has torn it loose… I'll try just that one…

Bitter! So bitter…

This frozen sister of the glaucous leaves has fallen; for the first time a cloud hides the sun; the birds mark it with a mocking catcall: the breeze dispenses a stale smell of cadavers and mourns the tender orphans. The Serpent exclaims: "I always liked them!" And Salammbô breaks her golden chain.

Tree of life and fruit of death.

But the flames of the pyre build in the darkness; the crimson of youth, this too-narrow diadem, the blunted blade and cabalistic manuscripts which have taught us nothing since our childhood when we divined their doctrine—let's burn them all, and this tress of multi-coloured hair as well.

The pale blue eyes invite silence; the Maia at the bottom of the sea has smiled upon me; I'll sleep between her breasts.

Doubtless it would be better to live. "Life is action and action, joy," says one philosopher. But a pale figure, so happily pale, with a halo of lilies which have wasted away, with a voice wherein flights of angels formerly passed, says to me: "Happiness is made from dreams."

I am inclined to agree; so then, so then my life, to me, is a frail dream-plant which I must constantly inspect for signs of essential growth. I do not allow "things" to distract me from these attentions, and if I must exhaust myself, I prefer to do so pruning my unreal flowers grown wild, without any goal, however vague, other than to infiltrate a little of their pollen into my heart.

I collect Chimera wings; already a certain number of them, indifferently set aside, have crumbled into dust between the leaves of so many deceptive albums at the bottom of a cupboard, still solid though a bit worm-eaten, this piece of family furniture of which I am proudest—it has already withstood so many assaults!

But a last Chimera, long sought, clawed me with bronze talons as I attempted to pursue it, and bore me away, a stranger, to a black twin-star previously unknown to the heavens of my dreams. I am so profoundly ravished by her, gentlemen, that your earth is no more than a shining candle to me. Perhaps that's why you see so many ill tidings in those phrases which I have forced myself to offer for your edification. Do not hold it against me; I am so far from you, and so befuddled by the many sombre marvels which flourish in this black twin-star.

Concentric parks of shadow undulate; and curl and uncurl their infinite filigreed foliage; black plumes of prosperous ostriches which, teased by a summery breeze, rain little flakes upon the dust of the blue paths; a clump of tulips interspersed here and there with gladioli, mimic prisms beneath the mystery of the diffuse light of an eclipse. In a basin, where the congealed tears from last year's stars freeze, a water as sombre as remorse dreams and deforms in itself the reflection of a pale face with no eyes.

Since no person was ever mirrored here, where can this face have come from?

A Prince, very old although young, plays airs upon an organ installed in the peristyle of a ruined chapel which madden the wind-driven sylphs of his soul; and throughout the golden night there swells on every side in response to him, the flute notes of the Great God Pan.

Walks along the dirty yellow inertia of the canals, endless stations in a viscous fog rent by the hoarse cries of manoeuvring locomotives; count the pick-axe blows of a navvy whose humble and vulgar physiognomy exasperates you, observe the grimaces of a monkey left tied there by a mountebank who gets drunk at the local cabaret. See how natural its grimaces are! With us (atavism and selection, you see!) it is an altogether more complicated sport; consider, for instance, the diagram of avarice and duplicity inscribed in the wrinkles of my hostess's carefully composed face as soon as the bill appears. Smoke... have a drink as well... Other days I contemplate, lost in thought, the sky all vernal and new, and the sun, at once floating and held fast in a vast blue and golden dream. Or I pick wallflowers from a flower-bed and scatter them to float—what a contrast!—upon the stagnant water in a tub swarming with monads and bacteria; but a dancing sunbeam riddles this corruption with emerald holes where little wings beat diamond-like with thousands of facets.

In the evening, I enjoy the concert of toads who spin

out oboe notes, answering one another from meadow to meadow. At length, rather than face that sullen old man squatting in a Vatican of shadows, who patiently awaits his hour: my genuflection and kiss upon his slipper—anything, anything rather than this sinister pontiff whose infallibility I will not accept: awareness of Reality and his cardinals: *Ennui*.

❦

Those eyes, yes; those eyes of her's... mazes which amuse my idle thoughts.

Those eyes: altars of velvet adoration stirred with rosy fires, and such a vision—among the low-pitched soundings of a horn—a turret, with sleeping lions of sable and gold, where a persecuted chatelaine grieves; lutes hum beneath the carefree fingers of parti-coloured pages; the palfrey of a Dark and Handsome beau whinnies toward the turret...

A little romance, those eyes; but that's a good thing, and then: the altar excuses it all.

Those eyes which alone can comprehend a spirit fit to cultivate, as is proper, the black flower Hysteria; those dark green mother-of-pearl eyes, all morbid and surprisingly phosphorescent, lanterns of the devil—angry because She hasn't been able to violate the Graal: the fiery steel and crystal soul of our most recent Parsifals...

You, so long ago, a giddy evening in the smart part of town.

Others, whom the spirit of Melancholy never touches with her wand, covet their unconscious cruelty; fierce metals with radiance from other stars whose unwonted flare no spectroscope can fix. At certain feverish hours, it is as if a wind from the Unknown has just brushed our foreheads.

One excellent fellow ignored her eyes.

Then another, and another: heaven vibrating violently in accord with stormy forges with long flashes upon the horizon, but which lightens, very pale, an unstrung necklace of pearls high above... An abandoned garden wholly impregnated with autumn, with its noisy wings of dead leaves where, through excess, an arrogant folly shakes the little bells to drive the guardian angels away from the soul of Eugene who, wearied, still strives to be drunk once more... Convulsive waves, grossly greenish, cadaverous paleness of a malefic moon rising, coil themselves upward from ulterior gulfs like serpents, like hissing basilisks... the others, so distant, blue blades jostling; then calm panoplies which would have been overthrown by the new, if only she hadn't doubted herself amid the rancours of the Valkyries... damn! Those eyes of Hers, so well known—too well known—waltzing and flashing around my thoughts...

But silence and sudden darkness... what has occurred, that Night should thus steal away before a sudden splendour?

Those eyes of Hers, the eyes of that dearest child sparkle amid the desolation of that first light! Divinely sombre lake, lake three times pure, shivering with impalpable white vapours which flee and are silvered over, oh so distantly, by a dawn of missal! The Sad Queen remains seated at the edge of those melodious waves and weaves who knows what fabric of disheartened gold, and dwells there mute and in profile since the doves have taken flight never more to return...

But to drown his heart in those eyes; to be lost there, and gather from those lips a few sobs from a choir of stars scattered in the sky which die so madly in the depths of the mysterious lake... this is what the Dream covets; it is the charm and grace of the infinite—and my soul can no longer escape from the net which Her looks have stretched. And my own eyes are two mirrors irreparably dulled, for I have been blinded by those other eyes being too much reflected there.

Real life floats about me like funeral veils.

But I no longer recognise myself very clearly—so weary, run aground on this faded settee whose springs groan like heretics put to the test. The stench of an ancient crime stagnates in the room; the curtains seem like tearful relations round a tomb; the furnishings creak in an alarming fashion; the fireplace freezes where two shrunken embers will not burn. And who with fuddled eyes watches for me from the depths of the glass?

I have a very clear perception of not being here; my *Me* is vibrating elsewhere—somewhere else completely: but where?

Meanwhile, the creature standing before me strolls her teasing fingers through her dishevelled red hair then reaches for her glass—always that infernal alcohol!—and bangs it down upon the table next to my own.

"Go on then, have a drink. What's bothering you?"

"Nothing... I was afraid and I am drunk. Do I see you?"

"Cheer up!... what're you looking for? Don't you hear the rain falling? You're not going out in weather like that are you?"

I empty my glass without answering and look around me: so much distress in everything!... And me, a hunted wolf, I tell you, a real wolf, this person in the mirror annoys me.

"What are you thinking about now?" she resumes, parting the folds of the dressing-gown which conceals, but just barely, her regally tawny nakedness.

"No, no... enough for today, my charitable friend... and then, if you must know, I'm thinking about my black twin-star, that dear wicked star from which I have been exiled for so long... If you only knew how much malice is gathered at my heart's core!"

"You're telling all this to me?"

"To your very self; but now I think it useless to embroider further upon this theme; I'm much obliged to you for your grief at my sufferings... but now I must leave you. I'm returning to my Island, and besides, I happen to like the rain."

And off I go without further ado, unsteadily, while she, so tranquil—indifferent?—lights up a cigarette.

I am content to leave there, and yet I shall soon return, most definitely.

An implacable scribe, Asmodeus, installs himself in a vast hall which is haunted by all the demons of Impurity. Upon granite slabs and with a stylus of iron, he inscribes the sins committed in all the wicked places where he raised the roof when my soul got coarsely, vulgarly drunk. Here on certain evenings I shiver to contemplate the cold lamp, so yellow, which lights his sinister task. For nothing in this world would I ever sneak a peak at that encyclopædia of my villainies—a mad longing would grip me to take shelter amid hair shirts and macerations if, upon further reflection, I could not prove that "all that" was not my fault, really not my fault given the madman that some unknown person gave me to look after, whom I have to keep amused, do I not?

Still, such an exoneration is perhaps a suggestion of the demons of whom I catch glimpses, grimacing through the sulphurous shadows of this hall.

If I consult this scribe?... I forgot that, as regards my wickedness, he is both deaf and dumb. Go, my sweet fool, I think it better for you to return down there from whence we came.

Is it true that these things will come to an end? My *Me* now weighs on me horribly, and this bantering double whom I have caused to well up so frequently, like a genie in its bottle, beneath the noses of people who thought they had a right to keep watch over me, now supplants me. And the garrulous brood laughs, thinking me droll.

Hide—in the pure nocturnal landscape of a fatidic dream...

Beneath the blue moon a soft prairie stretches out where campanula flowers thrive; in the middle, a well embraced by tormented ivy. Not a sound, not a breath, the kingdom of Calm!

Some nights I have leant my elbows against the parapet of this well wherein the black immobile waters send back to me, instead of my reflection, the image of the One from whom I am awaiting, without hope of obtaining it, a welcoming smile.

Yes, and before these magical waters I would gladly and for hours mingle with it a few tears, if I had not forgotten the years of workmanship that go into weeping... or hurl myself into that well?... But the image would break; and then an order emanated from Her eyes, sombre chalices, pushing me back. Then I recline on the soft grasses of the sleeping prairie; I surprise myself by picking a bouquet of golden campanula which I raise as an oblation to the moon—the very friendly moon which brushes my lips with the kiss of a blue moonbeam, coldly chaste... And caressing rhythms, the soul of the campanula, sing in the depths of my heart.

What compensation! No matter now that I am very ill...

Now, everyday life carries out another coffin; the Undertaker himself leads the mourning. And passers-by are astonished at the clean white shroud sprinkled with tigridea and exclaim: "What's this, then?"

No big thing: once again, a high-born soul returns to LIMBO.

Comte Robert de Montesquiou

Comte Robert de Montesquiou-Fézensac (1855-1921). An extremely wealthy, homosexual dandy, aesthete and *the* arbiter of taste for the more *outré* members of the aristocracy. Montesquiou inspired the three great fictional representations of his type (Proust's *Charlus*, Huysmans' *Des Esseintes*, Lorrain's *de Phocas*), and was their equal in real life. A mannerist poet of exquisite *tours de force*, the poems here are from *Les Hortensias bleus* (1894) a collection which, according to the author "presents in blue this life that others see in rose." *Portent* is dedicated to the glass-maker Gallé, and bears this characteristic epigraph from de Vigny:

Astonished by your pale and mystic glow,
Strong men grow weak and start to utter oaths.

The essay on Lalique (from 1897) is an example of his voluminous aesthetic appreciations.

When his Chauves-souris *in violet velvet first took flight, the question was posed in all seriousness as to whether Monsieur de Montesquiou was a poet or an amateur of poetry, and whether a life in fashionable society could be reconciled with the worship of the Nine Sisters or of one of them, since nine women are a good many women. But to hold forth about such matters is to admit that one is unfamiliar with that operation of logic which goes by the name of the dissociation of ideas, for it seems elementary justice to evaluate the worth or beauty of the tree and its fruit, the man and his works, separately. Thus we will not fret over unravelling the linen thread from this distaff, nor over enquiring into what the name of Monsieur de Montesquiou hid, and what his standing as a man moving in society might add, by way of the illusory, to the fame of the poet.*

The poet, here, is a "Précieuse..."*

And here, at last, is the real bone of contention with de Montesquiou: his originality is excessively tattooed. The beauty of this bard recalls, not without melancholy, the complicated figurations with which bygone Australian chiefs were wont to decorate themselves, but in truth he adorns his own work with a less naïve artifice; there is even a singular refinement in the nuances and in the design and in the amusing boldness of tone and line. He realises arabesques better than figures, and sensation better than thought. If he thinks, it is in ideographic signs, like the Japanese...

With half of his Hortensias bleus, *one could make up a volume, still quite thick, which would be almost entirely filled with fine, or lofty, or sweet poetry. The author of* Ancilla, *of* Mortuis ignotis *and of* Tables vives *would then appear as he really is, beyond all misrepresentation—a good poet...*

THE BOOK OF MASKS 134

ROBERT DE MONTESQUIOU

Succubus

Androgynously writhing on supreme
Brocaded purple, silver limbs entwine
A prostrate form, coagulating wine-
Dark lakes of blood with streams of milky cream.

Unfathomable, formless dazzling dream
That whirls a staring victim! Prophets shine
Auspiciously; yet drooping, sphinx-eyed, seem
To seal enigmas with a wondrous sign.

The priestess that evokes Apollo's gaze?
The Sphinx—that Oedipus, by solving, slays?
Or vampire, when the hour is drawing near

That midnight's chimes will bid spread sunken old
Tombs with these robes of ivory: each tear
Indelible on each stained velvet fold?

Portent

These fabled monarchs, who
Are crowned hydrangeas—blue
In fairest Flora's land—
With filigreed crests stand
Where convex petals grew.
Pale tears Pan sheds as dew
Drench gardens all unplanned.

They reached our coasts at last—
Regalia's pomp cast
Beyond the distant view
Of their unsullied blue

Unfathomable past
Where moonbeams held them fast
In robes her glow-worms grew.

These masters of disguise
Place masks across white eyes
When robbing roses' roles.
No whispered word consoles
The way that they surprise
Us when their spell belies
Their transmigrated souls.

If, fragrance lost, their air
Makes certain men beware,
And birds fail to rejoice,
What's rare means they're first choice.
Though prudent men take care,
We others adore their
Soft low and pearl-grey voice.

**Banality
(Dry-point)**

Bizarre is blameless; *special* spells delight;
All *oddness* thrills; *rare* earns an orison...
A blackbird's song's ecstatic if it's white
And, hearing it, my gloomy mood is gone.

Obscurity is piety in flight;
A blue-flamed iris—gliding regal swan—
Sets fountains gushing tears at its mere sight:
Half-smiles that jealous roses raise are wan.

What's *commonplace* is Revelation's beast:
Its vanquisher becomes my saint of saints
In precious triptychs limned with rarest paints;

Whilst genuflecting, rich robes at my side,
I'll give up flowing worlds for that unique
Blue solitaire Bavarian kings seek.
     —*Translated by Stanley Chapman.*

To the beauteous first Lapidary.
LA FONTAINE

Goldsmith & Glass-maker (Excerpt)

Lalique, a jingling resonance rhyming nicely with relic; predestined name for a goldsmith, for a carver of shrines and reliquaries, of redly glowing ciboria, of radiant monstrances, of jewelled candlesticks whose burning tapers reflect the fiery tongues of their candlemases in enamels and precious stones. Designer of gold-embroidered orfrays in which jewels star the brocades; skilful setter of gems and bejeweller of sacristies, aptly skilled to wire-draw a pyxis on the elongation of one of the nails of Christ or to outline it with an aura like the crown of thorns, imitating in it tears of sanguine jasper and a grief of pearls; able also to discover, as in Florence, the profile of a Caesar in the veins of an agate; of creating, as in Dresden, an entire Lilliput out of gemstones; and of draping, around Josephine's neck, Troy burning in a blaze of opal.

I have often had the impression that I saw that coquette from the *Thousand and One Nights*, who, despite the glass case in which her husband enclosed her, enumerated by as many precious rings the tally of her lovers—stretching out her hands to me in Lalique's show-cases. And, the hussy, how not to pardon her on account of the rings—excuses for her infidelities, those irresistible wedding-rings. Were not those swans swimming among the reeds the gift of some dying poet who offered up his swan-song in her arms? From another poet, this other cygniform inspiration: two of Leda's birds with intertwined necks, "the one black and the other white"; day and night. And those peacock-feathers with opalescent eyes, the proud conquest. For, it must be said, in homage, since it is also prejudicial to Lalique, that he is the master of irisations and the play of colours, the prince of pearls' waters and reflections. Vigilant friends have in vain summoned up risible or respectable superstitions, unaccounted-for ostracisms, tenacious fears, invincible prejudices; it is as if the sly jewel-setter takes pleasure in complicating, in perfecting his labours of *charms* and bewitchments. For the Fates are capricious and quickly changeable. Such a stone, said to be fatal according to the conjunctions of the times or the seasons, of sex or of age, by dint of infinitesimal variants transforms its evil spells into benefits. The milky opal imprisons turbid sentiments that you cannot, without injustice, attribute to the limpid designs of the transparent opal. For certain people, it is the actual peacock-feather that must be mistrusted. Its reproduction is benevolent. Here there is a complete ritual to interpret, full of artful dodges and compromises like the flesh of certain Lenten fowl. And I advise ladies of fashion, badly in need of signs and portents, to obtain from Mme de Thèbes, whose good graces and accommodating knowledge are unfailing, regular dispensations which permit them to reconcile complete security with the fascinating possession of one of Lalique's opaline amulets. For the self-willed will make use of Labradorite, however much it be filled with petrified butterflies' wings, only with regret; and you will not easily persuade him to plunge his hand into his bag of turquoises.

A Japanese lacquer, the most famous of all, the Kô-rinn, has already assimilated the whole rainbow of mother-of-pearl to bring into play its mauve, greenish or rosy rays in an infinity of marbled shimmerings. The cape of peacock-feather stares had also tempted him, and that strange death-agony of hydrangea-globes which curiously blends in their fading corymbs all of the nuances of the steely blue, the pinkish and the nascent green of their yellow shares.

But he, Lalique, the most audacious Prometheus, has truly stolen the flame. To lull it to sleep or awaken it in flashing pendants or in wanly gleaming ones, that is the art of this showman of fairy-tales full of fiery adventures. It is a whole garden of the Hesperides, fervent and glowing, that burns in the plates of this necklace, between these slender dashes of black enamel and these diamond leaves in whose shadows and white fires the red flaming fruits stand out more ardently. But the opal does not limit itself to embers; and there are still the clouded surfaces of stagnant waters in which the irises mirror themselves, in which boundless and minute landscapes are suspended from chains. Soap bubbles take flight from a flute-player's pipe, and they too are opals. For humanity has its role in these chosen necklaces, in these impassioned brooches. I have before me the most subtle of *aquarelles*; a design for a pin to bind heavy hair, and it reminds me of these lines:

> *It pleases me that worry*
> *Should gnaw at ivory,*
> *My hair, brown mantle.*

Massy pin, airy comb with long ivorine teeth surmounted by a creation of Blake, of Grandeville or of Wagner; of a butterfly-woman whose arms are the enamel wings of a *paon-de-jour*, half-opened along the length of a delectable body of Venus, whose hair, hewn in gold, streams with insects' wings and rolls with pearls.

This too is one of Lalique's obsessions, one of the chosen elements of his decor; that of hair. He coils it around faces in sinuous waves, fabulous also since he deranges its nuances to the point of giving them a greenish tinge, in just the way the Grand Albert prescribes, or makes it resemble that of the Queen of Sheba, of whom Flaubert wrote that it was "sprinkled with blue powder."

I might never be done with detailing and describing. A floral necklace of water-irises, themselves bent over threads of pearls whose drops are likewise those of that wave. Chrysanthemums in brown enamel, with a diamond at the centre, with leaves of gold filigree set out in the form of a narrow and pointed triangle like a Louis XV bodice-front. A pin made like a branch of fuchsia with drooping Chinese bell-flowers. Unused flowers, variegated insects, lilacs depicted from the front, from behind, and in profile, like that violet of Leonardo Da Vinci whose series of aspects multiplies itself in a masterly sketch in Venice. Projects for a series of tiaras for Sarah Bernhardt, who first gathered together in the ingenious goldsmith's flowerbeds the lunar Nile lilies of Cleopatra, the dewy lilies of The Princesse Lointaine. Designs that are themselves gems, truly giving flames to their diamonds, marking out the diaphanous paper with a complete scintillation.

But not only ornaments are hatched from the studios of this Parisian Cellini; many marvellous objects: goblets, comfit-dishes, handles for canes and umbrellas, pommels for sword-hilts. And, before leaving, to return to those show-cases of a genial artisan, it still seems to me that I see the hands of the oriental coquette gleaming there, fingers encircled by flowerets that are the nimbus of Queen Mab; and of the Queen of Sheba too, for it is indeed she whom I hear murmuring to me: "We shall look at the sun through opals!"

—*Translated by Andrew Mangravite & Iain White.*

139   EPHRAÏM MIKHAËL

Ephraïm Mikhaël (1866-1890). A poet and playwright, Mikhaël (real name Michel) worked at the Bibliothèque Nationale and died aged 25, his prose poems and other writings were collected and published by his friends after his death in 1890, which is where these two texts appeared. *Miracles* is also one of the poems translated by Merrill in his *Pastels in Prose*.

Since he left us only a very few too brief pages, the work of only a few years, since he died at an age where most of a noble genius still slumbered, an unknown perfume, in the closed calyx of a flower, Mikhaël is not to be judged, only loved. He was charming, though very proud, amiable, though sad and withdrawn; gentle, though he had to suffer in this life, either from the tiresome and the envious, or because he knew a fame as precocious as his talent...

In Miracles, *unbelief in the divine is analysed with a beautiful sureness of touch and with intelligence; almost everywhere, one senses a spirit, master of itself which insists upon endowing with form ideas that merit the form. He is above all attracted by stories that are meaningful and revelatory of a hermetic state of being: he loves magic and prodigies, creatures oppressed by mystery and sick from reason. He was an assiduous reader of Spinoza, who had taught him, in the apt words of Pierre Quillard, with a superior mysticism, "the vanity of joy and sorrow," and he came to appreciate equally the life and the nirvana-philosophy of the philosopher of his race. The masterpiece among his prose works is* Armentaria, *a poem of great purity, clearly aureoled by love, mystic and candid flower,* flos admirabilis! *There are lines in it like this one; Armentaria says: "Let us be pure in the darkness and go silently to heaven."*

It is enough to have written this small amount of verse and prose; posterity would ask no more if there were still room for those the Gods favour in the museum we vainly enrich for it, and which future barbarians will perhaps never have the curiosity to enter.

EPHRAÏM MIKHAËL

Miracles   It is in a rich and ancient city, on the shores of a cerulean ocean, in a strange city where, among obelisks and pylons, machines of war press and thunder. From a high terrace of marble, the poet Azahel contemplates the swarming of ambitious sails in the harbour. In the peaceful twilight, under the sky vibrant with the flight of swallows, he meditates upon the uselessness of the hours.

For he knows that in that city, where live wise men and sages and doctors of the law, he alone has recognised the infirmity of Reason, and he thinks of those who bear through the ages their ridiculous common-sense like a precious and heavy reliquary; and because he has disclaimed it, he glorifies himself in his heart.

And lo! among the crowd by the harbour, appears a stranger clad in a woollen mantle of noble folds and of ancient pattern. His eyes, like antique gems, seem to preserve the memory of primordial visions, and under his feet the stones quake as with dread.

When the poet Azahel had descended among the crowd, the stranger lifted his arms to heaven; and now he cries out, in tones that resound like the trumpets of the temples: "Men, I am a prophet of God. I have come to proclaim the Word, and those that will follow me I will lead, walking on the waves of the sea, towards the veritable Land of Promise." Then from the crowd arises a murmur of disappointment. Young men glance from the prophet to the sky where the vesper mist is thickening, and they pass on with negligent steps. The wise men watch in silence; and the merchants, having cast a last look at their good ships anchored in the peaceful harbour, shrug their shoulders and depart. A doctor of the law, however, has said with a smile: "Master, if thou art the envoy of God, show us some sign. Verily, couldst thou not, after the rite of the prophets, heal the dumb and blind!"

Near the harbour were two men—the one blind, the other dumb. The prophet laid his hands upon their foreheads, and the blind man opened his eyes, and the dumb man spoke in a loud voice. The prophet asked: "Is the sign sufficient, and do you wish to follow me?" But the crowd remains motionless, the blind man shakes his head, and the dumb man cries out with his newly-found voice: "I do not believe thee!"

The stranger therefore extends his confident hand towards the horizon which is now full of night, and repeats the sacred words of Genesis: "Let there be light!" and lo! in the Orient bursts a summer dawn.

Disconcerted, the doctors of the law consult with the wise men. But no one advances towards the sea.

Then, with the sadness of a vanquished angel, the great stranger goes and sits dreamily on the steps of an ancient temple, before the doors that have been closed for thousands of years. The crowd scatters little by little, the wise men and the doctors abandon the harbour, and as they return home they feel less troubled, because the natural night has returned. Azahel alone has remained near the closed temple, and he gazes upon the man come from yonder. If he were truly the Envoy! Oh, to recognise him, to bow before him, to follow him towards the chosen land! —But the spirit of Azahel is obscured by earthly ideas, and he can only think that the man is very fair because of his high stature and of his godly looks.

Suddenly the elder arises and walks towards the poet: "Azahel, thou hast loved a virgin who is dead. I will give her back to thee." Immediately, wrapped in funereal robes and coming forth blushing from death as from the coolness of a morning sea, a young woman appears. Smiling and forgetful of the divine secrets of the tomb, she opens her arms to her lover.

But he flies in terror through the silent streets; among the pylons and the obelisks and the images of the forgotten gods he flies, blinded by the miracle like a night bird frightened by torches. And it is only when he finds himself once more on the peaceful terrace of marble that he dares direct his gaze towards the harbour haunted by prodigies.

At that moment a mysterious light shines towards the Orient. Upon the pacified ocean the great biblical elder passes calmly, and the reflection of stars in the water borders his ways with a double row of diamonds. Now Azahel would fain arise and walk forth also on the miraculous waves. But he feels himself so heavy with reason that he cannot even lift his shameful hands towards the Envoy who returns. (Trans. Stuart Merrill)

Armentaria

That evening the spirit of the Lord visited the house and Armentaria died.

She had languished since the summer, but the sickness advanced so rapidly this day that the young woman didn't even have time to reach her own suite of rooms. She passed away in the oratory while she was at her prayers. A servant who was waiting for her at the door (because she was a captive from Thuringia and still a pagan) heard her corpse fall to the flagstones. Having entered, she saw Armentaria lying on her back, her arms spread wide. And by the will of God, the heavy crucifix of carved wood before which the dying woman prayed had fallen piously upon her dead breast.

Then there was great confusion throughout the entire house. The servants departed, in all haste, to find Armentaria's young husband, Florentius, for he proved to be absent that evening, having gone to comfort a poor man who was dying. The servants made their way to the poor man's hut and they said: "Master! Master! Your wife is dead." And Florentius cried out aloud and ran to his house.

The young girls of the neighbourhood had already gathered. They had carried Armentaria to her marriage bed. Some searched through the chests for white garments to adorn she who could no longer adorn herself. The others went down into the gardens which in the land of Neustria are barren and sad during this season. But a few precious flowers managed to survive there, because the virgins who were to be married in the spring watched over them anxiously until their wedding day. And they tended them lovingly each day. But now, without any regret, all those fiancées went to gather the finest flowers for the funeral bed; for they loved the young woman who had died.

While they were thus honouring Armentaria, Florentius arrived: "Leave, I beseech you," he said, "so that I may be alone with her." But Martial, the bishop, and Cresentius, the deacon, came forward. "The young girls will leave, but we, men of God, we shall remain here to console you." But Florentius rebuffed both the deacon and the bishop as well.

When everyone had gone from the house, Florentius, seating himself by the bed, began to weep unreservedly. He did not give way to violent sorrow, but allowed his tears to flow, slowly and almost peacefully. Then, in the silence, his sorrow elated him. And as though his wife were listening, he spoke to her: "Beloved virgin," he murmured amid his sobs, "beloved virgin!" And he kissed the cold pure hands that lay like sleeping doves surrounded by flowers: "Alas! Alas! Why did you withhold yourself from me in days gone by? Why did you not become my wife? Everyone believed us to be carnal lovers, aglow with sensual pleasure. And we, we lay side by side, our lips never joined in a kiss. Sometimes still… I remember… sometimes, your hand trembled in mine, didn't it? But with a sign of the cross you purified the hand that had trembled and we two slept side by side beneath the gaze of the Lord. I have suffered, Armentaria, I have suffered from a lengthy passion through your sweet volition, and no one has known our divine secret. Behold how even now they shroud you like a wife, you who will be greeted among the blessed virgins…"

Florentius slowly paced the funeral chamber. The odour of the flowers was heavy; the tapers also charged the air with perfumes. Florentius opened a window overlooking the fields. Then he thought about the men who were out there in their silent homes. Perhaps even at that moment they were embracing their wives, lovers sleeping together voluptuously. He saw those happy couples, dispersed as in a misty dream, and a mysterious pride rose within his heart. Alone among all those men he had been able to renounce those licit joys. He rejoiced, he felt the intoxication of saintliness welling up inside him. "I wish that they might know, he murmured to himself, I want to tell them of our secret."

But the dead woman raised herself upright from among those decaying flowers. A momentary flush had spread across her pale face, because it was an ineffable modesty that had awakened her. "Do not reveal that," she begged, beckoning towards her husband with asupernatural hand. "Do not diminish our glory. I want you to be like me, my beloved. Do not reveal that. Your silence will earn you great experience of love in heaven. My dear Florentius, divulge nothing. Virtue is complete only when it remains a secret. And it is little enough to keep secret, it is better still to deny it. If I had wanted to be revered on earth as a virgin, could not I have lived in seclusion near Randegonde? Long ago the bishop of Vienna, Avitus, wished to lead me off to that good queen. My dear friend, do you know why I refused? It seemed to me that virgins publicly consecrated to the Lord must take secret pride in their merit. Men know of their virtue and praise it. As for me, I would suffer it as a divine shame to be chaste in the eyes of all. What offends my virginal modesty is to have someone know of my virginity. It is for that reason, Florentius, that I have desired these sham nuptials. I wanted to be mistaken for a wife in order to be an unknown virgin. And now, my Florentius, I adjure you not to reveal our secret to those who will return. So that our souls may be blessed, renounce all glories and above all, that of being sanctified while on earth. Be pure in the darkness and go to heaven in silence."

Having wept for a long time, Florentius thought of those who had fallen asleep again, and prayed to the Lord. And peace returned to his heart. Dawn, a mild, sad dawn was breaking; the morning breeze extinguished the tapers. The bishop, the deacon and the women came and put Armentaria into a shroud.

Then the bishop, Martial, said: "Florentius, the servants of the church have come to remove the body of Armentaria. But you know, Christian, that death is but a brief and powerless separation. You know that you will see your wife again. Thus I do not address long and desperate farewells to you. Embrace her as though she were leaving on a brief journey, embrace as you did each morning on parting company." Florentius approached the bed docilely. He bowed before the bishop; everyone heard him respond: "I shall embrace my wife as I embraced her each morning." And trembling all over from his radiant lie, he approached her lips for the first time with his lips that had never touched hers.

145 Stuart Merrill

Stuart Merrill (1863-1915). Stuart Merrill was born in the United States, in the state of New York, spent his childhood in France, where his father was a diplomat, and returned to the USA to attend university at New York City's Columbia College (now University). Merrill had close ties to the New York branch of the Symbolist/Decadent movement in the United States—with Vance Thompson, Edgar and Frank Saltus he was a member of the circle of poets dominated by Edgar Fawcett. His work as a cultural ambassador culminated in his collection *Pastels in Prose* (1892). This anthology was the first really to bring the literature of the French Symbolists before the general American public in English language translation; the volume included prose poems by Mallarmé, Huysmans, Régnier, Quillard, Mikhaël and Villiers. He spent his adult life in France.

A lover of literature's sense of rightness of things is offended if he discovers that his admirations are not in accord with those of the public; but he is not surprised, he knows that they are the chosen of the hour. The public's attitude is less benign when it learns of the disagreement that exists between it, the public, obscure master of plaudits, and the opinion of a small oligarchic group: used to having two ideas linked, fame and talent, it exhibits a reluctance to separate them; the public does not accept, because it has a secret sense of justice or of logic, that an author can be illustrious by chance alone, or that an obscure author merits the light of day...

His verses, somewhat gilded, somewhat clamorous, truly glitter and ring for festive days and stately processions, and when the play of the sunlight fades, torches illumine the night to give light to the sumptuous cortege of supernatural women. Women or verses, they are doubtlessly embellished by too many rings and too many rubicelles, and their robes are embroidered with too much gold thread; they are royal courtesans rather than princesses, but we love their cruel eyes and auburn hair...

And so, one discovers in Stuart Merrill, the contrast and conflict between a fiery temperament and a too gentle heart, and in accordance with whichever nature flares up, one hears the violence of brass or the murmur of viols...

STUART MERRILL

Ecstasy I—sang He who bore the Lyre and the Sword to the generations drained by their many ancestors drenched in sin—am the Mage, holder of the ultimate secrets, who has gathered stars from the Tree of Universal Life.

And a thousand snakes with coruscating golden scales sprang forth from the sacred plants whose juice causes madness, and hurled themselves upon my armour and my shield blazoned with the sign of victory over their quivering crimson tongues.

I caused the vindictive anger of my sword to flash in the astral light and I drew out the divine Ode of the Rulers upon the seven chords; and the agony of the ruby-eyed reptiles hissed through the dolorous plain.

And I seized hold of the mane of the immemorial lying Sinner, the rosy flower of her sex opened tempting me beneath the starry darkness of the Tree where, wingless and mute, all the birds of Time kept vigil.

Subdued by my strength of knightly purity, she uttered to the heavens with a voice never heard till that moment, the dread word that revealed to me, like the storm's thunder, the mystery of the worlds of which our ancestors the giants spoke.

Since that hour of hours my archangel's soul has flown upon a hippogriff's musical wing, sinuous and fond, toward an Unknown that lies beyond our Unknown, like the Silence that is beyond Darkness!

And my pale hands tensed—stiffened by gems stolen of old from the Dragon's treasure—around the dazzling mysteries, hidden forever from the keen gaze of my brothers by the gods, fearing ineluctable folly.

Flying, galloping on high, O monsters of revelation, until
my lips grew bloody from biting the purple clusters which will be harvested upon the days of vengeance, Christ and Satan,

So that, pounding with my clamorous arms upon the adamantine gate of the seventh sphere where, with blades of white flame in their hands, the seraphim and the cherubim tower, winged by moon and helmeted by sun,

I am abler having accomplished my seven-fold destiny, to enjoy at last, in the paradise of asphodels and amaranths where day is night and night day, the perfect Life and the perfect Death, for an eternity of eternities!

Thus sang He who bore the Lyre and the Sword.

Apocalypse In the semi-darkness beneath the pale planet where the last light quivers, brooding over the secret of the earthly centuries, there's a vain tinkling of harps amid the garlands of the universal orgy of mankind.

Above the towers of the basalt palaces where the violet flames from tripods swirl toward forgotten heaven, the drunken kings, their throats flayed by laughter, rend with their nails the rough silk standards that their ancestors, on mornings of hope, had decorated with chimeras in flight.

And the queens whose fingers and arms are heavy with the most precious stones study parchments illuminated with sinople: tales concerning love, warfare, and death, of which they are scarcely able to make sense, their heads reeling beneath the weight of their ancient crowns.

All of a sudden, in the desert whose sands unfold to the gates of these damned capitals, the barbarian horde of the night, awakening the sound of the dulcimers, gallop through the field of shadows around the ramparts, where the steel sentinels sleep in the glow of torches pricked upon their lances.

A wind arises out of the wastes, and in the wind of this solitude the drunken kings and their foolish queens in their terror allow the rags of standards and parchment leaves to fall from the tops of the towers. They recall the shouts of the ancient prophets before the apocalypse.

Already the river from the East carries along in its currents—purpled of old with the blood of many multitudes chanting vengeance and victory—the bodies of vigorous men whose eyes, having read the secret of their destinies beyond, have forever filled themselves with fear.

They have had strange dreams in the blue mountains of silence where the Magi meditate, and wished, by way of a human pity contrary to that of God or of gods, to proclaim to the peoples grown pale through ancient sin the new good that the Book contains.

But the archangels, guardians of the secret, have struck at their heads with the flashing flame of their swords, because they attempted to break, before the appointed time, the triple seal upon the threshold of the Temple of the Light which is not to be broken except by the sceptre of the fatal Redeemer.

And here the drunken kings and the foolish queens at the sight of those corpses which pass by palely on the tide, and hearing the thunder of the barbarian cavalcade, begin to weep in the irremediable night; and their fingers suddenly raised seem to wish to pull from the sky its last remaining stars.

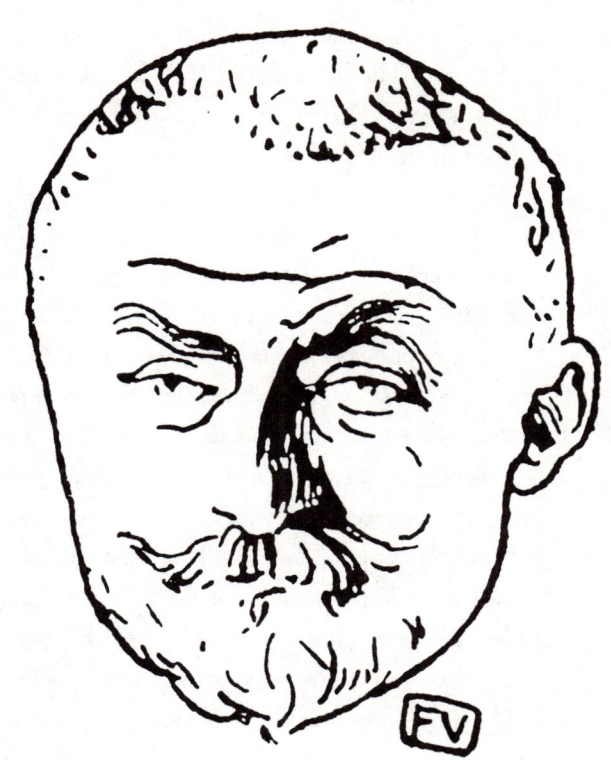

Joris-Karl Huysmans (1848-1907). The most important prose writer associated with Symbolism, Huysmans wrote the "bible" of Decadence, *A Rebours* (*Against Nature*) so beloved by Oscar Wilde, then *En Rade* (*Becalmed*—which is published in English by Atlas) and *Là-Bas* (*Down There*), in which his autobiographical hero explores Satanism. His later work reflects his conversion to Catholicism and, with exceptions, is less compelling.

Contemporary readers cannot fail to notice that the whole of Huysmans' *oeuvre* is pervaded with a misogyny that manifests itself as a profound disgust towards the body and even the entire biological universe. This theme underlies his earliest realist novels and prose poems (one included here, from *A Dish of Spices*, 1874), and equally his later works of Catholic piety. These concern either withdrawal and abnegation, or concentrate on other more dubious religious enthusiasms in which Huysmans' neurosis is able to express itself so eloquently: his famous essay on Grunewald's painting of the crucifixion, or the less well-known, but equally horrific, hagiography of St Lydwine (1901), an extract of which follows.

That same year, 1901, Huysmans became a monk, a few years later he suffered a terminal illness almost as horrific as that of St. Lydwine, which he bore with great fortitude.

Romance and Chambertin, Clos-Vougeot and Corton would parade before him abbatial ceremonies, princely banquets, the opulences of vestments brocaded in gold, blazing with light. The Clos-Vougeot above all used to bedazzle him. That wine seemed to him the syrup of great dignitaries. The label would glow before his eyes like those glorioles, radiating rays of light, that are placed in churches behind the occiputs of images of the Virgin.

The writer who, in 1881, in the midst of the slough of Naturalism, faced with a name read on a wine-list, experienced such a vision, must have worried his friends, making them suspect an imminent defection. A few years later, in fact, there emerged the unexpected A Rebours *which was, not the point of departure, but the consecration of a new literature....*

It is sometimes necessary, in order to entice the public toward very difficult subject matters, to simulate vague romantic plots, which one unravels according to one's own inclination, when one has said all that one wished to say. But the main point of days gone by has become an incidental, and an incidental more and more despised: writers ingenious enough or strong enough to succeed in a genre so much debased, capable still of spurring on with authority the jaded steeds of sentimentalities and adulteries, are very rare nowadays.

Besides, the aesthetic tends to specialise in as many forms as there are talents: amid a plethora of vanities, there are admissible vanities to whom one cannot refuse the right to create their personal norms. Huysmans is one of these: he no longer creates novels, he makes books, and he conceives them according to an original arrangement; I believe that this is one of the causes for which some still contest his work and find it to be immoral. This last point is easy to explain in a single word: for the non-artist, art is always immoral...

Now, tired out with having looked upon the hypocritical faces of men, he is looking upon stones, working on a supreme book on The Cathedral. *In this, if it is a question of feeling and understanding, it is a matter above all of looking. He will see as nobody has seen, because nobody has ever been granted a gaze so sharp, so penetrating, so perspicacious, so adroit at insinuating into the inmost recesses of faces, of rose-windows, and of masks. Huysmans is an eye.*

JORIS-KARL HUYSMANS

Saint Lydwine of Schiedam

Until her fifteenth birthday, Lydwine seems to have been a fairly healthy girl; her biographers merely inform us that while still young she suffered from the formation of stones and that she expelled a good number of calculi; but neither Gerlac, nor Brugman, nor à Kempis speak of her childhood afflictions; and it was only towards the end of her fifteenth year that the furious love of the heavenly Spouse descended upon her.

It was at that time she fell ill, and though the sickness never threatened her life, it left her in a weak condition that none of the potions or medicines vaunted by the doctors and apothecaries of the time could succeed in overcoming. Having grown remarkably feeble, she languished; her cheeks became hollow and the flesh melted away; she became emaciated to the point that she was nothing more than skin and bones; the attractive disposition of her features disappeared beneath swellings and hollows, and her complexion, once white and rosy, took on a greenish hue, before finally turning ashen. Her suitors were overjoyed at being rejected and she was no longer afraid to be seen in public.

However, as she was unable to recover her strength, she was confined to her room, where, a few days before the Feast of the Purification, her friends came to visit her. It was freezing hard at the time, and the river Schie, which runs through the town, together with the canals, was frozen over; everyone in Holland skates during such icy spells. Lydwine's young friends invited her to skate with them; but, preferring to be alone, she used the poor state of her health as a pretext for staying home. They insisted so much though, reproaching her for not taking enough exercise and assuring her that the fresh air would do her good, that, not wishing to oppose them further, and with the permission of her father, she eventually agreed to accompany them to the frozen canal behind the house where she lived; she had just stood up, after putting on her skates, when one of her friends, racing flat-out, collided with her before she was able to move herself out of the way, and threw her against a block of ice, one of whose edges broke an asternal rib on her right-hand side.

She was taken home in tears, and laid out on the bed which she would scarcely ever leave again.

The news of this accident soon spread around the town and everyone thought it his duty to express his opinions. Lydwine had to endure, like Job, the interminable chatter of those whom the misfortunes of others render loquacious; but those who were wiser, instead of rebuking her for having gone out, felt sorry for her, presuming that God must have had some special reason for having treated her so.

Her family, who were terribly upset, were determined to stop at nothing to make her better; although they were poor, they called in the most famous doctors in the Low Countries. They dosed her with an endless quantity of medicines and the illness only grew worse; as a result of this treatment, a hard, purulent tumour formed in the fracture.

She suffered martyrdom; and her parents were at a loss to know which saints to invoke next, when a renowned physician from Delft, a very charitable and pious man, Godfried de Haga (commonly called "Sonder-Danck", which in Dutch means, "My pleasure", because that is invariably how he replied to all those who were sick and whom he treated free of charge), called to see her. His views on therapeutics were the same as those expressed by Bombast Paracelsus, who was born a few years after the death of Lydwine, in his *Opus Paramirum*. Amidst all the more or less incoherent drivel inspired by his occultism, this astonishing man had seized upon the law of divine equilibrium when writing on the subject of the essence of God: "It is essential to realise that every illness is an atonement brought about by God and that until He decides that the atonement has been fulfilled, there is nothing that any doctor can do... A doctor may only be said to effect a cure when his intercession coincides with the end of the atonement decided upon by Our Saviour."

With these thoughts in mind, Godfried de Haga examined the patient and spoke with his assembled colleagues who were curious to know his verdict: "This sickness, my dear friends, is not within our powers; all the Hippocrateses and Avicennas in the world would lose their reputations here." And he added, in a prophetic tone: "The hand of God is on this child. He will work great marvels in her; I would to God that she were my daughter; if she were for sale, I would willingly give a weight of gold equal to my head for such a favour."

And so he departed, without prescribing a remedy; all the quacks lost interest in her then, and she obtained at least a short respite from having to swallow all those useless and expensive potions. But the illness was advancing and the pain became unbearable; she was unable to remain still whether lying down, sitting up, or standing. At a loss as to what to do, and incapable of staying in the same position even for a moment, she asked to be transferred from one bed to another, hoping this might relieve the acuteness of her sufferings; but all these movements only served to irritate the illness.

On the eve of the day celebrating the nativity of St John the Baptist her torments attained new paroxysms; she lay sobbing on the bed in an atrocious state of nervous exhaustion; at last, she could bear it no longer; the pain, throbbing and tearing at her, threw her from the bed so that she fell doubled up across the knees of her father who was seated weeping at her side. The shock made the abscess burst; but instead of opening towards the outside, it exploded internally, and the pus poured from her mouth. These vomitings shook her from head to foot and were so abundant that there was hardly time to empty the bowls into an enormous round pot before they were overflowing again. Finally, she fainted after a last effort, and her parents feared her dead.

She regained consciousness, however, and from that time the most accursed life imaginable began for her; incapable of supporting herself on her legs, and continually racked by this urge to change positions, she crawled around on her knees, dragged herself along on her stomach, or hooked herself around stools and the edges of furniture; burning with fever, she was possessed by unhealthy appetites, and drank polluted or lukewarm water which, contorted by terrible spasms, she ejected. Three years passed in this way; while, to complete her martyrdom, she was abandoned by those who had until then still occasionally come to visit her. The sight of her agony, her screams and groanings, the horrible mask of her face swollen with tears, all drove her visitors away. Only her family continued to give her support; her father's kindness never wavered, her mother, less resigned to her lot as sick-nurse, became irritable with her and, weary of her continual moaning, was often harsh with her.

The grief that she suffered, in addition to all her other misfortunes, at being obliged to submit to such tirades and reproaches would surely have killed her had not God, who seems to have still been in a state of some doubt about her until then, suddenly intervened on her behalf, and demonstrated, by means of an unexpected miracle, that He would not desert her and at the same time taught a lesson in mercy to her mother.

This is what happened.

One day two men were quarrelling in the square; after hurling insults at each other, they began to exchange blows until one of them, drawing his sword, fell upon the other who, lacking either in weapons or in courage, took to his heels; at the corner of the street he spotted the open door of Lydwine's home, and nipped in. Though his adversary had not actually seen him go in, he nonetheless suspected that he was hiding there.

"Where did he go? I'm going to kill him! Don't lie to me! He's hidden here somewhere!" he shouted, foaming with rage, at Lydwine's mother, who was standing, rooted to the hall-way, staring at him with terror.

She assured him that it was not so; but he did not believe her; and brusquely pushing her aside with his hand while uttering the most fearful threats, he forced his way in, entering even Lydwine's bedroom and ordering the sick girl not to conceal the truth from him.

Lydwine, incapable of telling a lie, replied: "He whom you are pursuing is indeed here."

At these words, Lydwine's mother, who had slipped in behind the man, could no longer contain herself, and started to hit her daughter, saying, "You little imbecile, how can you betray like that a man who is your guest and who might get himself killed!"

The furious man, however, neither heard nor saw anything that happened. Swearing aloud, he searched for his enemy who had become invisible to him, but who was standing right there in front of him in the middle of the room. Not finding him, he rushed out to try to recover his traces again, while his antagonist made off in the opposite direction as fast as his legs would carry him.

When they were both gone, Lydwine, who had received her mother's ill-treatment without demur, whispered: "I thought, mother, that simply telling the truth would be enough to save the man"; and her mother, admiring her daughter's faith and the miracle with which it had been rewarded, was filled with more generous sentiments, and from then on bore the troubles and burdens which her daughter's infirmities caused her with less resentment and bitterness.

It must be admitted that the continual attention required of her and her incessant harassment gave the good woman valid cause for ill-humour; all the more so because however excessive the infirmities of her daughter seemed already, they were almost as nothing to those which would ensue.

Soon Lydwine could no longer even drag herself about on her knees and clutch at the corners of baskets and chairs: she had to crouch on her back in bed, this time for ever; the wound under her rib which had never healed became inflamed and infected with gangrene; worms bred in the putrefaction, moving around under the skin of her stomach and forming three enormous ulcers as large and round as the bottom of a bowl; the manner in which they multiplied was alarming; they wriggled so much that to Brugman they appeared to boil; thick as the end of a spindle, their bodies were grey and watery with black heads.

The doctors were summoned again and prescribed that poultices made from freshly milled flour, honey, and the fat of capons, to which some counselled the addition of cream or a stock made from eels, all sprinkled with dried beef and reduced to a powder in an oven, should be applied to these nests of vermin.

These remedies, which demanded no little care in their preparation – for it was emphasised that if the flour was allowed to cool even a little the worms would not feed on it – brought her a little relief, and it was possible to pick out of her wounds between a hundred and two hundred of these vermin every twenty-four hours.

But, in fact, these medicines were only palliatives and had hardly any healing effect. A doctor from Cologne who had heard of her, perhaps from Godfried de Haga, who seems to have been a friend, appears initially to have been more successful, though when everything is taken into account he too probably only succeeded in making matters worse. He applied to her most purulent quarters a compress soaked in a mixture which he prepared by distilling certain plants picked only in dry weather when covered in dew from the woods. This preparation, blended with a decoction of centaury or millflower, gradually dried up the ulcers. This doctor was surely a good man because, so as to be sure that Lydwine would not be deprived of her remedy if he died before her, he charged his son-in-law, an apothecary by the name of Nicolas Reiner, to send her after his death all the flasks of the mixture that she needed to close the wounds.

But the moment came when none of these palliatives could be of any assistance, for the whole body of the miserable girl became raw; besides the bright red ulcers in which whole colonies of parasites were being nourished without being eradicated, a tumour, which turned septic, appeared on her right shoulder; this was the dreaded disease of the Middle Ages, ergotic poisoning or the sacred fire, which attacks the arm and consumes the flesh right to the bone; the muscles twisted and snapped, all except for one which retained the arm and prevented it from becoming detached from the trunk; Lydwine could not even turn on her right side now, and all she was able to do was raise her head, to which the infection had also spread, using her left arm. Terrible neuralgic pains assailed her, boring into her temples like a gimlet and beating ever more violently on her skull like a mallet; her forehead split in two from the roots of her hair to the centre of her nose; her chin became dislocated under her lower lip, and her mouth swelled; she lost the use of her right eye, but the other became so sensitive that the least glimmer of light would make it bleed; she also suffered from raging toothaches, sometimes lasting weeks on end, which drove her half crazy; and, finally, after an attack of quinsy which almost suffocated her, she began to lose blood through her mouth, her ears, and her nose with such profusion that the whole bed was soaked.

Those who witnessed this terrible spectacle wondered how so much blood could come out of a body which was so utterly exhausted, and poor Lydwine tried to smile.

"Since you all know so much more than I, tell me rather from where does the sap come which in spring swells the vine, so black and bare in winter?"

It would seem by now that she must have endured every possible ill. If one turns to the descriptions of her biographers, which I have had to tone down, one would think oneself in a hospital watching a procession of patients pass by one by one, all suffering from the most terrible diseases, the very extremities of agony, and the rarest nervous disorders.

Soon, in addition to her other infirmities, her chest, which until then had remained immune, joined in the attack; a livid mucus ran from her nose, then copper-coloured warts and carbuncles formed; the urinary disease, from which she had suffered in her youth but which had disappeared, returned and she passed calculi the size of small eggs; next it was her lungs and liver which became infected; her skin became cankerous and gnawed at her; and, finally, when the plague ravaged Holland, she was the first victim; two enormous boils began to grow, one under her arm, the other over the heart. "Two boils, that is fine," she said to the Lord, "but it seems to me that in honour of the Holy Trinity three would be better." A third boil immediately broke out on her cheek.

She would have been dead twenty times over if these afflictions had been natural; one alone would have been enough to kill her; nor was there anything more to try or to do to cure her.

The rumour of all these disasters which had so strangely fallen the lot of one person who, though mortally ill in every part of her body, still continued to live, spread far and wide. And if it brought her orthodox doctors who perhaps aggravated her troubles with doubtful panaceas, it was also the occasion of another visit from the good Godfried de Haga who had cared for her after her fall.

Godfried, whose initial prognosis had been as to the divine origin of all these ills, could only reiterate that his art was powerless to cure them; in the hope of bringing a degree of relief to the patient, he nonetheless removed the intestines from her stomach and deposited them in a basin; he cleaned and examined them, and replaced those which were fit for use. His diagnosis was that she was afflicted by a putrefaction of the marrow, which he attributed to the fact that she did not take salt with her meals; and he added, as he took his leave, that a new disease, dropsy, would shortly declare itself, which is exactly what happened; the dropsy appeared as soon as the ulcers, which had been dressed in the solutions and poultices of the doctor from Cologne, had healed. When they ceased to suppurate, the miserable patient began to swell, and regretted the exchange of one evil for a worse.

She endured this incredible assault of physical calamities for thirty-eight years; during all this time, she had not a moment's respite nor a single easy hour.

It is as well to remark here that her sufferings included two of the three scourges which came from the East and ravaged Europe during the Middle Ages: the consuming fire, a type of gangrenous ergotic poisoning which burns like a hidden fire in the flesh of the limbs, and until the bones split, and from which death provides the only respite; and the Black Death which, according to the observations of one doctor of the time, "declares itself by a continuous fever, external boils and carbuncles, frequently under the armpits, and results in death within five days."

There remains the third scourge however, that other source of despair throughout those centuries — leprosy.

This was all that was missing from the wretched girl's list of afflictions. God, who, in His Scriptures and in the lives of His Saints, appears to show a special concern for the "meseled" or leprous, healing them or employing their repulsive image to test the charity of His Saints, did not wish to put his pitiful servant to this last trial; but the reason for making this exception, astonishing as it may seem at first, is easily to be understood. Leprosy would have thwarted the Saviour's designs and rendered the development of Lydwine's holiness impossible.

It should be remembered that during the Middle Ages lepers were considered as incurable, and despite all their pharmacopoeia of hellebore, sulphur baths, the flesh of vipers, all used since antiquity, and arsenic, which had been tried by Paracelsus, the doctors had failed to cure a single one, so that, from fear of contagion, they were shut up in special hospices or isolated in wooden huts, which they were forbidden on the threat of the severest punishment ever to leave. They even had to wear distinctive clothes, a sort of grey frock or prison uniform, and to shake in their hand, which was always gloved, a tartavelle or rattle, to warn people from approaching. The leper was a pariah, having no legal existence, separated for ever from the world, and buried after his decease in a place apart.

The liturgy was terrible towards him; prior to his sequestration, the Church celebrated a Mass of the Holy Spirit containing the *pro infirmis* prayer in his presence, then he was conducted by a procession to the hut or lazar-house, if such should exist in the area, for which he was intended; the frightful prohibitions which would cut him off from all contact with the living were read to him, and three clods of earth taken from the cemetery were cast on to the roof, a cross was planted before the door, and that was the end of the leper.

In certain parts of France, the ritual used was even more sinister. The wretch afflicted with the disease of "Monsieur sainct Landre" only entered the church on the day fixed for his internment laid out on a stretcher and covered with a black sheet, as if he were already dead. The clergy chanted the *libera* and conducted the office for the dead. The leper did not stand up again until he arrived before the hut or lazar-house which was destined to shelter him and, there, with head bowed, he listened to the pronouncement of the sentence which enjoined him not to set a foot outside, to touch no one, and which even prescribed him to pass down wind of healthy persons, should he by chance come across such persons.

The rules concerning leprosy must have been broadly similar everywhere. A series of ordinances of this kind are preserved in the *Coutumier*, or Book of Customs, of the county of Hainaut, which, in the Middle Ages, was one of the provinces forming what is now the Low Countries. It is therefore certain that if Lydwine had been stricken by the disease, she would have been taken from home and, to all intents and purposes, buried alive; she would not have received the care of her mother and father and, after their deaths, of her nephew and niece, who would have been kept away from her for fear of the disease spreading; from that time on, she would have remained unknown, since no one would have been able to visit her, and the example that God wished her to set would have been forever obscured.

It must be noted, too, that this question of the care which was given to her appears to have received special consideration from Our Saviour. He overwhelmed her with torments; He disfigured her, substituting for the charm of her clear countenance the horror of a face swollen out of all recognition with a sort of lion's muzzle scarred by streams of blood and tears; He transformed her into a skeleton and raised a ridiculous dome filled with water on her impossibly frail stomach; for all those who see only outer appearances, He made her hideous; but, if he accumulated in her every visual disgrace, he intended that the nurses charged with dressing her wounds should not be disgusted and grow weary of their charitable offices because of the putrid smell which must necessarily accompany such wounds.

By continual miracle, He turned these wounds into a cassolette of perfumes; the dressings which were removed, teeming with vermin, exhaled an odour of sanctity; the pus smelled fragrantly, and her vomit gave off delicate aromas; and from this poor body swathed in lint whom He rendered so shameful by His exigencies, He wished that there should always emanate an exquisite atmosphere of seashells and spices from the East, a fragrance at once distinct and soothing, something both very Biblical and very Dutch, of cinnamon and spices.

—Translated by Terry Hale.

Chlorotic Ballad

Softly, draped in a hood of grey clouds, the twilight unfolded its misty tapestries over the melting purple of a setting sun.

She came slowly, smiling a vague smile, poising her thin figure in a white robe, quilted with red peas. Her cheeks were stained, for moments, with purple patches, and her long hair waved over her shoulders, tossing in sombre billows of white and red roses.

A crowd of youths and a throng of young girls watched her coming, fascinated by her cruel eye, her sickly smile. She advanced upon them, clasped them in her thin arms and furiously glued her lips to their mouths. They gasped and trembled all over; breathless, aghast, screaming with pain, they writhed beneath the wind of her kiss like grass before the breath of a thunderstorm.

Desolated mothers embraced her knees, grasped her hands and wept, with great sobs; but she, impassive, pale, her fixed eye filled with liquid gleams, her hands clammy, her breasts two darting points, repelled them, gently, and continued on her way.

One young girl crawled to the ogre's feet, clutching her breast with both hands, in dying agony, and spitting blood. "Mercy!" she cried, "Mercy! O Tuberculosis! have pity on my mother, have pity on my youth!" But the implacable ghoul hugged the girl in her arms and plundered the virgin lips for kisses, long drawn out.

The victim still quivered feebly; the other clutched her more tightly and dashed her teeth against the girl's; the latter's body convulsed weakly, then became cold, inert, while her cheeks mantled with glaucous tints and livid vapours.

Then the goddess fluttered heavily; pallid rays gushed from her eye-balls and bathed with bluish glazings the blanched cheeks of the dead.

Softly, draped in a hood of grey clouds, the twilight unfolded its misty tapestries over the melting purple of the setting sun.

—Translated by Samuel Putnam.

Pierre Louÿs (1870-1925). Louÿs' refined evocations, not to say re-inventions, of the society of Hellenistic Greece proved extremely popular both in France and the English-speaking world, especially due to the somewhat risqué nature of such works as *Aphrodite* (1896) and *Les Chansons de Bilitis* (1894). He lived his entire life in Paris, travelling occasionally around the Mediterranean coast where so many of his works were set. He had close friends among the writers of his day but otherwise kept himself rather apart from literary cliques except for that around Mallarmé.

The story here, from *Sanguines* (1903) perfectly contrasts his devotion to things Hellenic with *fin de siècle ennui*. Apart from his celebrated "public" writing he composed a vast hidden *oeuvre* ranging from scabrous, but satirical, poems often of epic length (*Le Trophéé des vulves légendaires* on the heroines of Wagner) to works of outright filth. These began to appear after his death, the first being his pastiche of a young lady's etiquette manual, a selection of which follows. It first saw publication in a strictly under-the-counter edition in 1930.

At this moment there is a little movement of neo-paganism, sensual naturism, eroticism at once mystical and materialistic, a return to those purely fleshly religions in which woman is adored even in the ugliness of her sex, because by means of metaphors one can idealise the misshapen and make the illusory divine...

But how deceptive is such a literature! All those women, all that flesh, all those cries, all that lust, so animal and so vain, and so cruel! The females nibble at cerebellums and eat up brains; thought flies, ejaculated; their souls ooze out as if from sores; and all those copulations engender only nothingness, disgust, and death....

And he has rightly foreseen that this book of the flesh logically concludes in death: the idea of death is joined to the idea of beauty; and the two images, entwined like two courtesans, die away slowly in the night.

PIERRE LOUŸS

A New Sensation

About four years ago, perhaps five, I used to occupy for several days a week an inconvenient but out-of-the-way and picturesque ground floor flat in a street which led at one end into the little park of Monceau: I took no interest in this detail, as the gate was closed every evening before midnight, and I was unable to go there at the precise hour when I enjoy walking in the open air.

One night, when I was there, in silent colloquy with two blue porcelain cats squatting upon a white table, I was trying to make up my mind between two methods of employing my solitude; I was either going to write a strictly regular sonnet while I smoked cigarettes, or I was going to smoke cigarettes while I contemplated the paper on the ceiling.

The important thing is always to have a cigarette in one's hand; objects must be enveloped in a heavenly and delicate haze which bathes both light and shadow, effaces solid angles, and by its scented spell imposes upon the restless mind a variable rhythm whence it may fall to dreaming.

That evening I both intended to write and desired to do nothing; in other words, it was an evening like all the rest; and it would assuredly have ended before a virgin sheet of paper and an ash-tray full of corpses, had not my thoughts been suddenly interrupted by an unexpected ring at my front door.

I raised my head. I was convinced that on Friday, the ninth of June, I did not expect any one at this hour of the night; but as a second ring followed close upon the first, I went to the door and unlocked it.

On opening the door I saw a woman standing there. She was wrapped in a voluminous mantle of natural serge, resembling a travelling dress, but figured with interlaced ornaments, like an opera-cloak. It was gathered about her neck by a circular, tufted trimming, above which her head just showed; it was a completely brown face, surmounted by light coloured hair. Her features were young and sensual, and had a slightly mocking expression; there were two very black eyes, a very red mouth.

"Will you please allow me to come in ?" she said, putting her head on one side.

I made way for her with the astonishment which can only be felt by a man who sees, at an hour when one scarcely receives any but the most intimate feminine friends, a woman enter his abode of whom he has not the slightest recollection, and who addresses him in familiar terms in the first words she utters.

"Dearest," I said to her timidly, when I had followed her into my room; "Dearest, don't be angry with me, I recognise you perfectly well, but unfortunately, somehow or other, I can't for the moment remember your name. Would it be Lucienne now, or Tototte."

She smiled indulgently and, without answering, took off her mantle. Her dress was of sea-green silk, adorned with enormous irises woven into the fabric itself; their stems rose tapering up her body as far as the square opening at the breast, which displayed both nipples bare. She wore on each arm a small gold bangle in the form of a serpent with eyes of emerald. A collar of large pearls in two rows gleamed upon her bronzed skin, emphasising the base of the supple and rounded neck.

" If you recognise me," said she, "it is because you have seen me in dreams. I am Callisto, daughter of Lamia. My tomb was left undisturbed for eighteen hundred years in the flowery woods of Daphne, near the hills where once stood the luxurious city of Antioch. But in these days tombs are great travellers. I was brought to Paris, and my shade followed the stone which held my delicate ashes. I slept for a long time, imprisoned in the icy vaults of the Louvre. I should be there still had not a great pagan, a venerable man, Monsieur Louis Menard*, who is the only man who remembers, today, the sacred rites and gestures, pronounced before my tomb the traditional words that can give a brief nocturnal existence to poor dead women. For seven hours, each night, I go wandering in your squalid city . . ."

"Oh, my poor girl!" I interrupted. "How changed you must find the world!"

"Yes and no. I find the houses black, the costumes ugly, and the sky mournful (what a singular notion that was of yours to come and live in such a climate!). I find that life is more stupid, and that people seem less happy; but one thing that absolutely astounds me is the reappearance at every step of everything I used to know. Really! In eighteen hundred years is that all you have done? Nothing more original? Nothing better, positively? Is what I have seen in your streets, in your fields, in your houses everything, absolutely everything? What a sorry business, my friend!"

The astonishment of my expression was a sufficient answer. She smiled, and went on to illustrate her meaning:

"You see how I am dressed?" she said. "I am wearing the robe that was buried with me. Look at it. In my time dresses were made of wool, yarn, and silk. When I returned to earth I thought I should find that all those ancient fabrics had not only vanished but been forgotten. I supposed (forgive me) that after so many years men would have discovered stuffs marvellous as the sun or the moon, and more voluptuous to the touch than the skin of a virgin or of a fruit. But no; what are your dresses made of? Wool, yarn, and silk . . . Oh, I know you have invented cotton goods, and you wrap up negroes in them, as you don't like the state in which those people walk about. I expect it is extremely moral of you . . . Are you very fond of cotton? Are you proud of discovering it? Personally I cannot even bear to feel the thing under my hands, it is so sticky and hangs so badly. Anyhow, have you any material which drapes better than wool? You have not. Anything finer than linen? Brighter than silk? . . . Tell me yourself."

She continued:

"In my time foot-coverings were made of leather . . . Slippers, coloured shoes, furred indoor slippers, and high boots were known . . . Your cycling shoes too, open, with a strap rather high up, that was a Phrygian fashion. Now look at mine; they are made of olive morocco, gold-tooled like a bookbinding. You had better admire them. You will not find any so fine where your lady friends buy theirs."

She went on again:

"In my time there were two precious metals used for ornaments: gold and silver. Have you people found a third? They were employed in the manufacture of necklaces, rings, bracelets, ear-rings, diadems, and brooches. I found all these articles again in the Rue de la Paix, identical with ours. We were acquainted with pearls, emeralds, diamonds, opals, moonstones, rubies, sapphires, and all the variously tinted silicas which come from Arabia and India today as they did then. Now, have you by any chance produced one precious stone in eighteen centuries? Just one, tell me just one, I beg of you! A stone I never knew, a ring I never put on my finger; a new jewel, even one mounted in gold, as mine are, since you have no rarer metal to offer me, but one that clasps a gem invented by yourselves?"

Her voice had gradually become more excited, until it assumed a tone of reproach and scorn. I made a gesture, a much calmer one.

"Callisto," I answered, "you seem to me to attach far too much importance to the ornaments that women load themselves with, and for which there is no excuse but that of employing, in their difficult selection and meticulous arrangement, a stagnant and idle existence. It is quite clear today, after ten thousand years of fruitless efforts by all nations, that a girl can never be made more beautiful by the art of the tailor, of the embroiderer, and of the jeweller, than she is at the moment when she displays herself naked as the Gods created her. I have no doubt that the Greeks were acquainted with that simple costume..."

"Better than your people are."

"You did not invent it: you need not flatter yourself. I recognise that nowadays it is disguised even more badly than when you were born; but does the difference between bad and worse amount to much? It is impossible to dress a woman. That is an axiom with which we cannot dispense. If aesthetic truths could be demonstrated theoretically, Monsieur Poincaré would have already proved mathematically that it is useless to employ the human imagination in the quest for a solution of this problem, which is as certainly chimerical as the trisection of angles. For my part I do not worry myself over a failure which is persistent because it is eternal; and I am content to admire a woman in her primitive purity (which is also immutable), with the antique emotion of those who touched the body of Helen."

She looked at me more steadily, bending her head towards me, and said slowly:

"Are you sure, presumptuous one, that women have not changed?"

II.

I do not know whether I actually saw, in my confusion, what she did immediately after uttering these words.

How she took off her rings, slipped down four bracelets, unfastened her necklace, and let her robes fall at the same time as her heavy hair, I really could not say. It was all so rapid and so dazzling that the recollection of it in my mind is that of a burst of splendour full of shadows.

Up till that moment I had not believed with conviction in the reality of my adventure. Apparitions, which were long supposed to be supernatural, and which are now with less reluctance considered as obeying certain profound and mysterious natural laws, exhibit themselves sometimes with the signs of a material substance which is not denied by any of our senses and which can mislead the most sceptical mind or even one simply forewarned against its improbability.

I had been wondering for the last hour whether I were not being mystified by one of the wilder of my lady readers; some foreigner, I thought, who is immodest and bold enough to visit, at night, a bedroom to which she has not been invited, no doubt wanting to make me forget the vulgar intention that has brought her here in the contemplation of the care that she has taken to dissemble it under a theatrical costume. I had answered her in the way that she seemed herself to suggest, with the indulgent reserve, in conversation, of one who through deference or curiosity is unwilling to tear away too soon the veil of a laboriously concocted and interesting comedy.

But as soon as she was naked, I understood that she had come to me from the depth of the past...

I remember very well that the moment I was certain of it I began, if I did not finish, all the movements with which an invincible religious instinct inspired me. I held onto my chair to prevent myself going on my knees, and I gazed at her with bent head, with a feeling as though I were committing sacrilege, and that so miraculous a personage ought not to be contemplated with eyes accustomed to behold living women.

Callisto was tall. The torso was spare and rounded, the waist high, the legs very long. Her limbs were articulated with a fragile nicety which enchanted me; and one could conjecture, even under the muscularity of her thighs, the dainty bones. Every hair had been plucked from her skin, but it was spotless, innocent of rouge, and shone as if just bathed, having a uniform light brown tint, almost black at the nipples, at the elongated borders of the eyelids, and in the short line denoting the organ of sex. I am really unable to explain why her beauty could not have been produced either in this climate or even in this age, for the evidence of it did not arise from the appearance of any particular detail, but simply from a harmony and perhaps from a kind of brightness about her. In order to assert a difference between her and the women of my own epoch, I was compelled to rely, without any other proof, upon my personal discernment, just as a collector distinguishes the genuine from the counterfeit without sometimes being able to show that he depends upon any special feature for the establishment of his conviction.

As if to place herself within my reach she lay down upon a couch.

"You might at least have been able to perfect the female form," she began again, with a smile. "And yet, as you see, the races of mankind have degenerated. Why do your physicians, who are contemptuous of ours, allow your mistresses, today, to be less beautiful than my sisters? The earth on which we live has not been swallowed up. The river Orontes still flows from the depths of the cedar wooded mountains. Smyrna survives. Sparta is dead, but Athens has been brought back to life. O vainglorious and sickly age, why dost thou substitute for the women of Ionian stock the mongrel Levantine, and why hast thou not created choice breeds of women as thou createst families of roses? Thou canst not. Thine experiment is that of a child. Ours was that of the Gods."

As she talked—for I was scarcely in a state of mind to argue with her—a terror such as one hardly ever knows except in some fit of cold shudders, when one is half asleep, constricted my temples. I trembled lest she should suddenly vanish, like something fluid, some empty flash of light, and I wondered whether it were only my sight that could have the illusion of her bodily presence; whether I could, by placing the end of my finger on the tender skin of one of her lips, touch her.

"Come along!" said she, laughing. "I am not a ghost. Give me your hand."

And, arching her loins on the couch, she drew my arm round her body, which rested, with a voluptuous weight, upon my fingers.

Then, with unflagging pertinacity, she resumed her lecture.

"A thousand years before my beauty existed, men coupled with women in practically the same way as goats did with their mates. You have read Homer? Neither Argos nor Troy knew any other pleasure except that of the simple and brutal act which satisfied the animals. Briseis was ignorant even of the kiss upon the mouth. Andromache never proffered her breast to other lips than those of her new born babe. Never upon the flesh of Helen's sides did an open and nimble palm arouse the thrill which is born of the caress of a human being."

She closed her eyes.

"And then, suddenly, in one day, the ancient East, where I was born, took from the Gods, like a fire that can never grow old, the only gift which distinguished them from the other inhabitants of the earth: they invented voluptuousness.

"O days of flowing sap! Youth of the world! For the first time the lips of a man and a woman abandoned the savours of fruits for those of each other. The great burning soul of Aphrodite inspired the bodies of lovers, and each day a new pleasure—a new pleasure, do you hear?—came down from blue Olympus into the wide beds filled with their enamoured cries. An unbridled intoxication ruled: from Babylon to Mount Eryx every perfume, every silken fabric, every flower, every art, and every woman joined the triumphal procession which entered upon the discovery of delight. Girls who were at last liberated from a hereditary barbarism became conscious of their senses and their desires, opened their nostrils to the rose, and their entrancing bodies to human mouths. For centuries the treasure of sensualities grew. In my time at Antioch and at Alexandria women were still adding to its riches. I, I myself, Callisto, daughter of Lamia, invented this . . ."

But I had started away from her.

She laughed.

"Now I've frightened you! Well, suppose you tell me something; come! While I was asleep in the grave for eighteen hundred years, what unknown delight has been your conquest? I asked you just now to tell me of a new pearl. Now I am asking you to tell me of some way of making love that I have not experienced. Doubtless, after all this time, some quite new kinds of enjoyment must have been made known. I await your invitation to partake of them."

She was firmly entrenched in the ironical positions she had taken up, and I could well believe that in her long nocturnal wanderings about the city she must have tried in vain to complete her education; and so I made no effort in that impracticable direction. I merely said:

"You must be patient. We began by forgetting everything, you see. Now we are making the old discoveries afresh. The process is called the history of modern civilisation. A few years after your death the world was involved in unprecedented calamities which might have proved irreparable. What happened was, first of all the birth and the singular fate of a religion which, at its origin, was morally admirable; but when it became distorted, it sterilised the effort which had been made by your race and sowed salt on the ruins of Athens. Next came the inroads of the barbarians; when the flood had rotted the wood of the vessel, the rats entered into it and gnawed it to pieces. That state of affairs lasted until the dawn of a new day when men saw arising from the East, like a ray of early morning light, the books which had been saved from the wreck and were being brought back from Constantinople. We took a hundred years to read them. Since the study of them began, life has gone on for barely three centuries. But time is on our side, perhaps. Give us time, Callisto."

She smiled mockingly.

"Will you find," she answered, "the tradition of Rhodopis in the byways of your museums? Have your archeologists, who understand so well the politics of Pericles and the strategy of Alexander, re-established the science of Aspasia and of Thais? Are they sure that the tomb where the delicate dust of Phryne lies at rest does not hide for ever the secret of a lost delight? I still possess that tradition. Would you like to know it? I surrender it to you..."

III.

Whatever may be the feelings of curiosity which the women who will read this fragment of recollections may experience, I shall not continue further with the description of what followed; first, because I have already written, on the evidence which I took from Callisto, a whole book with the title of *Aphrodite*; and, secondly, because a certain modesty would still perhaps prevent me from communicating in the first person the details of a night which was immoderately exciting.

Callisto rose about midday. She drew my attention quietly to the facts that the sun had already risen, and that we had to blame a perfect lighting system for not having observed it.

"You do away with Night, you no longer know Dawn," said she in a melancholy tone. "Once, the gleaming pageant of sunrise was the reward of long and exhausting vigils. But now you pass all your lives in a light without variations, and you no longer know, even, how to look upon the Dark."

I became anxious.

"Midday!.. But you told me that, for you, life was limited to the hours of the night. How am I able to keep you here still?"

"That is a matter of private arrangement between myself and Persephone," she replied, with a peculiar smile. "Let us talk. I have not yet finished reviling your epoch."

I was a little tired and, at the same time, nervous. "No more of that, I beg of you," I said. "Let us speak of ourselves, shall we not? Let us abandon the world, whether it is better or worse than it was... You are all that interests me."

"In that case, listen. You are not convinced. I shall continue until you confess. Really, I am returning very vexed from my second voyage on earth. I ought to have stayed in the grave with the dream of a purer age, in which I grew up surrounded by delights. I feel the need of telling someone what deceptions I have undergone in the course of my journey, and how angry I am with your century on account of all the surprises which it has not given me. I tell you, the world is a young man who promised well and who is in a fair way to spoil his life."

"I don't know . . . I think, all the same, that we have thought and created a great deal since your death. The century in which we live is not so very contemptible."

"It is! By reason, to some extent, of its impotence, but still more on account of its complacency. No! You are neither thinkers nor creators! You are Phoenicians, clever at reproducing models invented by my race, but you do not find them anywhere but in our civilisation, and you only exist in our shadow."

She gesticulated.

"Walk through the streets of Paris. On every side our eternal soul breaks forth in the facades of monuments, in the capitals of columns, and in the aspect of statues. After the construction, during the course of a barbarous and paltry Middle Age, of some wretched buildings which are already in decay (thank goodness!) you, the men of modern times, being incapable of creation, returned to our ruins; for the last four hundred years you have been making mosaics of stone with the fragments of our temples. One column discovered in Sicily begot two thousand churches and as many railway stations. You cannot even give a new architectural form to new requirements. You make, with the brass of your cannon, yet another copy of Trajan's column, and you erect concert halls in the style of the Corinthians. In succession to ourselves, sculptors of marble and founders of casts of bronze, you discovered nothing, not a single natural stone, not a single chemical alloy, which was better suited to reproduce the human form. And the solitary great sculptor you have had only became what he was because people discovered underground a torso by Apollonius, a headless, armless, and legless wreck; a piteous ruin, but a created work, that—a creating work. Schoolboys!"

She took two books from a shelf and threw them on the carpet.

"Your thought, like your art, is a parasite upon our corpses. It was not Descartes, it was Parmenides, who said that thought was identical with being. It was not Kant, it was Parmenides, again, who said that thought was identical with its object. And in these two phrases the schools of the present day are completely contained; they will never get rid of them. In all the directions in which your science becomes general—that is to say, philosophical—it rests, even today, upon the foundations which we laid. Euclid's masters settled once and for all the unalterable relations of line. Archimedes employed the integral calculus long before your Leibnitz, who is also indebted to us for his metaphysics. Instead of meditating on the fall of the apple, your revered Newton might have confined himself to reading a page of our Aristotle, in which his theory of universal gravitation had been set out two thousand years before. On the subject of the constitution of matter, which is the problem of God, Democritus knew as much as Lord Kelvin; his hypothesis is still the only one admitted. Finally, at this moment, when you are on the point of achieving the concept of a universal and central science, whose law would suffice to explain the entire collection of phenomena—what is this science, and what is this law? They are those definitively expressed, two thousand four hundred years ago, by Heraclitus. Fire becomes movement, movement becomes fire, and there you have the world. In two thousand years you have discovered neither—"

"We have discovered America," I interrupted patiently.

"That is not true!"

"Callisto, don't talk nonsense."

"I repeat and I maintain that America was discovered by Aristotle, and that this is not a paradoxical thesis but an historical and obvious fact. Aristotle knew that the earth was round, and (as you can read in his works) he had advised the exploration of the way to the Indies in a westerly direction, beyond the pillars of Heracles. Columbus took up the project again. But it has always been considered that the glory of a discovery redounds to the credit of the brain which conceives it, and not to that of the labourer who gives it practical effect. When Leverrier discovered Neptune—"

"Good," said I, in the last stages of lassitude. "At least you agree to that; we did discover Neptune."

"And suppose you did! Discover Neptune! You are an amazing person! Since yesterday I have been begging you to tell me of a new pleasure, a conquest on the road to happiness, a victory over tears. And you tell me you have discovered Neptune! I return to life after twenty centuries, anxious about everything, jealous of the marvels that I supposed to have been invented; wondering whether I shall not have to weep all through my ghostly eternity for too early an arrival in the world; and you tell me you have discovered Neptune! A pleasure! A pleasure! Of the mind, of the senses, what do I care! Am I to descend to the Elysian plains again without taking with me the thrill of a new sensation?"

She stretched out her hands . . . then added abruptly: "Besides, it was Pythagoras who discovered Neptune."

I collapsed. I had abandoned the struggle.

"Will you have a cigarette?" I asked.

"What?"

"I say, will you have a cigarette? Of course, I know, cigarettes too come from Greece, for it was Aristotle who—"

"No. I won't go so far as that. I confess that we were ignorant of that silly habit, which consists in filling one's mouth with the smoke of burning leaves. But I suppose you don't mean to offer me that pastime as a pleasure?"

"Who knows? Have you tried it?"

"Never! Why, are you one of the practitioners of that ridiculous business?"

"Sixty times a day. It is actually the only regular occupation with which I have agreed to burden my existence."

"And you like it?"

"I really believe that I should be content not to touch a woman's hand for positively a whole week, rather than be cut off from my cigarettes for the same period."

"You exaggerate."

"Hardly."

She became thoughtful.

"Well! Give me a cigarette."

"I was offering you one."

"Light it. What do you do? Inhale?"

"Girls puff at them; but that is not the best way. It is better to inhale, as a matter of fact. Take a whiff. Close your eyes. Now another . . ."

In a few minutes Callisto had reduced her little twist of oriental leaf to ashes. She threw away the half-finished stub, where the paint of her lips had left a reddish stain.

A silence ensued.

She even avoided looking at me. She had taken the square packet in her hand, which shook a little, I thought, as though she were agitated by a faint emotion, and after she had examined each of its four sides, she did not, I observed, return it to me.

With slow movements and with the care one uses in handling very precious articles, she placed it near the ashtray on the edge of a brightly coloured divan, and disposed her tawny person at full length beside it.

—*Translated by James Cleugh.*

Some Advice From *The Young Girl's Handbook Of Good Manners*

At the museum
It's best not to ask the curator why the hermaphrodite has both bollocks and breasts. This sort of enquiry falls outside his field of expertise.

In the pantry
Never tell the undercook to go screw a cooked chicken up the arse unless you have *personally* made sure he is not suffering from a venereal disease.

At the ball
A hard and fast rule: never grab the prick of your dancing partner *unless* he already has a hard-on for you. A quick glance at his trousers will prevent you from committing this embarrassing solecism.

Going visiting
Should some modest lady happen to mention: "My son doesn't work half so hard as your brother does" the correct response is not: "Just so, but never mind: he fucks twice as well." Panegyrics of this sort find little favour among Christian mothers, however sincerely intended.

At church
If you fellate a gentleman before communion, be careful not to swallow his come. Otherwise you will have broken your fast, which is strictly against religious practice. (Except on Fridays: sperm, like milk, is not classified by the church as a meat product.)

At the opera
You really shouldn't ask why the handsome tenor doesn't just get on and screw the soprano who has been singing all night as if she were sopping for him. They just don't do that on stage.

Your mother's lover
Should someone call by when your mother is engaged with her lover, and you are asked to present her excuses with: "I'm afraid my mother is indisposed": be discreet. Thus, if the visitor continues: "I'm so sorry, nothing serious I hope?" then "A prick up the arse" would be an unnecessary elaboration on your part. —*Translated by John Harman.*

167 Albert Samain

Albert Samain (1858-1900). Samain's habitual response to would-be biographers was: "*Ma vie n'a pas d'histoire.*"—he was not really exaggerating. Born in the provinces, he became a bank messenger at 14½, attempts to break into journalism failed and by 25 he had progressed to clerk in the Ministry of Education. He had some contact with the rowdier literary elements but, a profoundly classical writer, he found the new theories "troubling." His considerable literary success only began with the appearance of the *Mercure de France* which published him in its review and in book form.

Samain's sentimental conception of the joys of antiquity is very different from that of Louÿs! The present text is a severely edited version of the original: between the first paragraph and the final section given here, Hyalis falls in love with a mortal, Nyza. It is taken from his posthumous collection *Contes* (1902).

Albert Samain's sincerity is admirable; I think that he would have been ashamed of variations on sensations not explored through his own experience. Sincerity does not mean candour here; neither does it mean gaucherie. He is sincere, not because he acknowledges all his own thoughts, but because he thinks all the thoughts that he acknowledges; and he is simple because he has studied his art even to its innermost secrets and has helped himself to these secrets without effort and with an unconscious mastery.

But this poet who loved only the nuance, the Verlainian nuance, was able, at certain times, to be a violent colourist or a vigorous carver of marble. This other Samain, older, but no less genuine, is a Parnassian Samain, but always personal, even in his grandiloquence...

Such is this poet: powerfully delicious in the art of making every bell and every soul vibrate in unison: all souls are in love with this "infanta in robes of state."✻

ALBERT SAMAIN

Hyalis The Blue-eyed Faun (Extracts)

A little faun was born out of the union between a mortal and an Aegipan in the wind-thrashed forests of Mycalesia. His peculiarities, legendary to this day, clearly attested to the duality of his nature. He lacked the awesome strength of the forest gods, but his delicate feelings were more unbridled than his animal form might have suggested: a pelt less coarse and thick than the norm covered his flanks; his pointed ears and fine nostrils trembled constantly at everything around him; his gestures were spontaneous and carefree; when he smiled his cheeks would slowly become hollow, and the ingenuous look upon his face was ravishing at those times; but what truly excited surprised delight were his large, cerulean-coloured eyes, blue as the sea and the sky, always in motion casting afar their sweet, astonished glances like that first star shining in the East, before the sun has entirely set.

[...]

As daylight spread over the brownish heather, and he watched the far-off, sombre sea catch fire with the sun, Ydragone, the magician, tapped him on the shoulder. Ydragone was famous among the Pythonesses. Her philtres could determine the path of the stars, transmigrate the essences of metals, and cause the shades themselves to do her bidding.

"Why are you here?" she asked him.

"You know all things—don't you know that?"

"Of course I do. But Xylaos' daughter Nyza suspects nothing."

"Oh listen," he cried, "have pity, explain to me this thing I've been stricken with; it's like a desire no longer to feel, or see, or even be myself... isn't this the thing men call 'death'? O Ydragone, can you obtain this death for me?"

And he lifted a sorrowful face in which his eyes shone like coals.

"In truth," she said, "that which you ask for is impossible, because you are ignoring the fact that the blood of an Aegipan runs through your veins, and that is the immortal blood of a god."

"But your philtres are so powerful!" the faun murmured in a suppliant voice.

"Listen, your sorrow has moved me, and I wish very much to try out the effect of my enchantments upon you. But first you must bring me something to which you are attached—that pet lamb of yours, for example..."

Hyalis shuddered, and the little beast licked gently at his fingers.

"You can have him."

"Moreover, be aware that in order to attack your divine essence, I must employ terrible poisons. Hyalis, you will suffer horribly!"

"No matter. I'll come to you tonight."

The lair of the Pythoness was situated in the heart of the mountains.

It was situated in the depths of a circle of monstrous-looking rocks, where poisonous trees were reflected in dead water and the shadows looked as though they had been there forever. Vipers writhed in the black grass, twisted in knots, and hideous monsters came forth slowly from the pond and plashed in the mud with a noise dry as scales, shaking their many sharp claws. An odour of decay trailed through the air and the flames of the torches panted.

Hyalis arrived in the middle of the night. His face was pale, but his eyes were determined and filled with an unwonted light.

As he went leaping across the grotto, a great bald-pated bird with a human face and a grey and rosy belly shook two heavy and ponderous wings, and called out his name three times.

Hyalis, already pale, became frightened and paused, shivering, but Ydragone appeared, leaving him no room to retreat.

"You see," she said to him, displaying a bowl from which dense fumes issued forth, "I've finished preparing your philtre. Have you brought what I demanded of you?"

Hyalis, without responding, clutched his lamb.

The magician took it, extended it upon a stone, its head resting over the bowl, and raised a large knife. The lamb bleated softly and Hyalis covered his eyes.

Soon a strange mist diffused itself and the grotto turned completely red, the magnificent and terrible red of blood.

"Now then," said Ydragone, and approaching the faun, she presented him with a cup wherein a blackish liquid bubbled. "But listen to me, hear me well, and fix my words in your heart. When the cycle of the next moon is completed, on that same day, and at that very hour of completion, you will die. Drink."

And Hyalis took the cup and emptied it.

Immediately he fell backwards, emitting a terrifying cry.

It seemed to him that a fire arose and spread through his body, flowed in his veins, gnawed at his fibres, attacked his bones. His limbs contracted, twisted, like dry twigs in a flame. He rolled about on the ground, tearing off strips of flesh and tufts of hair with his fingers; and his suffering became so atrocious that Ydragone herself grew pale.

Suddenly he stiffened, becoming immobile; then the magician sprinkled a few penetrating drops upon him.

He reopened his eyes, breathing slowly; he rose...

His soul shivered in all its senses, agitated by confused sentiments like a forest at dawn where the sleeping birds awake with myriad joyous cries.

He took some steps, groping his way; his hands met the skin of the lamb, and he eagerly lifted its warm and curly wool to his lips. Then a strange sensation arose from the depths of his being like an irresistible wave that comes from the open sea and rushes to break abruptly upon the shore. His chest swelled with sigh after weary sigh, and suddenly, from his blazing eyes, a mysterious water spurted, falling in great drops upon his sorrow like a refreshing rain upon the parched grass of the prairies; and, filled with a delicious astonishment, he murmured:

"The gods know nothing of the pleasure of weeping."

From that day on, his existence modified itself in a singular manner. Thoughts that had endured so long no longer troubled him and his sorrows were less acute.

As a man standing on its bank can better admire a river's majestic course than one caught in its currents so Hyalis, less narrowly drawn to the obscure lives of the waters and the woods, embraced the forces and workings of the entire vast universe with a greater amplitude, drawn from his contemplation of the most profound impressions.

Now the eternal rhythms of the world, the silent course of the stars, the mobile and infinite sea, the silvery fires of the night succeeding the light of day, the beauty scattered everywhere in creation, from the neighing of rearing stallions to the streamlined flight of the larks filled him with a ravishing confusion.

Further, Ydragone's poison, pursuing its certain course, marshalled its forces slowly; and his soul, less nourished by the energies of his blood, leaned with a secret sympathy toward all forms of life which he perceived to be in decline. The agony of a slow twilight, the fatigue of a flower drooping between his fingers diffused through his finer sensibilities the most exquisite quiverings, and each day he fathomed with a finer charm the moving mystery of life.

One evening he watched a funeral cortege from afar: the pallor of the women beneath their long white veils, the dolorous brilliance of their eyes, the dismal slowness of the funeral hymns, the sudden invitation to embrace, so sweetly poignant as to be almost voluptuous; and he said to himself, pensively:

"The gods know nothing of the beauty of death."

Now, more than ever, he dreamed of the daughter of Xylaos, but his feelings had become transformed. He knew that it was because of her that he had lost the light but had gained the gift of inner illumination; and thus the regret at leaving the earth and the joy of suffering for Nyza formed in his heart a sad and impassioned mixture, which he savoured with an inexpressible sorrow.

Meanwhile, the new moon had all but run its course, and the time assigned him by the magician had arrived.

Like a man who is leaving on a long journey, assembling those things that he wishes to take, Hyalis passed the day in recalling to his memory his happiest hours; he remembered his childish games, his conversations with Glaucus, the dryads, the vastness of the forest and the sea, and the most insignificant details, arising suddenly within his memory, touched him more than all the rest. He watched his last evening falling upon the garden of Xylaos, upon the orchard which bordered a curtain of poplars with silver tips, upon a basin scaly and verdured where doves briefly touch down before flying off, upon the roof, upon the paths of fine sand where Nyza's footsteps lightly pressed themselves.

Little by little these things became effaced; the last sounds of the day gradually passed away... night had come.

The house beyond raised its pale facade and its colonnades connected by garlands of leaves. Hyalis cleared the hedge and advanced within the darkness. The scents of the flowers, revived by a recent rain, exhaled around him, pungently.

He bent down and recognised the rope with the wooden handles recently left there by little Callidice, and suddenly, he remembered the gentleness of the child, her gambols in the garden beneath the deftly turning rope, and her noisy joy when Nyza also consented to play, and their dance together, the bare arms at her waist. This memory of bygone hours touched his heart most deeply, and he silently touched to his lips the wooden handles polished by her charming hands.

He had now reached the gates where the servants slept. He stopped, his arm resting upon a column, and strained his neck in the darkness. His heart beat violently against his chest, and drops of sweat ran down his torso and the small of his back.

He listened: turtledoves began to coo nearby, then fell silent; the leaves of the garden moved with a long murmur.

Then, mastering the hesitation that made his knees shake, he cleared the doorstep and felt his way, groping toward a feeble light filtering from between the closed hangings.

He parted the drapes and inclined his head.

This was Nyza's room. A copper lamp in the shape of a bird spilled a pale light. At the back, upon a bed of cedar inlaid with ivory strips, the virgin slept.

Hyalis came forward, watching her. In the presence of this polished face, before those eyes sealed by sleep, a supernatural emotion agitated him, and the room surrounding him filled with divinity. Then, trembling and pale, he leaned over this visage and studied it carefully. A rosy and luminous blood in her veins traced a bluish network upon the fine membrane of her temples; a delicate lock of hair, which trembled at her slightest breath, caressed her cheek; imperceptible tremors passed over her immobile features, like those ripples that a breath of summer spreads over the smooth surface of the waters; and, at times, the furtive shadows of some sensation tugged at her lips, furrowed her brow and wrinkled the delicate nostrils of her nose.

But what melted Hyalis' heart was the fringed shadow of the long lashes upon her cheek, and, behind the finely moulded ear, the amber border of her hair, her hair as fragrant and mysterious as a forest.

Being able to study so closely one whom he had never before been able to approach made his head spin with a sort of vertigo, and immense chasms in his thought became evident, succeeded each other within him, as with the eyes of an eagle over a landscape that it dominates in its flight.

He leaned forward again; a breath, feeble and pure, passed over his face and he shivered: it was the sleeping woman's breath.

At regular intervals her white breasts rose and fell, and it seemed to Hyalis that now he was united with her, that he carried a bit of her divine soul poured out into his own body, that the rhythm of his life was at last in accord with that of his beloved.

Her exquisite mouth opened in the darkness like a fruit.

Then, goaded by irresistible desire, he brought his lips to Nyza's, as gently as he could, just enough to touch without waking her, with an almost immaterial contact.

Then he remained thus, immobile and with closed eyes.

An infinite peace coursed through his limbs; at the same time it seemed to him that his heart grew large, becoming vast and splendid, blue as the firmament on summer nights, where a thousand stars running in all directions in golden curves decayed.

The hour had arrived; Ydragone's poison struck him at the very source of his being. An icy cold enveloped him. Like an urn plunged into water, his soul filled rapidly with the smothering darkness, he uttered a long sigh, and his head, suspended over the virgin's breath, slid noiselessly upon the pillow.

Thus Hyalis of Mycalesia, the blue-eyed faun, died of love.

173 Jehan Rictus

Jehan Rictus aka **Gabriel Randon** (1867-1933). The circumstances of Randon's bizarre illegitimate birth have been made almost impossible to unravel by the author's, and his biographers', myth-making. It resulted, however, in Randon being subjected to a totally miserable childhood at the hands of a tyrannical and sadistic mother. She coerced him into excellence at school, but he ran away from home at 16 and began a life of utter deprivation in Paris, living rough around the markets of *Les Halles*. Eventually his educational qualifications got him a menial government office job and he had the good fortune to meet Albert Samain, who helped him materially and with publication. His existence was still precarious and itinerant, even as he began to make a small living out of journalism. He specialised in pro-anarchist articles, interviewing several of the most famous activists. It was partly his political stance that caused him to change his name and abandon Symbolism in 1895 to write *chansons* using popular language and *argot*. His most famous collection *Les Soliloques du pauvre* (1896) drew on his own experiences at society's bottom. He successfully performed these songs in the Montmartre cabarets for several years, using his extraordinary appearance (tall, cadaverous, a poverty-stricken dandy) to great effect. Despite the popularity of his poetry, especially among *poilus* during the war, his work went out of fashion and he led a penurious and forgotten existence thereafter, working on one immense unfinished poem for the last 12 years of his life. Our extract is a chapter from his only novel *Fil-de-Fer* (1907) an autobiographical account of his early life.

There was a rumour from Montmartre: something new was arising out of the throng of slangy and spicy monologists and fortune-tellers; someone, for the first time, was speaking, with an original and wayward abandon, for the Poor of great cities, the Parisian tramp, the tatterdemalion in whom there remains something of the Bohemian, the vagabond who has not lost all sentimentalism, the prowler in whom there is a touch of the poet, the unfortunate still capable of irony, the outcast whose rage evaporates in bantering curses, whose rage recedes if

Hope gleams like a wisp of straw in a stable,

whose bitterness is no more than desire gone rancid; in short the man who would wish to live and whom the egoism of the chosen casts eternally into outer darkness.

...Rictus's poor-man is certainly inclined towards anarchism. Since he is deprived of all material gratifications, great principles leave him cold. The Socialist in an overcoat and the Republican in a frock-coat inspire in him an identical contempt, and he can barely conceive how the poverty-stricken, smoothly deluded by fat politicians, can still listen without laughing to the shameful promise of a happiness as illusory as it is future.

...It is genuinely difficult for me to accept the patois, the argot, the errors in spelling, the elisions, everything that, offending against the form of the sentence or the word, of necessity impair its beauty. Or, if I accept it, that would be by way of a jest: now, art does not jest, it is grave even when it laughs, even when it dances. One must still understand that, in art, everything that is not necessary is pointless, and everything that is pointless is bad.

...All this does not prevent me from recognising the very individual talent of Jehan Rictus. He has created a genre and a type. He has set out to raise the everyday speech of the people to the level of literary expression, and in this he has succeeded as far as is possible; it is worth our while making a few concessions and departing, although for him alone, from a rigour without which the French language, already much flouted and scorned, would become the servant of mountebanks and buffoons.

JEHAN RICTUS

A chapter which will shine a vivid light on the ideas professed by La Marquise de Tirlapapan-Ribbon-Ribbette concerning education: The Axiom.

Madame de Saint-Scolopendre* employs a favourite axiom that is hers by right and which She constantly enunciates, in a majestic tone:

"Nobody other than myself has the right to beat my child!"

She could, Fil-de-Fer soliloquises, she could add that She discharges this right on the general behalf, that She acts, in a way, by delegation, and that, in the accomplishment of this task, none can replace her.

She alone, too, possesses the correct method, She alone knows the sensitive spots on the miserable anatomy of *her child* and those that must be spared, seeing that these last have been hardened by a daily tanning, already of long standing, which renders any chastisement illusory.

It is thus a privilege of justice, high and low, that Madame de Saint-Scolopendre, Marquise de Tirlapapan-Ribbon-Ribbette reserves to herself over Fil, and She is determined that nobody, let this be well understood, nobody shall deprive her of it!

What would become of us, great God! if Somebody usurped Our Authority to correct him.

Suppose, perhaps, that that other should strike not quite as hard? There and then, the prestige She retains in the eyes of that young human creature would vanish right away.

In any event, he'd go to the bad.
No, no, not that, Lisette.
Tender-hearted stroke a nettle, And it stings you for your pains.
It was now or never.

"Who's blacked your eye?" she asks Fil-de-Fer imperiously one evening as, slipping in, he presents a visage streaked with a few scratches and with his right eye slightly swollen

Fil, who had attempted, unsuccessfully, to hide the visible traces of a fight, and who feared a complementary thump on the other eye, the one on familiar terms with conjunctivitis, Fil blurts out:

"It was the butcher's little apprentice, but it doesn't matter," he pleads, "I knocked two of his teeth out."

"Ah! So that's it!" Madame de Saint-Scolopendre cries.

(Fil is already resigning himself to receiving the other shiner; for, in similar cases, this was his recompense: but no, She has another idea.)

"Ah! So that's it! Come with me. We'll see about that. Nobody other than myself has the right to beat my child."

Well now! There she is, embarked upon the exercise of her ordinary offices and prerogatives and, after all, not at all put out that the occasion should arise to win herself something of a reputation in the neighbourhood.

So, seizing Fil-de-Fer by the hand, she leads him unceremoniously to the butcher's.

She arrives at the opportune moment, the shop is full of customers. The assistants are busy cutting, weighing, wrapping cutlets and escalopes; one of them, artistically, with the point of a knife, is trimming a dressed brisket of beef; the butcher himself is boning a shoulder of mutton and giving it a resounding slapping; the shop is packed with housewives, waiting or making their way to the cash-desk: "A *pot-au-feu*, that'll be one franc seventy-five!"

As for the little apprentice, the cause of the impending fracas, he has been sent on some errands.

Irruption of Madame de Saint-Scolopendre, hanging onto her captive son and bursting upon them suddenly, like a cyclone. But at first they take her for a customer.

"What would you like, Madame?" —Death and blood!

Madame explodes in ferocious yells—which are incomprehensible, because She neglects to recount the tale of the little apprentice.

What She would like: *that nobody other than myself beat my child*, is that understood?

The butcher, the butcher's assistants, the customers, who are at a loss, stare at her, dumbfounded. What's this? Which of them would have beaten Fil? What's all this about?

But Madame de Saint-Scolopendre is providing less and less information.

She paces about, threatens, gesticulates, fumes, shakes her fist under the noses of each and all, two or three times gets her chignon caught in the legs of mutton hanging from the ceiling (the line of which, Fil reckons, resembles the backsides of children awaiting a thrashing), repeats her celebrated axiom, makes as if to leave, returns, begins over again, gathers the passers-by together in a crowd, creates an enormous, unforgettable scandal, without anybody making a move, so spellbound is her audience.

At length, her breath and her rage exhausted, She goes off in triumph, taking Fil-de-Fer with her, wretched and ashamed, wishing the earth would swallow him up.

And, as they dispersed, the gawpers—who remembered of the scene only the fateful apophthegm—the gawpers exclaimed:

"What a splendid mother!"

—*Translated by Iain White.*

177 HUGUES REBELL

Hugues Rebell, aka George Grassal (1867-1905). A rather forgotten figure whose fierce character mightily impressed his contemporaries. A rich Breton semi-aristocrat, he spoke several languages, travelled extensively and generally applied himself to exhausting his fortune by indulging in a lifestyle dedicated to satisfying his every appetite. He also worked obsessively at literature producing a substantial body of prose poems and novels of a more or less lubricious nature.

Arthur Symons offers this portrait in his *Memoirs*: "His force was frantic, almost elemental. An insensate thirst intoxicated him with the desire to drink in all the perfumes and all the madness and all the vice and vehemence that exist upon the earth, together with a frenzied appetite and an audacity which reminded me when I saw him now of Nero, now of Caligula, they gave to the man himself an exasperation which showed at least the atrocity of his nerves. He was one of those to whom love and hate were interchangeable words... He was an absolute type of Abnormality."

Unluckily for Rebell his fortune was exhausted before his life, he was rescued from starvation more than once by his friends, in particular Barrès, but died literally in a gutter in the Marais, then a particularly loathsome slum quarter of Paris.

The two texts here are from *Dizzy Spells* (1888).

At a time when small-minded plagiarists of the philosopher Seneca, stockbrokers, people's advocates, professors retired on an inheritance, millionaires, ambassadors, tenors, ministers and swindlers, when all the "republican royalty," hypocritically glad to be alive, are moved with a tender concern for the "lot of the humble," at the same time as they place their foot upon their necks, in times like these, it is pleasant to hear some frank words, and Hugues Rebell speaks out: "I wish to enjoy the life that has been given me, in complete accord with the whole of its richness, its beauty, its freedom, its elegance; I am an aristocrat..."

Transported into works of imagination, the aristocratism of Hugues Rebell becomes vague, merges wilfully with moral licentiousness. One is rather disconcerted....

This writer is liable to surprise us in more than one way with all he has in him by way of freedom of spirit, of daring flights of imagination. But even now his originality is visible and incontestable: he is one who prefers the silken mantle to the cotton shawl, the purple carpet to the socialist straw-matting, beauty to virtue, the splendour of the naked Venus to the "mournful eyes of pale Virginity."

HUGUES REBELL

Surprises Head leaned upon the upholstery of the carriage and bathed in light, my soul scattered amid things by the wild flight of the train, a kaleidoscope that unwinds moirés of fairy castles, landscapes upon landscapes; the sweet hesitation of my dreams against the white smoke, sylph-filled, folding in on itself, brushing up against the sun, and vanishing in the immensity of a close-cropped plain; a stream lost amid the great mysterious forest to the horizon with its soaring white wings; and, very far away, my heart raises its chalice toward the royal triumph of the violet archipelagos which swim upon a golden sky balancing—like an enormous lamp—a bleeding October sun; but all at once, the locomotive comes to an abrupt stop, collision of carriages, one against the other, in front of a brick pavilion, and above it all the blissfully ribald laughter of red faces with brown moustaches, indifferent to the pale beauties strewn about in the glory of a too divinely vaporous evening, consecrating their nullity with sparks of gold and flames.

My pretty little black cat, when I had given her a fragrant biscuit, in the guise of thanking me, sprang onto my hand, securing herself with steely claws so tenderly merciful that drops of my blood dripped onto the carpet. I then genuflected before her beauty and grace: "My pretty little black cat, barely a year old, and you already know that great maxim of our deepest human wisdom—give a slashing for a kindness; return evil for good!"

Always look for a woman beneath everything: setting great store by complementary arrangement and familiar with the art of dressing well, he wished himself to select for his well-beloved mistress the black silk bodice, narrow and low, which allowed her to bare her breasts; then he slipped in three real camellias which seemed to surge up as a laughing blossoming of flesh; lastly he rolled her blonde hair into twists and sprinkled over it, as if accidentally, tiny rose-buds; and then backed away to appraise reflected in the parquet floor: the feet sweetly shod in white satin, the tight silk of the blouse, the smooth and supple throat on which the light played with a softness of moonlight, when, about to raise his eyes from the shoulders of his beloved, he exclaimed, as though speaking to himself: "Truly, the costume goes far on this charming body, but fails, alas, to distract from the ugly face!"

A little lad in yellow rags beneath a rain that rattles the gutters, and makes the red bricks, the worn doorsteps, the doors without paint on the old houses with long roofs, shine. In the grey sky, the great chimneys of the factories spit billows of black smoke which the wind sways, tears and scatters on every side. Beneath an accumulation of filth, bones, shoes without soles, and gnawed-at rubbish, stagnant streams exhale putrid miasmas into the narrow streets.

The child remains motionless, his back set against a milestone, arms dangling, the fingers raw, with pinched lines and a face which looks like the legs of a lady crab from his beatings. He pushes on with plaintive cries, the same note prolonged for a long time, which he repeats, rising and falling an octave, as if his voice now loses its vigour, now acquires new force.

What's he doing there? From a low door giving access to a descending stairway, there appears, as if from a trap, a woman of uncertain age, olive-skinned, her black mop of hair poorly imprisoned in a grimy hairnet, which allows a few short locks entangled with white hairs, to escape from two large tears. From her darned and greenish slip slender waxy legs emerge, just like spider legs, plunging into sabots without laces; and her hands, riddled by warts, sticky as if with tar, are raised with menace and promises of chastisement in the direction of the motionless kid. Her yellow creased throat, overspread with hideous knobs which indecently overhang a blue and green striped handkerchief, emits a voice hoarse from drinking brandy: "Hark runt, I've a mind t' kick yer arse!"

The child, always against his milestone, continues to moan indistinctly. Confronted with this spectacle, delightful to a contemplative soul, I think about beautiful nuptials, snow-white and sunny, of rosy figures beneath white veils, caresses which this mouth stinking from wine and growling had been the object of in a wedding bed. I think too on the thousands of similar creatures who fill up the earth with their filth, their howls, and their ugliness, endlessly drawing from their obese stomachs miscarried beings, horrible and idiotic; and then I think back, with a beatific smile to those lovable amateurs of philosophy who, reclining upon soft divans, and inhaling the aroma of their tea, remark, in blessing the name of God: "Infinitely good and powerful Lord, everything is perfect in this, the best of all possible worlds."

My room! No ugly room furnished with bookcases and covered in dust! Your tables and chairs, however banal in carving and design, are as precious to me as the altar and the sacred vessels are to a priest, because they assist in the cultic ceremonies, with different mysteries but with the will of a holy spirit, that I celebrate in a triumphal fête. Simply: with the blinds of the windows lowered, I have attempted in a moment—rare magician—to efface the ugliness of ambient things; and I bid the occult world arise.

Sesame—open up! Rushing to the fore, foul and fat, are the grotesque *bourgeoisie* of Zola and Balzac, "wearing their stupidity like a crown," winking as if to say: "Hey! Aren't I a pretty booby?"

Falstaff* gets stewed in the company of Coupeau, Alcestis drinks with Timon, Homais embraces Thomas Diafoirus and M. Prud'homme, gigantic, upholds the standard of theory.

Avaunt! Driving out these ignoble monsters, with the roaring of the damned, flamboyantly red, twisting in hysterical convulsions, it's the *diaboliques*—Barbey* and Charles Baudelaire. Oh hell!

But the cymbals ring out, the indigo of Oriental skies opens up and the shining backdrops of Baghdad and Irmensul unroll, strewn with roses from Ispahan, and amid the standards, bugles and lances, a chariot advances pulled by caryatids with human hands, to which unicorns are harnessed, the rolling chariot wherein Herodias, the Queen of Sheba and Akedysseril * stand wracked in a luxurious embrace.

A cry (is it human?) boring into the azure, pierces through the banality of a popular refrain.

Sinister collapse, fading away of the dear phantoms who are my joy—back to my chamber in your vulgar forms! Hell! Yes! You, loafer who execrates the silence propitious to spiritual flights, and you, music-hall songbird, who contribute to the propagation of Nonsense, shouldn't the two of you really be whipped in some public place for making a criminal attack upon intelligence? At any event it's only wise to forbid the entryways of the streets to these shameless clamourers, these sacrilegious violators of that most sacred of temples, THE DREAM!

Night

Night. All alone by the fire which flares up momentarily, I am seated in an old armchair where my grandfather used to sit, and my lamp traces a luminous circle upon the ceiling. Alarming, this miserly brightness that reserves for itself so small a portion of space; and the shadow-filled draperies that have seen so much grief and joy, in passing, seem to shudder at the gloomy sniggering of spectres.

Silence, the silence of an empty house causes me anguish. For the doors must surely swing open, and faces will appear; but whose? Doubtless yellow, bony ones, exuding the rot of the tomb, gnawed at by hideous worms, the faces of those whom I once loved and those I think about in my waking hours.

Right next to my own, the room in which my mother died; above it, that from which they bore my sister, a few days before her final agony. I look to my right, to my left, and above me; and the alcove, the piled-up books, the big armoire all appear from their shadows; stars with the eyes of ghosts are fixed upon me. Then, in fear, I rise to bolt the door, because I sense that someone is prowling in the corridor; and that pale shadow passing the window—whose face was that, which vanished before my eyes?

Poor leeches! How is it that you are forgotten except when you come to terrorise us in visions?

Fear now seizes me; in this solitude I have the sensation of being brushed by the wings of a malefic angel, and stalked by assassins with knives; panic makes me throw the door open once more, I leave the house that is making me shiver and feel so bad tonight. On the frozen streets I wander through the sleeping city, beneath a street light whose shade—monstrous beast—crawls toward me when its sinister flame vacillates with each gust.

"Mister, Mister wait" the voices implored. —No not tonight, girls; I don't want to think any more tonight, and the sight of you distresses me. Instead I'll make tracks for the house of a certain rich courtesan whose luxury and beauty creates pleasure from distress. I hope she will be beautiful, as beautiful as Leconte de Lisle's Leila, or Salome, or Flaubert's queen of Sheba; above all I hope she'll have a face that's dream-like and filled with mystery—such as Baudelaire used to attribute to his exotic lovers, and Poe to his divine creations—Berenice, Ligeia, Eleonor!

Because I have been trying for hours to forget, and more than anything else, I must loose myself in ecstasy. When I was a child, I used to seek out the caresses of my sister, I used to love her words, so sweet, and all those sexless kisses, confidences passed between souls; but now, desperate for any tenderness, I have come here, drawn to a unique beauty.

···

After that vulgar prelude, I am here, restored by the odour of opopanax permeating the silken hangings of the salon and by the exquisitely vivacious face of my hostess, a desire is born within my soul, to see completely naked the body now buried in clothing. I want to undo long black hair and see what strange voluptuousness gleams in her pupils: and my eyes glide to her room where we may recline, plunged in a restless half-light, in its midst the triumphant whiteness of the bed spreads itself out.

My companion has guessed at my weary concupiscence; and, as soon as I plunk down my gold, she commences with real joy to strip off each piece of costume, piece by piece, in a moving wave of perfume.

I felt as though I'd soon have become bored, were it not for the knowing coquettishness of her apparel; the woman diminished in direct proportion to the progress of her unveiling; all but dropping away with the lace-work of her expensive cambric slip.

And yet, she *is* beautiful, as the veiled lamplight from a rosy globe brushes against her smooth white skin: bluish reflections flow through her abundant ebony hair, and her nostrils have contracted with pleasure... But I search her look—even upon the blood-red lips of this stranger—for the mystery I have loved, for that woman-beyond-women all men dream of—and I haven't found her here. This one has nothing, nothing for all her airs; she is as banal as her surroundings, her luxury is a parvenu's delight. Her gimcrack furniture apes the antique, her Japanese vases are strictly imitation, and her bronzes are either grossly lascivious or else stupidly sentimental.

And now, as she wallows upon the bed, awaiting my embrace, I calculate how soon I'll be able to leave her, when I'll be far from this woman who speaks nothing to my imagination. It's a strange joy that condemns itself to such repugnant embarrassments as these! But then it's the torture of these women to have to suffer either forceful violation or Almighty Hunger.

183   JEAN LORRAIN

Jean Lorrain (1855-1906). Born into wealth, he began as a painter, then turned journalist and man-of-letters. As a novelist and short-story writer he oscillated between the Naturalist and Decadent camps, his most famous decadent novel being *Monsieur de Phocas* (1901). A dandy, society lion, overt homosexual, ether-drinker; as a satirical journalist his pen was much feared and highly profitable. Always in the public eye, he had a scandalous and successful literary career until sued for defamation by the artist Jeanne Jacquemain who recognised herself in one of his novels: the court seized the opportunity to bring low one who had showed so little respect for society's proprieties, its vengeance took the form of punitive damages. The last ten years of his life were dominated by financial problems and failing health.

The nature of Lorrain's provocations are exemplified by the preface to a later work which bore this splendid dedication:

To human hypocrisy and cowardice: to the rapacity of the honest and the honesty of the self-made, to the self-appointed defenders of virtue, to the upholders of marriage and the other pimps who earn their rent from prostitution and morals, to the redressers of wrongs and the seducers of the innocent, to the matrons whose seclusion has remade their virginity, to those ranting detractors of the vices they have known only too well; I dedicate these pages of melancholy and dissolution—a dissolution of whose frightful anguish and incurable tedium they know nothing—in the firm expectation of, and flattered in advance by, the indignant cries which will rise up in their throats at this heart-rending chronicle of a slow and appalling destruction of the human spirit.

TO THE GREAT MEN OF MY TIME I DEDICATE THIS COMPASSIONATE WORK.

Despite de Gourmont's eulogy to *Dans l'Oratoire*, we have not used anything from this book of critical essays, which contain too many contemporary references, his comments apply to the entirety of Lorrain's output however. This text is taken from *Tales of an Ether-Drinker* (1900).

There must be things that are forbidden and things that are permitted, otherwise those hesitant or slothful in their inclinations would halt at the first vine-arbour, lie down on the first lawn they encountered. It is perhaps social morality that has created crime, and sexual morality pleasure. That a pasha should be virtuous in the midst of three hundred women! I have always thought that the destruction of Sodom was a voluntary immolation, the suicide of a people weary of always seeing desire implacably ripening in the tedious orchard of voluptuousness.

From this eternal fruit, Jean Lorrain, rather than devouring it whole, has manufactured syrups, jellies, crèmes, fondants, but blended in his pastry, I know not what unknown ginger, what unfamiliar saffron, what mysterious clove, which transforms this amorous sweetmeat into an ironic and heady elixir.

It seems to me that the masterpiece from that laboratory is Lorrain's little volume Dans l'Oratoire: *never did a work go farther in the meticulous dosage of sugar and cayenne pepper, of rose-petal jam and red pepper. Another "dish of spices"* more authentic and less innocent, it seems to be out of the pocket of one of those damned* abbés *capable of drinking sacramental wine from their mistress's slipper; a poisonous and smiling book, a deceptive breviary in which every vice has its rubric and its antiphony, and which draws its "lessons" from the martyrology of Lesbos....*

Born in art, Monsieur Lorrain has never ceased to love his native land and pay it frequent visits. If he has a weakness for the hussy, for excursions into the shady side of Parisian life, for elegant putrefaction, the world of "the obol, the plait and the washstand," the ravages of which a Greek rhetorician (Demetrius of Phaleron) has already chronicled in literature, if he has, more than any other, and with more talent than Dom Reneus, propagated the cult of Saint Mucosa, if (in an undertone) he has sung what he modestly calls "bizarre loves," it was at least in a language which, being of good breeding, smilingly endured his familiarities of a recondite Oratorian; and if certain of his works are comparable to those startlingly blonde women who cannot raise their arms without exuding an odour injurious to virtue, there are others whose scents are only those of fine literature and pure art; his taste for beauty has triumphed over his taste for depravity.

JEAN LORRAIN

The Gloved Hand
🙠

It was fairly late at night, after a bachelors' dinner-party. While putting away a good many goblets of sherry-soda, whisky soda and other American beverages, the talkers, some lolling on divans, others sitting on their haunches, propped up on piled masses of cushions, had slipped from politics and passing events, from the theatre and women, to the mishaps of morphine and ether; the case of Serge Allitof, obliged to quit Paris to escape from an obsession which, for him, made every human face seemingly take on animal features had for a good while afforded matter for the conversation and, from the monomania of this unfortunate fellow, constrained to seek refuge in the Midi from a Paris populated by men with the muzzles of wild beasts and women with fowls' profiles, they had gone on to pass in review all the nervous disorders cited, more or less, by doctors Charcot and Lombroso; all, in most instances, lesions of the brain giving rise to phenomena that are sometimes curious; naturally they took into account the factors of heredity and chance—the delicacy of the mental organism is such that the most apparently trivial incident may occasion the most serious troubles—and, the personality of each in the end gaining the ascendancy in the general conversation, in fevered and slightly modified tones the eight men met there together traded the most baroque confidences. It was a dismayed exchange of personal impressions of the terrors of childhood, of youth, and even of yesterday, accompanied by vaguely disquieting glances and automatic gestures.

"As far as I'm concerned," Sargine declared, "after eleven in the summer and nine in the winter, I can't hire a fiacre—a fiacre or *voiture de cycle*. I live on the Avenue de Wagram, near the Place Pereire. Without being all that far, it's not very close to the centre; to go home I unavoidably have to pass through some fairly desolate quarters; in those parts, you'll agree, on a foggy night in November, there are some pretty sinister avenues; leaving aside the Boulevard de Courcelles, there's nothing particularly amusing about the Boulevard de Malsherbes—and as for the Rue Cardinet!... Well now, let it be blowing or snowing, in the outer suburbs I prefer to make my way on foot, and I often have as much as fifty or sixty thousand francs about me. I'm well aware I have my revolver in my pocket, but a nasty encounter is a nasty encounter for all that, and a fiacre would cut all that short. But, there you are... Once I'm installed in that wretched coffin on wheels and the cabby takes to the deserted streets, before you can say knife, I go odd in the noddle and an unshakable conviction gets stuck in my head"—with his index finger he touched his forehead between the eyebrows—"one I've done everything to get shot of, and it's not in the least pleasant, that idea, I'll leave you to be the judge of that. No sooner am I trundling along through the dark streets than I'm certain that the cabby is masked; and what sort of a mask is the cabby wearing? A coloured mask, imitating human features, a false face, the *faulx visage* of the mercenaries of the sixteenth century: and what I saw of his flesh under the confining masses of his muffler and his collar becomes in my mind a face of wax or of cardboard screening the most abominable of schemes. Perched on that seat is a squalid footpad; that *faulx visage* is driving me, hell for leather, towards some horrible ambush. Only beyond the fortifications, in the sinister solitudes of Aubervilliers and Saint Ouen will that nightmare fiacre come to a halt, that accursed box on wheels whose cunningly contrived door resists all my efforts, that midnight hearse of which I can no more lower the sealed ventilator than force the concealed lock; and my hair stands on end, I'm running with sweat, choked with horror, already in my imagination murdered, robbed, battered about the head, left for dead, my brains spilling out in a pulp over the hard surface of the road. The fiacre stops, my worried cabby leaps down from his seat, opens the door: 'You all right, guv'nor? Drop off then, did you?' I find myself in the street, at the door of my house, still shuddering from head to foot; and I'm all too pleased to give the flabbergasted cabby a five-franc tip.

"So now you know why I go home on foot."

And, to a unanimous smile, in a toneless voice, Sargine went on:

"And all this is on account of having hired, one Mardi Gras evening, without noticing the fact, a cabby wearing a false nose, a poor inoffensive blighter who, to celebrate the carnival, had adorned his boozer's mug with the traditional pasteboard accoutrement. There was an accident; one of the harness traces broke; the repair would take five minutes and he thought it his duty to warn me; I was half asleep. I opened my eyes, and before me I saw that mask, that horrifying *postiche*...

at one o'clock in the morning, on the Avenue de Villars, behind the Invalides, and I having promised to return to a ball to dance a *cotillon* with a friend's wife. Picture. It was freezing hard that night, fit to split the stones, and the moon stood clear, clear as day, in a sky traversed by inky clouds; I took this to be a nocturnal attack and I pitched into the fellow.

"There you are; since then, I can't help it, it's more than I can do to take a fiacre."

To this de Martimpré countered:

"A fiacre after midnight... there, beyond doubt, you have a state of mind that would definitely put a damper on my evening excursions, I who live in Auteuil, and am not inclined, on any pretext, to go home by rail; for me that's something else entirely! It's in the first-class carriage, the second-class carriage, the first carriage above all, that I go off my head and become literally crazy in the bright lights. And the 12.40, the theatre train, hadn't I taken it often enough, and loved and blessed it time and time again before my little adventure of three years ago? Ah! Hadn't I many a time done as the inhabitants of Neuilly, Passy and Argenteuil do and thrown myself at 12.20 into a fiacre so as to be in the booking-hall at 12.40, and at ten past one at the Boulevard Montmorency, at the end of the line of the last train! It's rather more reassuring, all in all, that half hour in the carriage, than sitting all alone in a fiacre like a hearse, journeying across the equivocal steppes of the Avenue de Versailles with its shady bargees' and tramps' dram-shops, with their shutters closed but the windows still gleaming at one or two in the morning...

"Yes, it made my life a good deal simpler for at least ten years, the suburbanites' dearly-beloved western line: but then, three years ago, oh no! that was it! and it was no laughing matter! Nowadays I prefer to shiver, in the depths of winter, in my furs, my feet benumbed on the already frozen hot-water bottle of a night-time fiacre; and I'm not an ether-addict like Allitof, nor am I an old dotard like Sargine." And the latter having bowed low to indicate his gratitude, de Martimpré settled himself still more comfortably into his Hungarian-embroidered armchair, crossed his legs, one over the other and, in his habitual tone of unconcern continued:

"This is my little adventure. Before I begin, you will of course concede that there is nothing more unnerving—and I would go further and say macabre—than the lighting of the first-class carriages.

"On the Western Line it's quite terrible; it has a brutality about it that emphasises every feature, and distorts them all. It combines something of the arc-lighting in the morgue and the diffused lighting of an operating theatre. In it, every face is deathly pale; the eyes are hollow and the eyelids stand out in exaggerated relief, the nostrils are gorged with darkness and, in those faces, become like death's-heads under the luminous discharge of the lamps, the mouths of the majority are like black chasms. Every little plane of the face's surface, the slightest prominence of bone or muscle, takes on a disquieting relief and, little though the travellers' faces lend themselves to it, without any great effort of the imagination you might easily imagine yourself in a hospital waiting-room in the company of the sick, people in a thoroughly bad way; of stiffs, if you prefer, laid out in a dissecting-room."

"Charming, your prayer for the dying," one of those present remarked, "but a bit on the long side." De Martimpré smiled complaisantly, uncrossed the right leg he had placed over the left and, having resumed the same position in a reverse direction:

"I see we're agreed. You grant me the spectral and truly horrible aspect of the lighting in our railway-carriages. Now I'll come to the point.

"It was four years ago. I'd left the Théâtre du Port Saint-Martin where I had been present at one of the last performances of *Cléopâtre*. Oh! the Botticellian image Sarah evoked in those days, in her swathes of lamé, fastened here and there with turquoise scarabs and Egyptian jewels. Never had her resemblance to the Primavera of the famous Florentine fresco been so preciously underlined and, despite my lack of any taste for Sardou's drama, this was the tenth or eleventh time I had seen it, drawn as I was by the unforgettable plastic vision the great tragedienne presented.

"If I stress which play it was that I had left, it is to make plain to you my state of mind that evening—in no way gloomily inclined, very much to the contrary, seeing that a delicious artistic image still floated, almost living, before me. Thus it was that I climbed into a carriage that was almost at once filled—on the last train the compartments fill up quickly—and we were off. I had not so much as glanced at the seven travelling-companions chance had thrust upon me. On the theatre train there are always plenty of fur coats as far as the men are concerned and, as regards the women, not a few shimmering brocaded silk pelisses; the public, decked out in white ties, begloved and be-jewelled, is elegant enough—indeed positively varnished; and so I paid them no more attention than at any other time; we went on our way and, at every station, couples alighted, and the compartment emptied.

At Trocadéro I thought that I was alone; then I saw that, almost facing me, there was another traveller, dozing on the movable central seat: short, his shoulders hunched almost to his ears, the man sleeping there under the brutal light of the lamp was of a terrifying ugliness; a huge, pear-shaped head, broader at the base than at the apex, a prognathous face with enormous jawbones, its narrow forehead overgrown with shiny, greasy black hair; olive-coloured features, with drooping eyelids, heavy and puffy, the nose short and abrupt, with, in his greenish pallor, the tumid cushions of the pair of thick lips, hideously pendulous, one of those nightmare faces such as Goya has portrayed in his drawings of *comprachicos*, such as are seen in the portraits of the late Habsburgs in the museum in Madrid, the ugliness of the degenerates of a great line relapsed into the murderous ferocity of the brute.

"I watched this man: his fashion of sleeping was repulsive; his heavy eyelids did not quite meet, and between them one could see a little of the whites of his eyes; one would have sworn he was looking out at one from behind the lattice of his lashes; and while he snored, as if to reassure me, with a beastly, deep-throated snorting sound that it is more than I can do to describe, he held across his knees a long, black-gloved hand, a hand at once clenched and inert, immoderately long and extravagantly narrow, that seemed not to fit with the white cuff of his shirt and that certainly could not be the hand that belonged to his body.

"It was becoming an obsession: I could now no longer take my eyes off that hand; suddenly the man rose (it was after the Passy station and the train had just started moving again), took a few steps across the carriage and came to a halt directly in front of me. It was horrible. His heavy eyes were rolled back and the whites were staring at me; the man had thrust his hand into his pocket and, both his arms buried to the elbows in the depths of his overcoat, motionless, without uttering a word, he scanned me searchingly with his glassy eyes—and I saw then that he was asleep.

"Those were five minutes of unforgettable anguish. Oh! that *tête-a-tête* with that strange somnambulist in the silence and amid the jarring motion of that night-train! We were pulling into Auteuil; and the application of the brakes made my companion stagger on his short legs; he all but fell; groaning, he lifted his hands to his eyes and, as if coming suddenly to himself, he made his way to a door and tried to alight on the wrong side of the train. They were shunting and, recovering at last from my fright, I thought I ought to warn him. "Not that way, *this* way," I said, without touching his arm. He stifled another groan and, making no reply, rushed to the far door, which was open; he descended into the darkness... He was gone!

"What a strange traveller! I was about to alight in my turn when my foot struck against something soft; I bent down to look and found myself touching the hand, the horrible gloved hand the somnambulist had forgotten, immoderately long and extravagantly narrow, already cold, inert and clenched.

"It was the hand of a woman, freshly severed—for it was still oozing and left reddish marks on the cushions."

And de Martimpré added, in his languishing tone:

"That's why I never again took the 12.40 train!"

—*Translated by Iain White.*

Isidore Ducasse, Comte de Lautréamont (1846-1870). The known details of the life of this enigmatic figure are certainly few. He was born in Montevideo, his father being a secretary at the French Consulate; sent to France to attend boarding school; parts of *Maldoror* appeared from 1868 onwards; he died of unknown causes during the Commune. No likeness existed until the discovery of a photograph of him in 1977 (Vallotton's portrait was imaginary); only one copy of his second book, *Poésies*, survived from the first publication, the one deposited in the French national library.

De Gourmont was chiefly responsible for rescuing Ducasse's name from its Commune-era grave, an early champion of *Maldoror*, he also rediscovered the text of his second work in 1891. However, his interpretation falls in with the early romantic mythologising of Ducasse: he was reputed (with no apparent evidence) to have composed his books by candlelight at the piano, interspersing the phrases with dramatic musical discords.

It was left to later researchers to rescue Ducasse from madness. The Surrealists admired him unreservedly for his moral ferocity, fantastic metaphors and sudden flashes of dark humour. For them his desire to "inter reason itself" was proof of sanity not madness. The Situationists cited him as the inventor of *détournement*, and numerous other exegetes have laboured over the text of *Maldoror*. Not without result, for they have revealed a work elaborately constructed and carefully executed: far from the interpretation of de Gourmont and his contemporaries, who could hardly be expected to appreciate the prophetic nature of this book which seemed to appear as if from nowhere.

He was a young man of wild and startling originality, a sick genius or frankly a mad genius. Imbeciles go mad and in their madness an agitated or stagnant imbecility remains; but in the madness of genius often genius is left; the form of the intelligence has been affected but not its quality. The fruit in falling has been crushed; but it has kept all its perfume and all the flavour of its barely ripe pulp. Such was the fate of the amazing unknown, Isidore Ducasse...

Les Chants de Maldoror is a long prose poem of which only the first six songs were written... It is a magnificent, almost inexplicable stroke of genius, which will remain unique and from now on belongs to that list of works which, to the exclusion of all classicism, forms the abbreviated library and only possible reading of those whose ill-made spirits will not lend themselves to the everyday joys of the commonplace; or of conventional morality.

Alienists, had they studied this book, would have classified its author among those trying to pass themselves off as persecuted persons: he sees only himself and God in the world—and God thwarts him. But one might also ask oneself whether Lautréamont is not a superior ironist, a man moved by a precocious contempt for men to sham madness whose incoherence is wiser and more beautiful than run-of-the-mill reason. There is in it the madness of pride; there is in it the delirium of mediocrity. How many carefully considered and honest pages of good and simple writing would I give for these shovelfuls of words and phrases beneath which he seems to have wanted to inter reason itself.

THE COMTE DE LAUTRÉAMONT

The Second Song of Maldoror (Extract)

I sought a soul resembling my own and could not find one. I ransacked all the corners of the earth, but to no avail. Yet I could not remain alone. I needed someone to commend my nature, someone whose ideas resembled mine. It was morning: the sun rose on the horizon in all its magnificence, and behold, there also rose before my eyes a young man whose presence caused flowers to bloom in his path. He approached me, and offering his hand, said "I have come to you that seek me. Let us bless this fortunate day." But I replied "Be gone, I did not call you, I have no need of your friendship..." It was evening: night commenced to spread its dark veil across nature. A beautiful woman whom I could hardly distinguish also spread her enchanting influence over me, and looked at me with compassion; yet she dared not speak. I said "Approach, so I may clearly make out your features, for the starlight is not bright enough to illumine them." Then with modest gait and lowered eyes she trod the grass in my direction. As soon as I saw her I said, "I see that goodness and justice have made their home in your heart; we could not live together. Now you admire my beauty, which has dazzled many before you, but sooner or later you will repent having dedicated your love to me, for you do not know my soul. Not that I would ever be unfaithful to you: to she who gives herself with such trust, so freely, so do I give myself with equal trust and abandon. But get this into your head so as never to forget it: wolves and sheep do not look at each other with kindness." What then did I need, I who rejected with such disgust all that was most beautiful in humanity? I could not have said what I needed. I was not yet used to analysing the phenomena of my mind by those means recommended by philosophy. I sat on a rock near the sea. A ship had just hoisted all its sails so as to hold off from the land, and an imperceptible spot made its appearance on the horizon, and was gradually approaching, thrust onwards by the tempest and rapidly increasing in size. The storm was about to unleash its onslaught and already the sky was darkening, assuming a blackness almost as hideous as the human heart. The ship, a large man-of-war, dropped all its anchors, to avoid being swept onto the rocks of the coast. The wind whistled furiously from all four cardinal points, and tore the sails to shreds. Thunderclaps burst amidst flashes of lightning, yet they could not drown the sound of the lamentations to be heard from that floating foundationless house, that mobile sepulchre. The heaving masses of water had not succeeded in breaking the anchor-chains, but their blows had dashed a passage for the water into the ship's hull. An enormous breach: the pumps were unable to drive out the profusion of salt water which crashed in foam upon the deck, like mountains. The imperilled vessel fires distress-signals from its guns, but was sinking slowly, majestically. He who has not seen a ship founder in a hurricane, in the alternating flashes of lightning and pitch-black darkness, while those aboard it are overwhelmed with despair, knows nothing of the accidents of life, as you may well imagine. Finally a unanimous shriek of terrible anguish escapes from the vessel, while the sea redoubles its fearful attacks. It is the cry signifying the surrender of human hopes. Each envelopes himself in a mantle of resignation, and casts his fate into the hands of God. They huddle together like a flock of sheep.

The imperilled vessel fires distress-signals from its guns, but was sinking slowly, majestically.

All day long they have worked the pumps, but in vain. Night has come, deep and implacable, to add the finishing touches to this pleasant sight. Each man tells himself that once in the water he will no longer be able to breathe, for as far back as he can remember, there seem to have been no fish among his ancestors. Yet he urges himself to hold his breath for as long as possible, so as to prolong his life by two or three seconds; such is the vengeful irony with which he would confront death . . .

The imperilled vessel fires distress-signals from its guns, but was sinking slowly, majestically.

He does not know that the final plunge of a sinking ship creates a powerful folding-in of the swell upon itself; that slime and mud is mixed with the troubled waters, and that a pressure rising from below, a counterblast to the tempest wreaking its destruction above, stirs the watery element with sudden undertows and shocks. So in spite of the stock of self-possession which he has summoned in advance, this man—soon to be drowned—should, after more adequate reflection, be perfectly content to prolong his life in these whirlpools of the deep for only half a normal breath, at the very most. He will find that his supreme desire: to defy death, is quite impossible.

The imperilled vessel fires distress-signals from its guns, but was sinking slowly, majestically.

No, I am mistaken. It no longer fires its guns, nor does it sink. The nut-shell is utterly engulfed. O heaven! How continue living, after experiencing such delights! It had just been my lot to witness the dying agonies of dozens of my fellow-men. Minute by minute I followed the ebb and flow of their anguish. At one moment, the bellowing of some old woman, driven mad with terror, was at a premium. At another the mere howling of a child at the breast drowned out the captain's orders. The vessel was too far away for me to be able to catch distinctly the groans carried on the squall, but I made it seem closer by an act of will, and the optical illusion was complete. Every fifteen minutes or so—when a gust of wind stronger than the others carried the lugubrious plaints above the cry of the terrified petrels, and dislocated the ship with longitudinal splits that only increased the wailing of those who were about to be offered as a sacrifice to death—I plunged the sharp point of a steel rod into my cheek and thought secretly, "They are suffering more than I." Thus I at least had a means of comparison. I shouted to them from the shore, hurling oaths and imprecations. I felt they could hear me. It seemed to me that my hatred and my words crossed the distance, abolished the laws of sound, and arrived distinctly at their ears, deafened by the roaring of the enraged ocean! It seemed to me that they must be thinking of me and breathing forth their vengeance in impotent rage. From time to time I cast my eyes on the cities which slept on the land; assured that nobody suspected that a ship was about to sink but a few miles from the shore, with birds of prey as its crown and a pedestal of empty-bellied aquatic monsters, I took courage, hope returned to me: I was certain of their destruction! They could not escape! As an extra precaution I had fetched my double-barrelled gun, so that should any shipwrecked sailor attempt to swim towards the rocks, to escape his imminent death, I could frustrate his intentions with a bullet in the shoulder. With the storm at its height, I saw an energetic head with its hair on end swimming desperately through the waters. He swallowed pints of water and sank into the depths, buffeted like a cork. But soon he reappeared, his hair streaming, defying death as he stared at the shore. He was admirably self-possessed! A large bleeding wound, caused by some sharp hidden rock, was slashed across his fearless and noble face. He could not have been more than sixteen years old, for through the flashes which illumined the darkness a peach-like down could be seen on his upper lip. And now he was no more than two hundred metres from the shore, and I could easily observe his face. What courage! Such intrepid spirit! How the determined poise of his head seemed to defy fate, as he split the waves powerfully, their furrows opening reluctantly before him! . . . I had made up my mind beforehand. I owed it to myself to keep my promise; their last hour had struck for all of them, and not one must escape. Such was my resolve, and nothing would change it. A sharp report was to be heard, and the head disappeared at once, not to be seen again. I did not obtain as much pleasure from that murder as you might imagine; and it was only because I was sated with continued killing that I repeated it out of sheer force of habit, impossible to give up, but which affords only minor amusement. The sense of pleasure is soon blunted, hardened. How could I feel sensual excitement at the death of this individual, when more than a hundred others would soon parade before me in their last battle against the waves when the ship eventually sank? There was not even the thrill of risk in that murder, for human justice, cradled by the hurricane of that terrible night, was sleeping in the houses a few streets away from me. Now that the years weigh my body down I can say with sincerity, as a supreme and solemn truth, that I was not as cruel as men often said; but sometimes their wickedness persevered in its destruction for years on end. Then my anger was limitless; I had fits of cruelty; I became terrible to anyone of my species who should happen to meet my haggard stare. If it were a horse or a dog I let it pass: have you heard what I just said? Unfortunately I was in one of those fits on the night of this storm; my reason departed me (ordinarily I was equally cruel, but more prudent); and everything that fell into my hands on this occasion was doomed to die; I am not trying to excuse my sins. The fault is not all with my fellow creatures. I am merely pointing out as I await the last judgement, which makes me scratch my neck in anticipation. But what does the last judgement matter to me! My reason never departs me, I said that only to deceive you. And when I commit a crime, I know what I am doing: I did not intend something else! Standing on the rock, while the hurricane whipped my hair and my cape, I watched with ecstasy as the powerful tempest harried this ship beneath a starless sky. Triumphant, I followed all the vicissitudes of the drama, from the moment when the vessel cast its anchors to the moment when it foundered, a fatal garment dragging down into the bowels of the sea those who had clothed themselves in it as in a coat. But the moment was coming when I myself was about to participate in these scenes of natural disorder. When the place where the vessel had suffered the onslaught showed clearly that it had gone to pass its remaining days on the bed of the sea, then some of those who had been washed off it by the waves reappeared on the surface. They clasped their arms about one another, two by two and three by three; it was a sure method of not saving their lives, they hampered each other's movements and they sank like jugs peppered with holes . . . What is that army of sea-monsters which is rapidly cleaving the waves? There are six of them, their fins are powerful, and cleave a passage through the heaving billows. Out of all those human beings waggling their four limbs in that unsteady continent, the sharks soon make an omelette with no eggs, and share it out according to the law of the strongest. Blood mixes with water, and water with blood. Their fierce eyes are sufficient to light up this scene of carnage . . . But what is that other tumult of the waters, yonder on the horizon? Like an approaching water spout. What strength! I see what it is. An enormous female shark has come for a share of the duck's liver paté, and to partake of cold boiled beef. She rages, and arrives ravenous. A battle begins between her and the other sharks for possession of the few throbbing limbs which silently float here and there upon the surface of the red cream. She snaps her jaws to right and left, causing mortal wounds; but three living sharks still surround her, forcing her to thrash and turn in every direction to thwart their manoeuvres. With a growing emotion such as he had never before experienced, the spectator on the shore follows this new variety of naval engagement. His eyes are fixed on that brave female shark with such strong teeth. He hesitates no longer, puts his gun to his shoulder, and with his usual skill lodges the second ball in one of the sharks in the moment when it showed itself above the waves. Two sharks remain, who only increase their fury. The man with briny spittle hurls himself from the cliff into the sea and swims towards the agreeably tinted carpet, clasping in his hand the steel knife which never leaves him. Now each shark has an enemy to face. He advances towards his wearied adversary and, taking his time, he plunges his wetted blade into its belly. The mobile fortress easily disposes of the last opponent. The swimmer and the female shark whose life he has saved remain face to face. They look into each other's eyes for some few minutes, and each is astonished to discover the ferocity of the other's gaze. They swim round and round, neither letting the other out of sight, saying to themselves, "I was mistaken: here is another more wicked than myself." Then of one accord, in mutual admiration, they slide towards each other under the water, the female shark pushing the water aside with her fins, Maldoror beating the waves with his arms, holding their breath in profound veneration, each one desirous of contemplating his living double for the first time. Three metres away from each other, like two lovers they fell quickly against each other without any effort, and kissed each other with dignity and recognition, in an embrace as tender as that of a sister and a brother. Carnal desire quickly follows that demonstration of friendship. Two sinewy thighs clung tightly round the monster's viscous skin like two bloodsuckers, the arms and fins interlocked round the body of the beloved object which they encircled with love, while their throats and chests were soon only one glaucous mass redolent of seaweed; in the midst of the storm that still raged, in the glare of the flashes, their marriage bed a foamy wave, carried by a submarine current as in a cradle, and rolling over each other towards the depths of the abyss, they united in a long, chaste and hideous coupling . . . At last I had found someone who resembled me! Now I would no longer be alone in life. She, with the same ideas as myself! . . . I was face to face with my first love!

—*Translated by John Harman.*

Edouard Dujardin (1868-1933). Music and its connection with *vers libre* were Dujardin's main preoccupation. He was a co-founder of *La Revue wagnérienne* which championed the work of Wagner when any appreciation of "boche" culture was generally frowned upon. Dujardin became an active historian of Symbolism, chairing academic conferences on the movement and writing a study of the first appearance of *vers libre* (*Les Premiers Poètes du vers libre*, 1922). Dujardin's most famous work, however, is his novel *Les Lauriers sont coupés* (1888), it was there that James Joyce discovered the "interior monologue" which he later used in *Ulysses*. Three different translations have appeared over the years, including ones by George Moore and Stuart Gilbert.

The story here is from his first book, *Les Hantises* (*Obsessions*, 1886).

Having taken charge of the literary columns in the waning days of Naturalism, Edouard Dujardin led it along the two roads that had to rejoin later on, the one side leading toward Ibsen, the other to French Symbolism...

In the midst of these multiple activities, and even during the hours of his Wagnerian apostolate, Dujardin did not forget about himself: he wrote stories, poems, a novel and a dramatic trilogy, The Legend of Antonia...

"One day, as I viewed the faded portrait of a young girl in an album, someone passed who spoke a name...

"And so I knew you; having heard your name, you, I shall dream of you."

Thus begins a poem to the glory of this woman of dream whom one recognises, memory or vision, "adorable face," in many of the other pages in which she is the symbol of the ideal, the inaccessible. They are very sweet, these poems in lazily rhythmed prose and have great purity of tone; and Antonia always rises in the final lines, calling the poet to impossible loves...

As with his prose, Dujardin's poetry is always wise, prudent and calm; if there are lapses of language here, experiments in syntax that are somewhat daring, the thought is sure-footed, logical, reasonable...

From logic, sincerity, will, gentleness and sentiment, with the disinterested love for art especially in its most novel forms, come the words in which we can, I think, read the character of Edouard Dujardin. His literary works, although very wayward, remain always very personal; and that is a merit without which all the others are null.

EDOUARD DUJARDIN

The Iron Maiden 🙟

A woman once said to me:

"Now and then, the men we love and who belong to us escape us. Suddenly, even as we are speaking to them, we see that their gaze, suddenly vague, is fixed upon nothing at all. As we tidy a lock of hair, their spirit is flying far away; what are they staring at so wild-eyed? What new sensation, what new idea is fascinating them?... and then everything vanishes, the wicked vision effaces itself, and—there they are!—smiles, tenderness, attention. But we remain troubled and nervous, because we do not know the chimerical regions to which they have flown, and we tremble, lest they return, shuddering, from unknown depths."

That is what the woman said. After a moment's reverie I replied:

"Yes, now and then an extraordinary vision rises up before my eyes, sudden and clear; something terrible embraces my soul, and steals into my blood, my marrow, my nerves and my muscles. I remain, rooted in a vertiginous immobility, prey to an atrocious intoxication, fuddled with anguish. Then, just as a spark will sputter out, it disappears. The memory comes back, only much later, uncertain, as if in a dream. But in my soul, I retain a fear that, if the vision had been prolonged by even a fraction of a second, my reason might have succumbed to the delirium of the hallucination."

We fell silent. Just then a man, who was seated with his head bowed toward his knees in the corner of the artist's studio, revealed his face. His back was bent, his cheeks were pale and drawn, his face wrinkled and his hair grey, yet he did not seem to be an old man. He was tall and thin, his clothes were elegant, and his manners, careless. His eyes, which were very black, seemed to shine and sparkle when he became animated, at times a most disdainful smile caused his lips to part themselves. His body remained hunched, bent forward, his arms folded over his thighs; he made no gesture; his voice was halting, ironic. Finally, there was a sort of gloomy transport during which his eyes caught fire. And he said to us:

"Listen to the story I am going to tell you, and if it occurs to you that I myself am its hero, believe it or not as you please!"

"It was the habit of my hero to rove the world in the company of his beautiful mistress: the two of them were truly in love, parading together in joyful insouciance from city to city. They wandered through the voluptuous sites of Germany. Having crossed the heroic Rhine, the rolling hills of Baden, the Main with its melancholy dales, they now found themselves in the merry old streets of Nuremberg, with sweet loves of bygone days.

"That day they went to see the castle of Nuremberg.

"All along the sunny route, some strangers walked alongside in a pretty little caravan: through a few overheard words spoken in French they knew them to be fellow countrymen. There were two young ladies and their husbands. They joined together. And all of them, chattering and laughing, climbed, slowly, in pairs, toward the massive walls, where the pink parasols and flounces were reflected.

"In the castle they toured a museum of torture instruments. The full panoply of medieval punishments was there on display: racks, wheels, pincers, spits, bellows, and other devices both terrible and strange. Their aspect caused Lucy to press herself close against her lover's breast. He squeezed her pale hands more tightly, and dreamed of those poor wretches who were once put to the torture beneath the vaults. They studied the place in tender silence, and pity aroused their love so that their lips soon sought each other out in kiss after kiss.

"The guide returned to conduct the tourists into a hidden room: after a few moments, in the centre of the room, they distinguished a human form in the darkness, upright, a crudely formed statue of wood and iron, a woman in a great stiff cloak. The guide proceeded to pull at two doors which opened outwards from the centre of the statue, revealing within, a space large enough for a man. The inner walls and the two door-leaves bristled with long iron spikes. When the doors were closed, these points became transpierced and rent the eyes, cheeks, the bowels and all the rest of the condemned person's body.

"The little group of Parisians were silent. Lucy stole a peek from behind her gloved hands. She abandoned herself in her lover's arms, her back curved and quivering, while he, supporting her, and breathing in the slight warmth of her hair, studied the monster. Becoming accustomed to it, she unshielded her eyes, shook her head, and, all at once, she cried, noisily. Finally she exclaimed that it was too clever.

"The young woman approached it. She nonchalantly walked up to the statue, slapping the bloody inner wall with a glove, and, with her finger-tips she tested, humorously, the sharp points, undulled after centuries of usage. She posed before the opening in a winsome way, stooping, she inspected the interior; and, while the rest of the group amused itself with pranks, she, pluckily, through childishness, through the petty bravado of a rebellious girl, in spite of the guide's warnings, climbed in, cuddled herself against its terrible sides, allowing her parasol and her white and rosy skirts to become stuck to its cramped steel walls.

" 'Close it, and everything will be ended,' she said.

"And there she stood in front of her lover, laughing, between the two outstretched arms of the colossus, like an open coffin, ready for torture. That is how her lover—who tried gently, to restrain her, and called her mad, and scolded her—saw her.

"Then a haze arose inside his brain, it seemed to him as if the Maid of Iron had moved her arms. He seemed to see the Maid of Iron pulling in her frightful arms, and as she did so, closing them upon his adored mistress, and that she was enclosed there, her sweet flesh pierced, torn, crushed between the iron spikes, horribly shredded. He saw the horror of the gaping wounds, the punctured eyes, the gashed breasts, the blood trickling down the cherished flanks like from a sieve. Grimacing, he saw the face of his beautiful beloved, defiled, a spike staving in that mouth he had kissed, and this beautiful body that he had feverishly covered with his lips, this beautiful perfumed body from which he had breathed in every pleasure, he now believed, as a result of this sudden vision, he had seen kneaded beneath the nails of the Maiden of Maidens. And—mysterious magic of the heart—from this hideous contemplation which had so fascinated him with such a fierce pleasure, such an infernal and diabolical elation, his being became so fuddled at this point with the idea of her lost and himself damned, such was the extraordinary intoxication of these thoughts of horrific sufferings, that with a savage, hoarse cry, he hurled himself at the monster, and, with his own two hands, sealed his beloved mistress in the death-embrace of the iron Maiden.

199 Gustave Kahn

Gustave Kahn (1859-1936). Kahn founded *La Vogue* in 1886, the most successful review of early Symbolism and the first to publish Rimbaud's *Les Illuminations* and *Une Saison en Enfer*, as well as Mallarmé et al, he then founded *Le Symboliste* and edited *La Revue Indépendante*. Credited by Dujardin and others with the creation of *vers libre*, the form in which his first book of poems—which was already moving in the direction of Decadence—*Les Palais Nomades* (1887) was written. The prose poems included here are from this great collection and serve to introduce the themes explored by the verse in each section of the book.

...If there still remains, in some of his pages, a touch of rhetoric, it is because Monsieur Kahn, even at the feet of the Shulamite, has not given up the idea of surprising us with a mountebank's and virtuoso's endlessly renewed adroitness, and if, on occasion, he treats the French language as a tyrant might, this is because it has always shown him all the obligingness of a slave. To some extent he abuses his power, giving to certain words meanings that are unduly wide of the mark, bending sentences to a syntax that is too perfunctory; but these habits are not exclusively his own; he has borrowed from no one his knowledge of rhythm and his mastery of the newly recast verse-line.

Was Kahn the first? To whom do we owe vers libre?* To Rimbaud, whose Les Illuminations *first appeared in the pages of* Vogue *in 1886, to Laforgue who at that same time, and in that same precious little review—which was edited by Gustave Kahn—published* Légende *and* Solo de Lune, *and, lastly, to Kahn himself... and above all to Walt Whitman, who had then commenced to enjoy his majestic licence.*

This tiny Vogue, which today sells for the price of an illuminated parchment, was then read beneath the arcades of the Odéon—with such joy!—by timid young men intoxicated by the scent of newness that rose from its pale little pages!...

Words, words! without a doubt, but well-chosen ones and artfully mixed. Gustave Kahn is, above all else, an artist: which is sometimes a disadvantage.

GUSTAVE KAHN

Prose Interludes from **Nomadic Palaces**

Themes and Variations

In the lofty chamber, beneath candelabra blacken with smoke, in the lofty chamber, hermetic with the straight metallic pleats of heavy curtains.

The fumes descend, gyre, twist elliptically, striate and vanish in a midnight echoing with copper tones, dreams float heavy with flakes of smoke.

One night in the memory strewn with the dead of tentacular systems, and with the humus of the ancients, identical, sufferings are revived; the useless pagodas, constructed in haste from memories, have collapsed; and along rivers impassable for twenty years, the boats dismasted.

Ruins that vanish, implacable descent toward the abyss. Muted, the memory wells forth out of legends, and what was orchestral vapour becomes distinct, and a motif, come to the moment of living, cries out.

Recitative

A lull imposes itself, dreary and monotonous.

Tiresome, this slumbering of the idea. In bluish distance, memories glide along, so fragile, pale, melancholy.

In a theatre somewhere unknown; figurines pass in a sad apotheosis, bow, veer into oblivion.

Forcefulness lost, indulgence is at hand, and the remembrance of unforgotten moments of silence, haunted by sweetness and sorrow, consolers of memory.

Interlude

Ah! let the time come
When hearts fall in love.
  —ARTHUR RIMBAUD.

The evocative witchcraft of chance gives rise to similarities.

Memory vibrates, like an arrow feathered with sorrow; the vision, the very same, of identicals, flows in light and shadow. The chalk-line of streets, the quietening of market-places and squares, are evocative. Memory's sufferings are worsened. by simularities.

Present desire vaguely murmurs towards the past, towards the distant; chimeras unfurl in the taverns; and the bass of the harmonic development of peripatetic chance, the smiles and effaced timbres of another cycle; the similar arouses similar beings, only differently labelled.

And, without seeking the exit from the labyrinth, where the poor soul sleepwalks, perpetual rebirths, the perpetual awakenings of cravings, deceptive rebirths are revived.

captive, the one doomed to ill-chosen downfalls.

After the crisis and the calm, in the momentary silence, listen in all serenity to its voices, the voices of your times gone by.

Song of Temporary Insanity

The brief harmony beneath the bright branches is undone by slow sorrow.

The dispersed lassitude, which far-away hours entombed in the spirit, adjusts a winter cloak to the flesh not fresh enough.

Nothing survives this brief instant, the harmony evaporates in regrets, the act is dissonant, then is resolved, nothing comes alive again nor flowers anew.

Soon, towards the far-away buried hours, this moment too. Let us return to the necessary lassitudes.

Voice in the Park

Inflections of dear voices that have died.
—PAUL VERLAINE.

Fleeting are the times of love; enduring the hoppings of the little serf whose gaze you ennoble.

The long weariness of enslavements, and of muffled struggles and of feebleness. Its wretched, paltry irony is without a smile; a modicum of pity for the eternal

Lieder

And since everything is alike, all the suns of the years, all the sufferings of the days, hear the soul of legend rustle and fall.

    The old dream stirs in an affectionate atmosphere, with distant sorrows and facile forgivings; listen to your dead brothers smiling in time.

    Observe the legendary garden, the deep eyes briefly glimpsed, and the eternal roving ships, and the song that is heard on every road. Observe the motley garb of the wayfarers, and beneath so many robes, so many similar hearts.

Memorial

To the instant of luminous life, to the error sought out and cherished, crossroads of the voices of life, everything indefatigably returns.

    Regrets that might have lacked some sweetness. So beautiful is everything that is lost, so regretted everything exiled, so desired all that is expelled, in the evil hours of loneliness.

    To flee towards the past, and assert the veracity of the illusion, the feeble feats, and always and everywhere the recent past returns, troubled and devastated.

    Which first moment threw us, feeble, at the feet of clay; which ineluctable future commands that sorrow and silence be separated.

    Everywhere and always the recent past, the moment that perpetuates solitary fear.

Finale

And when will repose descend upon this poor being?

    Must he wait, his back broken, his eye lifeless, and the rags of his cloak in the pensive hands of a few regrets, here and there, which moreover he ignored.

    Collating scattered ephemeral glances, haunted by disgust, seated on the banal river bank, the ulcer of memory loathsome, will he see the heavy barges of his dreams forever crawling by?

    Weary of the glass and cup, of landscapes and of the human, cosily bending his brow to the memory of hands, calming hands, so small and so sharply sinewed, gaping on words that are lacking and no longer able to hear, a speechless Job, wreckage of his wreckage... Will the repose of this poor being be thus? Perhaps, for the poor fellow.

In the unconsoled hovel that's never decked out for any festival, the former masks are gathering dust in the corners, and boredom is expunging in greyness the useless tomes of the lovers of yesteryear; turning in the void.

Of surmised Babylon, of the country never born, enumerate only brute forces. The curtain of forgetfulness of preparatory deaths has fallen into the opacity of silence and is no more than a memory of the Moloch of adolescence.

The Phantasmagoria of the unelucidated times of childhood, the passing memory of the disappointed, the embers of the fires of yore, and blackness around the eyes, before the eyes, is this everything then? and the brutal undertow of who knows what ebb-tide.

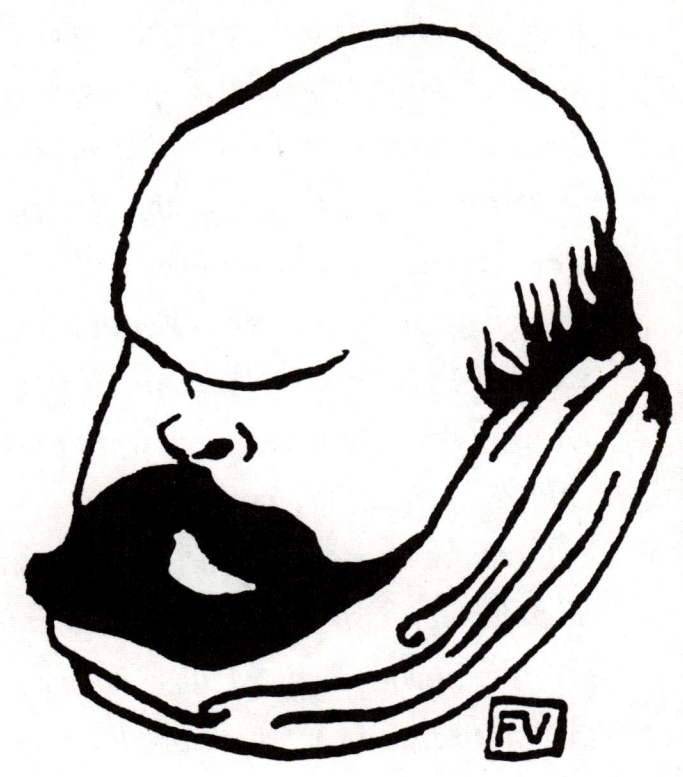

205 P. Verlaine

Paul Verlaine (1844-1896). Older than most of the other authors in this selection, Verlaine was a vital influence, not only through his later poetry but his encouragement and support of younger writers, especially, but not exclusively, in *Les Poètes maudits*.

He began publishing with the Parnassians, married, encountered Rimbaud and embarked on a messy homosexual relationship which took him around the less attractive parts of Europe on a drunken debauch which ended in prison when Verlaine shot and wounded Rimbaud. There he converted to Catholicism but lapsed frequently afterwards and became a familiar figure, absinthe-besotted, in the cafés of bohemian Paris. Nevertheless he somehow seemed able to pick himself up and return to poetry, composing numerous collections, including erotic lyrics which have made recent appearances in English. He was elected "Prince of Poets" on the death of Leconte de Lisle, but died himself of poverty and neglect soon afterwards.

His prose is scarce, the present tribute to Poe (from 1886) seems never to have been translated before.

Verlaine is a temperament, and as such, indefinable. Like his life itself, the rhythms he loves are broken or run-on lines; he accomplished the disjoining of Romantic verse and—having rendered it shapeless, having bored into it and unstitched it in order that he might allow entrance to a greater variety of things: all the effervescence that bubbled from his crazy head—he was, without desiring it, one of the instigators of free verse. Verlaine's verse, with its words split between lines, its incidences, its parentheses, naturally evolved into free verse; in becoming "free" it has only regularised its own condition...

To confess one's sins of action or of dream is not a sin; no public confession can scandalise a man because all men are alike and are tempted alike; no one commits a crime that his brother is not also capable of. That is why pious journals or the Academy took upon themselves in vain the shame of having abused Verlaine, still garlanded with flowers; kicks from the boots of scoundrels, and the sacristan as well, come to grief upon a plinth already of granite, while in his marble beard, Verlaine smiled from eternity, with the look of a Faun who hears bells tolling.

PAUL VERLAINE

> *It stands there, signpost of baleful highways.*
> CATULLE MENDES

The Signpost

Edgar Poe told me, one day, with that lucidity of expression which never deserted him in the midst of the greatest flights of his magnificent imagination, that, in his opinion, *the majority of our errors have their origin in the facility with which our mind exaggerates or underrates the importance of an object, because it is unable to grasp exactly the relative closeness or distance of that object.* —While doing justice to the considerable measure of obvious truth contained in that proposition, I could not forbear to contest the axiomatic form in which it was cast, which seemed to me to set on one side a whole series of facts no less interesting than those which seemed to me admissible in the judgement my shrewd friend had just pronounced. By that I meant the hallucinations, visions or transfigurations of everyday objects produced by the moral forces of our being, conscience, foreboding, memory, *and so on*, and I contended that these facts hardly admitted of a categorical explanation, and that the wisest course to pursue, when faced with them, was equivocation, if not acceptance, pure and simple, and respect. Since I had employed some warmth and perhaps a certain eloquence in setting out these ideas, Edgar Poe seemed to be listening to me with interest and, the conversation continuing on that subject, I went on to tell him a story about my youth which was not irrelevant to the matter in question. This is it:

"Business had called me to a little village a fair distance from Paris, so that it was a stretch of genuine countryside I had to traverse on foot after alighting from the train. It was June. They were tossing the hay, which spread an exhilarating scent in the cool air which the nine-o'clock rays of the morning sun were warming. I soon reached a rather large wood, through which there ran a broad, grassy walk, speckled here and there with pale patches of light. Song-birds, especially jays, were creating an uproar among the gently swaying beech-trees and, in the distance, one could hear the laughter of women, cheerful at turning the hay, of which wisps were flying up, soon to be snatched by the many swallows. On leaving the wood I caught sight of a signpost which stood there, just where it should be; for, not having been there for many years, I had rather forgotten the way. It was a signpost with four arms, set out in a cross. On each of the arms, painted white, as was the post, in letters of black, somewhat effaced by foul weather, was the name of a village as well as the number of kilometres to cover in order to reach it. It would take me a good quarter of an hour, and the road the signpost indicated was delightful. I followed it at a leisurely pace, and soon I saw the steeple of the little village of J——. Yielding, then, to an access of indolence, and tempted by the soft grass, I lay down on the ground, and I lay there for some time. When I rose, the air caressed my face, some birds pecking in a nearby field were chirping, big white clouds, pierced by the sun, were floating in the azure distance; the scent of hay came to me in heady whiffs and, deep down in the valley, between the trees, the thatched roofs and the tiles of the village where excellent relatives awaited me, gleamed. A thrill of delight took hold of me and I began thinking that, all things considered, here was happiness, and that it was a great mistake to live in towns.

"I got up and, instinctively, my eyes focused on the way I had come, while I stretched with that healthy pleasure that follows upon agreeable meditations. The wood, of which I have already spoken, was turning blue, some distance away, and, against that sombre background, the signpost, of which I now saw only the arm pointing in the direction of J——, stood out; in the state of mind in which I found myself, that pointing arm seemed to me a benevolent exhortation on the part of Destiny to be on my way and make haste to the goal of my journey. Which I did, with eagerness, and singing a sprightly final chorus, heard once in some hilarious light comedy.

"Three months later I left J——, retracing the road in question; this time I was no longer alone: a charming, run-of-the-mill love-affair had occurred in my life during those three months spent among the fields. I had lived, or rather we had been living happily, in all the conditions of security that could be desired, when I know not what brutal desire for sole possession made me resolve upon an "abduction."

"Prudence demanding it, we set out at night, on foot, comparable in the lightness of our baggage to robbers without booty, and happy as larks. A small bull's-eye lantern with a fairly far-reaching beam guided our steps. We held hands, conversing as we went. All of a sudden I felt my body bathed in a sort of cold sweat and, to the great astonishment of my companion, my prattling ceased. At the same time I began looking about us. It was a dreadful night. The sky, of an obscurity more livid than dark, was blotched here and there with pallid patches like vast stains of mildew. A few blurred stars were glittering uncertainly. Austere, in a place apart, Saturn gleamed red. The earth, sodden from many days of torrential rain, was treacherously slippery underfoot. At the same time something extraordinary was taking place within me: my conscience was reproaching what I was doing there and, for the first time, my liaison with the person accompanying me seemed like an evil deed. More, the imprudence and folly of that abduction was becoming self-evident to me. To all these arguments of the innermost heart, I could oppose only the justification of revolutions: *it is too late!*—and I was quickening our pace, grasping my mistress's hand more firmly, when the beam of my lantern raised up before my eyes the white spectre of a SIGNPOST whose arm, pointing towards me, imperiously called upon me to turn about and retrace my steps. The sensation of icy horror that sight evoked in me is hard to credit: the arm of the signpost was there, terrible and implacable in its immobility. I quickly turned aside my lantern and the sinister vision vanished; but the impression remained with me and, in the darkness, my eyes saw that thing, very near, and black against the grey sky. The wood was moaning lugubriously in the bitter wind. No longer able to bear the shameful terror, and taking as my pretext the very imminent departure of the train, I urged my companion to run and, ran myself, ran like a deer. A horrible impact pulled me up short: at the very least my whole shoulder was grazed if not broken. Nonetheless, so great was my fear, that I had fortitude enough not to raise a murmur. For it was the signpost that had—*as a last warning*—run at me so forcibly. We ran like madmen. About us the night continued appalling. Before long we plunged into the wood, an into the unknown.

"Several weeks went by, at the end of which I became the contumacious hero of one of the most shocking judicial dramas ever to have diverted the curiosity of the citizens of Paris. The investigating magistrate and the public prosecutor had no reason, this time, to "find the lady." The lady was there, in glass jars, along with sundry other pieces of material evidence.

"Maitre ———, the pleader appointed by the court, here made his justified reputation as an emotional orator. I, at that time, had hopped on a ship to America.

"I lived there for twenty years, by turns banker and cafe-waiter, journalist and swindler, I experienced every luxury and every ordeal, committed every crime, exhausted every passion, in a word, did everything. In Charleston, where I was a penny-a-line scribbler, I was for a long time Edgar Poe's opium-companion and, to a degree, his collaborator. Later, in my capacity as a slave-owner, I joined the Confederate army, in which I became a colonel. Proscribed after the capture of Davis, and to some extent involved in the Booth -Lincoln case, I made my way to Mexico at the height of the Second War of Independence during which, without taking any side, I placed myself at the head of a gang whose exploits still, at this moment, arouse fear and trembling in Matamoros, Oaxaca and Querataro. Grown rich, indeed immensely rich after this venture, I judged it appropriate to return to the United States to take advantage of the amnesties. On the banks of the Hudson, I built a cottage among the trees. I lived a very comfortable life there, I assure you, but—if it need be said at all—not always at peace with my memories. Just consider it! And reflect that I was often obliged to dream of the guillotine and of the gallows, that they had all but shot me near Guadalajara, and that I had spent months as a prisoner of the savages!

"But among all these terrible things there is none, when memory or sleep are unkind to me, none which fills me with so intense a terror, which so freezes the marrow in my bones and the blood in my veins as that white-painted signpost, seen long ago near a wood, in the beam of a bull's-eye lantern, one night when I was on my way to a railway-station in the company of a loveable young person."

—*Translated by Iain White*.

André Rouveyre, *Remy de Gourmont.*

211 G.-ALBERT AURIER

George-Albert Aurier (1865-1892). A poet and *prosateur*, Aurier contributed to most of the important Symbolist magazines during his brief life, and was a founder of the *Mercure de France*. He is principally recognised today as an important art theorist and wrote the first essay on Van Gogh (1890), then totally unknown. Articles on Gauguin, Pissarro, Carrière etc. followed, attempting to formulate the ideas underlying Symbolist painting. He edited a short-lived journal of his own *Le Moderniste*, wrote a couple of novels, short stories (for one of which he was prosecuted for outraging public morals), verse, and dramas before his premature death from typhoid, aged 27. Almost forgotten in this century, his works received renewed attention from the *Collège de 'Pataphysique* which devoted an issue of their journal to him in 1961.

This text is from the *Mercure* of April 1890.

Possessing a non-compromising temperament, that of ironic observer, and a tendency toward Rabelaisian joviality, Aurier found himself, during his early student years, taking part in a literary grouping which appeared, at least, to be utterly opposed to his inclinations... Aurier sinned less through omission than through youth, and if he demonstrated a talent which was, perhaps, less reliable than his intelligence, the faculties of the soul do not develop at the same time; and in him intellect flowered first and drew to itself the best part of his vital juices.

In his study of Gauguin he developed the elementary principles of Symbolist or Ideist art, which he summed up thus:

The work of art will have to be:

1. Ideist, *since its sole ideal will be the expression of the Idea.*

2. Symbolist, *since it will express this idea through forms.*

3. Synthetic, *since it will set down these forms, these signs, in accordance with a generally understood practice.*

4. Subjective, *since the object will never be considered as an object, but as the sign of an idea perceived by the subject.*

5. (and consequently) Decorative: *because decorative painting in its proper sense, as it was understood by the Egyptians, and most probably the Greeks and the Primitives, is nothing more nor less than the manifestation of art at once subjective, synthetic, symbolist and ideist.*

Having interpolated that decorative *art is the only art, that "painting could not have been created only in order to adorn the banal walls of man's edifices with thoughts, dreams and ideas," he still further imposes upon the artist the necessary gift of* emotiveness, *urging only "that transcendental emotiveness, so precious, so impressive, which causes the soul to tremble before the ever-changing drama of abstractions."*

When graced with this gift, symbols, which is to say Ideas, surge from the shadows, become animated, take on a life that is no longer our contingent and relative life, but an essential life, the life of Art, the being of Being. Graced with this gift, art is complete, perfect, absolute, finally real."

Doubtless, all this, at bottom, is a philosophy rather than a theory of art, and I will be suspicious of any artist, even one superlatively gifted, who applies himself to realize it through his works; nevertheless this is an exalted and possibly fecund philosophy and perhaps a few artists will be touched, even through their armour of unconsciousness.

...This was a man of more than ordinary talent, a superior spirit; he must not be forgotten: we can still read his novels, sample more than a page of his verse and, for a long time, his art criticisms will supply ideas, principles and a method.

THE BOOK OF MASKS

G.-ALBERT AURIER

Nocturne And it is still, as everywhere, as always, beneath this banal heraldic ceiling and amid the undistinguished sadism of these none too clerical stained-glass windows, it is still the same proud murmur of the crowd, the same inane lapping of the ocean—an ocean whose waves seem to be grotesquely anthropomorphised... The seaside resort of my soul, my poor sick soul!... Something, to tell the truth, like a psychological Trouville!...

Set amid the old carved-oak panelling, the threadbare Flemish tapestries strut on the walls their faded verdures, their dwarfish drunkards, their beery and sluggish gaieties, their whole charming gamut of calm subdued hues that, brutal and frozen, the keen diamond of an Edison lamp illumines... This dissonance enchants me. It enchants me as much as the little bomb-shaped chocolate-cakes, among all this very gothic furniture, and the disquieting cylinders of jet that adorn the surging sea of occiputs, as much as the cigarettes that smoulder between the unduly scarlet lips of those ladies over there, sumptuous and plaster-coated as the facades... Why inconvenience myself and not simply repeat: my soul has the colic. That such admissions involve ridicule, raillery, I know... In what way, though, are these simple words any more grotesque than the conduct of that well-known herbalist who, in the words of the poet, gave

Ipecacuanha to a cockatoo...

"Would you bring me something to write with, eh?..."

To write with? What's the point? In short, what's the point? Are the anthropomorphic waves not breaking over the epidermis of my soul? I'm at the seaside. Why should I write? And for whom? And to whom? What do I know? But I must do it! Certainly, I must. Ah! the eternal priapism of the writing desk!...

Look at them, male and female, taking their ease in the peace of their long-drawn-out deglutitions... Doubtless, through a slow endosmosis, their liquid brains are flowing away, bit by bit, with the beers gulped down... Their newly liquescent brains are running down into their bellies, and thence into the urinals...

As for me, just now, I feel as though myriads of tormenting flies' feet were titillating my trembling nerves, and my capillaries, and my medullae, and my fibres, and all the cells of my brain (above all those of the circumvolutions adjoining Rolando's cleft, where, as we know, Hetzig has located the psychomotor centres). Oh! The martyrdom!... The Others, they drink and digest... I hear their stomachs working very clearly... But it seems to me that, from minute to minute, their heads are growing smaller, smaller, smaller... Why then am I convinced that the resultant mathematics of all those minute vibrations that are imprinting upon my nervous system the tiny footsteps of flies' feet, mentioned above, is a very curious and even grandiose psychic phenomenon, comparable, for example, to an earthquake, a volcanic eruption, a cyclone, an aurora borealis? Why, too, do I presume that all these people who surround me, lips gaping, are bound to admire this spectacle, assuredly not at all banal, with the satisfaction of English tourists who have witnessed a lovely cataclysm?... But see how they are all laughing, and their laughter angers and devastates me like a blasphemy, or rather like an insolent imbecility! Certainly, all of that's far from being clear!...

Moreover, the mysterious endosmosis is accomplishing its work... From minute to minute, their heads are growing smaller, smaller, smaller... Look!... That gentleman over there already has no head, no head at all...

Ah! how they bruise my soul, all those walking sticks... creaturoids who do not seem to feel and who, indeed, do not feel the monstrous tortures of the flies' feet... My entire body is vibrating painfully, as a supposedly hypersensitive double-bass might under the bow of a madman.

Over there, in a corner, I catch a glimpse of three young lads, virginal and too pink, who are simpering and smiling. Their eyelashes are adroitly heightened with pastel, and their lips, with aquarelle. Their nails are as polished as priests' and their hands are boastful with gold rings. Their jackets, appropriately shortened, reveal voluptuous callipygies that are almost Hottentot. Why, from the first wink, I got this alexandrine which, for the moment, seems wholly sublime:

The eternal strabismus of stunted pansies!...

But, I think, perhaps its all for the best that these three young men have infamous morals!...

Be that as it may, this imbecilic crowd, this crowd of dolts self-absorbed with their bellies, is beginning to give me a nausea akin to that of sea-sickness.

She, alone...

But then, why those smiles at the contented stupidity of her neighbour? Why the indulgence of her smiles for her neighbour's obvious goitre? Can't she see even her neighbour's psychological goitre?... —Oh! My God, after all, what logical inference incites me to conclude that her pale mauve eyes are anything other than stony opals, unable to transmit the sensations of her soul? And does she even have a soul?... She prides herself upon her blonde hair, blonde as hemp, a little crimped, no doubt thanks to the artifices of curlers. That's all! Absolutely all!...

I feel myself slipping, slowly, into imbecility... The feet of those flies are as near as may be to setting the double-bass of my body vibrating no longer... Piano, piano, pianissimo!...

Amid the worn-out Flemish tapestries... Ach! those little chocolate bombs!... endosmosis!... the voluptuous callipygies! psychological goitres! and Her, and her hair! and all the rest!... In short, why all of this? Let's think it through... Think it through...

(A gap, a lacuna, a lethargy of perception. How many times have you endured it? How long did it last?)

Now, look there. She's speaking. She has a long nose, almost aristocratic, and a wide thin mouth, almost without lips, always laughing, pale as a scar, in the middle of her even paler face, of her pseudo-Anglo-Saxon face which has never known the stolid joys of roast beef... And all of it beneath an extraordinary flavescent wig, ruffled, as I had already said, by the perfidious artifices of curlers.

Oh! that horrible clicking of those dominoes...

She isn't very young. No, not a chance!... not at all young. Unless she has a soul; I don't know that, nor do you, nor does She, nor does anyone, not even God. Perhaps she's seen a youthful thirty-six autumns, or indeed forty, or even a hundred or more! But her skin is pale and, though a bit dried out from the face-paint, the bismuths, the magnesias and all the rest of the cosmetic gouaches, with no wrinkles visible to me, and her hair as blonde as her soul must be, in the event, I repeat, that she has one; and I feel that if her littler teeth, which the abuse of mercury has imperceptibly turned bluish, and her pale mauve eyes, cold and malevolent as opals, didn't laugh so insistently, amid the painful and pleasurable uproar of this stupid place, the monstrous goitre of her unspeakable neighbour, perhaps she might one day become a Sorceress, the sainted Sorceress a thousand times blessed whose divine philtre...

Time, gentlemen!...

215 Stéphane Mallarmé

Stéphane Mallarmé (1842-1898). Quite against his will Mallarmé became identified as the leader of the Symbolist "school." He was certainly one of its greatest poets and his works have acquired new significance in the light of modernism and its explorations of the limits of language and expression.

Mallarmé led a quiet life of unspectacular poverty and toil as an English teacher, interrupted occasionally by personal tragedies that deeply affected his work. His Tuesday evening *soirées* attracted the greatest artistic and literary minds of the day and became the forcing house for aesthetic theory over many years. Despite his enormous reputation, whose beginnings can be dated from his appearance in Verlaine's *Les Poètes maudits* (1883), Mallarmé's work is slender and fragmentary. He spent much of his life working on a vast project he called simply *The Book* which was intended to embody the totality of the world—hardly anything survives of this utopian enterprise.

La Fausse vieille is one of four *Contes Indiens* written in Paris and Valvins in 1893, but which remained unpublished until 1927. They are admittedly minor works of a major writer and owe their existence to the fact that Mallarmé's friend Mme. Méry Laurent was fond of a volume of Indian stories, *Les Contes et Légendes de l'Inde ancienne* by Mary Summer, whose style Mallarmé found wanting. This tale is therefore an imaginative re-writing of Summer's original version of an Indian fairy-tale, and has not been translated before. It is preceded by one of the most famous Symbolist poems ever penned, the so-called *"Sonnet in X"* whose arcane vocabulary is explained by the fact that the original French uses two very difficult rhymes: "x" (the mathematical symbol for the unknown) and "or" (in French: "gold," alchemical symbol of perfection).

Before he died, Baudelaire had read Mallarmé's first poems; he was disturbed; poets do not like leaving behind them sons or brothers; they would prefer to exist in isolation, and have their genius perish with their brain. But Mallarmé was Baudelairean only through filiation; his own precious originality soon affirmed itself; his Proses, *his* Après-midi d'un Faune, *his sonnets came forward, at over-lengthy intervals, to speak the marvellous subtlety of his patient, disdainful, imperiously gentle genius. Having voluntarily slain in himself the spontaneity of an impressionable being, the gifts of the artist gradually replaced in him those of the poet; he loved words for their possible meaning more than for their actual meaning and he combined them in mosaics of refined simplicity. One can easily say of him that he is a difficult author, as Persius or Martial are difficult. Yes, and like Andersen's gentleman who wore invisible threads, Mallarmé assembles gems coloured by his dreams, the lustre of which our care does not always succeed in guessing at. But it would be absurd to suppose that he is incomprehensible....*

Recently a question was posed, more or less in these terms:

"Who will replace Verlaine—who had replaced Leconte de Lisle—in the admiration of young poets."

Few of those questioned responded; two-thirds abstained, motivated by the absurd phrasing of such an ultimatum. How could it happen, in effect, that a young poet should admire, "exclusively and successively," three "masters" as diverse as those two and Monsieur Mallarmé—the incontestable choice? Thus, for reasons of conscience, many were silent. But I cast my vote here, saying: greatly loving and admiring Stéphane Mallarmé, I do not see that the death of Verlaine should be the proper occasion for loving and admiring him more today than yesterday.

For all that, since it is a strict duty always to sacrifice the dead for the living, and to give to the living, by a superaddition of glory, a superaddition of energy, the result of this vote pleases me and we who were silent ought perhaps to speak. What a pity if so many abstentions were to falsify the truth! For, informed by a circular letter, the press has found in this news an excuse for mockery and for finding fault in us, while, tossed on the inky waves of intellectual darkness, but victorious over the wreckers, the name of Mallarmé, inscribed at last on the ironic elegance of a racing-cutter, in full sail now derides the waves and the bitter-sweet foam of raillery.

STÉPHANE MALLARMÉ

*With Up-
Raised Nails...*

With upraised nails, chalcedonyx's hands
Lift midnight angst as an Olympic torch
While final Phoenix-glowing pyx's brands
Sear twilight's flickered dreams with fierce-licked scorch

On chiffoniers where no lone ptyxis stands,
Nor ash-free amphora to shade night's porch
(The lord's out fishing tears on Styx's sands
With it, to climax Nullity's debauch).

A glint, through open shutters, fades unwrought
To harmonise where unicorns once brought
Emblazoned sparks to sift a nixie's strands;

Expired and nude, the mirror sees her fraught:
Oblivion's dark frame affixes bands
Where astral septets evermore are caught.

—*Translated by Stanley Chapman.*

The Supposed Old Woman

In the kingdom of Mathura, comparable to a peacock's tail, where the sun, in place of flowers, half-opens eyes of emerald and of diamond, there lived beneath this gaze, two little princesses, their mother having died young. Their father, a rajah with a grey beard, employed all his wits to wed in a second marriage a very beautiful and very wicked young woman. Detesting her stepdaughters, maltreating them. This enamoured and domineered greybeard let things slide; each day brought its own torment. Their patience at an end, children resolve to run away; these two clever-heads, of fourteen and fifteen years, ripen a plan of escape beneath their curls. Eluding surveillance, they pass beyond the palace gates, those of the city and, on a moonlit night, the two daughters of the king walk haphazardly in the forest while the star with the tenuous ray chills their artlessness. Unacquainted with gadding about after adventures, as strolling actresses are, fright seizes them, they begin to have regrets.

Suddenly, a sumptuous palace presents its threshold, they enter there, rashly: habitation of a malevolent rachka and his wife who is in no way second to him. The hosts absent; the house, empty. These fugitives, dying of hunger, espy boiled rice on a silver platter, and they eat it with avidity. The meal finished, a great din arises of the ogre and his wife returning. The sisters flee onto a roof in the form of a terrace; where, through an opening prepared in the wall, they see, hear everything within. The appearance of the rachka, little reassuring: his eyes blaze, a bristling beard down to his knees, the enormous mouth gaped over sharp teeth.

"By the thousand eyes of Indra," he roars upon entering, "someone has been here, Madame, for I smell fresh flesh."

"Nonsense," the ogress insinuated: "who would dare to risk the darkness of this forest? And everyone for thirty leagues around fears us."

"I say again, Madame, I smell an odour that has already aroused my appetite."

"Your lips still have the odour of blood on them: didn't you just dine on some tradesmen you encountered in the jungle?"

"Have it your way. I'm dying of thirst and I'll go to the well to draw water; then I shall do my rounds, and nothing worthwhile will escape me."

You can well imagine how the princesses felt during this conversation!

The younger, of a composure marvellous for one of her years, as soon as the amiable couple tramped to the well, crept out softly. The ogre, already clumsy with a troublesome digestion, occupied himself with sending down the bucket, and his consort, bent forward, with controlling the oscillations of the rope. A gesture quick as a flash, from the courageous child, seizes each of the married couple by the heel, tumbles them: wild-eyed, they fall down the hole, struggle in the water, cry out with rage. Everything is silent, the ogre and his wife have ceased to live: we append no funeral oration. The house is overflowing with gold and silver, all that remains of the poor people the master has devoured to the bones. The children now possess these riches. With the superb residence, a single inconvenience: it is lost in the woods. In such a site, two young ladies such as Lotus-flower and Dew-drop become very vulnerable. One remained in the house to attend to the cares of housekeeping, the other led the flocks into the fields. That one, Lotus-flower, although the youngest, before she set out, directed a thousand suggestions to the elder. Chiefly not to forget to put the bolt in place, and "if someone knocks, be sure to show him nothing but a face powdered with coal dust, so that he does not discover your beauty."

Fortunately no one ventured into the accursed place. The darlings, by degrees grown familiar with their new situation, felt reassured together. Carried away by the ardour of the chase, the son of the King of Hastinapura*, one afternoon, passes before the dead rachka's palace. A prince of the city of elephants, in the flesh or sculpted in porphyry, having his strength and their endurance, is hard to frighten. His entourage remaining at a distance, he calmly walks in the direction of the dwelling, intrigued by its silence. The door remains closed to the pounding of his javelin, and the royal hunter, who is not patient, mutters and threatens. Dew-drop draws back the bolt with a timid hand, she holds out to the adolescent the bowl of cool water one offers travellers. Unrecognisable with her features masked by black dust, and tatters hurriedly rent on her clothing, one would have believed her to be the most vulgar of servants; the sly prince does not thereby let himself be taken in: he scents a mystery and, without drinking the proffered water, suddenly throws it in the princess' face. Her colour is restored, and her original bloom of youth. If his conduct was hasty, the lordly youth excuses himself as eloquently as only can a handsome lad suddenly struck by love. His heart, his hand and all his treasures he offers to the beauty; who is silent, intimidated, and thinking of her sister's return. Not for a moment does he admit of the idea that someone might refuse to be the daughter-in-law to a king. That blushing and those tears, he attributes to a chaste embarrassment and nothing more; he gathers the darling into his robust arms. A litter awaits them in the forest: Away to Hastinapura!—What! no time even to write a letter of farewell: a veritable kidnapping. To Dew-drop there comes a sudden illumination, she could leave behind a trail for her poor sister who would return to find everything deserted. She unthreads her necklace, tears a scrap of muslin and, in each shred wraps a pearl; this precious weight will fix the material to the grass. The journey of several days: all along the way she sows the pearls, dropping the last of them before entering the palace, the home of her future father-in-law. The portal of wood and mother-of-pearl closed, she dreams, in her heart, of the forlorn state in which Lotus-flower lives; then sobs within herself in unison with the fountain's jets.

The sun, its rays attenuated, was declining toward the west, there, when the shepherdess gathered together her flock; she is disquieted that, counter to a beloved custom, no one has come out to greet her; enters ere long, calls, searches in vain; and she tires herself out, only her echo awakened in the lonely house. The truth dawned on her: someone has carried off her companion. Rather than lament, she will sleep and postpone her inquiries until the next day. Astir, before dawn, a first pearl perceived in the lawn at the end of the garden, she recognises her sister's intentions. Walks directly along a route eked out by sunlight and in the dust. Sometimes she is more than an hour without finding any pearls. Out of charity some tillers give her some handfuls of rice and let her rest in the cattle-shed; in her headlong haste she has neglected to bring the least amount of money with her: this is no pleasure-trip. The beauty of the wandering princess exposes her to dangers, such as being carried off by some terrible person, lordship or robber, taken with dainty morsels. On one occasion she is benighted in a ditch when she is frightened by an old woman's corpse lying there, certainly dead of hunger: a skeleton with stretched skin. Overcoming her repugnance to it is worse for her than delicately lifting away the desiccated mask and washing it in a nearby pool: she had guided her blade so skilfully that it was like putting a hand in a glove; then, chopping off a stalk of bamboo, leaning on it, back bent, and head nodding, she made her entrance, that morning, into the streets of Hastinapura. Henceforth secured against any amorous approach. "What a wretched-looking female!" the passers-by exclaimed, turning away from her. Lotus-flower laughed beneath her wrinkles and tranquilly picked up a last pearl close to the palace; she had understood that her sister was not far away. She even attempted to get into the royal residence; the guards brutally drove her away. "What would an ugly brood such as yourself have to do with the grandees of the court?" "Another time" (she said to herself) "fortune will favour me more."

Meanwhile, to subsist—it was necessary—Lotus-flower took work with a farmer on the outskirts of the city. Heavy labour falling to her lot, nothing discouraged her, as hardworking as a daughter of the fields. The women pitied her and, because of her ugliness, treated her benevolently. For weeks on end the child kept her mask and her secret, an improbable heroism; but coquettishness must needs reassert its rights: and so, in the morning, early, she would steal away from the pile of grass, her bed, beneath the farmhouse's porch, to make her toilet in the crystal of the pond. Quickly to remove her borrowed skin, to plunge the voluptuousness of her countenance into the pure water. Her long hair flowing, thus, down her flanks, to comb it and tie it up again, to stick a red lotus there; because she has an immemorial fancy for that flower of her girlhood, with her very own name. Freely she would revel in the return of her image, the renewal of her memories, and make provision for herself, in secret, for a day's work. The old skin, washed, hung from a reed stem, dripped, fanned by the breeze. The day sparkles; it is necessary to become ugly again, to stoop, to go back to the farmhouse and labour like a beast of burden.

Now a circumstance unforeseen by Lotus-flower, her daily visit is little by little robbing the patch of water of its beautiful flowers; the king is greatly attached to it, is not long in taking note of the pilferage: this was an event that was noised abroad even in the council of ministers. The men of affairs racked their brains in regard to a means for discovering the theft. The second son of the rajah, a valiant young man, declared that he alone would take it upon himself to throw some light upon the affair. He would climb into a tree and, sheltered by the greenery, watch for the connoisseur of calyxes. That same night, this plan was executed: the heavens glittered with stars, the lake scarcely rippled in the breeze, stirring the king's lotuses without a petal falling.

At daybreak, the old woman appeared, whom the prince, in the streets of Hastinapura, had remarked upon as a paragon of ugliness. "Well now, there's an oddity for you, who'd expect to find coquettishness there? What need of flowers has that monkey-face... You're going to have me to deal with, Madame Thief." Amazement! The wrinkled yellow mask has just fallen, to reveal the softest, most childlike face that ever was seen: bewilderment seizes the prince. Who is this? An inhabitant of the heavens or the earth? So radiant an apparition had never yet haunted even his fancy.

The innocent thought herself alone and tranquilly exposed her entire body to the curiosity of the intrusive youth. She has come out from her bath, seated on one of the lower steps to the pool, while every drop evaporates, diamonds scattered over her: this supreme veil floats about her contours, wavers and vanishes like an idealised cloud, leaving her more naked. Presently she raises her arms, stretching herself as if to cause the roundnesses of her breasts to jut, soon she amuses herself by plashing the waves beneath her little white feet; it is as if, in their delight, a pair of doves were bathing. Then she slowly plaits her hair, black as the Indian bee. Now there are scarcely any flowers blooming in the basin; with a pert hand she seizes one of the last within her reach and, in the naïve mirror, she smiles and admires herself. The rajah's son misses none of this graceful coquetry: trembling, in order to see better, he pushes aside a bough of the fig tree in which he is concealed... Ah! the thief may gather all the lotuses that she wants with impunity: he doesn't dream of punishing her. Suddenly either the kohila has emitted its matutinal song or else a cry is uttered by Lotus-flower, the sun is blazing; the charmer has never been so tardy: in a minute she readjusts the mask and flees. On his feet, leaning against the tree, the prince snatches up the crumpled flower that the young girl has thrown to the earth: he is passionately in love and therefore disposed to every imaginable folly. Returned to the palace, he steps gingerly onto the terrace where the king holds counsel: "Sire," he blurts out without any further preamble, "I have fallen in love with the old servant who lives at the city gates, in the farmhouse of Your Majesty's tenant and, with your consent, I intend to marry her this very day."

The ministers, despite the respect due to sovereigns, were unable to suppress a gesture of astonishment. "What! This young man whom every eye follows with ecstasy when he passes, superb, in the streets; this prince who can possess the most beautiful women in the world; to have fallen into tastes so depraved!" The king himself remains dumbfounded at such a strange request: "You are losing your reason, my son!" he finally utters. "To marry this ancient beggar, a heap of abject bones, when the earth abounds with marvellous princesses! Would you dare to impose this shame upon our noble race, whose sons have received a share in this splendour?" "So be it, my father; you refuse me; I go directly to throw myself into the Ganges. May the gods pardon you for my death!"

The queen, informed, intercedes for her beloved son: they should satisfy this whim of a sick spirit, a passing fancy, even if it should prove lasting. The daylight slips away during these domestic tussles; the spoiled child finally triumphs. In the gleam of the candles, they go in search of the supposed old woman, who dares not refuse such an honour, is at a loss; the betrothed of a king! truly this was the penalty for making herself ugly, to arrive at such a result! at least she will take care not to remove her mask; the prince would see her as too beautiful for him to allow her to gad about the fields. He might forbid her to search for her sister, who more than ever, she wishes to find.

Two or three officers of the palace are present at the ceremony, which a venerable brahmin celebrates, a priest descended from the royal line. The prince is radiant; he leads his hideous spouse into the bridal chamber and, in that wheedling voice that men know to assume on these occasions: "My best-beloved," he entreats, "here we are alone at last; remove, I beseech you that sorry skin that conceals your divine features from my mouth." "These words are a mystery to me," the princess, who does not know that her secret is revealed, icily insists. "I wish, alas, that I were more worthy of you; but what you see here is what I really am." "Enough of these pleasantries that are wasting precious time. Coquette, you are mocking my tenderness. I am not a patient man, and I am usually obeyed. What! You won't obey me? That tries my patience too much. Cast off the infamy of that disguise or I'll slay you forthwith."—"Slay me then, Sir; I am truly sorry, but I cannot change my skin, even to please you."

Supplications, threats, all fail before her obstinacy. The groom resolves to lay at his wife's side; contact with this withered flesh evokes the memory of the nubile freshness that he glimpsed that morning: but, vivid as an imagination might be, it sometimes cannot efface reality.

That first night of marriage had its effect.

Before daybreak the princess, believing her husband to be asleep, slipped from the bed, to begin her ablutions in the alabaster of a neighbouring recess. The young man who was watching her rather than sleeping, furtively followed his wife and, seizing the famous skin that was lying on the floor, he flung it into a brazier where perfumes were burning: it crackled with a sound enchanting to his ear, and almost like kisses: "Burn, lying pelt," he hissed at it: "you've caused me vexation enough!"; and, turning, playful, to Lotus-flower, he jested: "You really are in a sorry state now that you're condemned to remain the most lovely and best-loved of women. Don't blush! I had discovered the secret of your beauty by the lustral lotus-pond, where I swore never to take any bride other than you."

A more heartfelt kiss than those of the night concluded the prince's speech to Lotus-flower, who allowed herself to be taken without a grudge. The palace resounded, as to the sacred echo of a gong, to the happy news: the princess, restored to her childhood, was solemnly presented to the gaze of the entire family. To speak of the joy of the two sisters upon recognising each other and falling into each others' arms would require the accompaniment of that most tearful of all musical instruments, one strung with the very strings of loving hearts: certainly, after so many adventures, they had merited happiness, which is silent.

Henri de Régnier

Henri de Régnier (1864-1936). Like Montesquiou and Villiers, Régnier came by his aristocratic airs naturally, being the descendant of French nobility. By virtue of his marriage to the daughter of the arch-Parnassian José Maria de Heredia*, Régnier had a foot in both Symbolist and Parnassian camps, his later works tending more to the latter. He was a regular at Mallarmé's Tuesdays and a very prolific and admired author in his day, his later works being now not much regarded.

The story here is from *Le Trèfle Noir* (*The Black Trefoil*, 1895), later republished in his collected stories *La Canne de Jaspe* (*The Jasper Cane*, 1897). The prose poem in italics forms the preface to this collection.

This one dwells in an old Italian palace whose walls are covered with emblems and figures. He dreams, passing from hall to hall; towards evening he descends the marble staircase and goes into the gardens, paved like courtyards, to dream his life amid the ornamental lakes and fountains, while black swans are uneasy in their nests, and a peacock, alone like a king, seems superbly to drink in the dying pride of a golden twilight. Monsieur de Regnier is a melancholy and sumptuous poet: the two words that most often ring out are or *and* mort; *there are poems in which this rhyme, both autumnal and royal, returns with an insistence bordering upon the alarming. In his latest collection one could no doubt number some fifty lines ending thus:* oiseaux d'or, cygnes d'or, vasques d'or, fleur d'or, *and* lac mort, jour mort, rêve mort, automne mort. *This is a very curious and symptomatic obsession, quite the contrary of a possible verbal indigence, symptomatic rather of an openly declared love of a colour particularly rich, and rich with a richness sad as that of a setting sun, a richness that is about to become nocturnal.*

Words impose themselves upon him when he wishes to express his impressions and the colour of his dreams; words also impose themselves upon whoever would define him and above all that one word, already written but which still returns, invincible: richness. Henri de Régnier is the rich poet par excellence—*rich in images! He has coffers of them, cellars of them, underground caverns of them, and a file of slaves incessantly carry opulent panniers to him which he empties, disdainfully, on the staircases' bedazzled steps, multicoloured cascades which gush forth, then calm themselves to form iridescent lakes and ponds. Not all of these are completely new. Verhaeren prefers, above the most exact and beautiful metaphors from the past, those he has himself created, even if clumsy, ill-formed. Monsieur Régnier does not disdain metaphors from the past, but he refashions them and appropriates them to his own uses while modifying their settings, while imposing new neighbours upon them, with yet unknown significance; if among these reworked images one does discover virgin material, the impression such poetry gives will nonetheless be completely original. In working thus, one avoids the bizarre and the obscure; the reader is not brusquely thrust into a labyrinthine forest; he regains his way, and his joy at gathering new flowers is coupled with the joy of gathering familiar ones...*

HENRI DE RÉGNIER

Preface *There are swords, mirrors, jewels, dresses, crystal goblets and lamps with, sometimes, the murmur of the sea outside and the breeze of the forests. Listen also to the singing of the fountains. They are intermittent and unceasing; the gardens which they enliven are symmetrical. The statue there is either of marble or of bronze; the yew is trimmed. The bitter smell of box perfumes the silence; the rose blossoms next to the cypress. Love and Death kiss each other on the mouth. Water reflects the foliage. Make a round of the basins. Go through the labyrinth; wander about the grove; and read my book, page by page, as though, with the end of your tall jasper cane, Solitary Stroller, you turned over on the dry gravel of the walk a beetle, a pebble, or some dry leaves.*

The Story of Hermagoras For a long while the Poor Fisherman was to be seen standing in his boat, motionless in the river's estuary.

The water passes slowly along the bulwarks and, coming from afar, from the depths of the sylvan and fertile earth, it carries along straw, drifting leaves, and maybe a flower too, herbs that stick fast to the boat or else swirl around in the backwash. The sky above this pale tide is grey; the sand from the banks goes out to rejoin the dunes along the shore; the boat rocks imperceptibly; it groans, suffering, worn out; the moan from its joints accompanies the sighs of the cable, his scrawny arms lift nothing but an empty net.

For days and even years he had often cast in vain. The fish were not to be taken there, though the Fisherman was

patient and careful to study the wind, the time of year, and the tide with the utmost vigilance that his shadow might not overtake the boat and never once did he see his reflection in the water.

Sometimes, weary of inaction, he rowed toward the high sea. The strongest waves awkwardly consoled his melancholy; the deep water turned green. From the open sea he saw the sandy coastline and the estuary. The wind sighed in the rigging all day long. The fisherman persisted at his task.

On those rough and unavailing days, he preferred the mediocrity of a derisory prize, fresh water fry, the calm of the current, the slow roll, the smooth, monotonous flight in which, one by one, straw, leaves, and a flower pass by.

Birds fly about him, having no fear. They were those grey larks with adventurous wingspans. The wagtails skipping upon the sand banks cry out to him persistently. He wishes to go with them to the vast lands of the interior where a different water murmurs from springs at which the herdsmen drink: the soft mud around the ponds is trampled by the beasts; the scent of hay mingles with the odour of the stables; there are hives of bees in the gardens and the haystacks are even with the thatch; in the little square field where one digs in the sun, there is nothing in front of him above the living hedges, but the sky. Sweat runs down the face in warm drops, and the shade of the trees is as refreshing as a drink from a fountain.

One evening dreaming thus while spreading his nets upon the sand around his beached craft, he heard someone speak to him. It was a stranger: his frame supported by a stick; his weary features and his fustian cloak resembled the twilight. The man asked to buy the nets and the boat, and even as he spoke, counted out in the darkness, one by one, the pieces of gold.

༄

At dawn, Hermagoras the Fisherman stopped in the middle of a vast sandy plain hemmed in by bluish grass. The river had rejoined him through a caprice of its meanderings, and its blue-green water flowed between islands whose reflections seemed to take root with the hair of their inverted trees. A bird flew out of a bush; butterflies fluttered about on their sleepy silken wings, pink and grey, a few as yellow as gold. Hermagoras felt the sum that he carried in a cloth bag and set off. Twilight came, and each evening the walker counted his humble treasure.

At the end of a day in which he had crossed swampy meadows, Hermagoras saw the forests. Their massive form shut out the whole horizon; everything within was silence and long shadows; sometimes the forest appeared to end and widen into a skirt; then he was about to run, but the woods recommenced below some ravine whose crest and trees like clefts in the sky had simulated this bright interval from whence one mastered the distant continuation of the undulating peaks.

For a long time Hermagoras heard nothing but the wind in these solitudes, but one day he recognised the echoes of an axe, and by following the sound, he came across woodcutters who were cutting down beech trees; further on he saw a roof and smoke, and he saw at last the land of which he had dreamt. The slow undulations of the hillocks, meadows alternating with wheat fields lined with poplars; sometimes he heard the piping of a flute; linens dried beneath the willows and, at evening, everything seemed so calm that he dared not tread upon the grass.

The little field was situated on the slope of a hill; square, enclosed by hedges. Hermagoras cultivated it carefully. He sowed in the deeply ploughed land. All winter long he was happy, but in the springtime, he saw that the neighbouring fields would be more fertile than his own. And so they were. The crop was barely enough for next season's sowing. The following harvest looked even more meagre: the birds attacked it fiercely and Hermagoras could be seen amid the sparse ears, standing, as he once did in his flat-bottomed boat, gesticulating and casting clods of earth at the pillagers.

Sometimes he deserted his garden and travelled the countryside: fertile harvests ripened on all sides and the privilege of his misery seemed even more bitter to him. The flock passed and he watched them disappear toward the horizon like the ships of old; their sails knowing all the winds and, through distant seas, they travel to rich lands where their holds become impregnated by the scent of their cargoes in order to enrich the powerful masters who, in residences adorned with coral and charts, calculate the tides and their ports-of-call.

The following year was such that Hermagoras gleaned just enough to be able to sow. He went through the fields bent beneath the sun. At last his sowings prospered; his field was gilded too, until one day, while he watched it preparing his prosperity the sky clouded over. The hail-storm broke; not a stalk remained upright, and Hermagoras, silent and pale with anger and despairs went off across the plain, his face deathly and his hands bloodied by the hailstones that had wounded them.

As he approached a spring in order to bathe his wounds, he saw a man lying at the edge, asleep. It was the same stranger who had once counted out pieces of gold for his boat and tackle; he still had the oars and the net, and Hermagoras, about to waken him so as to enquire about his fortunes, noticed a half-opened purse next to the sleeper; coins were shining; some of them glowed between the fingers of his closed hand; he must have been casting them into the water, because through the transparency one could distinguish them resting on the sandy bottom of the spring. The man slept forever. Hermagoras picked up the purse and, having walked all through the night and into the next morning, arrived toward noon in sight of a city.

The houses were clustered about a vast dome accompanied by other smaller ones. Palaces lined a wide river traversed by cambered bridges; trees intermingled with the houses; sometimes they were lined up along long avenues or spilled into gardens. The waters sparkled there. The streets were empty, deserted because of the heat.

Immense cemeteries surrounded the city; forests almost, by virtue of the cypresses standing at the corners of each tomb, all of which were either pyramids or blocks carved from stone. The first, those of the women, were adorned with roses. Their perfume, a mixture of flowers and foliage, was at once bitter and sweet, the scent of death itself. A solitary visitor passed slowly amidst the tombs. Her long yellow veil sometimes caught on the branches of a cypress or the thorns of a rose, revealing her face, which was delicately made up. Once she leaned over in order to read a name, and the medallions of her bracelet tinkled upon the marble, then she sat down and wept. Hermagoras approached her: "Why do you weep?" he said to her.

"Wayfarer," she responded, "where do you come from that you are in ignorance of my famous mourning? I am spoken of in distant lands and you alone seem to know nothing of me. You do not know who Ilalie loved. She loved that one who has departed. He is gone, and since then I wander through these precincts; he left one evening and abandoned me for poverty and wisdom. They say that he is now a fisherman beside a river, near the Sea!"

"I too have been a fisherman at the river's edge," Hermagoras responded. "I have laboured in an arid land and am tired of the ploughshare and the oar and I come here for gold and for love."

Hermagoras who had slept naked amid the river reeds and rested his head upon a stone in the furrows of the field, who had been whipped by the wind, stung by bees and barked at by dogs, lay upon beds of bronze and slept upon woven silk. He was fanned with palms and lulled by song; perfumes smoked by his bedside.

Those were amazing loves. And because there was a secret and a cowardly desire on the part of those she had rejected to at least see the lucky lover of a woman they had all desired, Hermagoras became famous and sought after. For Ilalie stalked through the dreams of those young men like a haughty statue. One morning she was discovered upon her couch, naked and indeed white as marble, smiling as though she had died of joy.

Hermagoras did not weep for her. They admired the superiority of his indifference, and rumours of the fabled elegance she had kept him in reached all the way to the queen. She inhabited a palace surmounted by a vast dome surrounded by other smaller ones. Hermagoras was ushered into her presence in secret, and he often went there evenings and remained until dawn. The queen loved him and, because it was as much her destiny as some disease, he became king, the one who had reigned being dead, beatified and idiotic, in the solitary pavilion where he had dragged himself slobbering upon the paving stones. The grave of the deceased consecrated the accession of the usurper; a few heads struck off consolidated the adventure. The arrogance of the parvenu was to believe in his own predestination. They prostrated themselves before him; he was bored.

One day as he crossed the great plaza of the city, in bright sunlight, crown on his head and sceptre in his hand, he noticed a man proudly erect, though dressed in rags, who smiled as he watched him. He recognised again the stranger who had purchased his boat, the sleeper whose purse he had taken, one evening, by the spring. Upon the order of the king they brought the ragged one before him.

"Why are you laughing?" Hermagoras asked. "What do you want of me—speak!"

"Oh king," the miserable one replied, "I was observing the shadow at your feet cast by your glory." And the king having lowered his eyes saw this shadow. A composite formed by his high crown, the rod of his sceptre, and the wings of his cloak, it was deformed, trapped, monstrous; in this chimerical form he appeared to be some aggressive but lowly beast, squatting at the feet of the triumphant one who preceded it.

King Hermagoras understood the beggar's allusion. He had, in this parody of his body, beheld the very image of his soul; and he wept. That very evening he fled from the city furtively and, upon passing by that spring where he had once robbed the sleeper, he threw his crown and sceptre into it. Finally he arrived at the tiny field where once he had laboured and, casting himself naked upon the hard earth, he let himself die there.

That year, an extraordinary harvest was heralded throughout the countryside; children lost themselves in the wheat. Only one little field remained barren; it was situated upon a hillside, uncultivated and full of brambles, green on surrounding yellow, but when they had cut all of the neighbouring wheat closely, they saw that, all alone, an enormous stalk had grown there and they discovered a skeleton. The arms were spread in the form of a cross and the miraculous marvel was growing from the skull. A stranger from among the harvesters, one who worked for wages, came forward, plucked the stalk, then, on his knees, bowing, he kissed the ivory mask on the mouth. They watched him do this in silence and, when he failed to rise, they found, on touching him, that he was dead!

—*Translated by Antony Melville & Andrew Mangravite.*

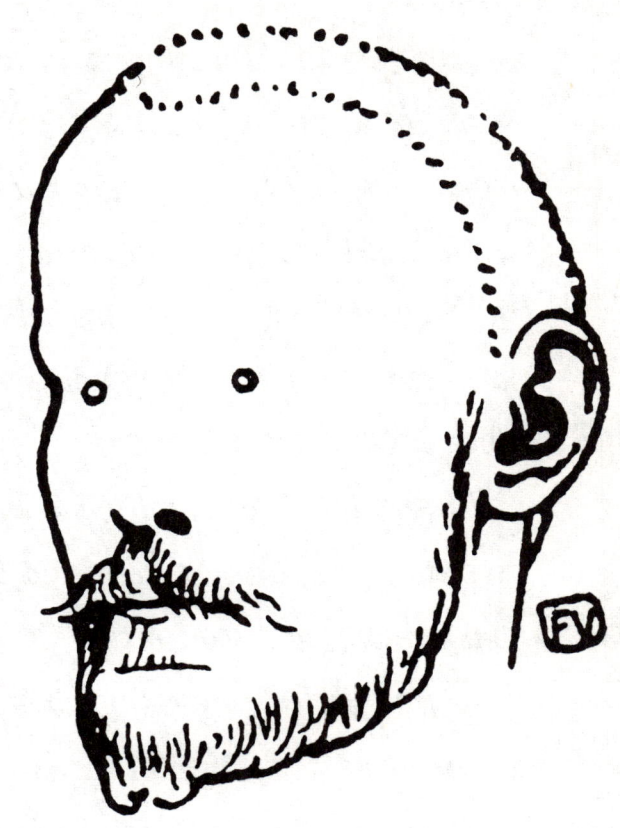

229 JULES RENARD

Jules Renard (1864-1910). A miserable childhood, followed by military service, then increasing success in journalism: Renard's subsequent career seems to have progressed with remarkable ease. One of the founders of the *Mercure de France*, he contributed to most issues over many years. *Poil de Carotte* (1894) and other novels crowned his success. He moved with his family to a small village outside Paris where he presided as famous author and town councillor.

These prose poems are from *Histoires Naturelles* (1896) which had a wide circulation and went through a number of editions, including ones illustrated by Lautrec and Bonnard; the first text was quoted in full in de Gourmont's essay.

Jules Renard has given himself this name: the hunter of images. He is a singularly fortunate and privileged hunter, because, alone among all his confreres, he does not bring back animals great and small, but new prey. He disdains everything that is known, or he ignores it; his collection is only of rare and even unique pieces, which he does not trouble to lock up, because they belong to him in such a way that any thief's attempt to steal away with them would be in vain. So keen and distinct a personality has something disconcerting, irritating and, according to a jealous few, excessive about it. "Do as we do, draw from the common treasure of old accumulated metaphors; it's quick, and very convenient." But Jules Renard doesn't care to go quickly. Although very hard-working, he produces little, and above all, little at a time, like those patient engravers who prepare the metal plate with a geological slowness...

JULES RENARD

Family of Trees

It was after traversing a sunburned plain that I met them.

They do not dwell by the roadside, on account of the noise. They inhabit the uncultivated fields, beside a brook known only to the birds.

From afar they seem impenetrable. As soon as I approach, their trunks disperse. They receive me prudently. I may rest and refresh myself, but I understand that they watch and mistrust me.

They live *en famille*, the oldest in the middle, the little ones—those whose leaves are just budding—about them, here and there, but not straying far.

They put off dying for a long time, and they prop up the dead till they fall to dust.

They touch each other lightly with their long branches—like the blind—to assure themselves that all are there. They gesticulate with anger if the wind storms to uproot them. But among themselves no dispute. They murmur only in accord.

I feel that they should be my true family. I should soon forget the other. Little by little the trees would adopt me, and to merit it I should learn what needs to be known.

Already I know how to watch the passing clouds.

I know also how to keep my place.

And I know, almost, how to hold my peace.

Chimney-swallows

Each day they give me a lesson.

They stipple the air with cries.

They draw a straight line, put in a comma, then brusquely, a dash—

They set the house in which I live between fantastic parentheses.

Swift, so swift that the sheet of water in the garden cannot mirror their flight, they mount from cellar to cockloft.

With light pen-feathers they scrawl inimitable flourishes.

Then, two by two, in accolade, they meet and mix and become but a blot of ink on the blue of the heavens.

Only a friend's eye can follow them, and though you may know Latin and Greek, I—I can read the Hebrew written in the skies by the chimney-swallows.

Snail

Stay-at-home in the season of colds, giraffe-neck drawn in, the snail bubbles over like a full nose.

When fine weather comes he takes the air, but knows no better way of walking than on his tongue.

Dragon-Fly

She nurses her ophthalmy.

From bank to bank of the river simply dips her swollen eyes in the fresh water.

And flickers as if flying by electricity.

Toad   Bred of stone, he lives under a stone, and there will dig himself a grave.

I visit him often, and whenever I lift his stone, I dread finding him, and dread also that he may no longer be there.

But there he is.

Hidden in his dry, clean lodging, his very own, he fills its every corner, fat as a miser's purse.

When the rain drives him out he comes to meet me. A few clumsy jumps, then he sits on his haunches and stares at me with red eyes.

Though the harsh world shuns him as a leper, I squat down and put my human face close to his.

Then I overcome the last remnants of repulsion and stroke you—toad.

The course of one's life offers harder things to swallow!

Nevertheless, yesterday I was tactless. He fermented, oozed: all his warts had burst.

"My poor friend," I said, "I don't wish to hurt your feelings, but—Lord! you are ugly!"

He opened his toothless mouth, gave a soft, warm gasp and replied, in a slightly English accent:

"And you?"

Ants   Every one resembles the figure 3.
                And there are so many...
So very many of them...
3333333333333 ...to infinity.

Bats   The night, poor dear, will wear herself out with working.

Not on high, among the stars, but at ground-level, skirt dragging among the pebbles and tree roots, in the depths of noisome tunnels and stagnant cellars.

No corner where a fragment of Night does not penetrate. Thorns pierce her, colds chap, mud besmirches. And every morning, when Night arises once more to go, tatters fall from her, caught here and there by chance.

Thus bats are born.

They owe their intolerance of daylight to this origin.

At sunset, when they take to the air, they unstitch themselves from the old beams, where they drowsily hang by a claw.

Their awkward flight disturbs us. On whaleboned, featherless wings, they throb about us, guided less by their useless wounded eyes, than by their ears.

My friend hides her face, I turn my head aside for fear of their obscene contact.

They say they would suck our blood till we die, with an ardour greater than love's.

Such exaggeration!

They are not wicked, they don't touch us.

Daughters of the Night, it is only lights they hate, and, with the brush of their little funereal shawls, they seek candles so as to blow them out.

Spider   A small black, bristly hand, clutching a fistful of hair.

All night, to the moon's signature, she affixes her seals.

—*Translated by John Harman.*

233 Barrès

Maurice Barrès (1862-1923). Barrès' early novels, collectively titled *Le Culte du Moi*, explored an individualist-anarchist position close to that of Max Stirner, otherwise the bulk of Barrès' works are essays that read almost like novels, a highly felicitous form for a writer as concerned with ideas as he; his total *oeuvre* runs to many volumes. His works written while under the spell of Symbolism include *Sous l'oeil des Barbares* and *Du Sang, de la volupté et de la mort* (1894, from which our excerpt is taken).

Barrès soon moved to the far right. As a Catholic Nationalist his outraged protestations during World War I: *"They have dared to bomb our churches!"* were the frequent target of derision from the left. One of the most famous of the Dadaist actions in Paris after the war was their trial of Barrès for his betrayal of his earlier ideals, which, along with his remarkable literary style, had been much admired by them.

A great many young men have believed in Barrès; and even a few who are not as young as he. But what is the significance of this? It was certainly not unscrupulous ambition pure and simple. Here we find, in a youthful intelligence a primitive nobility which finds it unconditionally repugnant to hand over to life the forces of his activity: to arrive, yes, but toward a victory and through battle. As an aim Monsieur Barrès indicated the full possession and full enjoyment of one's self; as a means, the winning over of the Barbarians who surround us, blocking our way, opposing, by their mass, the development of our activities and our pleasures. Too intelligent to concern himself with what goes by the name of social justice, too shrewdly an egoist to dream of destroying privileges into which he wished to enter, he had the people open the door of the fortress, which the people then believed they had taken.

I do not believe that Barrès has ever written a book, unless perhaps at his début, or even a page, of totally pure art, in absolute disinterestedness, and this is a true originality and a very rare merit in occasional writings (in the elevated sense that Goethe gave to the term) but they have, with their value as ideas and as egoist propaganda, a literary value equal to that of works of artless beauty....

Some followed Monsieur Barrès only as far as the cult of the individual, inclusively; they propagated about them an individualism that was somewhat unsociable but which has borne fine fruits; they taught (this is again from Goethe) that the best way of bringing about universal happiness was for each to begin by creating his own happiness—a fancy that must be worked over with patience to extract from it a definitive thought; finally they came in this way to know the elements of an idealism of the sentiments: Monsieur Barrès has certainly rough-hewn a good many intellects. Other disciples went further in the understanding of their master and they learned that to achieve the happy life—which, as in Seneca, requires much gold and much purple—one must please, and that to please one must give the appearance of making one's thought coincide with what is generally felt.

...The danger of extreme opinions is that, issued from the brain that engendered them, as from a flower in which they are agreeable, they go their way, insensate seeds, to decay in the harshest of terrains to produce grace and flowers.

MAURICE BARRÈS

Hate Conquers All

One can learn a lot about hatred on the benches of the Assembly. Very few displayed it during the long months when it was powerless, but, in December of 1892, I saw it, in flashes, contorting various faces. Panama, Panama!... I saw just such a speechifier pause, choked by a spasm of delight, when an adversary passed, his eyes anxious, his cheeks pale, and down-in-the-mouth. Hatred, like a beast emerging from its lurking-place, became evident to me in the eyes, between the teeth of those vanquished the day before.

And I recollected a harsh story from the Spanish civil wars.

In Seville, in 1869, there was a rich widow of noble birth, one of those women who spend their time in the shops, with a fine taste in clothes and further enlivening their charm with a pleasing air of companionship. The elegant folds of her dress were those of a Parisienne, but, beneath it, her slightest movements revealed the national *salero*, that type of violent suppleness, very necessary in order to heighten desire in those Andalusian torpors, and which betray a spirit tense as a coiled spring.

Her father sat in the assemblies as a member of the Carlist group, which should be understood not in a monarchist sense, but in a patriotic one. Of a race that, through the Inquisition, had delivered itself from the Jews and Protestants, he would not stand for a foreigner on the throne. In 1850, he failed in the elections, during which the worst insults were showered upon him, because he possessed valour. His daughter, still a child, knew the anguish of awaiting the newspaper and opening it on a jumble of improbable scandals, there being always some filth that sticks. One of her brothers was crippled in a duel. Then, in 1869, with Don Carlos opening up the Northern Campaign and the party active in Andalusia, the police implicated the old politician in a shocking case involving vice. In broad daylight, he was dragged through Seville en route to prison, where he died, choked by his desire for vengeance.

Without delay, the young woman crossed the whole of Spain in order to rejoin Don Carlos in Navarre. Behold the avenger! In her mind's eye, this prince was as beautiful as the day—as the day on which she would make her enemies weep. She ran to him, her little fists clenched, in the fevered state that she might have experienced in running to the hanging of her father's traducers and assassins.

She had a great deal to fear and to suffer on those narrow paths of Navarre, because the Carlists who held them were of a thieving temperament and they plagued even women. In like manner they carried enormous pairs of scissors in their belts that were used to clip mules, but which they used to cut off the long hair of the Basques suspected of "liberalism."

Finally the coach, escorted by brigands through the high rocks and along the narrow torrent, broke cover in the grim little town of Estella, the fortress of Carlisa.

"Don Carlos is at confession, he will receive the sacrament tomorrow morning," they tell her, with all the myriad pleasantries of soldiers, all those volunteers who were thronging the dark arcades about the public square, and whose bold stares, in that sad hour of the setting sun, were even more frightening than their talk.

Having gained refuge, after much searching, in a miserable "fonda," from which she wrote to Don Carlos, she expected to await the daylight without further complications. This was to reckon without the drawbacks of a town in which there are more men than women. A dozen chiefs were gathered together on the ground floor and, having drunk a great deal and kicked up a rumpus, they even grew weary of violating the tavern-wench, as they had been accustomed to doing for the past fortnight, and so commanded that the stranger-woman be brought to them—their drunkenness causing them to confuse stranger and enemy in their minds.

She had no option but to go down to them. Her long hair, loosened for the evening's toilet, bore witness that she had sufficiently established her loyalty in the face of the volunteer's scissors, but these debauchees had nothing more in mind than another seduction. After activities it would be ignoble to mention, nearly all of them violated this elegant young woman whose cries brought no aid, because, in Estella, as soon as the bells of the angelus died away, such protests were all too ordinary.

At dawn, left all alone, her soul and her body defeated, but more touching now for having suffered so many affronts, she made her way to the king.

This prince of twenty years, and very sensitive as regards women, was deeply moved by such harassment. He wiped away the dregs of wine from the hair of his young partisan; for the lack of women who might assist her, he took it upon himself to undress her and to carry her, completely exhausted by now, to the only bed in that poor house, the still warm royal bed.

Incapable, in her affliction, of keeping pace with so many sentiments at the same time, she could only repeat to him:
"Such a way to treat me, one of your own!" Pressed against the energetic breast of her king, this person of twenty-six years fell into a state of sleepy confidence. A girl deprived of her father, a young woman unloved, a royalist insulted by liberals, she had so greatly desired this protector! And, out of an entirely natural modesty, she dwelt more on grievances in Seville than the more recent outrages.

The investigation that was set in motion established in less than an hour that the culprits were the most popular and vigorous chiefs of Don Carlos' band. If they had been lowly soldiers, they would have been executed without delay. But it is reported that the young woman said to the pretender, who perhaps was hesitant: "A score of good soldiers can restore more of my honour than these have taken from me." A thoroughly admirable response.

What is certain is that Don Carlos called the men together, and six of them being found, upon his questioning them, to be bachelors, he invited the young woman to choose which of them she would accept as a husband.

"Sire," she asked him, "to which of them will Your Majesty give the command of the province of Seville?"

And foreseeing an interrogation: "The fact is," she said, "that having two vengeances to pursue, I wish only to abandon one in order the better to satisfy the other."

Upon the assurance that the husband of her choice would receive as a wedding present full power over the province of Seville, she claimed the first braggart who had molested her. They were married that same morning, at the mass at which the king received Communion. But Don Carlos, upon leaving the service, commanded the new husband to embark upon a perilous mission. The chivalry of a young husband who desired that so agreeable a woman should remain at liberty.

She would, it seems, have had little to attach her to her rough-and-ready husband. But that is to misunderstand the fitness of purpose of a passionate being. After two days, when the Carlist returned, exhausted, his bayonet bent and his clothes slashed by sabres on his untouched breast, she accompanied him to his tent to wash away the blood and dust in which he was covered. He had strangled liberals with his bare hands! And, in the intoxication she experienced in inhaling from upon him the scent of the slaughter of dead enemies, she forgot the stench of the wine and those breaths by which, at their first encounter, she had been sullied: she gave herself over completely to the image of a Seville soon to be terrorised.

Eventually, the rogue was hanged at Pamplona. He was possessed of every low quality and had not a scrap of virtue. But it is less their qualities than their common hatreds that bind people together. Abhor such a man? Ah! how strong a reason to love one another!

Hatred is not a base sentiment, if one really takes the trouble to consider that it martials our strongest energies in a unique direction, and that thus, necessarily, it gives us an admirable disinterestedness in other matters. Completely seized by a hatred, we are capable of pardoning trivial affronts, as follows from this story of the young woman who pardoned twelve of them.

5229. - CAMARET (Finistère). - Manoir de Boultous - Propriété du Poète St-Pol Roux

Saint-Pol-Roux aka **Pierre Paul Roux** (1861-1940). Something of an outsider even during the Symbolist period, Roux was admired by Villiers (who coined his nickname: "The Magnificent"), Maeterlinck, Huysmans, Mirbeau... From the outset he rejected the dogmatism and asceticism of his contemporaries, urging them not to turn their backs on life but to render it more "magnificent" and indeed to "correct God" by constructing the world anew through a poetic language driven by the imagination. In practice this meant a plethora of metaphors that fuse the abstract and concrete, uniting disparate aspects of reality and exposing relationships that are normally concealed.

In the 1890's Roux published the first of three volumes of *Les Reposoirs de la Procession* (from which the prose poems here are taken) and then devoted himself to *La Dame à la Faulx* (1899), an extraordinary tragedy on death which was never performed, despite a long campaign on its behalf by his most illustrious contemporaries.

Disillusioned with literary Paris, Roux left in 1898 for the far western tip of Brittany, where he built the astonishing *Manoir de Coecilian*, in which he lived for the rest of his life. Here he became a legendary figure, both to the local inhabitants, for his generously eccentric behaviour, and to a new generation of poets ready to appreciate his works, even though, after 1907, he was unable to find a publisher: many of these works are only now appearing for the first time. The Surrealists admired him greatly (even forgiving him his frequently Christian themes!), and organised a famous banquet in 1925, which ended in a pitched battle between Surrealists and Symbolists. His death followed the ransacking of his beloved *Manoir* by German soldiers, some three months after one of them had assaulted his daughter, Divine.

One of the most prolific and astonishing craftsmen of image and metaphor. Huysmans, seeking a new expressiveness tried to concretise spiritual, intellectual ideas, giving his style a rather too heavy precision and an artificial brightness: "decayed souls" (as though they were teeth) and "cracked hearts" (like old walls); this is picturesque, nothing more. The reverse of this process is more attuned to the stale desires of some to impart vague sentiments and an obscure sort of consciousness to things; it remains faithful to pantheistic and animistic traditions, without which art and poetry are impossible, being a deep well at whose source all the rest replenish themselves with the pure water transformed by a lesser sun into gems livelier than an elfin ring. Other "métaphoristes," like Jules Renard, run the risk of seeking out the single redeeming image, that one isolated detail which transforms and becomes the whole through the transposition and exaggeration of metaphors in everyday use; finally, there is an "analogical" method which, whether we wish it or not, modifies the usual meanings of everyday words. Saint-Pol-Roux combines all of these procedures and encourages them to co-operate in the formulation of images which, though always novel, need not be always pretty.

...Saint-Pol-Roux is endowed with imagination and a nasty but exuberant sensibility. Even if all these images, some of which are quite ingenious, follow the poet's lead throughout Les Reposoirs de la Procession, *reading such a work as this will be difficult, for smiles will too often intrude upon one's aesthetic musings; but these are slight flaws, lightly scattered about, and will hardly shatter for good the harmonies of these richly-coloured, clever but serious poems.* Le Pèlerinage de Sainte-Anne, *written almost entirely in images, is free from any blemish and its metaphors possess multiple meanings, yet are bound together in a logical manner; it is the very type and paragon of a poem written in rhythmic and cadenced prose. In the same volume, the* Nocturne *dedicated to Huysmans is nothing more than a vain chaplet of incoherent catachreses in which ideas are devoured by a frightful herd of beasts. But* L'Autopsie de la Vieille fille, *despite a defect in tone, but* Calvaire immémorial, *but* L'Ame saisissable *are masterpieces. Saint-Pol-Roux plays upon a zither whose strings are perhaps too tight; a slight adjustment of his clef would allow our ears to rejoice profoundly.*

SAINT-POL-ROUX

For Mme. Sarah Bernhardt

The Pilgrimage to Saint-Anne's

Five earthenware Lads, with skin of cliffs, with eyes the colour of subsiding sea, go, arm-in-arm, toward the painted chapel where the good Saint smiles pleasantly in an old-fashioned way.

In their Sunday best, marjoram-scented, their five Fiancées of dainty chinaware accompany them, arm-in-arm, pretty toys whose apple cheeks shine—for they are in their stays, gloomy whalebone from vile orifices; healthy seamen are destined for their beds.

Then the young garland marches toward Saint-Anne's, through the childish land, past flax and mills, hives, buckwheat, millstones, manors, plates of brown bread, cows, sheep and grandfatherly goats bleating.

And, living souls, the people arrive at the chapel in which has been painted, in ancient fashion, the good Saint smiling.

They come, these sons of the waves, to present their offerings; they come to present them to the Sponsor with the subtle seaweed-coloured eyes, the Sponsor of sailors, who saves them from the hungry wolves of the Northwest wind, who guides their great wooden sheep to Cornwall's fold.

See how they search the bottoms of their pockets during the greeting of the bells, see how they seek those golden or silver hearts pledged to the reefs which have clothed in mourning those Fustian women going to weep at the fountain...

See them searching there for gold or silver hearts, but meanwhile, tired out en route, the sweet Fiancées with their long sheaves of hair stretch themselves out upon the grasses and the moss.

But they do not find gold or silver hearts inside their pockets, at the greeting of the bells, they find, at bottom, only coral, tinder, and their medallions; but hearts of gold or silver, none at all.

Surprised, and paler than a surplice, they realize immediately that they must neglect an ex-voto for their village.

Then the sailors mourn, docile pilgrims, none of whom wish to make widows for the gifts that the Saint with the subtle seaweed-coloured eyes sends them as rafts on those fragile voyages—how pious one becomes before departure over blue seas beneath a splendid cross of mast and yardarm.

In the breeze, ever low, Fiancées of marjoram-scented porcelain are already asleep.

•

All at once, necks craning, the five earthenware Lads draw from their waists five knives more brilliant than five Lorient sardines and proceed, on tip-toe toward the five sleeping virgins.

Their ears, tangled among blonde tresses, resemble shells drawn from the sable waves.

As if in jest, the five Lads kneel before the pretty ones who dream on the grass that is as green as frogs.

Each young man having undone a blouse and a bodice wherein twin knobs of Quimper laugh, and beheld those living breasts, they made subtle signals, with chandelier eyes, and steel sardines plunge down into the source.

Spurting suddenly, from the rose, freshness of ancient foam... one would think it a rose blush made by reflected light, from the bulwark's iron sides, or that they had eaten blackberries and raspberries, from gullet to gorge.

At last their hands plunge into fair bosoms and draw forth five Hearts, five Hearts beating like sails.

In the breeze Fiancées of marjoram-scented porcelain sleep forever.

Then flesh is sewn up—with a thread of kisses through a needle of teeth—and the blouses and bodices, wherein twin knobs of Quimper laughed, close... the five earthenware Lads enter the painted chapel to offer up the Hearts, the Hearts beating like sails, to the Saint of the subtle seaweed-coloured eyes who guides their great wooden sheep through the hungry wolves of the Northwest wind to Cornwall's fold.

•

Alas! the sweethearts with their long flowing hair will no longer return once they have gone from the mosses and the grass.

All depart hence, depart along blank roads which unfold from the villages in which the men coo.

They summon them by name: Yvonne, Marthe, Marion, Naic and Madeleine.

But the beauties do not turn around; Yvonne, Marthe, Marion, Naic and Madeleine... and the villains run far away.

In the distance their caps, at first seagull wings, turn to wings of butterflies, then snow flakes cast on the horizon...

The five earthenware Lads fall down in a swoon, while the five Fiancées of marjoram-scented porcelain vanish.

•

No longer possessing their hearts, they ceased to love: Yvonne, Marthe, Marion, Naic and Madeleine.
Quimper, 1890.

For Joris-Karl Huysmans.

Nocturne   Darkness speaks.
    It might remind a schoolboy of that Appian charcoal which is only put right after many a blunder and buffeting.

    The frivolous breeze has decamped, having fixed her imperceptible tresses into a chignon which will turn the heads of the mills; but she has quite forgotten her little girl, a breezelet fit for dolls.

    A magpie nesting in a chestnut tree opens and closes its wingsinvitingly.

    Silence fastens its clasps meanwhile, and a grit of insects—most indiscreet of make-ups—lingers upon the contours of the earth.

    The vines compose themselves, as if the apoplectic falling

of the sun had taken away their desire to smile. Through bowed hours the trees seem lost in contemplation; the rascally rocks dream all alone.

Isn't this darkness mystery's own colour?

A final flock of crows passes by: a cemetery on the wing.

A bat scatters its extinguishing strokes upon the first lamps to show themselves, as if with an unsatisfied thirst. Its flight, a hybrid of hesitations between muzzle and wing, evokes, through its angles obtuse then acute, a ruler opened then folded up again by a velvet-ribbed carpenter.

Already, on viol-bridges of grass as well as by caresses, moths imitate cool stars.

Flowers are no longer distinguishable, but their perfume—a song for the nostrils—reveals them like a prayer offered up by the grasses.

This egalitarian vesper makes off with my coloration, leaving me a victim drowning in an atmosphere of sans-culottes.

Since darkness submerges our appearances, wouldn't it be better, when twilight falls, to be without eyes, nails, hair, skeleton or flesh—like a soldier unlucky in battle—and, with senses alone preserved, to be left wholly as spirit?

As if from an outraged sense of decency, the houses are shut up; the silken worms from the chimneys dry up among the tiles. Like Chinese shadow-plays, people taking to their beds are revealed; certain images, set down in a long-ago Book of Hours, revive at the memory of my hand.

From a house in which a dowry is being plotted through fine rains of tears The Maiden's Prayer arises: some young lady with tapering fingers is taming those decaying ivories, the flats of a modern-day Tarasque.

And then, a mastiff, vicious trinket of the portal, spits its catarrh against a hand cart—pushed by a blaspheming stone mason—which has in passing broken down.

•

Darkness speaks...

...a summer's day viewed through dark glasses...

...a funeral where an engagement is announced.

What if white hairs were to snow down from who-knows-where?

What if they were stolen from invisible swans or else from souls just barely visible?

What if they were the immense robe of a widow whose breasts, just now caressed, will henceforth weep vain milk? What if the dead should shun their winding-sheets? Do they weep over their nullity when, at rare times, the pool of their regrets overflows?

These hypotheses tear my eyes and my skull to pieces!

Then a dancing of spiders breaks out across my skin so that everywhere... shivers?

No doubt caused by the dismal immobility of those poplars...

Ah! there—from the decapitated windmill: a celestial shaft arising!—the orphaned motions shoot up to deliver their captive members from the dungeon of my Imagination!

Suddenly, a childhood fear invades me, inflaming my desire to take refuge in Nurse's skirts. If I were to open my mouth, maybe you would see my heart aflame.

Hasn't this underwood spewed the salty fellow out to you, mutely grasping the intolerable tongue in his fist?

See—as if sleepwalking, I find myself before a precipice. Am I a bon-bon then, that the abyss yawns for me with a glutton's desire, a permanent appetite?

Then the ecclesiastical cyclopses of stone, with hoary eyes, chant bronze alexandrines over all those things darkness gives itself to in lingering mantles.

Within me a naïve apprehension of secular death tightens the cords of my arms which feverishly cross themselves on my person.

Purely by chance life is offering me a mugful of air, father Adam's cognac. Regaining my balance, I laugh sonorously—but I recall: sometimes courage is nothing but the shining armour of fear.

And now the whole of nature is a negress in a chemise

powdered with hoarfrost.

•

Darkness speaks.

Duped by this semblance of dawn, the cocks sound their laborious whooping cough off into diverse barns. The grooms grouse in the straw before their work begins. But they have a venerable reply-in-kind of their own; a quick wink at the half-nocturnal union with the needles allows them to bury themselves in that Image-making which does not see itself when eyes are closed.

Eye of the firmament, I travel on.

And my steps press their weight into excrement fallen from the Omega of louts who are without embarrassment or anxiety.

In the hollow of the valley, between the breasts of the hills, the pool stagnates, blurred like the eye of an androgyne. Here, on the bank, the two-horned tamarisk mimics Hamlet on the Battlements; there amid the rushes, knowledge sets a filigree ambush for jolly fauns.

At the water's threshold and from all directions the frogs, leaves of living salad, bleat airs while the toads, fat cannons, deign to drop a rare note in baritone.

Unexpectedly, a jeering snake spurts from a hollow elder tree and menaces the green gossipers with the draaught of his passing.

Plic! plac! ploc!

Confronted now by the pool's ironic wrinkles and long-nosed reeds, the serpent returns to the obscurity of his failure.

The dog has fallen silent, his catarrh cured by sleep; the cock no longer sets his sonorous corn-poppy in the button-hole of the hour; but once again, far away now, the tardy cart, guided along by that Capuchin of the Conveyances whose discipline lacks silence, breaks down.

Darkness has spoken.

Saint-Henry, 1888.

For Emile Bergerat.

The Autopsy On The Old Spinster   Upon the marble lay the aged and waxy corpse: one might have said a soul, solid and perceptible.

Three medical students in white aprons, pipes in their jaws, with the air of a decisive tribunal, jeered.

—O neighbour to the church with a green thumb for missals!... O honeysuckle in the flax of a nun and a coif of the valley!... O spokeswoman for dead leaves in the breeze!... O virgin without a shift!

One wanted to see: could this be true?

And those impious ones spread wide the legs of the aged and waxy corpse, as they would the needles of a compass to make a calculation...

THE BIRD HAD NOT MADE HIS NEST.

Having been thus disappointed, the students give voice to this song of the cock:

—That doesn't prove a thing—fear of the big belly that attends the suckling-sin might have discouraged her; or, if a prudent and wise gourmand, the hypocrite might well have kept company with her greenish-blue desires behind drawn venetian blinds, but we proceed to be instructed!

They were about to conduct a subtle autopsy—an autopsy of the senses as it were.

Lisping insects at twilight, the invisible steels—sharp tongues of vipers—immediately conjugate the corpse.

Winding from the pipes, cunning fumes, shaped like a moustache one might twirl, hang in mid-air in incredulous waltzes.

•

Her Feet revealed pilgrimages to the green hill where the Firmament, under the seal of her fleeting toes, inspired a bouquet of consoling rain. From the Hands emanated the frequent and capricious touchings of blessed objects and caresses of a rosary.

Inside her Nostrils were the fragrances of incense, of hawthorn, of candles, of sepulchral herbs, of precious bone buried in glass coffins.

Behind her unsullied Teeth were found the savours of hosts, of fish with white flesh, of eggs—and an abstinence from wines and from all dainties.

Her eyes exhibited, in shapes of diaphanous streamers, looks expressing ceremonies of celestial-hued chasubles, processions with laudatory banners, and similar compassionate visions in which flourish a Virgin with lilies, a Saint Peter with the keys, a splendid baby swathed in the breath of an ass.

The Ears yielded up many a sonorous ingot of Angelus, precepts of the flesh, organ notes and praises; but also, dimly, as though hardly heard, these words already fifty years old... tired words! And useless, from the lips of a proud herdsman who passed one morning, marriageable, beneath the innocent and candid window: "Madelon-Madeleine, humbly I adore you; take this shepherd and his sheep, if my love is for you!"

•

Going down into the Heart disclosed the breasts, so nibbled by the teeth of her hair-shirt.

A perfume of rectories gushes forth.

Then the heart appeared, pierced through by seven swords like the Mater Dolorosa.

They knelt then, reverentially, amid the pipes fallen from their jaws—and three signs of the cross, made by three red hands upon three white aprons, vaguely recalled three Knights of Malta...

Saint-Henry, 1891.

For José-Maria de Heredia.

The Immemorial Calvary ❧

The good breeze of reverie wafted me into adventure, amidst the thatched roofs, over the solid river of roads that borders the tender hope where those living distaffs, the sheep, graze.

On all sides beneath the metal cocks, in the divine keeps, the gross pennies of existence, jingling to a uniform rhythm, beat down the windmills' sails and the ploughs' fins.

All alone, I went, giving way only once before the naïve old coach: a wasp with a whip for its stinger, which flies about from town to town, and gathers the animate booty that the hive of the city will soon collect.

At a certain bend in the road, doubtless a meeting place where conscripts made their farewells, I suddenly came upon Calvary.*

The Christ had to be guessed at, he was so worn!

Here he was set up hard by an ancient yew with little berries like drops of blood.

But I was greatly distressed because Jesus seemed to suffer all the more in his decrepitude. He was no longer anything more than something hanging there: like a long forgotten scrap of stone, and still more ancient, like a lad from before the Age of Lances and Nails.

Great Flowers of Solitude slumbered all about.

I said:

"How I pity you, crucified one, in your devastation!... But why such skinny misery?... Why are you hanging, beautiful and grand, from a Sycamore of granite where I barely see you with the eyes of my soul? Answer me, o fraternal father: will the form be layers of dust that the housewifely wings of the Birds of Time might in passing raise? Or else have you been carved from the salt of tears, and will the long raindrops dissolve you? Speak, paternal brother!... You spoke well, in the time of palms, to the Woman of Samaria."*

Jesus answered me...

Oh! he did not speak, no longer living lips, tongue, mouth, oh! he did not speak... but the scrap of stone was swarming with bees, and each bee was a vowel with two wings for consonants.

Now I understood this honey:

"No, it isn't the rain, it isn't weather! Although I've been here for centuries, erected by the pious women who would be very old if they still lived, and who are, in Paradise, very young to be dead. No, it isn't the weather, it isn't the rain! although it has oftentimes rained for the pleasure of the flowers and the glory of the apple-trees! No, that's not it! But, they have come to this cross-road for years and years, all the morose have come here. For years and years spiritual mendicants with withered flesh have come on pilgrimage to me; and all, clambering up the marches of Calvary, feverishly kiss my health-giving image."

"In truth, Jesus, the presence of those kisses manifests itself in the absence of stone that has been worn away by the passing lips."

"There's more to it than that. Each kiss defines the sorrow that set it there. Thus the Mad kiss my brow, the Blind my eyes, the Dumb my mouth, the Deaf my ears, the Lame my legs, the One-armed, my hands and arms, and my heart receives the kisses of the Magdalens. These sufferings brought together signify Suffering Humanity in its entirety, and their scattered kisses contribute to the same goal in wearing away my benevolent stone."

"This goal, what is it, Word made swarm of bees?"

"It is my Soul! my Divine Soul which ingeniously hatches out under a terrestrial form. For them it is admirable Hope, and if one day they were not able to harvest it beneath the plough of their kisses, these pilgrims might adore the blasphemous tares and forever loose their faith in Paradise."

"O Divine Soul!" I cried out lost like a divine lover. Then, clambering up the marches of Calvary, I embraced the sycamore redeemer and full of ardour I kissed the scrap of stone at the places I believed to be the eyes, the hands, the feet, the heart, the brow—for, the poet is the whole of Suffering Humanity.

So numerous were my kisses that the image disappeared, and at last the Divine Soul gushed out through the worn-out form, the Soul for years and years expected by the spiritual mendicants with withered flesh...

My heart, suddenly ravished by this premier diamond of invisibility, opened just as would a fanatical sunflower faced with the sun.

And I had to remain there, virginal, immutable, from age to age.

I alone had seen the great Flowers of Solitude.

For Henri de Régnier

The Perceptible Soul Under the blood-tinged tiles of the Market in my village—a pyramidal carapace supported by four pillars bedecked with onions, garlic, tayoles and garish headscarves—a Mountebank set up his stage.

In the background, to the right, to the left, from the high floor of the stage the motley Eccentrics tread, got up like affected birds or magic frogs, a childishly painted backcloth hangs, upon which: Naine, a princess, marrying King Géant; an Explorer in a cornflower-blue greatcoat, a yellow umbrella under his arm, being gobbled up by a crocodile the colour of tender grass; a Redskin writhing in the abominable colic of a reptile with oysters for scales, and other parodies of terror.

In front of the platform two crazy musicians. The one squats doubled-up on an ass metamorphosed into a drum, the other, evoking for me a derisive caricature of St John Chrysostom*, thrusts out and retracts great copper lips: a resonant hailstorm like the rays of the meridional sun tumbles down from the metallic bell, and this braying trombone complements the drum.

Now, on the down-to-earth stones, a flock of smocked Yokels, congealed with ecstasy, breathless, with hearts hopping to escape through the shady lozenge of their mouths, watch the tumblers demonstrating their fantastic skills with dazzling capers...

I began thinking that the simple ones must have valued these extraordinary manifestations greatly, as being without doubt the finished print of the infinite, the visible geometry of the invisible, the perceptible pantomime of the mystery, the divulgation of the hieroglyphics, the presumable or suggestive demonstration of theorems rebellious to their puny brains, in other words the spectacle, at a ready price, of things too difficult to grasp, the divine Thule of the dream unexpectedly placed at the mercy of the profane, the impossible glimpsed, the beyond surveyed and valued, the absolute monetised; I came to the conclusion that the crowd was delighting in the sadly evident fatigue of the jugglers and gymnasiarchs, become the final repose and the joy of its being, having, for its proper and victorious satisfaction, only to superficially observe.

Then:
—These Yokels, shut up in the vale of the contingent amidst the very hour of their banal life, I purred, these inhabitants of the transitory present are unable to relish decently the fruits of my reason sufficiently for their age since it partakes of forever, vassal to the future and of the past: both eve and fecund morrow of the arid moment. The eyes and the ears unique to their bodies brush past gaping, neither seeing nor hearing my enigma, accessible to the capable senses of a subtle spirit alone, ostensibly devout and served by that fiancée of genius, comprehension. But if I even attempted to invite them to understand me, the multitude would indeed shun my divine leprosy. It appears then that Charity, too sweet to the wayfarer, legitimate light of the poet, who divines the disinterested virtue of alms, terrifies the basely imperious philistine, the eye of dread beholding a sack of coals roaring, in which a sack of diamonds smiles. The bringer of good news inspires the mistrust of the prisoners of customary dogmas, and this sage seems malign, hideous, illogical: a phantom!

A clown on the platform jeered.
The keyboard of her pert little face played the whole scale of grimaces; the histrionic mouth puckered into a pout like a chicken's arsehole or stretched from ear to ear, in such a way that the Yokels, beautified by the gradual rainbow of laughter, span round in the hurricane of apish antics.

For my part, I continued:
—When all's said and done, one is always the enemy. Rational grounds—and how!—because, truly, we are: they the immediate fatherland, myself the exile. At each approach I represent to them the one who returns from a supernatural terrain, masked in a superhuman idiom; so my good news falls fallow upon their inhospitable sands: I am the Voice, but they are the Desert.

A rope-dancer, flitting nimbly through the void in the guise of a dragonfly now set the horny-handed ones a-yelling in amazement—and a swift, inspiring light invaded me.

I had found the translation zone, in which we would be able to understand each other.

Venturing out to take refuge under the boards, in an

obscurity propitious to enchantments, I enjoin, with the imperious will of a god, I enjoin my soul to appear—*to be*.

Suddenly a fabulous Girl springs forth from the clay of my potter's wheel!

My wisdom took the place of her beauty, my passions vivified her form with truth; and so perfect was the living image that I believed her clad in bitter foam.

Quickly I led her away behind the childishly painted backcloth. In a costume emanating—a dawn of tulle—from a half-opened trunk, I clothed my soul, then I cast the psyche, like a handful of fortune, upon the empty stage.

The exclamation of the crowd, at seeing her appear, was a formidable silence

Then my Soul, with a seraphically nimble frolic through the *turns* somehow resolved by limbs of the breeze, translated herself, defined herself, revealed herself to the eyes of the Yokels, breathless at the sight of the adamantine salutation as if they had suddenly been bent over a mine of treasures.

She is (by virtue of the hereditary and common interpreter, the *sign*, understandable to lesser intelligences) a kaleidoscope in which, in a faithful interpretation, the essence formulates itself, transcendence makes itself accessible, the abyss makes itself feasible, idea makes themselves figurative. Each pirouette, each massive arabesque is the exoteric equivalent of translated esotericism; each gesture, as if traced by white chalk on a black slate, is the adequate and spontaneous contour of an abstraction; and that evokes thoughts of the First Idea that the alphabet of intermediary stars, sooner or later deciphered, will divulge. In the twinkling of the eye, a thousand eagles of metaphysical wind are restrained, birdlimed by the frost of the formal drawing of miraculous lines.

Thus, through that web of facile phenomena, my fastidious Soul vulgarises herself through the artifice of a transposition familiar to the Yokels whose entire bewitched being stands attentive, on the threshold of their eyelashes; and see how, by means of this commentary suited to their relative comprehension, they proclaim my nature, heretofore negligible and ostracised, a charitable and necessary truism.

Such is the success that the Yokels now desire and piously glorify this soul, completely reviled by all the brutality of their ignorance: from each spectator long-stemmed flowers of admiration take flight to caress and bless the wonderful creature. The rude hands, like cymbals, crash out eulogies, while, on the platform, the supple psyche strips off the leaves of her revelatory algebra...

Finally, drunk with genuflections, the Yokels roar: "Enough, for mercy's sake, rare Girl!... We're already reeling, and our enthusiasm is so ardent that it's going to consume us if you don't cease these marvels!..."

Lenient, my Soul bowed to the delirious multitude, and armed with a glazed earthenware plate, she went down to undertake the customary collection, with the material idea of putting a value on apotheosis.

But, so as sufficiently to pay the Icon, and also so as henceforth to see no more of her, the Yokels removed their eyes from their sockets and gently placed them in the proffered plate.

Then, groping their way with canes, the Yokels dispersed—with my vision in their memory.

Saint-Henry, 1888.

—Translated by Andrew Mangravite & Iain White.

249   FRANCIS POICTEVIN

Francis Poictevin (1854-1904). The mysterious and gnomic works of Poictevin, so accurately portrayed by de Gourmont, record a quest which ended in disaster: his mental collapse in 1894, and confinement in an institution until his death. He continued writing even then, but he was forgotten, except by a few friends, and these manuscripts have never been published. His books, which are not novels, nor travel diaries, nor *récits*, but some intermediate form, appeared with perfect annual regularity between 1882 and 1894. In them Poictevin contrived to chronicle a psychological and spiritual journey by means of observations of the external world: they are perfect demonstrations of Symbolism, everything here is symbol clothed in the skin of appearance. With hindsight his obsessive and repetitive observation of detail, verging on synaesthesia, can be seen to foreshadow his illness.

A Christian mystic and hyper-aesthete, Pocitevin shared these characteristics with his close friend Huysmans, but applied them to his works in a unique way. Unfortunately for this anthology the impact of his books is cumulative. He has never before been translated into English.

The texts here form two consecutive sections from *Derniers songes* (1888).

Like all writers who have reached an understanding of life, that is to say its immediate uselessness, Francis Poictevin, although a born novelist, promptly renounced the novel. He knows that everything happens, that one fact is not in itself more interesting than another fact, and that "the manner of expression" alone matters....

The author of Tout bas *and* Presque *would have been able, like all the rest, to arrange his meditations into dialogues, to order his sentiments into chapters cut at random into slabs of lines, to insinuate into sham-living characters a few animated gestures and have them convey, through noticeable genuflections upon the flagstones of a known church, the efficacy of an unacknowledged creed: in short to write "Mystical Novels" and to vulgarise for the "literary journals" the practice of mental prayer. By this means his books would have acquired some popularity, which he certainly lacks, because, if few writers are so esteemed, few, among those of evident talent, are less well known and less seen in the bookshops. But in order to interest us, and almost always excessively, Poictevin disdains all artifice outside of the artifice of style, a trap into which it is agreeable for us to fall...*

He visibly strives to go to the heart, to penetrate even to the vital centre of the flower-head of the hortensia. Everywhere he seeks out the soul—and he finds it. No one is less of a rhetorician than this stylist, for the rhetorician is he who dresses up in stylish garments those solid commonplaces apt to support all the vulgar herd of tawdry ornamentation, while Monsieur Poictevin would make a phantom still more diaphanous, a rainbow, an illusion, an azalea-flower; this, for example: "Would the hand of a consumptive, in the angustation of its near-translucency, calm, not indolent, but which no longer feels, less exalted than before and indulgently returned, appear to warn?"

Yes—how subtle he is!—And why not write "like everybody else?"

Alas, that is forbidden him—because he is a mystic, because he senses new affinities between men, and things, and God, and because, veiled by the painful perfection of a form in which grace takes great pains over minute details, Poictevin is spontaneous. But there are, no doubt, things he has not transcribed, not daring to, doubting his ability to capture its true, unique, very rare, unpublished essence!...

Everything, in effect, in a work of art must be as yet unknown, even the words, in the way they are arranged, to bring them round to new meanings—and one sometimes regrets having an alphabet known to too many illiterates.

A disciple of the Goncourts, the preciosity of whose writing he has still further heightened, Monsieur Francis Poictevin has refined his work to the point of immaterialisation. And in that lies his genius, the expression of the immaterial and the inexpressible: he has invented the mysticism of style.

FRANCIS POICTEVIN

Jacques:
Dreams,
Reveries
❧

That night he dreamt a black fowl was obstinately pursuing him. It was larger than an ordinary fowl. Where the head should have been, in the severed neck, there was a hole like a scooped-out eye. In the room, some pieces of furniture and even one or two people were obstructing my circling flight. And I felt saddened, with a sort of fury at being unable to escape this terrible creature. Yet I did not allow myself—despite the fowl almost constantly brushing against me, and feeling in anticipation its clawing at me and suffering already the pain of it—I did not allow myself to be caught.

In another dream he found himself in the upper tiers of an enormous amphitheatre, open to the sky and divided into quite unequal proportions. The arena was still empty: the crowd was waiting, inattentively animated. The neighbourhood, so to speak, in which I saw myself confined, almost perched, was occupied by sick people wearing workmen's shirts, printed calico dresses, with head bandages on their brows like people in hospital, and these men and women, seated promiscuously, rather stooped on the whole, were looking malevolently in my direction: that bourgeois dressed all in black, holding himself aloof, as if apart from their furthest rank. Soon I divined a confused murmur rumbling in their breasts, and already faces were becoming tense, in an ugly fashion, bearing down on me, against me. And, to flee them, before they singled me out with an indubitable precision—for presently, I sensed it, there would be no point whatever in my making myself look small on this spot—I slipped, somehow or other, behind those hostile beings, along the back of the highest tier and finally crept into an angular and roofed passage. But there a wan, uneasy light immediately made me fear I would be trapped. From second to second my fear increased, a terror now that they might discover me. And, through the thin wall of the fortunately sinuous corridor, there infiltrated to me the anhelation of the crowd confusedly muttering.

That night, in a dream, he was with an old friend, long since not seen, in the Luxembourg Gardens where, when we were reading law we liked to meet to read pages of the great poets. But in my nebulous, febrile vision the park was levelled; extended into a solitary space, there remained only a supposition of the phantoms of trees, offering no obstacle to walking nor to seeing. Our gait had about it a morbid languor. I saw that I was very thin, and I regretted that my friend had retained his former appearance, rather stout despite his good breeding and his extremely well-informed intelligence. And, while we conversed to no purpose, able to convey only the certainty of our double isolation, impenetrable one to the other, I felt myself fading away into an irremissible weeping grief. And about us the breezes were as if dead.

It was that night in the environs of the Place de l'Étoile, on the corner of an aristocratic and somewhat isolated street. Very close to me I heard an unfamiliar voice which caused me no surprise, as if previously I had wished to hear it, and yet that voice was literally unknown to me. "What does it avail you," it said to me, "to be so calm and observant, if you pass by like that without a word of commiseration?..." It was a person difficult to put a name to, at once humble and wise. The lucid eyes, of a lustreless grey, with a chaste aura faintly brown, reddish, possessed a depth of truth, they were gentle, transversely they were intersected by a thin veil of obscure transparency. The face had a matt quality, as if drained of colour, and bespoke a suffering reabsorbed in thought. The hands, pallid with purity, seemed in their apparent whiteness intermingled with a blackish tinge, to indicate they were in no way idle. Dressed in grey, her dress of no importance, she was neither a child nor a dwarf, although she was simple, small and singular, and wholly engaging. She reminded me of nothing hitherto experienced. Fundamentally her import had about it an obsolete bewitching quality of someone superannuated and prone to previsions. Suppose, I thought on waking, I were to encounter her one day. But no, comparing the dream-vision and the recollection remaining of it, I already sensed it evaporating, near-irrecoverable in the limbo of the awakened memory.

Finding oneself by chance in the situation just described with someone whose sentiments moreover have rather escaped you, it immediately seems to youthat your spirit not only perceives these latencies, but actually realises at that moment what the other must then be experiencing. Might that not be a proof that the visible side of beings is adequately attached to their substance, that the one and the other are identical?

That compels one to observe diminishing within oneself the esteem one has for somebody to whom one owes gratitude.

There are those whose disagreeable gaze gives one the impression that one is traversing their brain, ill-naturedly reduced in size.

At times the very small child, in its first few months, face raised, feet and hands in the air, fists clenched, eyes like a clouded glass, has a physiognomy that is ineffably inarticulate, as if with a happy infinity. If, then, one tries to caress it, it is obvious that this is a disagreeable distraction; even the presence of its mother seems intrusive, she is disturbing it in that speechless expansion with that which our dimmed eyes can no longer discern in the atmosphere, etherically peopled for the baby with higher things absent for ourselves.

Perhaps our black cat, with eyes of chrysoprase encircling two variable black pearls, cat slipping unexpected, wheedling and cautious, alongside objects, and whose splendid fur has at its tips reddish glints, likes to stop, to crouch on the mantel shelf almost next to the clock so that her somnolent reverie might in some way be regulated by the sound hidden in that box, sound of a shifting fixity.

That night my trousers, left tossed on an easy-chair, bothered me. I lit the candle again. Those legs: divergence, sagging, the factitious vestige not perhaps so much of my personal vanished legs as of a different form becoming distorted, out of kilter, imprecisely suggested.

Sounds horrifically slow and heavy of the nightsoil-carts, when one wakes in bed, disturbed by that squalling of shaken, jolted paving-stones. The sleeper, who ordinarily is dreaming, imagines himself in a hell hallucinatorily augmented by the darkness of the hour which itself is barely awake. In a muffled commotion, deafening and distracting, that juddering movement ignobly troubles the morning's final darknesses. And the fearfulness of the odour divined within and beyond the thundering of those carts.

Under the electric lighting I am walking on the asphalt of the Champs Élysées, preceded by my strangely double shadow. A blackish shadow enclosed within another, so to speak, of glass, as if the soul had slipped into the external form and inwardly all that remained was a dark emptiness. And it seems to me that it suffers within my long, doubled shadow which is fleeing, shabbily, coldly white, somewhat dirty, skimming the asphalt. All around truncated shadows, forked, twisted, of branches, oscillate, rigid.

That man, barely in his forties, of a leanness by no means delicate, greying already, his beard sparse at the sides and crinkled towards the point, eye-sockets constricted with dull eyes not unaccustomed to gleaming, that unhealthily lively man, usually well turned out, sometimes accosts me before I catch sight of him; he converses with me familiarly, as if resuming a conversation interrupted the day before, his words quickly insistent in his toothless mouth; without transition he makes off again and I remain a second, watching that back which seems to be hastening towards business not to be missed. However the fellow would no doubt have wished for himself what he was telling me of another: not to eat, he scarcely fancied that at all, but to absorb liquid... that he preferred.

In the waiting-room of an important newspaper a man in his fifties, his large and long limbs emaciated, remained seated, leaning forwards, on the settee opposite me. His features had about them that haggardness that already almost caves in on itself. One sensed that the pulled-down cuffs of his high-buttoned frock-coat concealed the absence of linen. His eyes, not precisely lowered, looking before him almost at random, told of disappointments experienced, always foreseen in vain. In his inobdurate bearing he exhibited a lassitude beyond enervation, lacking any further impatience. When at length the solicited journalist arrived, our man got to his feet, still a trifle bowed, in a sort of disgusted humility.

In the Café de la Régence, one afternoon, as we were entering, a painter and I, we saw, seated in a corner at a table with papers on it, a man still young, fairly slender, an opera-hat on his head, wearing a dress-coat, and a mauve satin cravat, blond and pensively sedate, his complexion unspoilt; we observed that man, all things considered a well-bred sort. He ceased writing, began again. In his buttonhole was displayed a decoration of the same hue as the cravat, flower or ribbon, who's to know. The people, the painter told me, call them, you know, those gentlemen, "scented fops." For my part I was interested in a minimum, the essential thing fundamentally, in the uncertainty I thought I found in that individual, less affected perhaps than disguised and unhappy.

On the Champs Élysées, of an elderly buck preceding me by a few paces, all I saw, in a ridiculously inverse direction of thoughts from behind the head, was the waxed tips of his moustache.

A woman, already old, whose nose rather contradictorily drooped rather like a beak, yet flabby.

In a wine-merchant's, the shopkeeper's voice seemed to me to be corked and to be at one with that forty-year-old, fairly well-groomed citizen's leaden skin.

Have you noticed how one listens sometimes almost complaisantly to persons who displease you and tell you vexatious things? One even begins, at those times, to speak as they do, with an admixture of good faith. Deep down in your being, however, a voice, personal and alien, confusedly reproves you.

Certain scents one feels to be of an acute subtlety, but veiled as in a muslin; they reach you almost sifted, and one fears they are becoming stale.

There are many oranges with a granular, florid skin, in short, commonplace. Some are smooth and muffled in a faint dampness. Peeled, the quarters of oranges of an oriental provenance resemble a sober light, a matt amber daylight, an odorous daylight.

The petals of the eucharis, a fragile cup-shape, are of a whiteness shaded with humidity, sumptuous, from which, proud, there exhales a like perfume. At the heart, a discreet blue fire subsists, peaceable.

Under my gaze that oscillates before a cat's-eye, Rue Royale, there shifts in the midst of the precious stone, between one of its sides, brownish-yellow, and the other, marsh-green, there shifts, phantasmally, a perfectly oblong shadow. And it makes as if to divide, and is no more than a minute swarming, and in my immobile vision it is already blending again into the suffused stone that lights up, but dimly.

In another goldsmith's window three diamonds, grouped—the third, slightly lower, surmounted by an ultramarine sapphire. This triple, luminous stone of non-diaphanous water is unified, for me, into a family shining with an inviolate purity. But the sombre sapphire dominates, spaciously alone.

In the window of a pharmaceutical laboratory. At a point on a small, wide-mouthed glass bottle a glimmer of green light settled; uneasily deeper, somewhat turbid, amidst the other similar bottles behind. Close by, a tubulated balloon-flask contained, as if frozen, a minute residue of silver powder. In another narrow, rather long glass container, some fallacious gum had the lustreless appearance of horn. But I made off, almost fleeing from the obfuscated eyes of black pills that aroused thoughts of hideous and dubious poisons.

In the cellars of the Panthéon, in the round corridor where the custodian-guide, his lantern in his hand, lines up the close-packed visitors in a file, the low vault describes a uniformly turning curve. The echo of the custodian's voice rolls and reverberates. And this absurd repetitive sound and that curve, bare stone, smooth, insipidly whitish, leave you bewildered at their illusory flight.

Parisian Landscapes Sometimes, under a clear winter sky, in the Seine more grey than green, trunks of trees immerse their shadows; they make way for each other, Licette mused, like swimmers; the water wets them without traversing them. On other occasions, mused Jacques, it was as if thin, impregnable and glassy laminae were barely floating beneath the surface.

Today the Seine, under a a fine wind-borne rain, was rolling along, yellowish, with meanders of shadow shading towards purple in, as it were, a surreptitious transparency. At some steps where horses are led to drink, the water breaks up, it halts, it wishes, so it seems, to take rest; and here it forms wavelets, long undulations only barely hollowed out, hesitant rolling waves: then, momentarily everything stirs again in a quickly lost eddy. And so there the waters do not so much go astray as coagulate. Lazy ripples that come together, and finally inconclude.

Amidst the nitidity of the snow on the lawns of the Champs Élysées, the shadows of the tree-trunks lie stretched out, a trifle bluish, soft, hardly transparent but veiling still the whiteness beneath in a velvety lack of lustre.

This morning the statues on the fountains of the Place de la Concorde were like negroes, blacker still in the frozen fullness of their mantles. Curved behind them, the fountain recalled some Chinese representation.

In the basins of the Rond-Point, among the lumps of slowly dissolving snow, melting ice, a greeny, steeped crystal; one senses it growing dim. Frozen tears hang from the fountains, inwardly brilliant.

Under a dismal afternoon sky, in the thawed and leaden water of those basins, the reflection of the low, bushy fountain had a whiteness of melting ice.

On the sterile snow in the Jardin d'Acclimatation, ornamental white ducks, not too fat, with small orange-yellow feet, are illuminated as if from within. A sort of melted light within those bodies of unruffled feathers and which gives an impression of expanding.

That morning, the air still not completely clear, the Seine had about it dubious charms. The ill-tarred blackness of barges against the green water, barges immobile or slipping along on tow; circles of water against the smoothed stone piles, in particular the blackish-violet shadows under the arches, a sort of luxury that hides itself away and makes off to be swallowed up in a neutralising green, and finally the reflections of the trees close alongside that seem not asleep, but awake and watching, and, above all, close to La Samaritaine, dormancies of quiet water, almost level, intermittently shifting slightly and faintly bestirring themselves in a deliciously chilly shivering. Next, a sewage-pipe discharges its filthy ochre, turgid, from the wall of the quay below the Conciergeries; one imagines a liquefied exhalation of all kinds of crimes—the ultimate dissolution of the pestilences of that Palais de Justice is making its way towards the ocean. And, under the dissipating mists, the pointed roofs and the round towers reappear, implacable, immured, dry as law-digests.

Under the arches of the bridges, a few stones of a slightly mildewed whiteness among the others, black. They seem phosphorescent, almost like rotten wood exuding light.

Morning. Between the bare walls of the houses, above scraps of wasteland, the white-coloured smoke of a factory-chimney was slowly drifting in tufts towards the mist-pale sky where, suddenly floating, ill-concealed, a globe appeared, seeming less of a sun than a moon. And that vaguely gleaming speck was quickly effaced, receding into the sky's high and even expanse. Along the Avenue d'Iena the purply-russet tree-tops were sprouting, bushy in a drab sparseness. Further on, almost above the Seine, faint wisps of factory-smoke were still insensibly merging into the sky, itself of a molten silverishness in places. The river, a faintly dulled green, flowed along in a billowy haste, eddying in ebullitions behind the arches.

Through that late-March afternoon, on the Place de la Concorde, among the gusts of contrary wind, and warm, and damp, interrupted gusts, recommencing, halted, off once more, as it were, towards the clouds, there were ripples wandering from moment to moment across puddles on the ground, infrequent passers-by, discords rather, hand on hat, coat-tails turned back or skirts pliant; in the sky a drama, resplendent and obscure: there, banks of clouds decking themselves out in rather fake gilt bindings, at the zenith severely sombre fragments, elsewhere, in the distance, stretches of subdued violet-tinged silver, faded towards the far horizon between the fine lines of blackish branches. The eye willingly returned, almost above the square itself, to some uniform whitenesses, intimately dissolving, steppes across which there slowly passed small, high, frayed, fluid-grey clouds. About us, irritating, carriages were threading, some of the fiacres' scrap-iron jangling, raucous; and the obelisk, a washed-out pink, was disconcerting in its unshaken fixity. Only the steeples of Sainte-Clotilde were at one with the spirit of the scene: narrow openings in their greyer stone seemed, in their ascending diminution, mystically to look out from the depths of an ancient sky.

That evening, from the Rond-Point, under the rain at the moment of sunset, in one of the lateral avenues, the not yet indistinct lines of the slightly moving tree-tops were receding towards the distant east of a sky almost magically blue.

That Easter Monday, the first fine evening of Spring, from the Place de la Concorde, I was watching the sun, vanished in a crimson glow to the left of the Arc de Triomphe. It was becoming indistinct, as if in a faded mist. Above, the rosy tints of the clouds were expiring in a violet display from instant to instant shading away into a pale lilac evanescence in the depths of the heavens.

That evening, after an intermittent day of hail and sun, from the Pont de l'Alma, to the left of the sunset, some clouds were massing their bushy, almost tenebrous summits, aureoled in too dazzling a gold. Then, a little more to the left, there was a curious crystal patch, imperceptibly bluish and already tinted grey; small clouds hung there, indecisively straying, still adding a velvety tone to their frail lilac.

That morning of shifting clouds, on the broad bank of the lake in the Bois de Boulogne, the moving water was encroaching less deeply into that greenery, not extending into it. From the swaying of the tops of the pine-trees, a murmur was welling up, it swelled, spread out, for a few moments became that place's soul. And small drops of rain fell, interweaving, fine, as if suspended and instantly reabsorbed, percolating into the atmosphere. A white swan on the lake advanced towards the stroller, then, faced with his empty and uselessly friendly hand, it turned, disdainful, floating along on its way.

That first morning of May, under a calm sky of timid rain, there was no dragging oneself from the parapet of the Pont-Royal. Behind the arches, after the foam-flecked swirlings of the water, among the broken agitation of its little waves, the Seine continued in smooth, rather placid sheets, slowly undulant. And thus the river communicated to the soul the indefinite gliding trepidation of its silence.

Through the glass screen on the *terrasse* of a boulevard café, the budding trees, the bases of their trunks apparently dissipated, take on an almost pallid mitigation of imponderables against a hazily blue sky. It is as if they were able to traverse it, and they appear, airy forms, like surprising, desired visions from the world beyond.

In the Montmartre cemetery that morning, in the blue sky, where the as yet not vertical sun made the emptiness around it still more limpid, in its very background that sky remained ashen. An almost harsh immensity, yet more desolate against the new foliage. And it blocks off the stars.

—*Translated by Iain White.*

257 Paul Fort

Paul Fort (1872-1960). A prolific balladeer over many years, Fort was an exceptionally popular poet in his day, not only with the public but also with his peers, who voted him "Prince of Poets" in 1912. His poems now seem very dated however.

Fort was most important as one of the founders of Symbolist drama at his Théâtre d'Art which functioned for four years before becoming the Théâtre de l'Oeuvre in 1894, where Fort's influence continued to be strong. In 1905 he founded and edited the review *Vers et Prose* which lasted until the outbreak of war. This, the last great Symbolist review also rather tentatively embraced the nascent modern movement.

This story is from his first small publication, *Plusieurs Choses* (1894).

This one makes ballads. For the present, nothing more, nor less, need be demanded of him. He makes ballads, and wants to make ballads still, and to go on making ballads. These ballads scarcely resemble those of François Villon, or of Laurent Tailhade; they resemble no one else's.

Printed like prose, they are written in verse, and superlatively animated. This typography has given amiable critics the illusion that Paul Fort has discovered the squaring of the rhythmic circle and resolved the problem that tormented Jourdain, of writing a literature that would be neither prose nor verse; there is a good deal of easy grace in this compliment, but it is only a compliment. If the line that separates verse and prose has been stretched, in these last years of literary development, to an almost invisible thinness, it nonetheless persists; to the right, prose; to the left, verse; non-existent for those who pass, their eyes unfocused, it is there, and indelible, for those who see. The rhythm of verse is independent of the grammatical sentence; it places its strongest emphasis upon sound and not sense. The rhythm of prose is dependent upon the grammatical sentence; it places its emphasis upon sense and not sound. And as the sound and the sense are only rarely able to coincide, prose sacrifices sound and verse sacrifices sense. This is a summary distinction which can, provisionally, suffice...

PAUL FORT

The Queen of Queens & her Lover the Great Blue Lake

On account of her being bathed there from a tender age, a Queen, beautiful as a thousand queens, loved a great blue lake. To see the two of them, it was as if their souls were as limpid as their faces. The one, sparkling with silver-blue facets and lying silkily in a casket of reeds, of moss and of small pink flowers; the other, with her body of a red dragonfly—her velvety body—and her coal-black, diamond-studded hair, how beautiful they were, and more than beautiful! But the lake often grew angry and did just as he wished with the Queen of Queens.

Ah! How many knights envied the fate of the lake with his treacherous waters! How many came, of an evening, in their white damascened breastplates, proudly helmeted, their swords aflame, to combat that too happy lover, and were drowned in the cold maw of their rival! How many, in songs, wept unaffectedly for that beautiful princess ravished from men's senses!

Now the blue lake became very proud of his conquest, and on feast-days one could see him amorously lifting up his lady-love's marvellous boat; and then everybody believed him happy. Oh! The deceptive delight of feast-days! The beautiful lake was the world's most demanding lover—he had already obtained from his beautiful lady-love her bracelets, her crown, jewels of every sort that were thrown to him from the tops of towers, with which, in silence, he adorned the depths of his waters.

One day he demanded more. —"I love your red finery, O my divine mistress," he said to the Queen. —"Slit the throats of your best soldiers over my waters, give me the best blood in your realm to dye my blue tunic. I too wish to be clad in red velvet!"

The princess, who was good at heart, tried to dissuade the king. To no avail. The idea was anchored in his mind more firmly than the big ships in the port. She did indeed think to deceive the lake's cruelty and, the first night, they slit the throats of a hundred and twenty lambs at the windows of the six towers on the banks of the lake. —But the wicked lake wanted the sacrifice in broad daylight, knowing full well that, in flowing, this blood had not damned him and had not damned his lady-love.

Thus the captivated mistress had no choice but to send for her finest warriors and have them killed in the flower of their youth. For three days, at sunset, three hundred were slaughtered, perhaps more. And, believe me, fifteen would have died for the queen. But the six towers where they drained the blood from the poor heroes were dyed, as was the lake and the sun. The country round about became red, and the white brows in a convent of nuns fifteen leagues distant also were tinged with red.

The terrified people trembled, but, taking pride in so beautiful a queen, they were silent. —And then, their blood was brown, coarse blood, hardly of a delicacy to tint a great blue lake bright scarlet, generally the colour of the blood of noblemen.

The red lake was not long in coming to understand that one thing was lacking to enhance his colour. —His pretty mistress confined her svelte waist in a broad belt of pure gold. One evening he said to her: "To love you better, I wish to resemble you greatly. Have a bridge in gold filigree-work made, as long as my waist, from the shore where you love me to that shore there where a black fox is going by." — "Wayward lover, can you not ask of me a thousand years of kisses on the edge of your waves? Do you not realise the immense girth of your waist? And that, between the shore where I love you and that one there, there is more than three leagues? Only the Celestial Artificer could erect here an arch great enough to contain you—he who covers two oceans with a rainbow." — "I must have that belt," the lake roared, rising up indignantly, "or I will inundate your realm and refuse you henceforth the youthfulness of my heart." Again she had to comply—and it was the turn of the poor villagers.

Two thousand and one perished, and fell into the cruel waters of the wicked lake.

But, when the people were already hatching plots—one night, gripped by a terrible frenzy of love, the terrible lover bellowed to his mistress that he must have her body, her beautiful body, to kiss it and stifle it for joy in his innermost depths, even in his red mud.

Oh! How many then bewailed and came running! But the window of the Royal Tower opened and, already, the red body of the Princess appeared... And in his delirium, the lake stretched out his hideous waves, like arms.

All at once fanfares, sweet as violets, sweetly made themselves heard and, in the midst of a cortège of beautiful ladies and handsome lords, softly coloured in the softest of tints, Amadis de Gaule, the good knight in whom the poor must put their trust and to whom all beautiful ladies confide themselves, on his proud battle-charger, all in armour, opened with the edge of his sword the Tower of the Queen of beauties, who then fell on his two arms as on two strong and tender reeds.

Then the lake blasphemed and foamed! And, the troop fleeing, that was carrying away his lady-love-queen-of-beautiful-days-gone-by, in a single wave he emptied himself in its wake and died, dried-up, on the plain, for having wished for too much. And he felled the three great towers, among them that of the judge Coictius, who at that very moment was reading the *Metamorphoseon libri* of that great master of love, Ovid.

While, in the distance, the fanfare of new days was almost dying away.

—*Translated by Iain White.*

Hello, through the absolutism of his faith, is indeed a representative of believing humanity, of the humanity which, hardly having sown, bends, already anxious, over the secrets of the furrow; but there is a curse on the womb of the earth; it is perhaps rotten since the murder of Abel. The seed does not ripen. And man begins again to throw seed into the rotten soil; he pours blood into it, he thrusts his heart into it, he buries his soul there, he descends, complete, into that miraculous tomb, and there, untroubled beneath the terrible covering of sterile weeds, he awaits, an incorruptible seed, the hour of divine germination. ...God is leaning over us. He is observing us as we observe an ant-hill. If they fall, too heavily laden with the burden of the chosen cross, he lifts up the believing ants, the ants that are pure in heart, and even those ants who are sinners but in whom the breath of sin has not extinguished all the flames of love. God speaks to his favoured ants; he encourages them; he predicts the future to them; he reveals to them the cataclysms whereby the wicked will be warned and brought to repent, if there is still time. Hello, an ant of good-will, halts on the slope of a straw and renders unto God his loving gaze.

...Hello is a Christian and a Catholic absolutely; he is a genius at belief; he believes spontaneously, without effort, but with the energy of a boatman carried along by the current of the river, and who believes in the current of the river. He knows that life is carrying him along, and he knows towards which country. The landscape along the banks hardly interests him, and it does not interest him as a landscape. When he has seen a line of willows, of reeds, of poplars, he closes his eyes for a long moment and meditates on the significance of trees, of bushes and plants. Having meditated, he understands, for he is qualified to understand everything, and he understands in a way contrary to that of a man of science. The how of things does not concern him; he seeks the why, and he always finds it, always satisfied by the simplest explanation, the eternal explanation with which the believer contents himself: God has wished it so.

...Ignorant, he is credulous: not having read him, he supposes that the admirable Darwin is a rascal after the fashion of Voltaire. He despises him, to exalt Benoît Labre and Monsieur Dupont (de Tours). Not having principles other than principles exterior to himself, he does not judge; he accepts and explains. He has donned the faith as one dons a vestment; he is decked out in superstitions as if with lucky charms.

...But Hello, who possesses genius, is not genius. He will not (like Samson) carry the gates of his prison to the mountain-top. His prison is the faith. He lives there, he is happy there. Rather than breaking the gates he adds new locks to them. Samson is the rebel; Hello the believer.

Ernest Hello (1828-1885). After a childhood spent on a large Breton estate, Hello went to Paris to study law, which he abandoned for ethical reasons. He immersed himself in theology and founded a newspaper, *La Croisée* in 1859. After its failure two years later, and in part due to his chonic ill-health, he returned to the family seat where he devoted the next thirty years to writing: meditations, essays and some short fiction. This story is from *Contes extraordinaires* (1879).

ERNEST HELLO

The Night-time Washer-woman. A Fantastic Tale

The gulls are settling to roost on the deserted strand: their cries, piercing and harsh, and cold as the night, are audible in the village of Saint-Adrien. But in the farmhouse where the Plernick family (we are in the depths of Brittany) are gathered together, only one person is listening.

The peasants do not hear the sounds of nature, and if one of them perceives a harmony between the plaints of their soul and those of the tempest, that one is well on the way to no longer being a countryman.

Under the chimney-piece, his day's work done, old Plernick is eating a porringer of buckwheat porridge: next to him, his wife is silently twisting her distaff.

In a corner of the room, by an emptied cider-glass, a young man is sleeping, his head in his hands and his elbows on the table; he is the two old people's son-in-law. Anna, his wife, is attending to the day's last tasks, putting the cottage to rights, preparing for the night; but I suspect I see in her eyes a certain liveliness of the glance, and in her gestures a vivacity alien to the peasant. She is working with a vigour that seems to originate in her inner self, and from time to time she pauses. Is she listening to the gulls on the coast, to which she was not listening yesterday? Perhaps she is!

The door opens and a fifth person enters, a child of fifteen, poorly dressed, in tatters, a farm-girl they have taken on to do the heavy work: her name is Yvonne.

This child looks nobody in the face.

Without shifting from his place, the old fellow sets his porringer down close to her and lights his little pipe to have a smoke.

Pierre—that is the young man's name—has just woken up. He rises.

"Where are you going?" says the old man.

"To the Dolmen, to see to the nets," Pierre replies.

"There won't be any fish tomorrow, and it's not safe to go near the Dolmen this evening," the old fellow continues.

Breton peasants never expect an explanation for anything. Pierre sits down in the place he has just vacated.

The young woman looks up and gazes at the old man: she wants to question him, but her father's look silences her. The little girl addresses the old woman, without for all that looking at her, and says:

"What's going on, then, this evening, at the Dolmen?"

The old man tries to impose silence on his wife with a gesture she does not understand; and, sighing as old people do when they abandon themselves to memories of their young days, she makes ready to speak at length and, conversing half with herself, half with the others:

"I saw it, my children," she says. "They called that woman the *Mother of Money*, because, they said, money bred in her house. You'd give her ten francs: at the end of the year she'd give you back a hundred; a hundred and she'd give you back a thousand. It's as true as I'm telling you. All the poor people brought her their savings. It seems that when you went into her place you had to give an owl that was perched on the door something to eat. It often happened that it bit you until the blood came. But lots of people made their fortune until the day came when the old woman told the people who came to ask for the interest on their money:

"That's it. There isn't any more!"

"As you'll imagine, the news that the Mother of Money was no longer paying out spread through the district like wildfire. The poor people were losing everything at the same time, capital and interest. And I myself, if the curé hadn't put me on my guard, I'd have done as the others did. Nobody hereabouts slept that night. I'll never forget the day that followed, as long as I live. They broke into the old woman's house. She seemed to be deaf and dumb; she made no answer, other than that the money was no longer there. They searched the house, in the bed, in the cupboards, they ripped open the mattress, they even looked in the joints between the boards, all without saying a word. But their faces were pale.

"They found nothing.

"After the first chill of terror, there came a sort of fury. There were cries, tears, curses! I can still see, right in front of me, a woman who came to me, out of her mind, tearing her hair, howling like a wolf, and throwing herself at my knees as if it had been in my power to help her. She no longer knew what she was saying. In a voice that rent my heart, she cried out: "I beg you! I beg you! My husband's going to kill me! I hid my savings with her, so he wouldn't drink them in the dram-shop. I told him they were still in my cupboard. He's going to ask me for my daughter's dowry and I've nothing to give him. I won't be going home any more." And, ripping her clothing, the woman climbed up on the Dolmen, from which she threw herself into the sea. They found her in the morning, at low tide, her body all mangled.

"And these difficulties were felt on all sides, from morning till night, from night till morning. People no longer spoke, they only wept. The countryside was like a cemetery. They didn't kill the old woman, and moreover, they still took care not to offend her, because one always hopes. They would approach her with a suppliant air; but she, without answering, would stand there in the fireplace: one hand on her shovel, the other behind her back, she had a look about her of having some new horror in store; when she did utter a sound, it was a sort of sneering giggle.

"One day she decided to leave the district. The peasants chased after her with pitchforks. Men, women, children, everybody joined in, as they do with mad dogs, and they caught up with her by the Dolmen. "To think I can't just kill her, once and for all!" an old woman yelled, lowering her arm, pitchfork in hand. The blow struck home on her right temple. The Mother of Money collapsed, bloodied, and leant against the great stone. They all fell back: they were frightened by their vengeance, because they all believed in God. But it was too late. The old woman never got to her feet again.

"That was forty years ago, my children. But it seems that, every seven years, at the full moon in December, at midnight, those who go and look at the Dolmen see, in the moonlight, an old woman in rags standing up erect on the stone. She lets out plaintive cries. Then, all of a sudden, she takes some silver *ecus* out of her pocket and slowly walks down to the sea. She dips the silver coins in it, washes them, washes them again, looks at them in the moonlight, still washes them. Then she draws from her dress a kitchen-knife and cuts open her breast; and, howling, she washes the silver with her blood; she stiffens her arms and tears at her silver as if it were cloth, looks at it, sharpens the point of her knife on the Dolmen, enlarges the wound she has just made, tears furiously at her breast as if the cold steel were invigorating her; when she is drenched in blood, she amorously embraces the *ecus* and immerses them in the red blood.

"They say that then she turns slowly in all directions and looks about the countryside around her, and that those who call her see her enter their home. She stretches out a hand;

she stretches out a hand, they put an *ecu* in it once again, as in former times. Next month, they are rich; but take care for the seventh year! It seems that some have seen her come in merely for thinking about her. They say she hears evil desires the way dogs catch the scent of the dead."

The old woman stopped speaking and there was silence in the room. The old man said nothing. Pierre was asleep again. Anna was melancholy.

Given over to evening's dangerous thoughts, to the frailty of that uncertain hour, she was lulled by that vague hope that believes itself still innocent because it does not know where it is going. "If you were rich," the voice that always lies whispered in her ear, "there would no longer be poor people hereabouts, and it is you who would renounce the modest prosperity you enjoy."

But she recognised the accent of the tempter. Accustomed to examining her conscience and to subduing her passions, she had amassed, as little occasions offered themselves, in daily struggles, those forces that make ready for great victories. She had often enough vied with temptation to treat it in advance as vanquished. Besides, she knew the way: she made the sign of the cross.

As for Yvonne, her eyes were shining. She too knew life's difficulties. She was accustomed to defeat.

"Suppose one was rich like that one who just got married today?" she said. "Suppose one had a big house and servants?" She was speaking to herself, casting a bitter glance over her torn clothing, as if she regretted the party-clothes of the celebration she had left: then her expression became vague.

The family went to bed. The two old people lay down as they always did. Anna went to sleep happily: after having felt in the course of the day the first perturbations of desire, she pressed herself tenderly against her happiness, took refuge in him; she was savouring that joy, hidden like all great joys, and which has only God as its witness, the sweet and immense joy of inward victories; in that moment she loved all mankind.

Yvonne got into bed without having prayed. She felt alone. Still not taking temptation seriously, she amused herself by letting herself be tempted: her eyes were fixed on a gold coin she had taken into bed with her; she had brought that coin—the first she had ever had in her possession—back with her from the celebration. Who did she get it from? That I do not know; but I know that she took pleasure in hiding it among her sheets, then taking it out to see it shining.

"You haven't put out your candle, Yvonne," the old mother shouted from her bed.

"I'm putting it out, I'm putting it out," replied the child who, obliged to renounce her joy, was gripping the golden coin in her hands, fiercely and lovingly, as if she had it in mind to infuse the metal into her blood. She snuffed out the light. Midnight chimed on the Ploemeur church-clock. The twelve strokes rang out slowly in the silence of the night. The young girl picked up two pebbles she had instinctively placed within reaching-distance and struck a spark so as once more to see the yellow of the gold glittering; she felt both pain and pleasure; she abandoned herself to a species of agreeable swoon; her eyes lit up: what was going on in her inmost self?

The gold was enticing her as the reptile does the bird, the abyss the one who leans over it, the sight of blood the wild beast. The spark was extinguished. "Now would be the time," Yvonne thought. She felt that uneasiness that precedes a fall, comparable to a step that will lead one to despair. Then she hid herself under the bedclothes to hide from some gaze that had followed her in the gloom. About five minutes later she heard a key creaking in the lock. And she felt herself going pale in the darkness.

"Come in," she thought.

She saw nothing, but she distinctly heard the sound of a gnarled stick, like those on which old people lean. Then a cold hand touched her on the neck. In the next room, Anna was sleeping peacefully. Next morning, when Yvonne was dressed, Anna said:

"I no longer see the golden cross you were wearing round your neck."

To hide her pallor, Yvonne made a show of looking for something in the cupboard.

"Perhaps I lost it yesterday when I was dancing," she said unconcernedly; but her voice was tremulous.

II.

This is what happened at the big house on the day of the celebration.

Jean Kernorak married the beautiful and charming Louise. The peasant guests sang in the open air, in the sunlight, to the sound of the old Breton bagpipes, wearing their holiday clothes, with the serious ardour of Breton festivals. Jean and his wife, who were singing, beautiful and confident as youth, paused and greeted an old man, collapsed rather than seated in a black wooden chair. It was the father of Jean, of the happy Jean and the beautiful Louise. The old man turned away his head, as if the sight of his children were odious to him.

The pallor of that man was livid; his hands were trembling, thick, clammy and cold as those of people to whom nothing is repugnant; his pendulous lips denoted the hideous frailties of a hasty and vacillating nature; he gave the impression of displaying, with I know not what pleasure, the deformities of old age and illness. It was as if, by his wild beast's posture, by the shamelessness of his dress, he had intended to put a stop to the impetuosity of happiness. His body seemed lifeless; life had taken refuge in his gaze, in which a sombre fire sparkled. That gaze attested to all life's vices, swarming in the bosom of death, in a heart already frozen. He watched the young people laughing about him with that smile peculiar to those who always hope to see joy sullied and innocence lost; then, lowering his eyes, he stared at the ground like a man reflecting on the past. He was grieving over a daughter he had lost, and he no longer heard what was going on around him; in his life he had known only one affection: he had loved his daughter, if it is permissible to use such a word of such a man.

That child, dead at twenty, had nonetheless found the time to be a monster. With her, and with her alone, the old man had had nothing to hide. He opened up to her, he found in her the complement to himself, he lovingly fostered the still young vices of she whom he had formed and in whom he hoped to live on. He had counted on her to carry to completion the deeds he had envisaged; she had not disappointed him.

When she died, he felt that the most living part within him was extinguished. Hating the happiness of others, the sun and the blue sky, he went over again in his mind the summertime of his life—the days when his daughter was still alive.

The woman Hourra, the Mother of Money, was his tenant. He would often shut himself up with her for hours on end in some secluded corner. Only his daughter was allowed to enter. It appeared that an abominable amity and a mysterious interchange united those three beings.

All of a sudden the old man got to his feet, as if he had returned to the days of his first youth.

"My daughter!" he cried.

And he threw his arms about Yvonne, who was passing by.

"It's not all over then?" he said in a muffled voice. "She was telling me the truth—she who knew secrets—that my daughter wasn't dead, that I'd see my own flesh and blood again."

And, galvanised by a horrible tenderness, the old man seemed about to forget his infirmities and take part in the celebrations.

"Yes, you're my daughter," he cried. "Nature doesn't make two people so alike! Come! Come with me!"

And he hurried her away to his house.

One particular day, rising from his meal, Jean, the young bridegroom felt himself smitten with an unaccustomed headache. Next day he no longer felt it, but he was still pale. This pallor got worse and, after a month, without great pain, without any known illness, he said to his young wife, who no longer dared to look at him:

"Louise, I want this countryside, full of memories, to be my last resting-place. When you see it's the end, have them carry me, I beg you, next to the clog-makers' cottage. Forgive my father, and don't revenge my death. Don't interfere with what's bound to happen."

The young woman believed he was delirious; and besides, despair does not seek to understand.

"Listen," said the sick man. "don't you hear anything?" Louise listened.

"It's as if there was somebody speaking in the room that used to be my sister's."

"You're right," said Louise. "And yet I've heard that nobody has been in there since she died. The door's been blocked up."

Louise was by the window. Without recognising her, she saw Yvonne, crossing the courtyard. The sound ceased.

Louise went into the blocked-up room; she remained there for a long time. The young woman returned to her husband's room, asked how he was, and got no response. She left the room on tiptoe. But these precautions were pointless; her husband would never again be bothered by any sound. Perhaps he had made an unavailing effort to call out.

Meanwhile his father displayed neither surprise nor sorrow at that strange death; but he became more sombre and before very long himself died, cared for by his daughter-in-law, Louise, and also by Yvonne, Yvonne the darling of his heart, to whom he left everything in his will.

III.

Seven years have gone by. The big house has a new owner.

What has become of the two old people, Pierre, Anna, and Yvonne? As to Pierre and the old people, don't ask me. Those who play no part in conflicts have no history.

This is what was happening in the big house.

The domestics were laughing, drinking, singing at a well-laden table. A cry was heard.

"Won't we go and see?" said Marie, the younger of the two servant-girls.

"Ah, who cares," said another domestic. "He shouted out like that, our rightful master down there, the one who inherited everything, and she managed to see to it there was nobody there to help him. It's a business that won't be cleared up for a long time yet."

"Be quiet," said Marie. "Don't say things like that."

"I know what I know," the man replied.

Harsh and unjust to her staff, Yvonne had made herself generally hated. She had made use of riches in the way those who have desired them immoderately do.

"Go and have a look, then." said Jeanne. "Who knows but that that cry won't be the last?"

"Go yourself, if you fancy," answered Julie, who had turned pale.

The door opened and a woman entered. It was Anna. Anna had never entered that dwelling without having been seized by that peculiar chill, which you perhaps know, and which is like the freezing caresses of an invisible hand. Likewise, she never returned home without experiencing a feeling of joy and security. In her cottage she knew that charm of simplicity that sometimes takes possession of our hearts when we traverse a village we regret having to leave so soon. Simplicity is touching. In Anna's presence the domestics adopted a gravely contrite air.

"How is she?" the young woman enquired.

"Not at all well, my poor lady," said Jeanne. "Every day she's paler than the day before, and the doctors don't understand the first thing about what's wrong with her."

"And you leave her alone?" said Anna.

Nobody replied.

"Madame," said Jeanne in a subdued tone, "I wouldn't advise you to go in there."

Without replying, Anna started off in the direction of Yvonne's room, and Jeanne followed her, almost involuntarily.

When they were alone:

"Jeanne," said Anna, "You ought to admit to me you didn't dare sit up with her any more. I'd have replaced you."

"I watched," said Jeanne, "really I did."

They reached the sick woman's room. Anna opened the door, despite Jeanne, who instinctively held back her hand. Yvonne was lying on her bed, pale as the living never are, as the dead are only infrequently. Anna held a mirror to the colourless lips: the mirror remained clear.

Between the two women there was a terrible silence.

"If there's something about this that's more terrible than death, tell me the secret on your oath," said Anna to Jeanne.

"If you want to know, it's for you to give me your oath," Jeanne said to Anna.

"Speak," said Anna.

"You're not to repeat what I'm going to tell you to anybody. They'd laugh at me."

"Go on then, speak."

"That night, I was watching over Yvonne. At midnight I woke up. I was cold. I heard a little noise. I saw a light, but I thought it was the night-light that lit her room, the way it does every night. I got up to give her something to drink. Intending to warm some lime-flower tea, I went up to the night-light and I saw it was out. And yet there was still a light in the room. Then I looked by the bed and I saw in the alcove, I saw just like I see you, and in the place where I see you (Anna flinched involuntarily), I saw an old woman with wild eyes, like an owl's eyes. I wasn't sleeping, I'm not mad, and I'm not lying. Yvonne was struggling with her. The old woman was holding out a little golden cross to her, drawing it back and giggling, while this one here," Jeanne said, pointing to the dead woman, "while this one here was trying to grab hold of it, and she said: "Haven't I paid you for this nasty little thing that's not worth a couple of brass farthings?" Then the old woman came up close. She rooted about with her nails in the woman's chest, round about the heart, saying: "Now would be the time, my pretty one: the moon is rising, there's a few drops left, near the heart, and I need them for my washing ."

269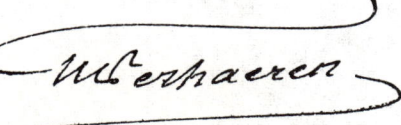

Émile Verhaeren (1855-1916). A Belgian, he studied law but abandoned it for literature, writing for *Le Jeune Belgique* after a period travelling round Europe. His early poems were deeply pessimistic and his incipient depression was becoming problematic until he married in 1891 and discovered an interest in social problems. He became a socialist along with his friend Eekhoud and this period coincides with his most Symbolist works, including *Les Villages illusoires* (1895) from which the *vers libre* poem *Rain* is extracted. With Maeterlinck he was the most famous Belgian author of his generation, his later collections of poems became simultaneously more mystical in thought and more naturalistic in expression, returning to evocations of the landscape of his native Flanders. The outbreak of war shattered his vision of a more equitable world and he stooped to penning patriotic verse. He was killed in an accident in Rouen railway station. The story is from a posthumous collection *Cinq Recits* (1920, but dating from much earlier).

The word most characteristic of Emile Verhaeren's verse is hallucinated. *From page to page this word crops up; one entire collection entitled* Les Campagnes hallucinées *has still not delivered him from this obsession; exorcism was not possible, because it is the nature and even the essence of Emile Verhaeren to be the hallucinated poet. Taine* said, "Sensations are hallucinations that are true," but where does the truth begin and where does it end? Who would dare to circumscribe it? The poet, who has no psychological scruples, neither lingers over nor takes care to separate the true hallucinations from the false; for him, they are all true, if they are acute or clever, and he recounts them with ingenuity—and when the account is set down by Emile Verhaeren, it is very beautiful. Beauty in art is a relative result and is obtained by a variety of the most diverse elements, often the most unexpected. Of these elements, only one is permanent and stable; it must turn up again in all the combinations: and that one element is novelty. A work of art must be novel, and one recognises the novel quite simply as that which gives you a sensation not yet felt.*

If it does not give that, a work, however perfect one judges it, is everything that is the worst and most contemptible; it is useless and ugly, for nothing is more absolutely useful than beauty. With Verhaeren, beauty is made up of novelty and might; this poet is a sturdy character and, since the Villes tentaculaires *surged forth with the violence of a telluric upheaval, none would dare contest his position as a great and glorious poet. Perhaps he has yet to achieve completely the making of the magical instrument he has forged for twenty years. Perhaps he has not yet attained complete mastery over his language; it is inelegant; he permits his most lovely pages to grow dull with inopportune epithets, and the most beautiful poems entangle themselves in what was once called prosaism. Still the impression remains, of grandeur and might, and yes: this is a great poet...*

ÉMILE VERHAEREN

The Horse-Fair at Opdorp

Every year, in June, there is a spectacular horse-fair —and sleek and well groomed are the exhibits—in the little village of Opdorp, on the boundary line between Flanders and Brabant.

Around a wide mall with smooth-shaven green grass and elm, ash, and willow trees, is the circle of houses—their walls like white coats, their roofs like red caps—and they gaze at each other with the bright eyes of their spotless windows. At one end of the oval stands the church with its steeple and glittering gold weathercock, and about the church lies the humble unfenced burying-ground.

The village is sleepy, sedate, unpretentious. Men go about their monotonous work unhurried, putting forth their leisurely hands as if to unravel the precious web of time without tangling it.

On week-days an aroma of butter and cheese streams out of the cellars. At night the herds of cows wind slowly home from the ponds and pastures. Behind them the drover whistles his tune. There is a loud mooing and lowing. A gate creaks open and shut. No other sign of animation save, on Sunday, the church bell promising a richer, better life. The people crowd to mass, vespers, and compline. On Monday the village relapses into tedium and pursues its regulated and monotonous round.

But the annual fair makes Opdorp famous. In the first grey of morning awkward foals are to be seen gangling into town at the heels of their mothers; then come formidable stallions led with a halter by peasant lads; then the work brutes, obstinate and powerful slaves which have survived God knows how many struggles through the thick Flemish mud.

They file along past the booths, and the jackpuddings frighten them with booings, thwack them on the rumps with lath swords, joke about their coarse

breed and make merry over their woolly tails and their hoofs, big and round like immense mushrooms and looking the more cumbersome for their matted fetlocks. A battle rises between peasants and clowns. The former lash out their fists with right good will, the latter deftly skip away and counter with a mocking flick on the nose. There is deafening uproar within and

without the placarded tents, and in the streets and lanes the mingled whinnying of the horses and the thud of the rattling gallop on the pavement. As soon as the trumpets, trombones, and bass drums make themselves heard the festival turns into an orgy. It is as if the entire village had been transformed into a gigantic wreath of clamour in which shrill squeals, insolent whistles, and yodelling catcalls represent the lurid flowers.

Nevertheless, notwithstanding the fun and excitement, the fair is less and less frequented. People have a reason for staying away.

In their times the bishops of Ghent and Tournay sent their riding-masters to this fair, the abbots of Aberbode and Perck found here the choicest of their animals, and above all, the undertaker of the little city of Termonde, every five years, sent his handsomest hearse, drawn by four lean, seedy black mares which after several years of hard service must be replaced that the pomp of a well-directed funeral might have nothing to fear from critics.

As soon as the coming of the hearse was heralded, the jackpuddings jumped back onto the stages and outdid themselves in follies. Four gilded skeletons hung at the sides of the vehicle; one clown reached out and chucked them under the chin, another thrust flowers between their fleshless ribs The musicians with swelling cheeks, blew their most doleful funeral march. Excited monkeys frisked chattering up and down the standards of the booths. The snake-charmer, wrapping her boa constrictor around her waist, seized the monster's head and turned it, with wide open jaws, toward the dark vehicle approaching.

The equipage proceeded slowly past the grotesque; cynical masquerade. The plumes and black hangings brushed the tawdry bunting and shamed the staggering posters and flaring streamers. The hearse was full of good-for-nothing boys and girls of the streets, dancing and pushing each other around the trestles which at other times served to sustain the coffin. In front of the church a couple of sextons were added to the retinue. And that the sacrilege might be complete, the dead lights burned ghastly and unnecessary.

The hearse stopped at the inn of the Three Kings. As soon as he had unhitched, the driver sold his horses, which looked at the knacker with furtive eyes. The

hearse driver quickly bought four others without haggling over the price, because the undertaker of Termonde was rich.

And hardly was the landlady paid, a glass hastily emptied, the harness furbished up, the girths lengthened to fit the plump new animals when the rejuvenated equipage set itself again in motion, the seats and running boards occupied by street boys and church wardens. It went back the way it had come, but this time the masqueraders ceased their buffoonery and stood respectfully as if awed by its now formidable appearance. Women could be seen crossing themselves. Death, which a moment ago had limped along forlorn and superannuated, now seemed to step forth trim and jaunty to combat.

It happened, it must have been twenty years ago—and since then the annual fair has been as if accursed—that the new horses were fiery and ungovernable and dashed through the village like a tornado. They darted around the booths and among the stands and further along, on the highway, they took fright at a wayside scarecrow and ran away. The people who had climbed into the hearse were panic-stricken. A few, to avoid the danger, jumped off into the soft earth of the roadside embankments, others, huddling against each other, uttered such unearthly cries that people rushed out of the farmhouses wringing their hands and imploring heaven. In broad daylight, with flying curtains and pelting wheels, the hearse, a living black clatter, hurtled past. The lamps jostled their supports, the cross, jolted out of its standards, was shaken from

right to left and from left to right, the silver fringe became entangled in the bushes, and black tatters were left hanging on the branches.

From the ramparts in Termonde the approaching whirlwind was observed. Great was the terror. Particular anxiety was felt for the church wardens, worthy dignitaries not nimble-footed enough to jump out of the way.

The mad hearse traversed the entire city. There were shrieks and cries. The panic spread from house to house, from quarter to quarter. Women, stretching out to aid their own imperilled boys and girls, were caught up and carried along on the dashboards. An old man was run over. The streets were rapidly emptied. Pale faces were pressed to the windowpanes. People ran along, breathless, behind the hearse. The bell-ringer in the main square thought to ring the alarm-bell, but

death ran too quickly and in its lightning flight soon struck the opposite end of the suburbs.

The mad horses, white with foaming sweat, bloody-muzzled, stopped for the first time at the wall of a cemetery. One of them fell down heavily. A little girl was killed. A church warden had his leg broken. All the others sustained some injury. Only the driver came off unhurt, without so much as a bruise, and as his horses, for their part, had recovered from their fright, he, in the end, laughed over the adventure.

But the townsfolk could not so easily be reassured. What unhappy event was foreshadowed by this significant accident? Prayers and devotions were redoubled. To no avail.

During the interminable winter the city was devastated by an unknown fever, and the Scheldt overflowed three times. The streets through which the hearse had come were the most heavily smitten. The path of affliction extended straight back to Opdorp.

How quickly the neat little village lost its aspect of peace! Every day there was a death. This lasted for months and months until the cemetery had to be enlarged. Even today the recollection of this black event has not been dimmed: it is even said that in a few years the famous fair of Opdorp will have to be stricken out of the calendar.

—*Translated by Keene Wallis, illustrations from woodcuts by Frans Masereel.*

Rain

Long as unending threads, the long-drawn rain
Interminably, with its nails of grey,
   Athwart the dull grey day,
   Rakes the green window-pane—
So infinitely, endlessly, the rain,
The long, long rain,
     The rain.

Since last night it continues unravelling
Down from the frayed and flaccid rags that cling
   About the sullen sky,
   The low black sky;
Since last night, so slowly, patiently,
Unravelling its threads upon the roads,
Upon the roads and lanes, with even fall
     Continual

Along the miles
That between meadows and suburbs lie,
By roads interminably bent, the files
Of waggons, with their awnings arched and tall,
Struggling in sweat and steam, toil slowly by
With outline vague as of a funeral.
Into the ruts, unbroken, regular,
Stretching out parallel so far
That when night comes they seem to join the sky,
For hours the water drips;
And every tree and every dwelling weeps,
Drenched as they are with it,
With the long rain, tenaciously, with rain
   Indefinite.

The rivers, through each rotten dyke that yields,
Discharge their swollen wave upon the fields,
   Where coils of drownèd hay
   Float far away;

ÉMILE VERHAEREN

And the wild breeze
Buffets the alders and the walnut-trees;
Knee-deep in water great black oxen stand,
Lifting their bellowings sinister on high
   To the distorted sky;
As now the night creeps onward, all the land,
   Thicket and plain,
Grows cumbered with her clinging shades immense,
   And still there is the rain,
   The long, long rain,
   Like soot, so fine, so dense.

   The long, long rain,
    Rain—and its threads identical,
    And its nails systematical,
Weaving the garment, mesh by mesh amain,
Of destitution for each house and wall,
   And fences that enfold
   The villages, neglected, grey, and old:
Chaplets of rags and linen shreds that fall
In frayed-out wisps from upright poles and tall,
Blue pigeon-houses glued against the thatch,
And windows with a patch
Of dingy paper on each lowering pane,
Houses with straight-set gutters, side by side
Across the broad stone gables crucified,
   Mills, uniform, forlorn,
Each rising from its hillock like a horn,
Steeples afar and chapels round about,
   The rain, the long, long rain,
Through all the winter wears and wears them out.
Rain with its many wrinkles, the long rain
With its grey nails, and its watery mane;
The long rain of these lands of long ago,
The rain, eternal in its torpid flow!
            —*Translated by Alma Strettell.*

277 Villiers de l'Isle adam

Auguste Villiers de L'Isle-Adam (1838-1889). An aristocratic dandy by inclination, the loss of his family's fortune condemned him to poverty, only sometimes ameliorated by the products of his pen. A precursor of the Symbolists rather than a participant in the movement, his early plays were hardly commercial ventures and he therefore wrote a great number of stories for journals (*Cruel Tales* being the best-known collection in English). His great drama of ideas *Axël* and a philosophical "science fiction" romance *L'Eve future* are also both translated. During his last years he was frequently saved from starvation by the subscription of his fellow writers. He lived with an illiterate "charwoman" (as his biographers would have it) and conducted a death-bed marriage with her to safeguard the future of their son. He wavered in his Catholic beliefs, frequently altering the pessimistic tone of *Axël* according to his present state of mind. When stomach cancer was diagnosed and he realised he might never finish his life's work he turned against God, even planning a lawsuit against Him in protest!

This self-contained story (which is dedicated to "the lovely indifferent ones") is taken from *Tribulat Bonhomet* (1887), his satire on bourgeois positivism and the illusions of progress.

Some love to repeat, an awkward testimony to a piously troubled admiration, and even to base paradoxical articles upon this maxim: "Villiers de l'Isle-Adam was neither of his place nor his time." That seems atrocious, for after all a superior man, a great writer is inevitably, through his very genius, one of the syntheses of his race and his epoch, the representative of a momentary or fragmentary humanity, the mind and the mouth-piece of a tribe and not a fleeting monster. Like Chateaubriand*, his brother in race as well as in glory, Villiers was the man of the moment, of a solemn moment; both of them, with differing views and under diverse appearances, re-create for a time the soul of the elite: the one by giving birth to Romantic Catholicism and that respect for the ruins of tradition; and the other, the idealist dream and the cult of interior antique beauty; but the one was still the proud grandsire of our ferocious individualism; and the other still teaches us that the life around us is only clay to be worked. Villiers was of his time to the extent that all of his masterpieces are dreams solidly based upon science and modern metaphysics, like L'Eve future, or Tribulat Bonhomet, that enormous, admirable and tragic buffoonery, wherein all the gifts of the dreamer, ironist and philosopher converge to make up perhaps the most original creation of the century...

VILLIERS DE L'ISLE-ADAM

Swans understand the signs.
VICTOR HUGO, *Les Misérables*.

Swan-Killer   In the course of reading Natural History books, Doctor Tribulat Bonhomet, our illustrious friend, had learned that "a swan really does sing before dying." In fact (he recently acknowledged to us), ever since hearing this music, it alone could help him endure the disappointments of life, and everything else seemed to him nothing more than a Wagnerian din.

"How did he manage to procure this dilettante's pleasure?" Here's the answer.

On the outskirts of the ancient walled town in which he was living, this practical old man had, one fine day, discovered in a centuries-old, abandoned park, beneath the shade of the great trees, an old sacred pond—a gloomy mirror upon which some twelve to fifteen of those serene birds glided—and had dreamily studied the surroundings, contemplated the distances, observing above all else a black swan, their elder, who slept, sequestered by a sunbeam. Throughout each night this swan kept its large eyes open, burnished a stone in its long rosy beak, and, at the slightest movement signalling some danger to those whom it guarded, it would, with a motion of its neck, roughly toss the alarm stone into the lapping water, into the midst of the white ring of slumberers: and the troop, guided once more by this signal, would fly off into the gloom of the deep walkways, toward some far off sward where some fountain reflected grey statues, or to some other asylum known to them by memory alone. And Bonhomet watched them in silence for a long time, smiling at them, too. Was he—ever the perfect dilettante—dreaming even then of hearing that last song with his own ears?

Sometimes—at the stroke of midnight on a moonless autumn night—Bonhomet, troubled by insomnia, would suddenly rise and dress himself specially for the concert he hoped to hear. The doctor, bony but lanky, first concealed his legs in enormous rubber boots that stretched, seamlessly, into a full but bulky, almost impenetrable frock-coat; a pair of steel gauntlets, taken from a suit of medieval armour, glittered upon his hands, gauntlets that he was pleased to have acquired at the price of thirty-eight sous—on a whim!—from a passing pedlar. This done, he clapped on his large modern hat, blew out the lamp, descended, and, the key to his lodgings snug in his pocket, set out for the edge of the abandoned park, like any other citizen.

At length he ventured down gloomy paths towards the desired singers' retreat—toward the pond whose water was not deep, and everywhere well-sounded, and nowhere reached higher than his waist. And beneath the canopies of leaves that bordered the banks, he muffled his footsteps, feeling for dry twigs.

Finally reaching the edge of the pond, slowly, very slowly—and without a sound!—he made his way through the water with unprecedented caution, such caution that he scarcely dared to breathe. Exactly like a music-lover straining to hear an imminent cavatina. So that, in order to complete the twenty steps that separated him from his dear admired virtuosos, it actually took him between two and two-and-a-half hours, so afraid was he of awakening the careful vigilance of the shadowy watcher.

The breath of the starless sky plaintively agitated the lofty branches in the darkness surrounding the pond. But Bonhomet, without allowing himself to be distracted by the mysterious murmuring, drew imperceptibly ever closer, so much so that, towards three in the morning, he found himself a half-step away from the black swan without his ever having taken the slightest notice of his invisible presence.

Then the good doctor, smiling broadly in the darkness, softly, very softly, barely touching it with the tip of his medieval index finger, raked the still surface of the water, in front of the watcher!... And he raked it so softly that the watchful swan, though forewarned, did not judge so slight an alarm worthy of throwing the stone. It listened. Its instinct, in the long run, being vaguely impressed by the *idea* of danger, its heart, alas! its poor ingenuous heart began to beat frightfully—which redoubled Bonhomet's jubilation. And now the beautiful swans, one after another, shaken by that sound from the depths of their slumber, stretched their heads out sinuously from beneath their pale silver wings— and, from beneath the weight of Bonhomet's shadow, were imperceptibly enveloped by their anguish, having who knows what confused consciousness of a mortal peril menacing them. But, in their infinite delicacy, they suffered in silence, like the one keeping vigil—unable to take flight, *because the stone had not been tossed!* And all of the hearts of these snowy exiles began to beat in a muffled agony—*intelligible* and audible to the enraptured ear of the excellent doctor who, knowing full well himself that its *moral* cause was his simple proximity to them, took delight, as if from a peerless itching, in the terrific sensation to which his immobility made them submit.

"How fine it is to encourage these artists!" he said very softly to himself.

Almost three quarters of an hour that ecstasy endured, one which he wouldn't have traded for a kingdom. Suddenly, the ray of the Morning-Star glistened through the branches, illumined, unexpectedly, Bonhomet, the black waters and the swans with dream-filled eyes! The watcher, filled with terror at the sight, let fly the stone... —Too late!... Bonhomet, with a great horrible cry, which tore away his syrupy smile entirely, hurled himself, claws raised, arms wide, into the ranks of the sacred birds! —And the embraces of the steel fingers of this modern warrior were rapid; the pure snowy necks of two or three of the singers were traversed or broken before the radiant flight of the other bird-poets. Then the souls of the dying swans exhaled themselves, oblivious of the doctor, in a song of undying hope, and deliverance and love, toward the unknown heavens.

The rational doctor smiled at this sentimentality, of which he did not, as a serious connoisseur, choose to savour anything except for: THE TIMBRE. Musically, he prized nothing except for the singularly sweet *timbre* of those symbolic voices, which vocalised Death like a melody.

Bonhomet, eyes closed, breathed the harmonious vibrations into his heart: then, staggering, as if in a spasm, ran aground on the bank, stretched out upon the grass, on his back, in his heavy and impermeable clothing.

And there, this Maecenas of our era, lost in a voluptuous torpor, savoured anew, and to his very depths, the memory of the delightful song—though tarnished by a solemnity out of fashion in his eyes—of his beloved artists.

And, reabsorbing his comatose ecstasy, he pondered in this perfectly middle-class manner on his exquisite impression until sunrise.

281 Marcel Schwob

Marcel Schwob (1867-1905). A scholar (particularly of Villon), linguist (and anglophile), poet and novelist, Schwob was immersed in books from an early age. He was a valued friend to a wide circle of writers: Valéry, Jarry, Mallarmé, Stevenson, Meredith, Barbusse, Colette, Louÿs, etc. His life was fairly uneventful, broken only by great encounters: with his future wife, the actress Marguerite Moreno; and with Louise, whom he called Monelle, a young consumptive girl "of the streets" whom he met in 1891: their relationship lasted two years until her death.

His grief pervades *The Book of Monelle* with an atmosphere of loss and nostalgia; when it appeared in 1894 it was an immediate, if modest, success and quickly became identified as the "golden book" of the movement and as "a condensation of all the Symbolist characteristics."* All this is perhaps surprising since *Monelle* is a very odd book; as autobiography, it is as resolutely fictional as Schwob's collection of biographical inventions *Imaginary Lives* (1896). It begins with a section *The Words of Monelle*, which are certainly sayings that she can never have uttered. The second section *The Sisters of Monelle* consists of a number of barely connected stories which seem intended as symbolic representations of aspects of Monelle and her relationship with Schwob (four of these are included here, the others have the titles: *The Egoist, The Voluptuary, The Faithful, The Dreamer, The Romantic* and *The Selfless*). The last section, *Monelle*, describes their encounter, again in heightened mode.

The final text here is from one of Schwob's numerous short story collections, *Le Roi au masque d'or* (1892).

The world is a forest of differences; to understand the world is to know that there are no formal identities, an evident principle and one which realises itself perfectly in man, since the consciousness of being is nothing other than the consciousness of being different. There is, then, no science of mankind; but there is an art of mankind. Marcel Schwob has said things concerning this which I would like to declare definitive, this one for example: "Art is the opposite of generalised ideas, it describes only the individual, desires only the unique. It does not classify; it declassifies..."

The particular genius of Marcel Schwob is a sort of tremendous complex simplicity; that is to say, through the arrangement and harmonising of an infinite number of precise and correct details, his tales offer the sensation of a unique detail; in the pannier of flowers there is a peony, and that is all that one sees amid the annulled others; but if the other flowers were not grouped around it, one would not see the peony...

Marcel Schwob's books encourage one to meditate, after they have pleased by way of the unexpectedness of their tones, upon their words, their faces, their garbs, their lives, their deaths, their attitudes. This is writing of the most substantial sort, from the decimated race of those who always have upon their lips some new words of goodly fragrance.

MARCEL SCHWOB

The Perverse

"Madge!"

The voice came through the little open doorway. Within, the great oaken shaft of the windmill rose from the floor and passed through the roof; it turned slowly and grumbled like an old man at work. The great cloth-covered sails of the mill revolved in their monotonous rhythm. Somewhere below two great stone beasts struggled and fought against each other so that the old mill groaned and trembled to its very base. Every five seconds a great long shadow cut across the room. The ladder which mounted to the loft was covered with flour dust.

"Madge, are you coming?" The voice rose above the sounds of the mill.

Madge stood with her hand resting on the oaken shaft; a strange sensation came upon her as its vibration ran up her arm and then over her body. Through the doorway there stretched before her the great flat country. The hillock on which the mill stood was as bare as a shaven head. The four great sails as they turned swung close to the ground and the long black shadows which they cast seemed to be ever in some futile pursuit of one another. Donkeys unnumbered had scratched their flanks against the poorly cemented walls while their masters had waited for flour, until now the plaster had worn away and left exposed the great grey foundation stones of the mill. At the base of the knoll, a roadway marked by dry and hardened wagon ruts led to a large pond where flame-red flowers grew.

"Madge, we are leaving now!" came the voice.

"Well, leave then," Madge replied under her breath.

The door of the mill screeched as some vagrant breeze swung it farther open. Madge watched the donkey's long flapping ears as it tentatively nibbled the short grass. A huge flour sack was slung across its back. The old miller and his son poked the donkey from behind and set off down the rutted road. Madge remained alone.

When her parents had found her one night lying on her face stretched out across her couch, her mouth filled with sand and charcoal they had called in the village doctors. Their advice had been to send Madge into the country where she would work hard each day, so hard that in the evenings she would be too tired to think of such things. However, since she had returned to the mill she had fled every morning at daybreak up into the loft where she watched the great turning sails for hours on end.

There was a creak and a clatter as someone raised the latch of the great mill door, and Madge shivered from head to foot in nervous excitement.

"Who is there?" she called down from the loft.

"May I have a drink? I am very thirsty," a feeble voice answered her.

It was but an old beggar of the countryside. Deep in his pack Madge could see a loaf of bread.

"It is too bad that he is not hungry as well," Madge thought.

She liked beggars as she liked toads, beetles and slimy white worms; they all fascinated her with some unknown horror.

"Wait a moment!" she called down.

She descended from the loft and stood before the old man.

"You are very old," she said, "and you are very thirsty?"

"Yes, my good child," answered the old man.

"Beggars are always hungry," Madge said, "and I like to help them. Wait a moment."

She pulled a flake of plaster from the wall and nibbled at it thoughtfully for a moment.

"No one is here and I have no glass but there is a pump in the yard."

She pointed to the curved iron handle above the well. While the old man pumped and held his mouth under the spout Madge slyly took the loaf of bread from his sack and hid it in a pile of flour.

But the old man got no water from the well for it was dry and when he returned to Madge she said:

"Down the hill there is a large pond. The poor may drink there."

"Though we are poor we are not animals," the old man replied.

"No," said Madge, "but you are as unfortunate. If you are hungry I will steal a cup of flour and give it to you. Then this evening with water from the pond you will be able to make some dough for your supper."

"Unbaked dough!" said the old beggar. "Thank you, child, but a kind person has today given me a loaf of bread."

"And what would you do if you had not the bread? If I were as old as you, my poor man, I would drown myself. Those who have drowned themselves are very happy. It is a lovely death! I pity you, old man."

"God be with you, child," said the old beggar and as he turned to go down the hill, he muttered in his wavering voice, as if to himself: "I am so very weary."

"You will be hungry tonight," Madge cried after him. "You will be hungry, old man. If your teeth are bad you must dip your bread in the water of the pond. It is very, very deep."

Madge listened to the last echoes of his footsteps and when they had passed she took the loaf of bread from the pile of flour and looked at it. It was black bread from some poor peasant hut; now it was spotted white with the flour.

"Pouf!" she said. "If I were poor I would steal good white bread from the bakeries."

When the miller returned he found Madge lying with her head on some flour sacks. Close in her arms she clutched the loaf of bread, her eyes bulged, her cheeks seemed fallen in and the scarlet tip of her tongue hung between her tightly closed teeth as she imitated what she thought a drowned person must look like.

After they had eaten supper Madge asked her father:

"Once upon a time, a long, long time ago, was there not an enormous giant who lived in this mill and who made his bread from the bones of dead men?"

"That is only a fairy-story," her father said. "But under the hill on which this mill is built there are caves cut from the solid rock, and a society from the city wants to buy my land and dig out these caves. Perhaps some day I will tear down my mill and sell the land to these people; then they may poke about to their hearts' delight among these old tombs and caves. They should find enough old bones to keep them busy for a long time."

"Bones grind easily? Yes? The bones of the dead...?" said Madge. "More easily than wheat, father? And the giant made very good bread from the dust of the bones and he ate the bread—yes, he ate it."

The young boy Jean shrugged his shoulders. The turmoil of the mill slowly ceased. The wind no longer turned the great sails. The great stone beasts ceased to struggle and pressed silently each against the other.

"Jean told me a long time ago," continued Madge, "that with a loaf of bread and quicksilver the bodies of drowned people can be found again. You make a little hole in the loaf of bread and pour some quicksilver into it and then throw it into the water and it will come to rest above the body of the drowned person."

"What should I know of all this?" the father answered. "And anyway, young lady, these are not things for a girl of your age to be occupying her mind with. What stories to tell a girl, Jean!"

"But Madge asked me about these things," replied the

boy. There is no quicksilver here," said Madge, "so I will put a leaden bullet in this loaf of bread and perhaps I will find a drowned person in the pond."

Seated before the mill door Madge awaited the coming of evening. Under her apron she concealed the beggar's loaf of bread with a little leaden bullet embedded in it. The old beggar surely must have become hungry and then drowned himself in the pond. She would find his body, and like the giant, she would grind her flour and knead her dough with the bones of a dead man.

The Savage

Just after daybreak Bouchette's father led her into the forest. While he felled a large tree she sat near to him and with fascination she watched the axe bite deep into the wood, showering a fine hail of chips and bark: sometimes the moss-covered bark flew farther than she thought it could and the little fragments would brush against her face. Timber! her father cried as the great oak began to sway and then with a subterranean rumble and loud crackling, slowly fell to the ground. Bouchette was a little sad when she saw the forest monster stretched out in the clearing, its branches wounded and shattered.

In the evening there shone through the deep shadows a burning circle where the little turf-covered charcoal mounds flamed in the darkness. It was time, Bouchette knew, to open the wicker basket and to set out for her father the little stone jug of wine and the loaf of brown bread. He lay back upon the deep pile of broken branches and ate slowly. Bouchette had her supper when they returned home. Now she ran here and there through the trees marked to be cut, and if she thought that her father had not been watching her she hid behind the trunk of one of the larger ones suddenly to spring out and cry: Boo!

Nearby there was a dark cave which the people of the countryside called Sainte-Marie-Gueule-de-Loup. The entrance to this cavern was choked with brambles and from its deep passages one could ever hear great rumbling echoes. Standing on her very tiptoes Bouchette would examine the cavern from some considerable distance.

One morning in late autumn when the frost-burned trees of the forest were still bathed in the soft rosy light of early dawn, Bouchette saw something green moving before the cave of the Gueule-de-Loup. It had arms and legs and a head and appeared to be a little girl about Bouchette's size and age.

Bouchette was afraid to approach the little green girl. She did not dare even to call out to her father. She thought that this was one of the strange people who answered when one called down into the black hole of the Gueule-de-Loup. She closed her eyes, fearing to stir from the spot and half-awaited some sinister attack. While she stood thus she heard a faint sob near at hand. The strange little green thing wept. Then Bouchette opened her eyes and she was sorry for the little girl. She looked intently at her green face, sweet and sad and wet with tears and the two nervous little green hands which pressed against the throat of this extraordinary child.

"Perhaps she has fallen and the grass and trees have stained her hands and face," Bouchette muttered to herself.

With a childish courage she crossed the fern-clustered brake until she stood beside this singular person. Two little green arms stretched out to Bouchette through the withered brambles.

"She is like me, save for her curious colour," Bouchette thought.

The weeping little creature was half dressed in a sort of tunic made from forest leaves sewn together. It was truly a little girl but a little girl of the shade and colour of some exotic wild plant. Bouchette imagined that her feet must be deep rooted like a tree in the ground. But this was not so for she moved slightly.

Bouchette caressed her and ran her hands through the little creature's hair and took her by the hand. The little green thing, still weeping, allowed herself to be led away by Bouchette. She seemed not to know how to speak.

"My good God! A green devil!" cried Bouchette's father, when he saw this little creature. "Where do you come from, my child? Why are you green?" And then because of her silence: "Can you not speak?"

Bouchette and her father could not tell if the little green child had heard them.

"Perhaps she is hungry," said the woodsman, and he offered the child some of his bread and the stone jar of wine. She turned the bread about in her hands and then let it fall to the ground; the stone jar she shook that she might listen to the gurgling sound of the wine.

Bouchette begged her father not to leave the poor creature in the forest during the night. The little turf-covered charcoal mounds gleamed one by one in the early evening and the little green child trembled as she saw their flames. When she entered the humble cottage where Bouchette lived she fled from the candle flames. She could never accustom herself to fire and whenever any one lighted a lamp she uttered a cry of terror.

When Bouchette's mother saw this strange child she crossed herself: "God help me," she said, "if she be a demon, and demon she must be for of a certain she is not a Christian."

The little green child would touch neither bread nor salt nor wine, and from this it could be clearly seen that she had neither been baptised nor had she ever received the communion. The curé was sent for and he crossed the threshold of the cottage just as Bouchette was offering the little green child some raw unshucked beans.

The child seemed very happy, and with her finger-nails she slit open the first pod which came to her hands. By chance this pod was empty, and thinking herself deceived the little girl began to cry again until Bouchette opened a full pod for her. For some time she sat there in the firelight nibbling the beans and watching the priest.

Later they brought in the village schoolmaster, but he could not make her understand a single human word, nor pronounce a single articulate sound. She wept and she laughed and she uttered strange and unintelligible noises.

The curé examined her very carefully, but he could discern nowhere on her body any mark of the demon. On the following Sunday she was taken to the church but she manifested no signs of inquietude save that she moaned when she was sprinkled with holy water. She did not recoil before the image of Christ upon the Cross, but as she passed her hands over the wounds upon the Holy Body and the cruel marks of the crown of thorns she seemed afflicted with a deep sorrow.

The people of the village were very curious about her; and some of them feared her. Despite the commands of their curé they always spoke of her as the "Green Devil."

She ate only fruit and the seeds of things, and whenever any one handed her an ear of corn or a stalk she broke them open and finding nothing she would weep from disappointment. Bouchette could never seem to teach her where to find the grains of wheat or the cherries and her self-deceptions and disappointments were ever the same. Imitating Bouchette, she soon learned to carry the wood and water, to sweep the floor of the little cottage, to help with the washing and even to sew, though indeed she could never touch cloth without a little shudder of aversion. But she would never light the fire, nor for that matter would she ever approach close to the hearth.

When Bouchette grew up and her parents wished to hire her out in service she grieved, and in the evening with her head hidden under her bed-clothes she wept softly. The little green girl looked with piteous eyes upon her poor little friend. In the morning she watched the great sad eyes of Bouchette and her own eyes filled with tears. In the night when Bouchette wept she felt a soft hand brushing through her hair and cool lips pressing against her cheek.

The last evening before Bouchette was to go away and

while her father and mother slept, the little green girl caressed her weeping friend and took by the hand. She opened the cottage door and stretched her arm forth into the night. As long before when Bouchette had led her to the houses of men, the little green child now led Bouchette by the hand toward some unknown liberty which lay beyond the night.

The Pre- destined

From the day that Elsie was tall enough she would stand every morning before her mirror and say: "Good morning my little Ilsée." Then she would purse her lips and kiss the cold glass. The girl in the glass always seemed to come toward Elsie. In reality she was very far away. Ilsée, ever more pale than Elsie, raised herself from the depths of the glass, a prisoner with frozen lips. Elsie pitied her for she seemed so sad and grievous. Each morning her smile was like a sallow dawn haunted by some nocturnal horror.

Nevertheless Elsie loved and talked to her friend:

"No one but I ever says good morning to you, my poor little Ilsée. Kiss me! Today we will go for a long walk, Ilsée. My lover will come for us, and you will walk with us."

Elsie turned away, and the little Ilsée fled into the shadows of the mirror.

Elsie showed the girl in the mirror her dolls and her dresses.

"Play with me, and show me your dresses," she said.

Ilsée seemed jealous, but lifted her dolls for Elsie to see, and they were pale; her dresses, and they were discoloured. Ilsée never spoke; she seemed content only to move her lips when Elsie talked to her.

Sometimes Elsie was fretful and like a little child became angry with the silent Ilsée.

"Naughty, wicked, Ilsée!" she would cry. "Will you not answer me ? Will you not kiss me ?"

At such times she would beat with her hands against the mirror, and a strange hand, which seemed attached to nobody, would appear before Elsie's hand. Never could Elsie touch the girl in the mirror.

But always during the night Elsie would forgive the girl of the mirror, and in the morning, happy to find her friend again, she would jump from her bed to kiss her and to murmur: "Good morning, my little Ilsée."

When Elsie became engaged she brought her betrothed to the mirror and said to Ilsée: "This is my lover. You may look at him, but you must not look at him too long. He is mine, but I want you to see him. When we are married I will let you kiss him with me every morning."

Elsie's lover laughed and the Ilsée in the mirror smiled also.

"Is he not handsome this man that I love?" asked Elsie.

"Yes! Yes!" Ilsée seemed to say as her head nodded in the mirror.

"If you look at him too long I will never kiss you again," said Elsie. "I am quite as jealous as you, my friend. Goodbye, my little Ilsée."

In the same measure that Elsie learned love and happiness, Ilsée became sad, for her friend no longer came to kiss her in the morning. She was forgotten. Elsie no longer looked at the girl in the mirror but her fiancé saw her.

"Oh!" said Elsie. "You no longer think of me, villain. You can only see Ilsée. She is a prisoner; she will never come to you. She is jealous of you; but I am more jealous than she. Do not look at her, my love, look at me instead. Wicked Ilsée of the mirror, I forbid you to speak to my love. You cannot go to him; you never can be with him. Do not take him from me, wicked girl. When we are married you may kiss him with me. Laugh, Ilsée. You will be with us."

Elsie became jealous of the girl in the mirror. On the days when her betrothed did not come to see her she would cry out: "You have driven him away, you have frightened him away with your ugly face. Wicked Ilsée!"

Elsie tacked a piece of soft white linen over the mirror and just before she hammered in the last little nail she lifted a corner of the cloth and said: "Good-bye, little Ilsée of the mirror."

Yet even with the Ilsée of the mirror shut away Elsie's lover seemed estranged. "He no longer loves me," thought Elsie, "he comes no more, and I am all alone. Where is Ilsée? Has she gone away with him?"

With her gold scissors Elsie snipped a little hole in the cloth and looked deep into the mirror. She saw only a white shadow. She has gone away, thought Elsie.

"I must be patient," Elsie said to herself, "or the Ilsée of the mirror will be jealous and sad. I will wait and my lover will come back to me."

Each morning Elsie, half-asleep, seemed to see the head of her fiancé on the pillow beside her face. "Oh, my love," she would murmur, "you have come back to me? My dear one . . ." Her hand ever stretched out, to touch only the empty sheet.

"I must be very patient," Elsie said to herself.

A long time Elsie awaited her fiancé, until her patience melted into tears. Her face became lined with wrinkles. Each day, each month, each year had left its mark upon her.

"Oh, my love," said Elsie, "I begin to doubt."

Elsie cut the linen cover she had tacked over the mirror; beyond the pallid frame appeared the glass hidden behind deep stains. The mirror was furrowed with translucent lines, and here and there where the silver backing had fallen away she saw only deep shadowy lakes.

Ilsée stood behind the glass. Like Elsie she was dressed in black, and her face was thin and drawn and marked and spotted by those blind patches of the mirror which did not reflect. The mirror seemed to have wept.

"You are sad even as I am sad," said Elsie.

The woman in the mirror wept and Elsie kissed her and said: "Good-bye, my poor Ilsée."

Upon going into her room with her lamp in her hand, Elsie was surprised for Ilsée, a lamp in her hand, came through the doorway toward her, and she seemed sad. Elsie placed her lamp on a little shelf above her bed. Ilsée placed her lamp there likewise and sat beside Elsie.

"I understand now," thought Elsie. "The Ilsée of the mirror has been delivered. She has come to look for me. I am going to die."

The Insensible

The Princess Morgane loved no one. Hers was a frank ingenuousness and she preferred to live among her flowers and her mirrors. She amused herself by putting red roses into her hair and then looking into one of her many mirrors. Since she but mirrored herself in the regard of others she never saw either young men or young women. Cruelty and voluptuousness were unknown to her. Her black hair fell about her face like a shadowy veil and hung between her and the rest of the world. She desired only to love herself, but the reflection of herself which she saw in her mirrors was frigidly calm and distant; her image on pools and lakes was sad and pale and her image upon the surface of streams and running water was elusive and trembling.

The Princess Morgane had read in history books of the famous mirror of the little Snow White which could speak and wherein one might foretell one's death. She knew the story of the mirror of Elsie, and Ilsée who had come from the mirror and killed her friend. She knew the adventures of the terrible mirror of Miletus which caused the Milesians to strangle themselves as the night faded into dawn. She had seen the mysterious painting in which the lover holds a naked sword before his betrothed to protect her because in the dusk of the evening, while walking, they had come upon their own spectres: and doubles are ever the sign of impending death. Yet despite this Morgane did not fear her own image for she had never seen herself cruel or voluptuous but always candid and veiled. The great sheets of polished green gold and the heavy liquid surfaces of bright silver never quite revealed Morgane to Morgane.

The priests of her country were geomancers and worshippers of fire. They would put sand into a square shallow box and there trace cabbalistic lines; by means of their parchment talismans they could predict the future and calculate events which were yet to occur, and they possessed a great black smoky mirror. One evening Morgane resorted to the priests, and as an offering to the Gods she threw three little cakes into the sacred fire.

"Look," said the geomancer and he held before Morgane a mirror whose surface was limpid black.

Morgane looked deep into this mirror and soon a clear vapour seemed to rise from its surface. There appeared a golden circle of light and then an image came into her vision which ran lightly and soon disappeared. Then she saw a square white house with long windows and under the third window there hung a great bronze ring. And all about the house there was nothing but desolation and a waste of grey sand.

"There," said the geomancer, "is the hidden place where the mirror of truth will be found; but our science can tell you no more—neither where this place is nor how to explain all this that you have seen."

Morgane peered even more intently and threw three more cakes into the fire, but the image trembled before her eyes and then became obscure; the square white house vanished and Morgane found herself looking vainly into an empty black mirror.

The day following, Morgane wished to set forth in search of the place she had seen in the black mirror. It seemed to her she remembered the dismal colour of the sand and so she departed and her course was that of the sun. Her father gave her a rich caravan, with mules belled in silver and Morgane was carried in a litter whose sides were lined with precious and famous mirrors.

Thus Morgane crossed Persia, and she examined all the houses she saw in the desert's isolation as well as those built near the oases: houses where bands of travellers stopped and houses of which men spoke ill wherein women sang through the night and beat musically upon pieces of metal the while.

Near the border of the kingdom of Persia she saw square white houses with long windows but never did she see a bronze ring hung from one of them, but she was told that the house with the ring would be found in the Christian country of Syria farther to the west.

Morgane passed the level banks of the river which bordered the country of the great marshes where the liquorice forests are believed to be. Here she saw strongholds carved from single rocks. And in the sunlight beside the path of the caravan women sat with twisted cords of reddish hair bound across their foreheads. These were the people who capture the great bands of wild horses and whose lances are tipped with silver points.

Farther along this way there was a mountain inhabited by brigands who drank, in the honour of their gods, strong liquors made from wheat. They lasciviously worshipped great green stones of a curious shape and within circles of burning brush they practised an obscene ritual of prostitution. Morgane greatly feared these people.

Still farther along this way was a subterranean city of black men who were only visited by their gods while they slept. These people chewed the fibres of hemp and covered their faces with powdery white chalk. During the night those who became drunken with the hemp rove the necks of those who slept that they might send them to their nocturnal divinities. Morgane greatly feared these people.

Even still farther along this way was the desert of grey sand where the plants and all that grew, and the rocks and all that was, were of the same grey colour as the sand. At the edge of the desert Morgane found the square white house of the bronze ring.

She had her litter lowered to the ground, and the mule-drivers unloaded the mules. It was an ancient house built without the use of cement and the blocks of stone were whitened by the sun. However, the owner of the house could tell Morgane nothing of the mirror for he had never heard of it.

In the evening, after they had eaten of their scanty store of thin wafers the owner of the house told Morgane that the house of the bronze ring in ancient times had been the palace of a cruel queen, but that she had been punished for her cruelty. She had ordered that her people cut off the head of an old religious who lived alone in the great desert and who with many good words was wont to bathe the feet of travellers, in his stream. Soon after this was done the cruel queen perished and with her, all her race. The chamber of this queen had been walled up, but the owner of the house showed the Princess Morgane the doorway blocked with great stones.

Toward the middle of the night and after the travellers had retired the Princess Morgane woke her mule-drivers and bade them break down the wall across the doorway of the ancient queen's chamber. And with a small iron lamp in her hand she entered through the powdery breach which they had made.

The servants of Morgane, hearing a cry, quickly followed the princess. She was kneeling in the middle of the room before a hammered copper basin filled with blood and in the basin she peered with ardent attention. The owner of the house raised his arms in prayer and horror. For in the closed room the blood in the basin had not evaporated since the cruel queen had placed there the head of the old religious.

No one knows what the Princess Morgane saw in the mirror of blood, but along the way of her return her mule-teers, their grey faces turned toward the heavens, were found assassinated one by one, each night, after they had entered her litter. Later people called the Princess Morgane, *Morgane le Rouge*, and she was known as a famous prostitute and a terrible slaughterer of men.

—*Translated by William B. Meloney.*

The Death of Odjigh

In those days the human race seemed on the point of extinction. The sun's orb was as cold as the moon. An eternal winter cracked the earth into fissures. The mountains that had arisen, vomiting the earth's burning entrails to the sky, were grey with frozen lava. Parallel or radiating cracks traversed the regions; subsidences, suddenly opening huge crevasses, swallowed things up and long files of erratic blocks were to be seen slowly sliding towards them. The gloomy air was spangled with a transparent lacework of ice-crystals; the universally spreading silver appeared to be sterilising the world.

Save for some traces of pale lichen on the rocks, there was no longer any vegetation. The world's bones were stripped of their flesh, which is made up of the earth, and the plains lay extended like skeletons. And the wintry death attacking first life of the lower kinds, the fish and the sea-creatures had perished, imprisoned in the ice, then the insects that swarmed on the creeping plants, and the animals that carried their young in ventral pouches, and the semi-aerial creatures that had haunted the great forests; for, as far as the eye could see, there were no longer any trees or any greenery, and no living creatures were to be found but those that lived in caverns, grottoes or dens.

Thus, from among the descendants of men, two races were already extinct; those who had lived in nests of lianas at the tops of great trees and those who, in floating houses, had lived retired in the middle of lakes: the forests, woods, copses and thickets that had bestrewn the glittering earth, and the surface of the waters were as hard and gleaming as polished stone.

The Beast-hunters who knew the use of fire, the Troglodytes who could burrow into the earth to reach the interior heat, and the Fish-eaters who had laid up stores of marine oil in their holes in the ice, still held out against the winter. But animals were becoming rare, caught by the frost the moment their muzzles touched the ground; and firewood had all but been exhausted and the oil was solid, like a yellow rock with a white crest.

Nevertheless a wolf-hunter called Odjigh, who lived in a deep den and possessed an immense axe of green jade, heavy and redoubtable, had pity on living creatures.

Living on the shores of the great inland sea whose furthermost reach expands to the east of Minnesota, he turned his gaze to the northern regions where the cold seemed to be gathering. In the depths of his grotto of ice he took the sacred pipe, hollowed from a white stone, packed it with fragrant herbs from which the smoke rises in curls and blew the divine essence onto the air.

The curls mounted upwards, and the grey whorls inclined to the north. It was to the north that Odjigh, the wolf-killer, commenced to march. He covered his face with a furry racoon-skin, pierced with holes, the tail of which waved above his head like a plume; from a leathern thong about his waist he had hung a pouch filled with dried meat mixed with fat: and, swinging his green-jade axe, he set out towards the thick clouds piled up on the horizon. He went on his way, and about him life was dying out. The rivers had long been silent. The opaque air carried only muffled sounds. The masses of ice, blue, white and green, resembled pillars flanking a great road.

In his heart Odjigh grieved for the wriggling of the mother-of-pearl coloured fish among the meshes of fibre-woven nets, and the serpentine swimming of the sea-eels, and the ponderous gait of turtles, and the sidelong running of gigantic, squint-eyed crabs, and the lively sighing sounds of terrestrial beasts, shaggy beasts with a flat beak and clawed paws, beasts covered in scales, beasts speckled in various fashions pleasing to the eye, beasts fond of their young, agile in their leaping or strange in their gyrations, or venturesome in their flights. And above all animals he mourned the passing of the fierce wolves with their grey fur and their familiar howling, being accustomed by the red light of the moon on foggy nights, to hunt them with club and stone axe.

On his left there now appeared a beast of the sort that lives in a den dug deep in the soil and lets itself be drawn backwards from its burrow, a skinny, mangy Badger. Odjigh saw it and rejoiced, without a thought of killing it: keeping its distance, the Badger advanced abreast of him.

Then, on Odjigh's right, a wretched hollow-eyed Lynx suddenly emerged from a gully among the ice. It looked sidelong at Odjigh, fearful and slinking in its anxiety. But again the wolf-killer rejoiced, marching between the Badger and Lynx.

As he advanced, his pouch of meat slapping against his side, he heard behind him a feeble, hungry howling; and turning to the sound of a voice he knew, he saw a bony Wolf miserably treading in his footsteps. Odjigh took pity on all those creatures whose skulls he used to split. The Wolf hung out his steaming tongue, and his eyes were red.

Thus the slayer continued on his way with his animal companions; the subterranean Badger on his left and the all-seeing Lynx on his right, and behind him the famished Wolf.

They reached the centre of the inland sea which was to be distinguished only by the endlessly green colour of its ice. And there Odjigh, the wolf-killer, seated himself on a boulder and placed before him the stone pipe. And before each of his companions he placed a block of ice which he hollowed out with the blade of his axe, after the manner of the sacred censer breathing forth smoke. He packed fragrant herbs in the four pipes: then he struck the fire-making stones together, and the herbs caught fire, and the four meagre columns of smoke arose.

Now the grey whorl that arose before the Badger bent towards the west, and that which rose before the Lynx bent towards the east, and that which arose before the Wolf curved to the south. But the grey whorl from Odjigh's pipe rose to the north.

The wolf-killer started once more on his way. And looking to the left he was saddened, for the Badger that can see below ground, was going off towards the west; and looking to the right, he regretted the all-seeing Lynx that was making off to the east, although in fact he thought that, each in its way, those two animal companions were prudent and well-advised.

Nevertheless he went steadily on, behind him the red-eyed, starving Wolf on which he had taken pity.

The mass of frozen clouds to the north seemed to reach the sky. The winter was becoming still more cruel. Cut by the ice, Odjigh's feet bled, and his blood froze in black crusts. But for hours, for days, for weeks, for months perhaps, he continued, sucking at a little dried meat and throwing the leavings to his companion, the Wolf that followed him.

In a vague hope, Odjigh continued on his way. He felt pity for the world of men, for the dying animals and plants, and he felt himself filled with strength for the fight against the cold.

And, in the end, his path was blocked by an immense barrier of ice that, like a chain of mountains whose peaks were lost to view, sealed the sombre dome of the sky. As they tipped into the solid expanse of the frozen ocean the great ice-floes were a limpid green; then, in their congested heaping-up, they grew cloudy; and, as they rose higher, they appeared an opaque blue, like the sky in the summers of times past: for they were composed of fresh water and of snow. Odjigh took his green-jade axe, and he cut steps in the escarpment. In this way he climbed to a great height, where it seemed to him that his head was enveloped in clouds and that the earth had fallen away. And on the step just below him, the Wolf sat and confidently waited. When he thought he had reached the summit, he saw that it was formed of a glistening, vertical blue wall, and it was impossible to go further. But he looked behind him and he saw the living, hungry beast: pity for the living world gave him strength.

He plunged his jade axe into the blue wall and hewed away the ice. Multicoloured, the fragments flew about him. He hacked for hours and hours. His limbs were yellow and wrinkled from the cold. His pouch of meat had long since been shrunken and empty. To appease his hunger he had chewed the fragrant herbs he smoked in his pipe and, all at once disbelieving in the Superior Powers, he had thrown the pipe and the pair of fire-making stones into the void.

He dug on. He heard a sharp grating sound, and he cried out, for he knew that this sound had come from his jade axe-blade that was about to split with the great cold. Then he picked it up and, no longer having the means to warm it, thrust it fiercely into his right thigh. The green axe was tinged with warm blood. Sitting behind him, the whimpering Wolf lapped up the red drops as they fell.

And suddenly the polished wall burst open. There was a great blast of heat as if, on the far side, the warm seasons were stored up at the bar of heaven. The aperture enlarged and the powerful blast engulfed Odjigh. He heard all the little shoots of spring rustling and he felt the summer's blazing heat. It felt to him as if in the great tide that lifted him off his feet, all the seasons were returning to the world to save life from extinction. The tide bore with it the white rays of the sun, and the caressing breezes and the clouds laden with fecundity. And in the breath of warm life the black clouds gathered and engendered fire.

With the clap of thunder there was a long bolt of flame, and the resplendent shaft, like a red blade, pierced Odjigh to the heart. He fell against the polished wall, his back turned to the world towards which the seasons were returning in the river of the storm: and the hungry Wolf, climbing up timidly, set his paws on Odjigh's shoulders and began gnawing at the back of his neck.

—*Translated by Iain White*.

OMITTED AUTHORS

The following authors from The Book of Masks *have been omitted from our selection, either because their entire* oeuvre *consists of poetry, or because the editors were unable to discover interesting texts.*

Henry Bataille, Victor Charbonnel, Louis Dumur, Max Elskamp, André Fontainas...

René Ghil, The Goncourts, A.-Ferdinand Herold, Henri Mazel, Francis Vielé-Griffin.

NOTES

Page 4. **Jarry:** The cause of this quarrel is described in the introduction to the Atlas Press edition of Jarry's novel *Visits of Love*.

Remy de Gourmont

14. **Germinal:** Zola's novel of 1885, one of the great works of the Naturalist movement, is an account of a miner's strike.

14. **Nightsoil-works:** A play on words here in the original French, which reads: *à moins que contre les basses oeuvres*. The public executioner used to be called the *maître* or *exécuteur des hautes oeuvres*; with a touch of gallows-humour the nightsoil-man or cesspool-emptier became the *maître* or *exécuteur des basses oeuvres*.

14. **Max Nordau,** whose study *Degeneration* (1893) weighed the new literature in the balance and found it wanting.

Paul Adam

24. **New photographs:** de Gourmont is, of course, referring to X-ray photographs.

27. *Les Veules:* The Weaklings.

Jean Moréas

30. **Benoît de Sainte-Maure** was a 12th Century poet who wrote a verse history of the Norman dukes at the behest of King Henry II. **Jacot de Forest**, 13th century epic poet, author of the *Roman de Jules César*.

30. The *Chanson de Saint-Léger* is probably the *Vie de Saint-Léger*, one of the earliest French poems to be preserved.

34. **IV:** There is no section III in the original (and only) edition, so this is presumably a misprint.

Léon Bloy

38. From Philippe Jullian, *Dreamers of Decadence*, p. 78, and Mario Praz, *The Romantic Agony*, p. 408 respectively.

38. Praz, *op. cit.*

André Gide

48. **Gide adds this note**: Truths dwell behind the Forms—Symbols. Every phenomenon is the Symbol of a Truth. Its one duty is that it manifests it. Its only sin: that it prefer itself.

We live to manifest. The rules of morality and aesthetics are the same: every work that does not manifest is useless and, for that very reason, bad. Every man that does not manifest is useless and bad. (Raising oneself a little, one may perceive that all manifests—but one must recognise this only later.)

Every representative of the Idea tends to prefer itself to the Idea it manifests. There lies the fault. The artist, the scientist, must not prefer himself to the Truth he wishes to express: there lies his whole morality; neither the word nor the phrase, to the Idea they wish to demonstrate; I would almost say that this is the whole of aesthetics.

And I do not claim that this theory is new; the doctrines of renunciation preach nothing different.

For the artist the moral question is not whether the Idea he manifests might be more or less moral for the greater number; the question is whether he manifests well. —For everything must be manifested, even the most baleful things: "Cursed betide he who spreads scandal," but "It is necessary that scandal be spread." —The artist and the man who is truly a man, who lives for something, must first have made the sacrifice of himself. His whole life is no more than a preparation for that.

And now, what to manifest? —That one learns in silence.

49. Gide adds a second note: Have you grasped what it is I call a symbol? —*Everything that appears.*

Paul Claudel

52. Quoted in Jean Cassou, *The Concise Encyclopedia of Symbolism*, p. 177.

Laurent Tailhade

62. See Philippe Oriol, *A Propos de l'attentat Foyot*, Fourneau, 1993.

Pierre Quillard

69. **Triumpant Beast:** Allusion to the works of Giordano Bruno, renaissance philosopher burnt by the Inquisition; it was his name for the Catholic church.

Rachilde

74. **Marceline Desbordes-Valmore** (1786-1859), actress and lyric poet, was one of Verlaine's original *poètes maudits*.

Alfred Vallette

85. **Tonneau:** Also known as the *Jeu de Grenouille*, the game of *tonneau* consists of a sort of table pierced with various holes: the players throw small metal discs into the holes, each of which is worth a different amount of points (the discs reappear under the table in sloping compartments marked with the number of points scored). The largest scoring hole (1000 points) is decorated with a frog into whose open mouth the player must cast his disc.

86. **The Two Perches:** *Une Perche* in French can mean either a "perch" or a "(thin) pole."

Félix Fénéon

90. **Louis-Auguste Blanqui** (1805-1881) was a revolutionary agitator and founder of the Blanquiste Party. He was instrumental in bringing down the Second Empire after the Sedan *débâcle* and was active in the Paris Commune (March-May, 1871). Sentenced to prison for life following the Commune's suppression, he was paroled in 1878.

Georges Eekhoud
102. *Sans-culottes:* originally used by the aristocracy as a term of contempt for those revolutionaries of 1789 who had forsaken their traditional breeches in favour of trousers.

103. The name **Chardonnerette** derives from the French *chardonneret,* "goldfinch," derived in turn from *chardon,* "thistle"—the classical plant of vacant lots and neglected field-edges. In autumn flocks of goldfinches feed greedily on the seed-heads of thistles.

105. **Virginities** etc: The original French has *Dépuceleur,* a conflation of *épouiller,* "to delouse," and *depuisler,* "to take a virginity."

105. **Phalanstery:** the name of the utopian socialist communities envisaged by the somewhat eccentric philosopher Charles Fourier. Alfred Vallette's house was called *The Phalanstery.*

Arthur Rimbaud
122. **The various interpretations of** *Voyelles* is the subject of an entire book by Etiemble: *Le Sonnet des Voyelles, de l'audition colorée à la vision érotique,* Gallimard, 1968.

122. **Château Rouge** remains obscure, though the context implies a dubious nightspot.

122. **Vita abscondita:** a life lived in hiding.

Robert de Montesquiou
134. A *Précieuse* was the French version of a Metaphysical Poet: rather closer to Donne or Marvell than to Herbert.

Pierre Louÿs
160. **Menard:** Louis Menard, author of *Rêveries d'un païen mystique* (1876).

Albert Samain
168. **Infanta in robes of state**, refers to *Mon âme est une infante en robe de parade,* the famous opening line of the first poem in Samain's first book *Au Jardin de l'Infante* (1893).

Jehan Rictus
175. *Scolopendre* = centipede.

Hugues Rebell
181. **Falstaff** etc: the references that follow are to various literary drinkers, misanthropes and bourgeois philistines.

181. **Barbey:** Barbey d'Aurevilly, dandy and author of *Les Diaboliques,* with Baudelaire, one of the important forerunners of Symbolism.

181. **Akedysseril** etc: Queens, cruel and Asiatic, from works by Mallarmé, Flaubert/de Nerval and Villiers de l'Isle-Adam respectively.

Jean Lorrain
184. **A Dish of Spices:** title of Huysmans' first book.

Gustave Kahn
200. *Vers libre:* Although a literal translation of the term would come out as "free

verse," this would be quite misleading since English free verse is much freer than anything envisioned by the French Symbolists. While *vers libre* abandoned the rigid rules of Classicism, with its strict accounting of syllable and metrical patterns, it did not abandon at least a species of rhythm and retained rhyme, albeit sporadically.

Stéphane Mallarmé

217. **With Upraised Nails..:** Mallarmé constructed this Munch-like picture around the mysterious word *ptyx*, which he included in desperation when limiting himself to two rhymes. The OED gives the English equivalent as *ptyxis*, which is even trickier to rhyme.

The inevitable compression caused by trying to squeeze a quart-sized Petrarchian sonnet into a pint-sized semi-Shakespearean one only compounds the difficulty. This version—which has two-and-a-half rhymes in place of the original two—can only give a shadowy reflection of the great original. [Translator's note]

Mallarmé, in a letter to Henry Cazalis (July, 1868) had these comments to make concerning this poem—themselves salient to the theory of Symbolist poetics and which perhaps give an indication of the rarefied converations that occurred at Mallarmé's soirées: *I have taken this sonnet, of which I once dreamed, from a projected study on the word: it is inverse, that is to say the meaning, if it has one (but I should console myself, it seems to me, for the contrary, thanks to the measure of poetry it contains) is evoked by an internal mirage of the words themselves. In letting oneself murmur it many times over one experiences an almost cabalistic sensation. It must be admitted that it is not very "plastic," as you require of me, but it is as "white and black" as possible, and it seems to me to resemble an etching filled with dream and emptiness.*

For example, a nocturnal window open, the two shutters fastened back: a room with a person in it, despite the air of stability the fastened-back shutters present, and a night made up of absence and questioning, without furniture save for an indication of indistinct console-tables, a mirror-frame, bellicose and dying, with its stellar and incomprehensible reflection of the Great Bear, which alone links to the sky this dwelling abandoned by the world.

I chose this subject for a naked sonnet reflecting back on itself in every way; for my work is at the same time as well prepared and hierarchically ordered, representing as it can the universe, that I would not have been able without troubling any of my tiered impressions to subtract anything from it—for no sonnet tallies with itself.

219. **Hastinapura**, known as the City of the Elephants, lay in bygone days on the banks of the Ganges. [Author's note]

Henri de Régnier

224. **José-Maria de Heredia** (1842-1905): a Cuban-born French poet, one of the first (and best) of the Parnassian poets. From 1901 until his death, he was Keeper of the Bibliothèque de l'Arsenal, the second most prestigious library in France.

Saint-Pol-Roux

245. **Calvary:** the reference here is to a roadside crucifix, the word Calvary being the Romanised version of Golgotha: the site of the crucifixion.

246. **Woman of Samaria:** cf. John IV, 7ff.

247. **St. John Chrysostom:** the name means "golden-mouthed."

Emile Verhaeren
270. **Hippolyte Taine** (1828-1893) was a philosopher, historian, aesthetician and critic, but also the principal theorist of Naturalism.

Villiers de L'Isle-Adam
278. **Vicomte François René de Chateaubriand** (1768-1848) was one of French Romanticism's "big guns." Born, like Villiers, into an ancient Breton noble house, he was officer, tourist of the North American frontier, sometime favourite of Napoleon, minister of state under Louis XVIII and politician. As a writer, he is remembered more for bits and pieces than for the whole of his oeuvre.

Marcel Schwob
282. Cassou, p. 271, & Praz, p. 237, respectively.

COPYRIGHT ACKNOWLEDGEMENTS

Works by Saint-Pol-Roux: *Le pèlerinage de Sainte-Anne, L'autopsie de la vieille fille & L'âme saisissable* from *Les Féeries intérieures*, tome III of *Reposoirs de la Procession*, © 1981, Rougerie, éditeur; *Calvaire immémorial* from *La rose et les épines du chemin*, tome I of *Reposoirs de la Procession*, © 1980, Rougerie, éditeur; *Nocturne*, from *De la colombe au corbeau par le paon*, tome II of *Reposoirs de la Procession*, © 1980, Rougerie, éditeur.
Works by André Gide © 1912 Eds. Gallimard.
Works by Félix Fénéon © 1948, Eds. Gallimard.
Works by Paul Claudel, Francis Jammes, Gustave Kahn, Henri de Régnier & Alfred Vallette: © Mercure de France.
Apologies: we have been unable to trace the copyright holders of some texts and would like to apologise for this involuntary omission here.

BIBLIOGRAPHY: Books in English

GENERAL SURVEYS:

ADAMS, Robert Martin, *Nil*, O.U.P., 1966.
ANDERSON, David L., *Symbolism: A Bibliography of Symbolism as an International and Multi-Disciplinary Movement*, New York University Press, 1975.
BALAKIAN, Anna, *The Symbolist Movement*, NY, 1967.
BOWRA, C.M, *The Heritage of Symbolism*, Macmillan, NY, 1967.
BRADBURY, Malcolm & MACFARLANE, James [eds.], *Modernism*, Penguin Books, 1976.
CASSOU, Jean, *The Concise Encyclopedia of Symbolism*, Chartwell Books, Secaucus, NJ, 1979; Omega Books, London, 1984.
CHADWICK, Charles, *Symbolism, The Critical Idiom*, Methuen, London, 1971.
CORNELL, Kenneth, *The Symbolist Movement*, New Haven, Conn., 1951.
DELEVOY, Robert L., *Symbolists and Symbolism*, Skira/Rizzoli, NY, 1978.
ENGELBERG, Edward, *The Symbolist Poem*, E.P. Dutton, NY, 1967.
FOWLIE, Wallace, *Poem & Symbol, A Brief History of French Symbolism*, Pennsylvania State University Press, 1990.
JULLIAN, Philippe, *Dreamers of Decadence*, Pall Mall, London, 1971; Praeger, NY, 1971.
JULLIAN, Philippe, *The Symbolists*, Phaidon/Praeger, NY, 1973.
LEHMANN, A. G, *The Symbolist Aesthetic in France 1885-1895*, OUP, Oxford, 1950.
LUCIE-SMITH, Edward, *Symbolist Art*, Thames & Hudson, London 1972; Praeger, NY, 1972.
MILNER, John, *Symbolists and Decadents*, Studio Vista/Dutton, London/NY, 1971.
PRAZ, Mario, *The Romantic Agony*, 2nd Ed., O.U.P., 1970.
QUENNELL, Peter, *Baudelaire and the Symbolists*, 1929.
SYMONS Arthur, *The Symbolist Movement in Literature*, London, 1899; E.P. Dutton, NY, 1958.
THOMPSON, Vance, *French Portraits*, Badger, Boston, 1900.
TUCHMAN, Barbara W, *The Proud Tower*, Macmillan, NY, 1965.

TRANSLATIONS (COLLECTIONS)

GEROULD, Daniel [ed.], *Doubles, Demons, and Dreamers. An International Collection of Symbolist Drama*, Performing Arts Journal Publications, NY, 1985.

HOUSTON, John Porter & HOUSTON, Mona Tobin, *French Symbolist Poetry*, Indiana University Press, Bloomington, 1980.
LOWELL, Amy, *Six French Poets*, Macmillan, NY, 1916.
MERRILL, Stuart, *Pastels in Prose*, Harper, NY, 1890.
SHIPLEY, Joseph T, *Modern French Poetry*, Greenburg, NY, 1926.
STABLEFORD, Brian, *The Dedalus Book of Decadence*, Dedalus, UK, 1990.
STABLEFORD, Brian, *The Second Dedalus Book of Decadence*, Dedalus, UK, 1992.

Dedalus Press have a sizeable catalogue of titles in this field, it may be obtained by writing to: Dedalus, Langford Lodge, St. Judith's Lane, Sawtry, Cambs. PE17 5XE, England.

FORTHCOMING

HUSTVEDT, Asti [ed.], *The Decadent Reader*, Zone Books, NY, Fall 1995.

A massive anthology that probably will not be for sale in the UK due to copyright restrictions, for information contact: Zone Books, 611 Broadway, Suite 608, New York, NY 10012.

SAINT-POL-ROUX

A permanent exhibition devoted to the life and work of Saint-Pol-Roux has recently opened at the municipal library of Châteaulin. They publish a large illustrated catalogue *La Verbe et la Lumière*, (from which our photograph of the master outside his chateau was taken) which is exceptionally good value at 120FF including postage. It may be ordered by sending a cheque made out to La Mairie de Châteaulin at the Bibliothèque Municipale, 7 quai Robert Alba, 29150 Châteaulin, France. Our thanks to the editor of this catalogue, Alastair Whyte, for his help with the present book.

Note: Atlas publishes a larger selection from *Pauses in the Procession* in our Printed Head series.

PAST & FORTHCOMING ISSUES OF THE ARKHIVE

ARKHIVE 1: DADA BERLIN

THE DADA ALMANAC. *Edited by Richard Huelsenbeck, Berlin, 1920. Introduced and annotated by Malcolm Green & Alastair Brotchie. Translated by Malcolm Green, Barbara Wright & Derk Wynand. Illustrations, biographies, etc, 176 pps. £12.99. (In print.)*

THE DADA ALMANAC was assembled by Richard Huelsenbeck, one of the foremost Dadaists from the very inception of Dada to its end, and published in Berlin in 1920 at the high-point of Dadaist activities in the German capital: the *Dada Almanac* was and is the most important single Dadaist publication. Containing a wide range of poetry, polemics, essays, manifestos and deliberate confusions, not only does it present the vast range of Dadaist literary production and experimentation on an international scale, it also reveals many of the apparent contradictions which lie at the heart of the movement. Apart from its suppression during the Nazi period, the German edition of this book has never gone out of print.

ARKHIVE 3: GEORGES BATAILLE & ACÉPHALE

ENCYCLOPÆDIA ACEPHALICA. *Two important collections of texts by authors associated with Georges Bataille and his secret society Acéphale. Introductory essays, photographs by Boiffard, biographies etc, approx 150 pps, for publication Spring 1995 in UK, Autumn 1995 in USA.*

This anthology will collect together two series of texts taking the form of enclopædias assembled by Bataille and the authors associated with the review *Documents* and the later *Acéphale* group. Both cover the essential ideas of Bataille and his associates: sacred sociology, eroticism enmeshed with death, the spasm of the revolutionary project, the nature of power and the imposibility of politics, etc. Humour, sardonic and ironical, is far from absent in these remarkable redefinitions of the most *heterogeneous* objects or ideas. The *Documents* group joined together artists, authors, sociologists and ethnologists (among the most important of their time) in a literary and philosophical adventure; the *Acéphale* group was more mysterious: even its membership is only vaguely known, and its activities remain a secret to this day.

The following issues may appear in a different order from that given here.

ARKHIVE: THE OULIPO & ITS OFFSPRING

AN OULIPO COMPENDIUM. *Edited in collaboration with Harry Mathews & Thieri Foulc. Translations by Harry Mathews & others. Illustrations, maps, games, biographies, manifestos etc. 176 pps, Autumn 1995 (provisional).*

The OULIPO was founded in 1960 by the author Raymond Queneau and the mathematician/chess-player François LeLionnais, originally to investigate the possibilities of combining mathematics and literature. The group's preoccupations soon widened to include all aspects of "constrictive form" in writing; it has met monthly for 30 years now and publishes its own *Bibliothèque Oulipienne* (more than 50 publications) as well as anthologies of their collective activities. Members include Duchamp, Calvino, Perec, Arnaud, Caradec, Roubaud etc.

ARKHIVE: FLUXUS

AN ANECDOTED TOPOGRAPHY OF CHANCE. *Daniel Spoerri, in collaboration with Robert Filliou, Emmett Williams and Dieter Rot, illustrations by Topor. 160 pps. approx, Spring 1996 (provisional).*

FLUXUS was a loose association of American and European artists operating throughout the sixties and seventies, and the present book is the result of a long-term collaboration between four of its most perceptive and good-humoured participants. It not only personifies the whole Fluxus spirit, but also constitutes a semi-autobiography of an important section of the movement.

ARKHIVE: VIENNA ACTIONISTS

DIRECT ART: BLOOD, ORGIES, MYSTERIES. *Edited by Malcolm Green in consultation with the artists. Manifestos, action scripts, handbills, posters and photographic documentation by Günter Brus, Otto Mühl, Hermann Nitsch and Rudolf Schwarzkogler. 192 pps.*

Viennese Actionism more or less spanned the ten years of the sixties, a period in which its main protagonists—Günter Brus, Otto Müehl, Hermann Nitsch and Rudolf Schwarzkogler—performed in some 150 actions which shocked, fascinated and nauseated well beyond the borders of Austria.

This anthology will offer the chance of a major reappraisal, for it will concentrate on primary material which is unpublished or almost totally unavailable. The three living artists are giving their support to this project.

ARKHIVE: COUNTER-CULTURE

THE BEST OF IT. *Edited by Miles. Selected texts, pictures, complete bibliography. 256 pps.*

IT (International Times) was the most important UK underground periodical of the sixties—it ran for seven years and 167 issues. IT embodied and directed all the liberational politics, culture and philosophy of this period and gave exhaustive coverage to the growth of new left and alternative politics and culture: virtually all the influential authors, musicians, artists, and thinkers of the period from both Europe and the USA appeared in its pages, many for the first time, either as authors or interviewed. The editor of this selection was IT's co-founder, a member of the original editorial board, and a regular editor/contributor throughout its turbulent existence.

ARKHIVE: THE COLLEGE OF PATAPHYSICS

THE TRUE, THE BEAUTIFUL, THE GOOD: A TREASURY OF PATAPHYSICS. *Edited by Alastair Brotchie and Antony Melville in collaboration with Paul Gayot and Thieri Foulc. 200 pps.*

THE COLLEGE OF PATAPHYSICS came into mysterious existence in 1949 and began publishing a quarterly review whose three series (*Cahiers, Dossiers, Subsidia*) continued to appear until 1975.

The College soon attracted to its ranks an unparalleled group of artists and writers. Its publications constitute a massive archive of material relating to post-war culture in France: Atlas is the first and only publisher to be given access to this material. Parts of this anthology have already appeared in our *Printed Head* series, in addition this **arkhive** will contain a generous selection from the reviews, a history of the College, its manifestos, Organigram, Calendar, and the Testament of Dr. Sandomir, among other works.

ARKHIVE: AVANT-GARDE HUMOUR

A HISTORY OF DERISION. *Edited and translated by Iain White, 240 pps. approx.*

This volume of the series identifies a certain tradition of French humour and its interaction with avant-garde writers and authors over a period of 150 years. Many of the characteristics of avant-garde art and writing: abstraction, subjective viewpoints, distorted logic, and all the other provocations that modernism inflicted upon the cultural establishment, were prefigured by writers and artists who thought of themselves as humorists, unaware of the formal inventiveness of their work.

ARKHIVE: LE GRAND JEU

THE GAME OF DEATH (& WRITING). *Edited by Michael Richardson, 180 pps. approx.*

LE GRAND JEU was a magazine assembled by a group of artists and writers broadly sympathetic to Surrealism, but who wished to explore other, more transcendental, areas of the human psyche. From their early teens the two most prominent members of the group, René Daumal and Roger Gilbert-Lecomte, had experimented with near-death states using various drugs and other methods. These concerns were allied with revolutionary politics and lyrical expression of the highest order. They declined to join the Surrealists and their reputation has been eclipsed by this refusal, especially in the English-speaking world.

ARKHIVE: UBU

THE CENTENNIAL UBU. *Edited by Alastair Brotchie, plays, texts, essays, hagiography, bibliography, iconography, 180 pps. approx.*

UBU has reigned for 100 despicable years. His schoolboy authors, and principal promoter Alfred Jarry inadvertently gave birth to a creature of mythical proportions out of what began as a satire on a particularly inept school-teacher. Ubu has fascinated a wide variety of artists, thinkers, and authors since he burst on the stage in 1896 in a production which initiated a theatrical revolution. This compilation will trace the history of Ubu, offer interpretations, both dramatic and critical from the 1890's to the present day, and contain an extensive iconography, as well as printing translations of all the remaining Ubu material by Jarry.

OTHER ATLAS PRESS PUBLICATIONS

Some Atlas titles are available only by ordering direct. We have published works by more than 200 writers over the past eleven years, details are in our free catalogue, available from:

BCM ATLAS PRESS, 27 OLD GLOUCESTER ST., LONDON WC1N 3XX